TOKYO GHOUL

東京喰種

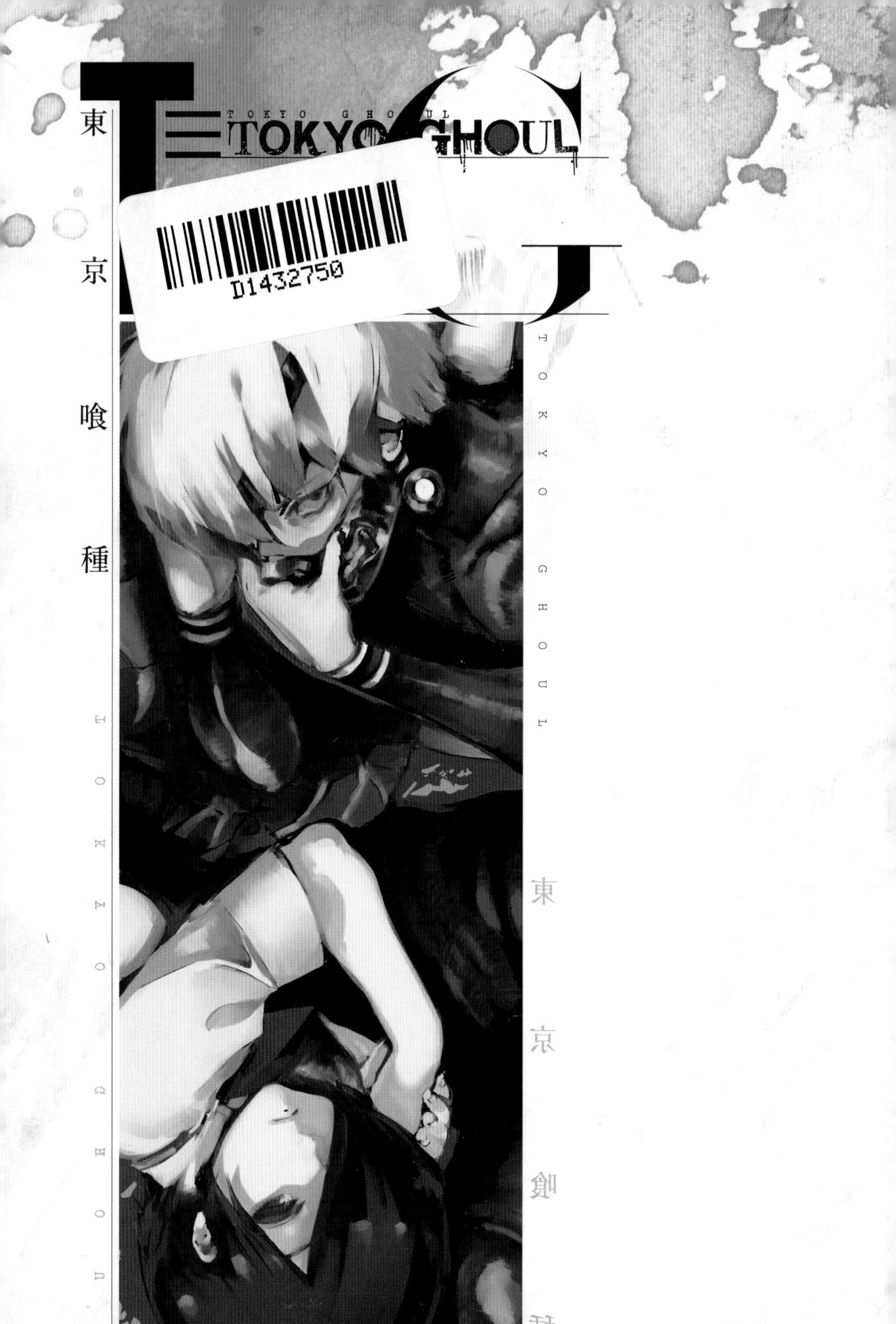

T O K Y O G H O U L

東京喰種

T O K Y O G H O U L

T O K Y O G H O U L

JUZO SUZUYA / REI

鈴屋什造（**スズヤジューゾー**）/ 玲（**レイ**）

BORN June 8th   Gemini

Ex-CCG Academy Cadet
CCG Main Office Rank 2 Investigator   20th Ward

BLOOD-TYPE: AB

Size: **160** cm   **47** kg   FEET **23.5** CM

Likes: Candy, playing, hunting Ghouls, mom

Hobby: Body stitching, disassembling, drawing

Quinque: Scorpion 1/56: Bikaku Rate/B

His first Quinque, given to him by Shinohara. Shaped like a small knife. Used in practical training in the 24th Ward. Taken from the CCG warehouse. Now has all 56.

13th Ward's Jason: Rinkaku Rate/S+

A Quinque made from the 13th Ward's Jason. Equipped with a Kagune that stretches out from the blade.

KISHO ARIMA

有 馬 貴 将 （ **ア リ マ キ シ ョ ウ** ）

BORN December 20th   Sagittarius

CCG Main Office Special Investigator   24th Ward Commander

BLOOD-TYPE: ?

Size: **180** cm   82 kg   FEET **27**.5 CM

Quinque: Yukimura 1/3: Kokaku Rate/B

A Quinque issued by the CCG and used while he was in high school. Later handed down to Hirako.

Ixa: Kokaku Rate/S+

Attacks with lance mode, defends with shield mode. A well-balanced Quinque with a transformation feature.

Narukami: Ukaku Rate/S+

Condensed Rc Cells are released like lightning. Has a tracking mechanism. Extremely difficult to evade.

SUI ISHIDA was born in Fukuoka, Japan. He is the author of *Tokyo Ghoul* and several *Tokyo Ghoul* one-shots, including one that won him second place in the *Weekly Young Jump* 113th Grand Prix award in 2010. *Tokyo Ghoul* began serialization in *Weekly Young Jump* in 2011 and was adapted into an anime series in 2014.

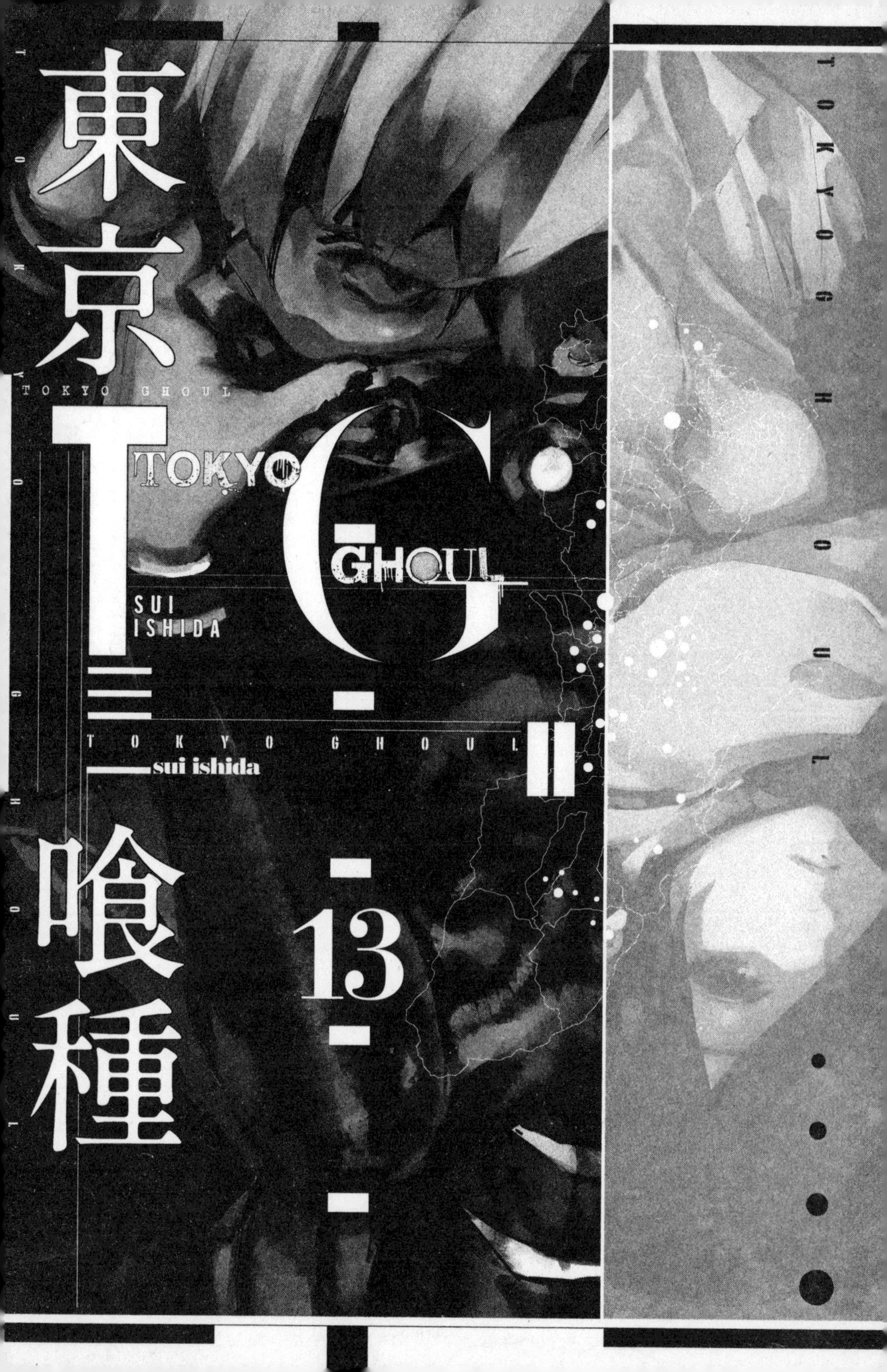
東京喰種
TOKYO GHOUL
TOKYO GHOUL
SUI ISHIDA
TOKYO GHOUL
sui ishida
13
TOKYO GHOUL
TOKYO GHOUL

TOKYO GHOUL SO FAR

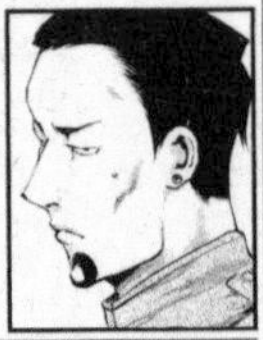

KAZUICHI BANJO

Former leader of the 11th Ward who admires Rize. Former member of the Aogiri Tree, but joins Kaneki after the fall of the 11th Ward.

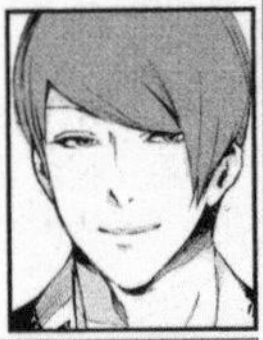

SHU TSUKIYAMA

A Gourmet who seeks the taste of the unknown. Obsessed with Kaneki, who is a half-Ghoul.

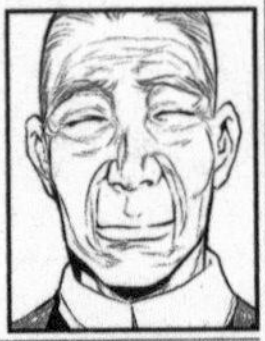

YOSHIMURA

Owner of Anteiku. Guides Kaneki so he can live as a Ghoul. Often works with Yomo. Shrouded in mystery.

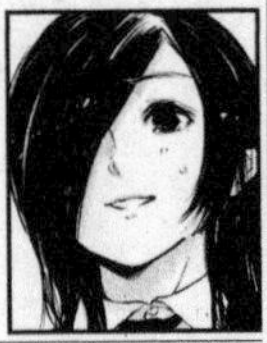

TOUKA KIRISHIMA

A conflicted heroine with two sides, rage and kindness. Ayato's older sister. Lives with the conflict of longing to be human. Hated investigators in the past...?

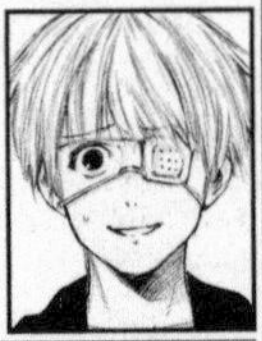

KEN KANEKI

An ordinary young man with a fondness for literature who meets with an accident, has Rize's organs transplanted into him and becomes a half-Ghoul. Struggling to find his place in the world. After being abducted by the Aogiri Tree and enduring Yamori's torture, the Ghoul inside him awakens.

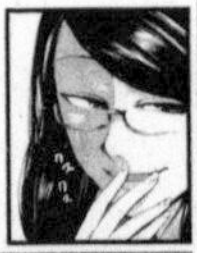

RIZE KAMISHIRO

Freewheeling Binge Eater who despised boredom. Previously lived in the 11th Ward. Met Kaneki in the 20th Ward and then had an accident. There are rumors she used an alias to hide her true identity.

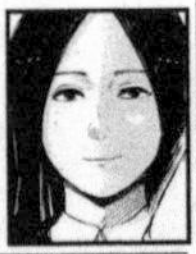

KAYA IRIMI

A longtime Anteiku server. Supports Yoshimura with her exceptional senses.

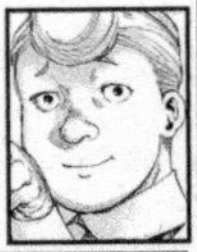

ENJI KOMA

A longtime Anteiku server. Was once known as Maen. Renowned for his coffee.

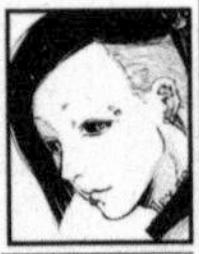

UTA

Owner of HySy Art-Mask Studio, a mask shop in the 4th Ward. Looks out for Kaneki.

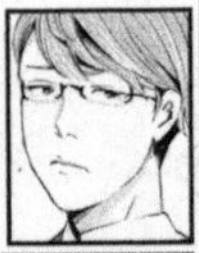

NISHIKI NISHIO

Studious. Adept at blending in with humans. Has a human girlfriend and a compassionate side.

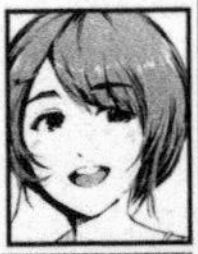

HINAMI FUEGUCHI

An orphan whose parents were killed by the CCG. Admires Kaneki like an older brother.

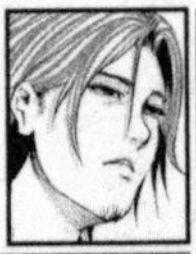

RENJI YOMO

Does not appear out in the open that often. Taciturn and unfriendly, but is trusted by many. Frequently works with Yoshimura. Concerned about Kaneki's condition.

[GHOUL]

A creature that appears human yet consumes humans. The top of the food chain. Finds anything other than humans and coffee unpleasant. Releases a highly lethal natural weapon unique to Ghouls, known as Kagune, from their body to prey on humans. Can be cannibalistic. Only sustains damage from Kagune or Quinques that are made from Kagune.

AOGIRI TREE

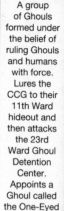

A group of Ghouls formed under the belief of ruling Ghouls and humans with force. Lures the CCG to their 11th Ward hideout and then attacks the 23rd Ward Ghoul Detention Center. Appoints a Ghoul called the One-Eyed King as their leader.

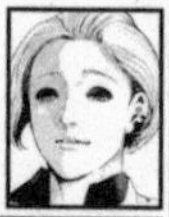

NAKI

Escaped from Cochlea. Worshipped the late Yamori like a god and mourns his death more than anybody. Plans to torture Kaneki for driving Yamori to his death.

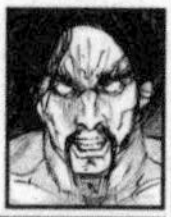

MATASAKA KAMISHIRO

Deeply trusted ex-6th Ward leader known as Shachi. Active behind the scenes for the Aogiri Tree after escaping from the 23rd Ward Ghoul Detention Center (Cochlea), but…?

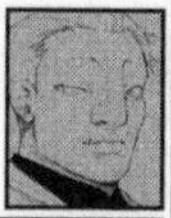

YAMORI
DECEASED

Possessed unrivaled combat skills. Feared as the 13th Ward's Jason for his brutal nature. Confined and tortured Kaneki, but was eventually defeated.

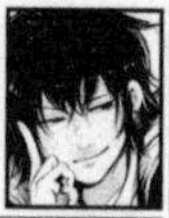

AYATO KIRISHIMA

Touka's younger brother. Even more hot-blooded than his sister. Recruited by Aogiri because of it. Has disdain for his sister and the 20th Ward.

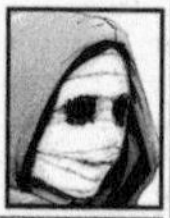

ETO

Origin unknown. Often seen with Tatara.

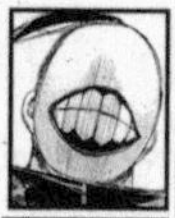

NORO

Direct subordinate of the One-Eyed King. Silent and mysterious.

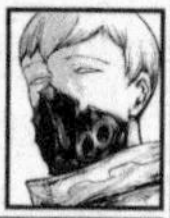

TATARA

Direct subordinate of the One-Eyed King. Boasts high combat capabilities, but…?!

CCG GHOUL INVESTIGATORS

A government agency founded by Tsuneyoshi Washu. Develops Ghoul extermination specialists at the Academy to maintain peace in the wards. Its principal functions are the development and evolution of Quinques and the eradication of Ghouls from Tokyo.

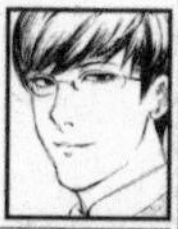

KISHO ARIMA
(SPECIAL INVESTIGATOR)

Personally recruited by Chairman Washu and joined the CCG under special dispensation. Accomplished many distinguished achievements and climbed up the ranks with exceptional speed.

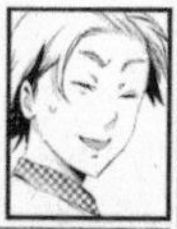

HIDEYOSHI NAGACHIKA

Kaneki's childhood friend with a strong interest in Ghouls. Begins working for the CCG. Recognized by Marude and promoted to investigator assistant.

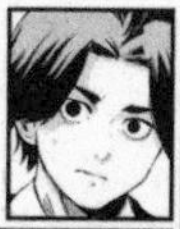

SEIDO TAKIZAWA
(RANK 2 INVESTIGATOR)

Joined the Bureau the same year as Juzo. Respects Amon and Arima.

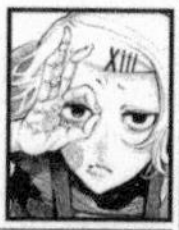

JUZO SUZUYA
(RANK 2 INVESTIGATOR)

An eccentric who joined the CCG under special dispensation. Enjoys killing and longs for Quinques with high lethality.

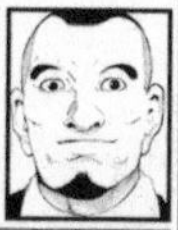

YUKINORI SHINOHARA
(SPECIAL INVESTIGATOR)

Ex-Academy instructor. A onetime colleague of Mado and Amon's drill instructor. Appears easygoing, but…

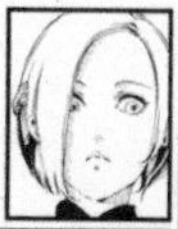

AKIRA MADO
(RANK 2 INVESTIGATOR)

Amon's new partner and Kureo Mado's daughter. Graduated the academy at the head of her class. Always calm and collected. May have a love for weapons like her father.

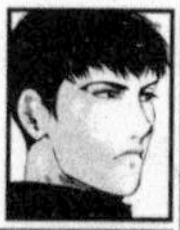

KOTARO AMON
(SENIOR INVESTIGATOR)

An investigator with a very strong sense of justice. Determined to eradicate Ghouls. Dedicated to avenging Mado's loss through his battle with Kaneki. Has a complicated past of being raised by a Ghoul.

Summary

Kaneki, an average student, is fated to live as a Ghoul when Rize's organs are transplanted into him. While questioning and struggling with the existence of creatures that take human lives to survive, he searches for how the world should be. One day while at Anteiku, he is abducted by the Aogiri Tree. While being held captive and viciously tortured by Yamori, he accepts that he is a Ghoul. He later relocates to the 6th Ward with Tsukiyama and Banjo in pursuit of Dr. Kano, the doctor who turned him into a Ghoul. However, after acquiring an uncontrollable power gained from feeding on his own kind, he wounds a friend. Upon the advice of others, he decides to return to Anteiku. But now the CCG has finally tracked down the suspected leader of the Aogiri Tree, the Owl!

東

京

種

TOKYO GHOUL

TOKYO GHOUL

SUI
ISHIDA

C O N T E N T S

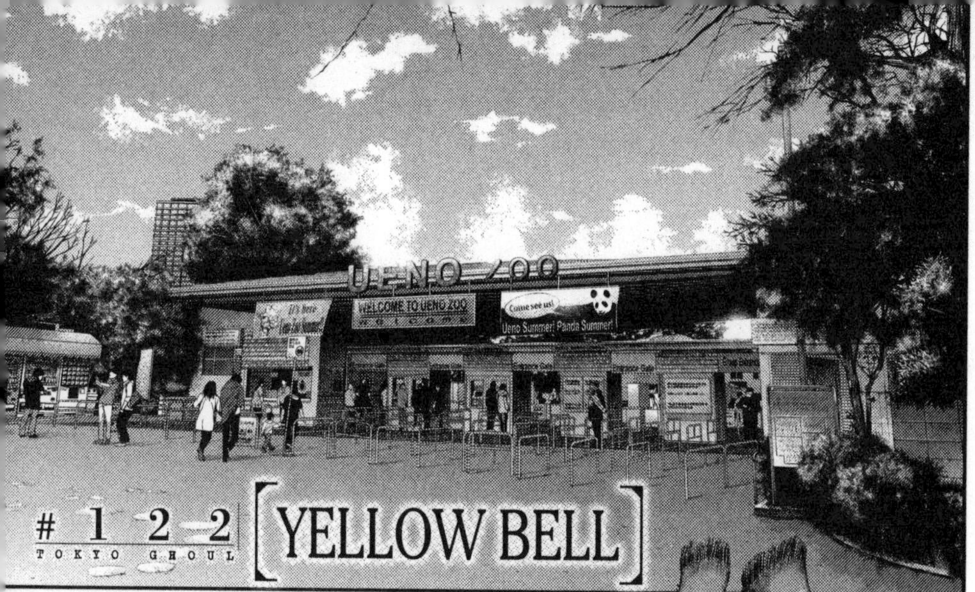
UENO ZOO
WELCOME TO UENO ZOO
Come see us!
Ueno Summer! Panda Summer!
#122
TOKYO GHOUL
[YELLOW BELL]

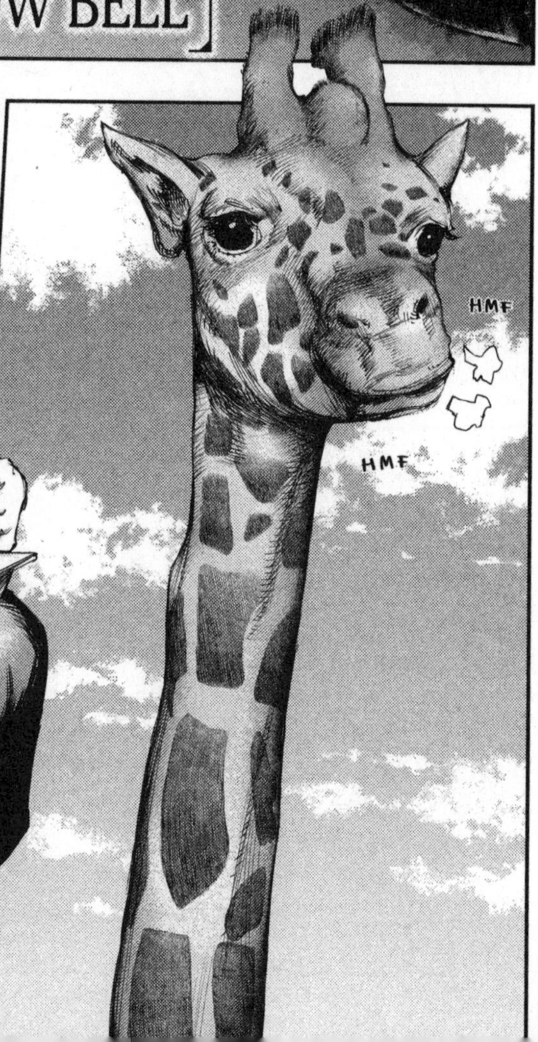
HMF
HMF

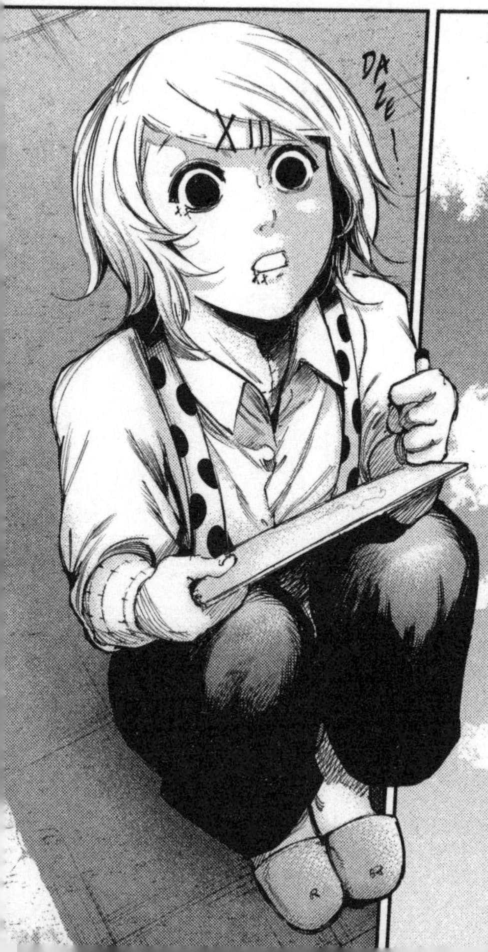
DAZE!

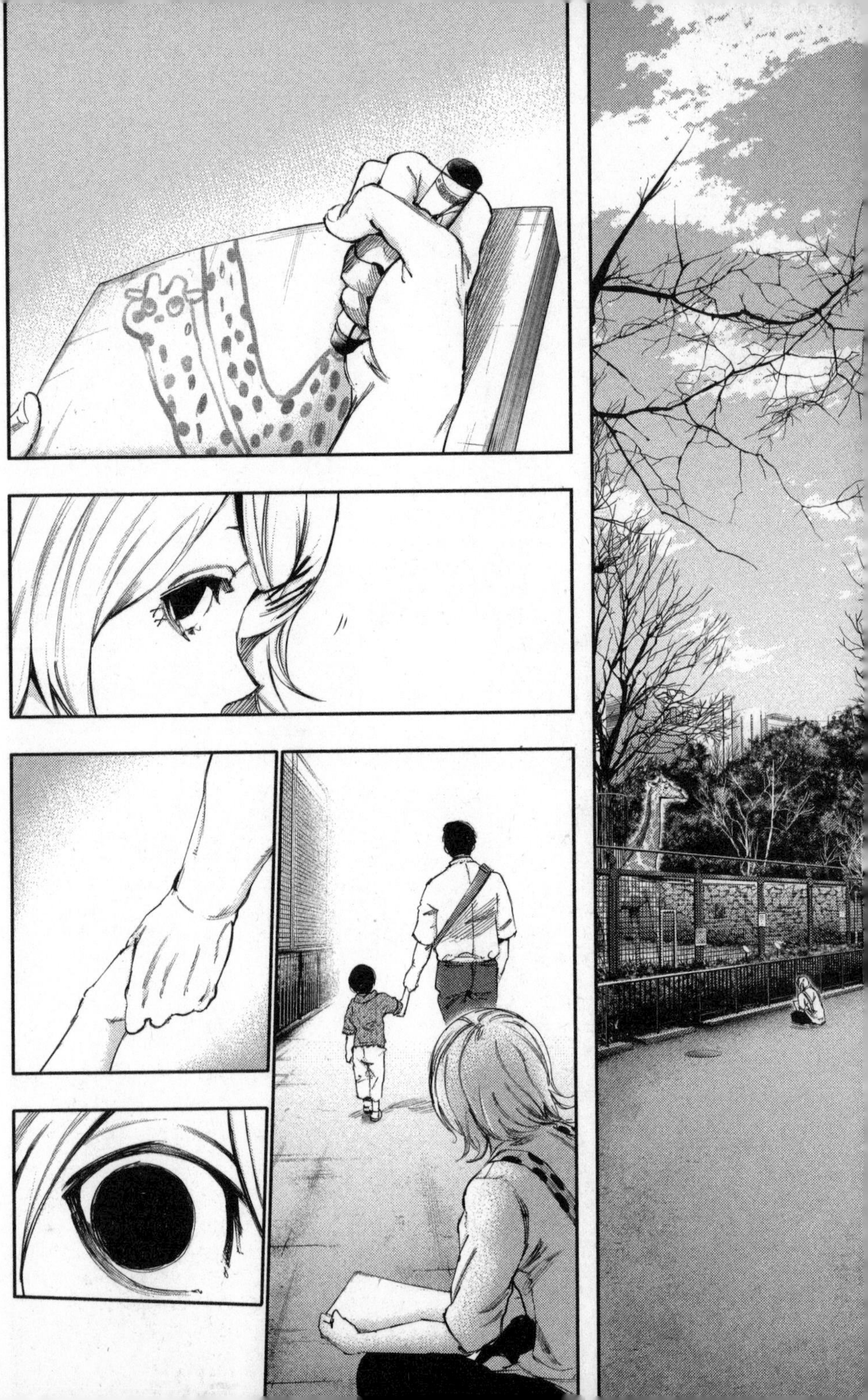

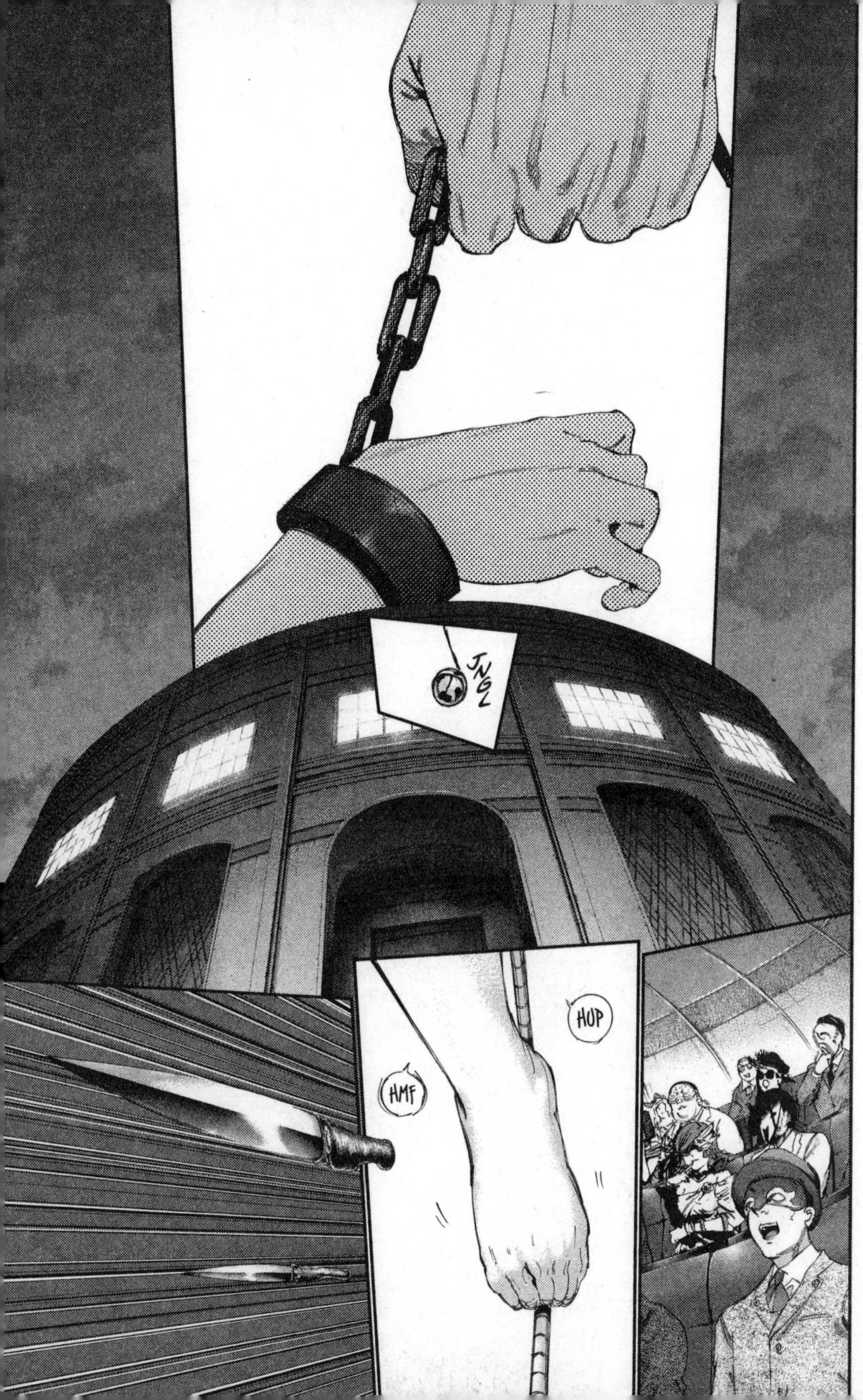
JNGL
HUP
HMF

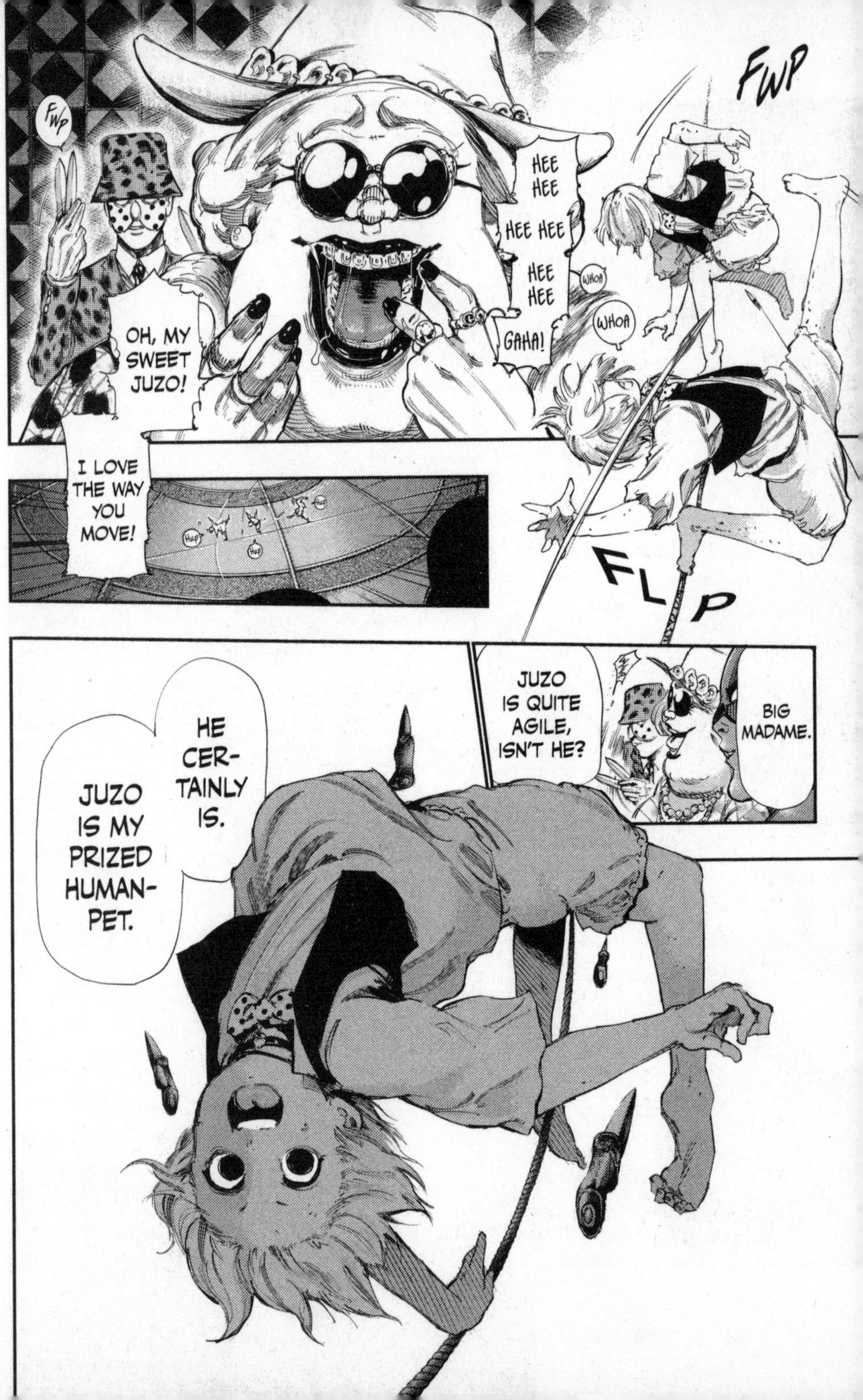
FWP
HEE HEE HEE HEE HEE HEE
WHOA
WHOA
GAHA!
FWP
OH, MY SWEET JUZO!
FLP
I LOVE THE WAY YOU MOVE!
HUP
HUP
HUP
JUZO IS QUITE AGILE, ISN'T HE?
BIG MADAME.
HE CER-TAINLY IS.
JUZO IS MY PRIZED HUMAN-PET.

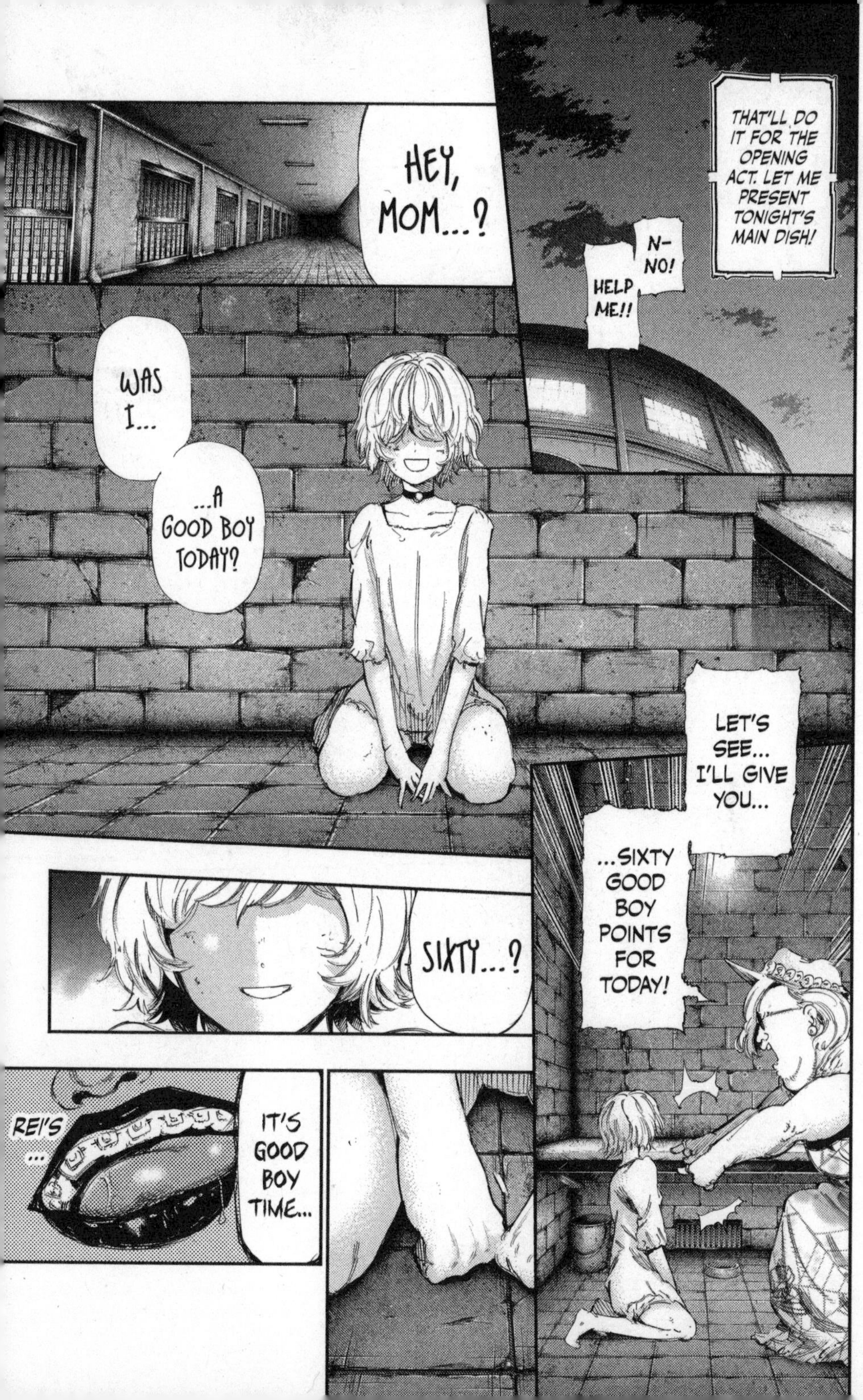

THAT'LL DO IT FOR THE OPENING ACT. LET ME PRESENT TONIGHT'S MAIN DISH!
N-NO!
HELP ME!!
HEY, MOM...?
WAS I...
...A GOOD BOY TODAY?
LET'S SEE... I'LL GIVE YOU...
...SIXTY GOOD BOY POINTS FOR TODAY!
SIXTY...?
IT'S GOOD BOY TIME...
REI'S...

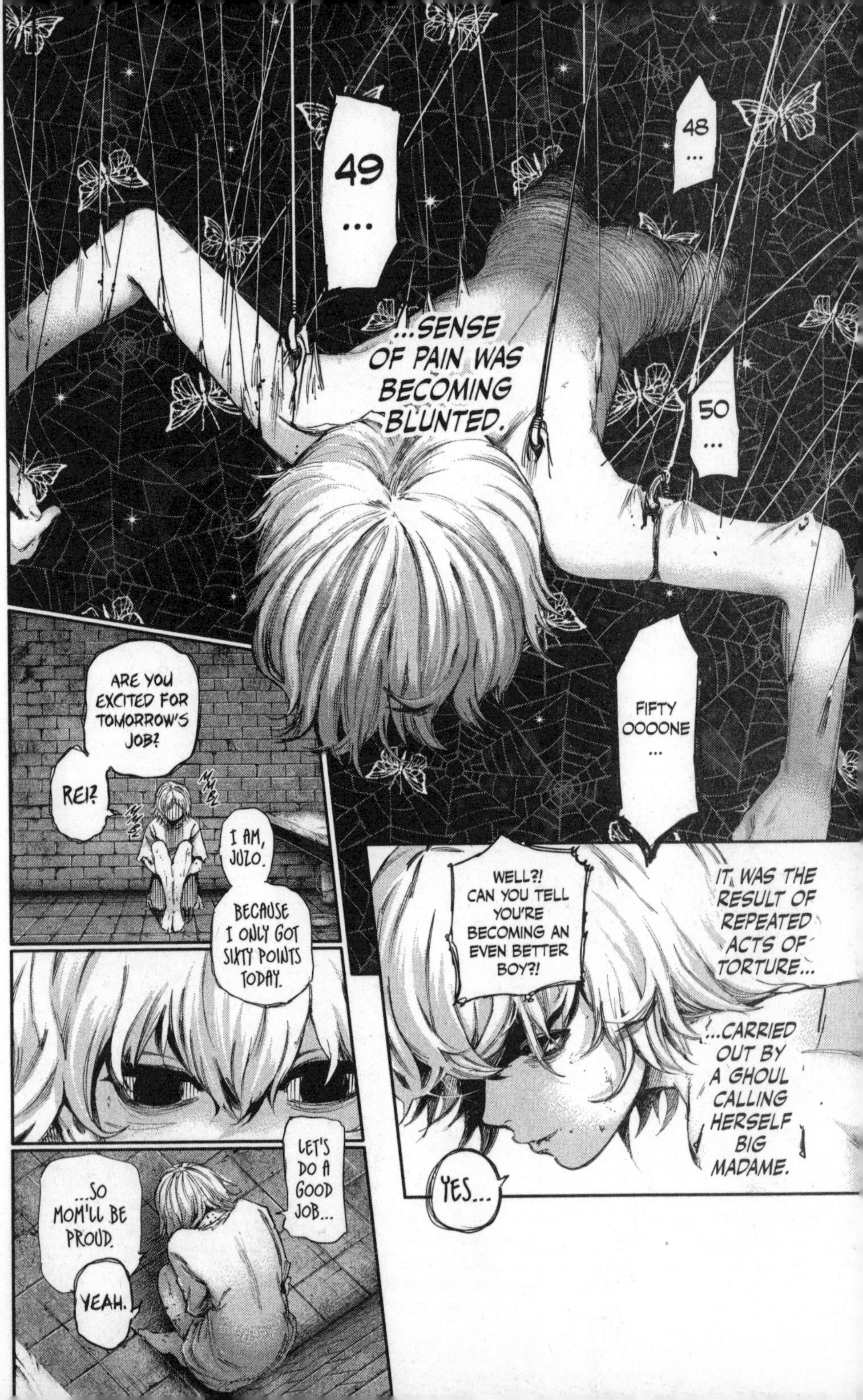
48 ...
49 ...
...SENSE OF PAIN WAS BECOMING BLUNTED.
50 ...
FIFTY OOOONE ...
IT WAS THE RESULT OF REPEATED ACTS OF TORTURE...
WELL?! CAN YOU TELL YOU'RE BECOMING AN EVEN BETTER BOY?!
...CARRIED OUT BY A GHOUL CALLING HERSELF BIG MADAME.
YES...
ARE YOU EXCITED FOR TOMORROW'S JOB?
REI?
I AM, JUZO.
BECAUSE I ONLY GOT SIXTY POINTS TODAY.
LET'S DO A GOOD JOB...
...SO MOM'LL BE PROUD.
YEAH.

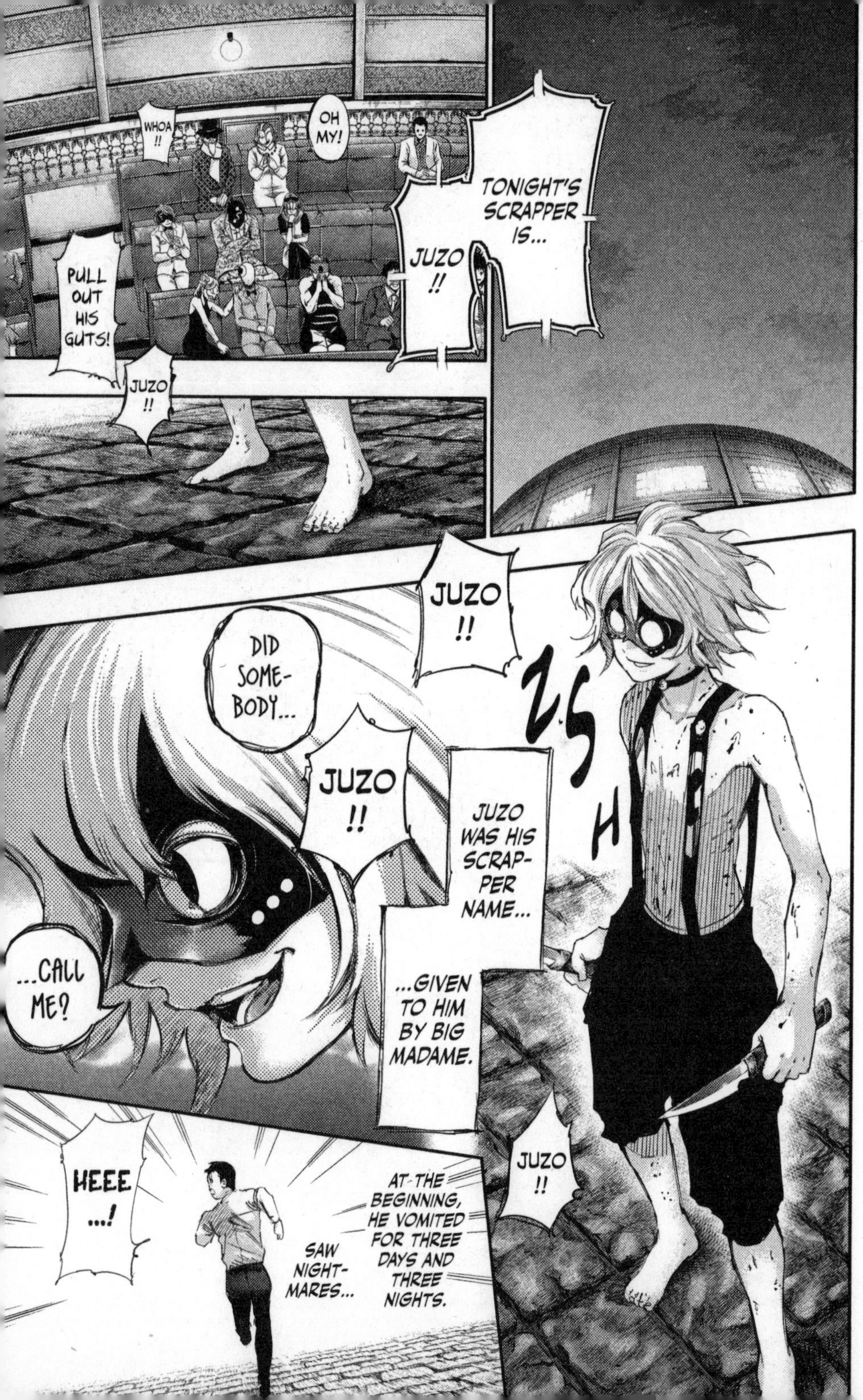
TONIGHT'S SCRAPPER IS... JUZO!!
OH MY!
WHOA!!
PULL OUT HIS GUTS!
JUZO!!
JUZO!!
ZSH
JUZO!!
DID SOMEBODY...
JUZO!!
...CALL ME?
JUZO WAS HIS SCRAPPER NAME...
...GIVEN TO HIM BY BIG MADAME.
AT THE BEGINNING, HE VOMITED FOR THREE DAYS AND THREE NIGHTS.
SAW NIGHTMARES...
HEEE...!

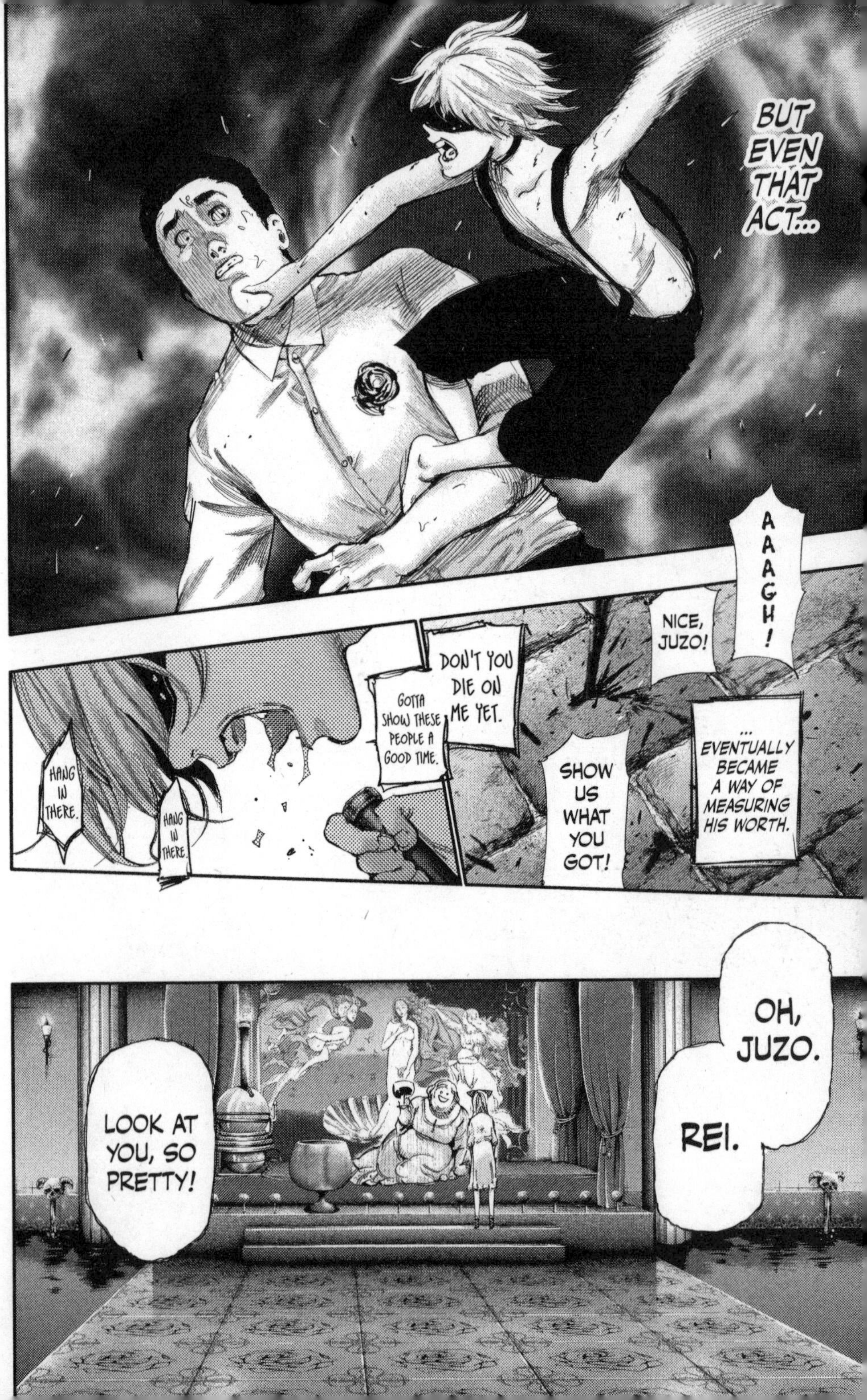
BUT EVEN THAT ACT...
AAAGH!
NICE, JUZO!
... EVENTUALLY BECAME A WAY OF MEASURING HIS WORTH.
SHOW US WHAT YOU GOT!
DON'T YOU DIE ON ME YET.
GOTTA SHOW THESE PEOPLE A GOOD TIME.
HANG IN THERE.
HANG IN THERE.
OH, JUZO.
REI.
LOOK AT YOU, SO PRETTY!

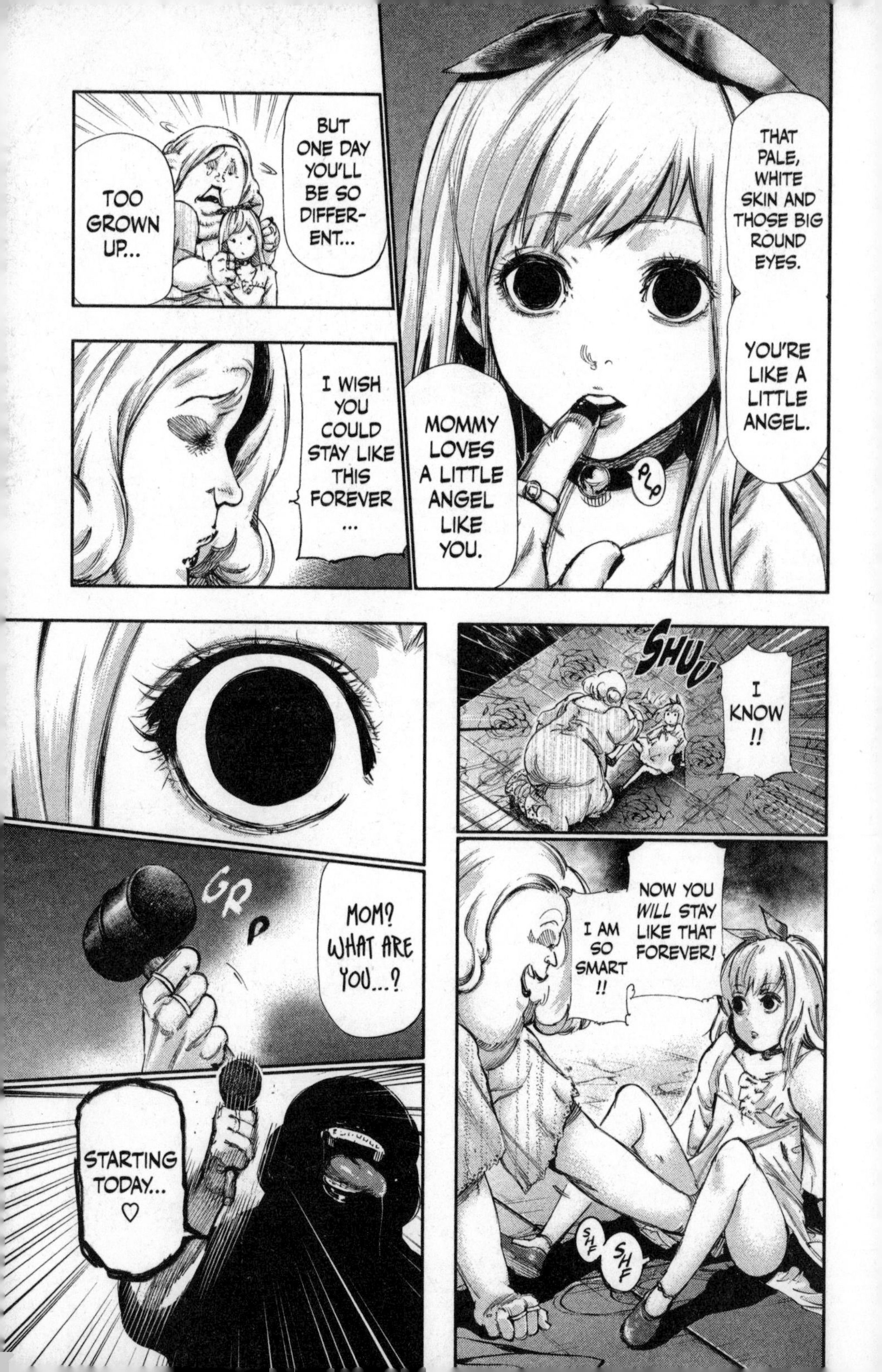
THAT PALE, WHITE SKIN AND THOSE BIG ROUND EYES.
YOU'RE LIKE A LITTLE ANGEL.
MOMMY LOVES A LITTLE ANGEL LIKE YOU.
PLP
BUT ONE DAY YOU'LL BE SO DIFFER-ENT...
TOO GROWN UP...
I WISH YOU COULD STAY LIKE THIS FOREVER ...
SHUU
I KNOW !!
NOW YOU *WILL* STAY LIKE THAT FOREVER!
I AM SO SMART !!
SHF
SHF
GR
P
MOM? WHAT ARE YOU...?
STARTING TODAY... ♡

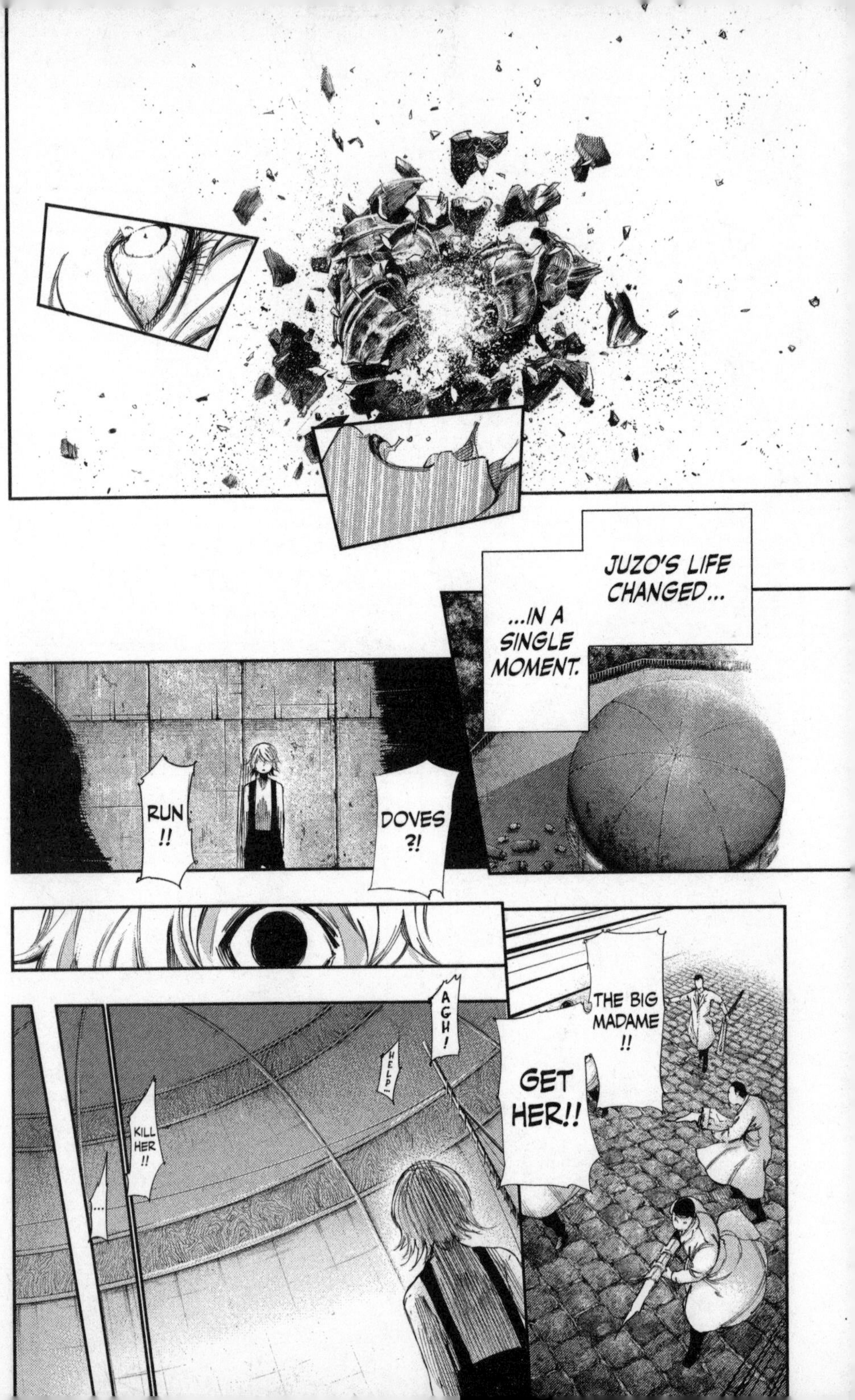
JUZO'S LIFE CHANGED...
...IN A SINGLE MOMENT.
DOVES ?!
RUN !!
THE BIG MADAME !!
GET HER!!
AGH!
HELP...
KILL HER !!
...

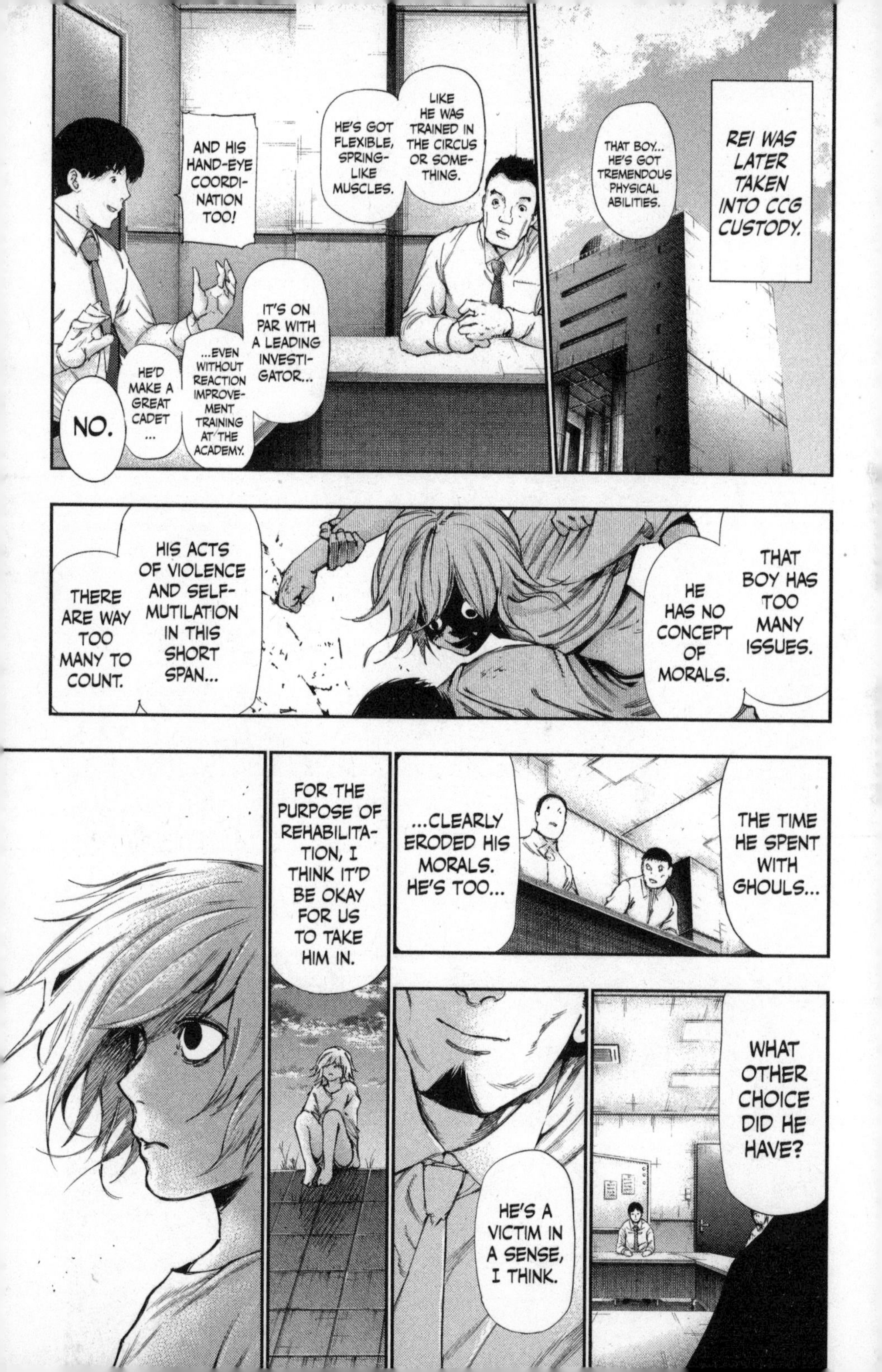
REI WAS LATER TAKEN INTO CCG CUSTODY.
THAT BOY... HE'S GOT TREMENDOUS PHYSICAL ABILITIES.
LIKE HE WAS TRAINED IN THE CIRCUS OR SOMETHING.
HE'S GOT FLEXIBLE, SPRING-LIKE MUSCLES.
AND HIS HAND-EYE COORDINATION TOO!
IT'S ON PAR WITH A LEADING INVESTIGATOR...
...EVEN WITHOUT REACTION IMPROVEMENT TRAINING AT THE ACADEMY.
HE'D MAKE A GREAT CADET...
NO.
THAT BOY HAS TOO MANY ISSUES.
HE HAS NO CONCEPT OF MORALS.
HIS ACTS OF VIOLENCE AND SELF-MUTILATION IN THIS SHORT SPAN...
THERE ARE WAY TOO MANY TO COUNT.
THE TIME HE SPENT WITH GHOULS...
...CLEARLY ERODED HIS MORALS. HE'S TOO...
WHAT OTHER CHOICE DID HE HAVE?
HE'S A VICTIM IN A SENSE, I THINK.
FOR THE PURPOSE OF REHABILITATION, I THINK IT'D BE OKAY FOR US TO TAKE HIM IN.

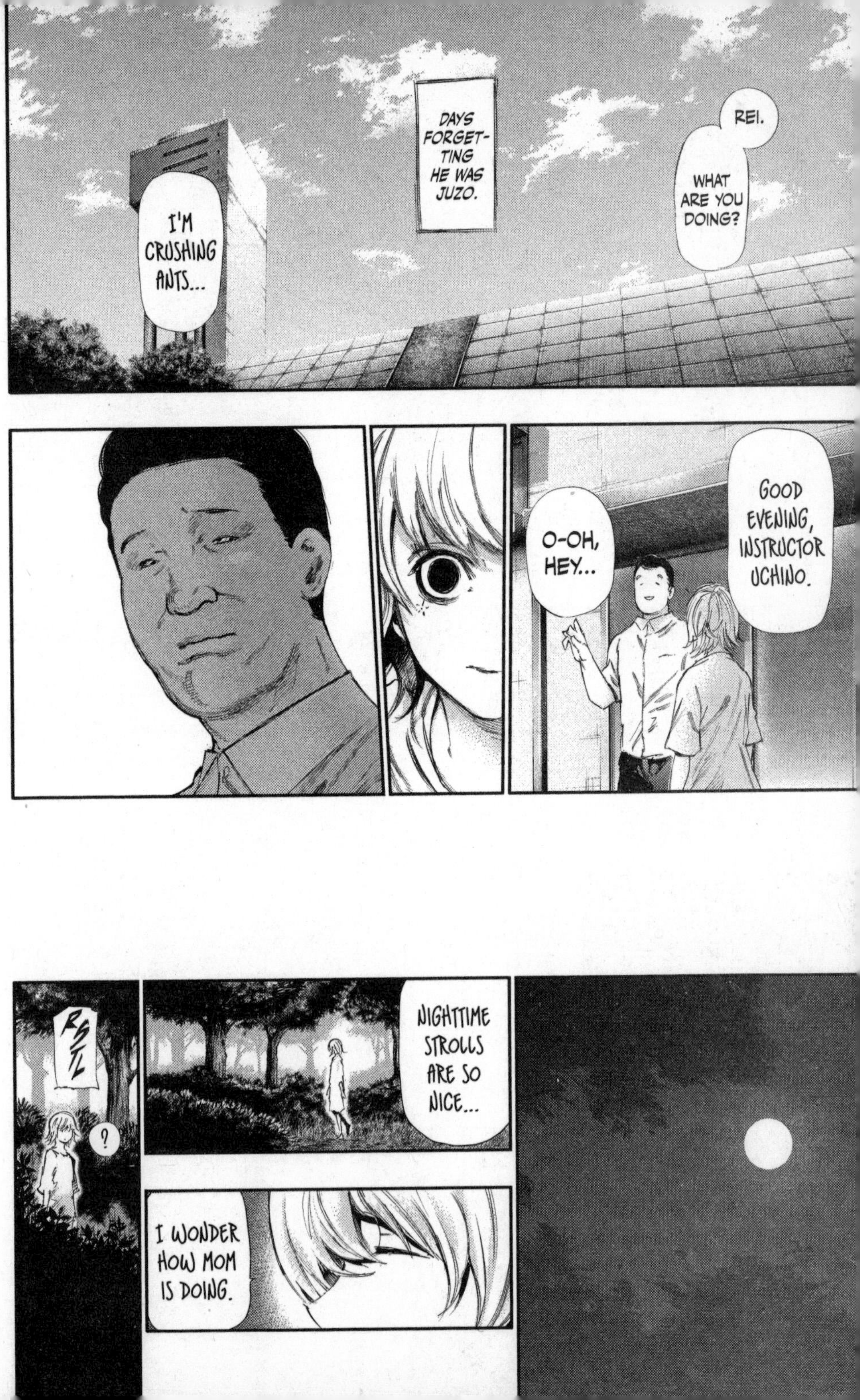
REI.
WHAT ARE YOU DOING?
DAYS FORGET-TING HE WAS JUZO.
I'M CRUSHING ANTS...
GOOD EVENING, INSTRUCTOR UCHINO.
O-OH, HEY...
NIGHTTIME STROLLS ARE SO NICE...
I WONDER HOW MOM IS DOING.
RSTL
?

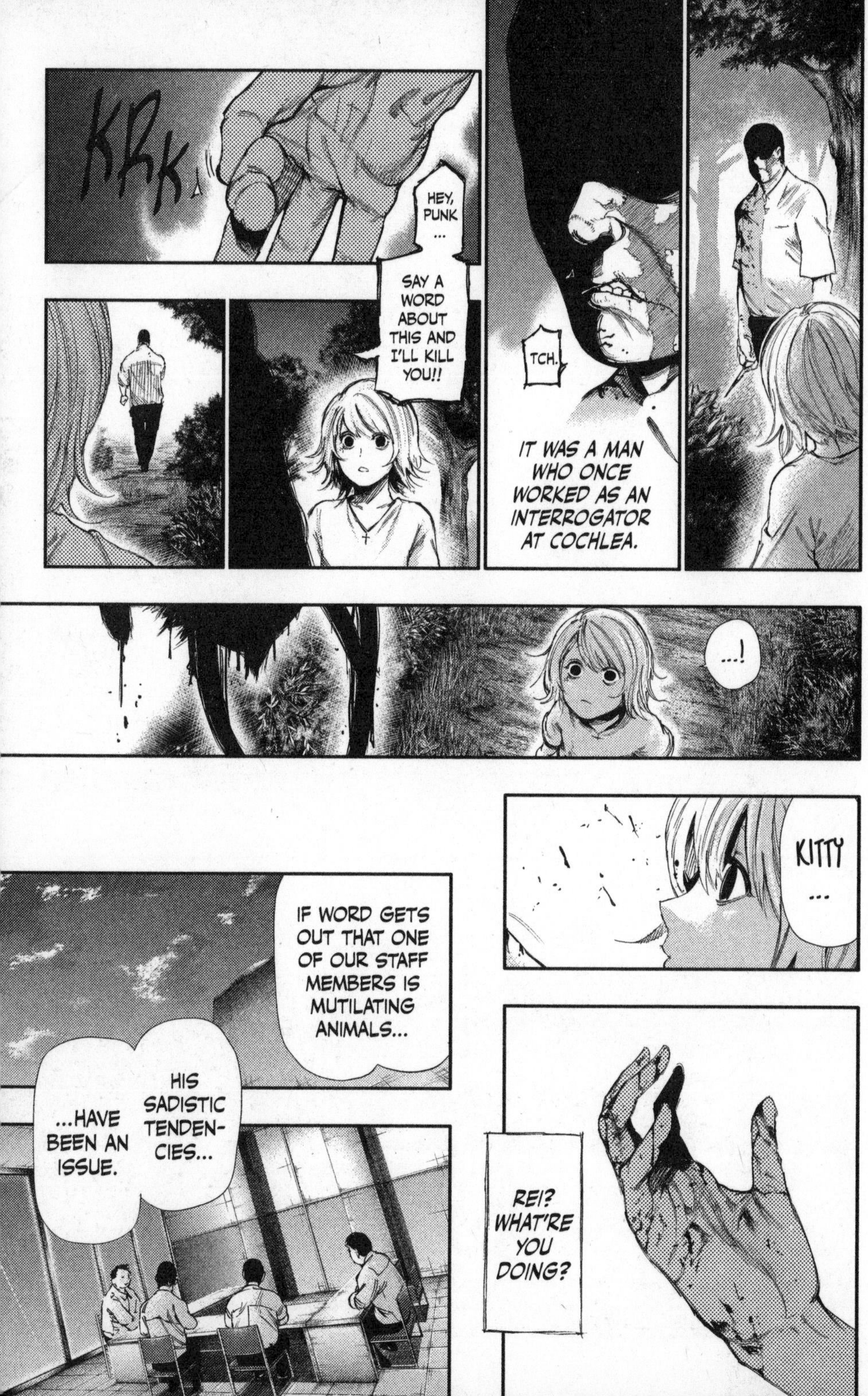
TCH.
IT WAS A MAN WHO ONCE WORKED AS AN INTERROGATOR AT COCHLEA.
KRK
HEY, PUNK...
SAY A WORD ABOUT THIS AND I'LL KILL YOU!!
...!
KITTY...
REI? WHAT'RE YOU DOING?
IF WORD GETS OUT THAT ONE OF OUR STAFF MEMBERS IS MUTILATING ANIMALS...
HIS SADISTIC TENDENCIES...
...HAVE BEEN AN ISSUE.

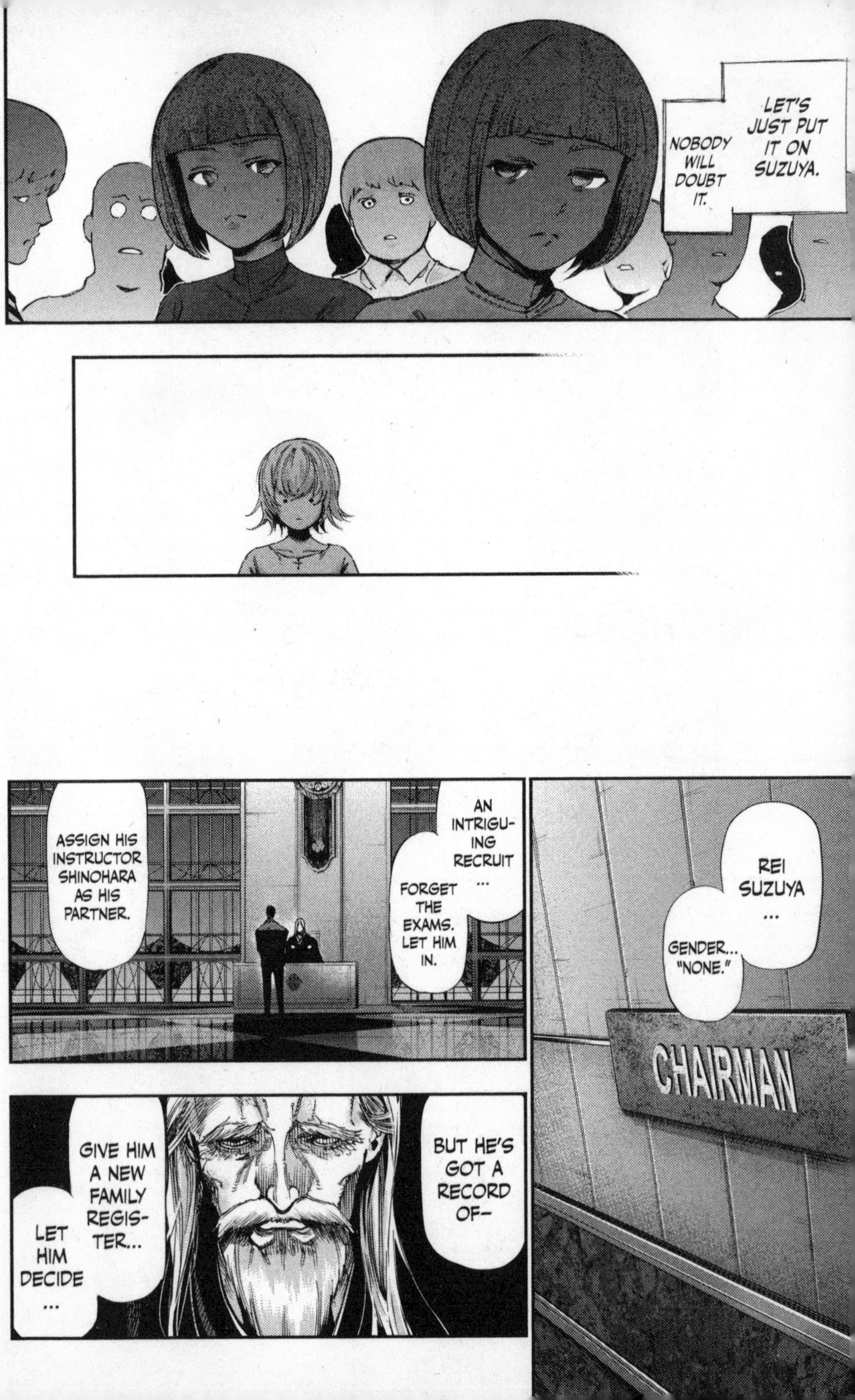
LET'S JUST PUT IT ON SUZUYA.
NOBODY WILL DOUBT IT.
REI SUZUYA ...
GENDER... "NONE."
CHAIRMAN
AN INTRIGUING RECRUIT ...
FORGET THE EXAMS. LET HIM IN.
ASSIGN HIS INSTRUCTOR SHINOHARA AS HIS PARTNER.
BUT HE'S GOT A RECORD OF–
GIVE HIM A NEW FAMILY REGISTER...
LET HIM DECIDE ...

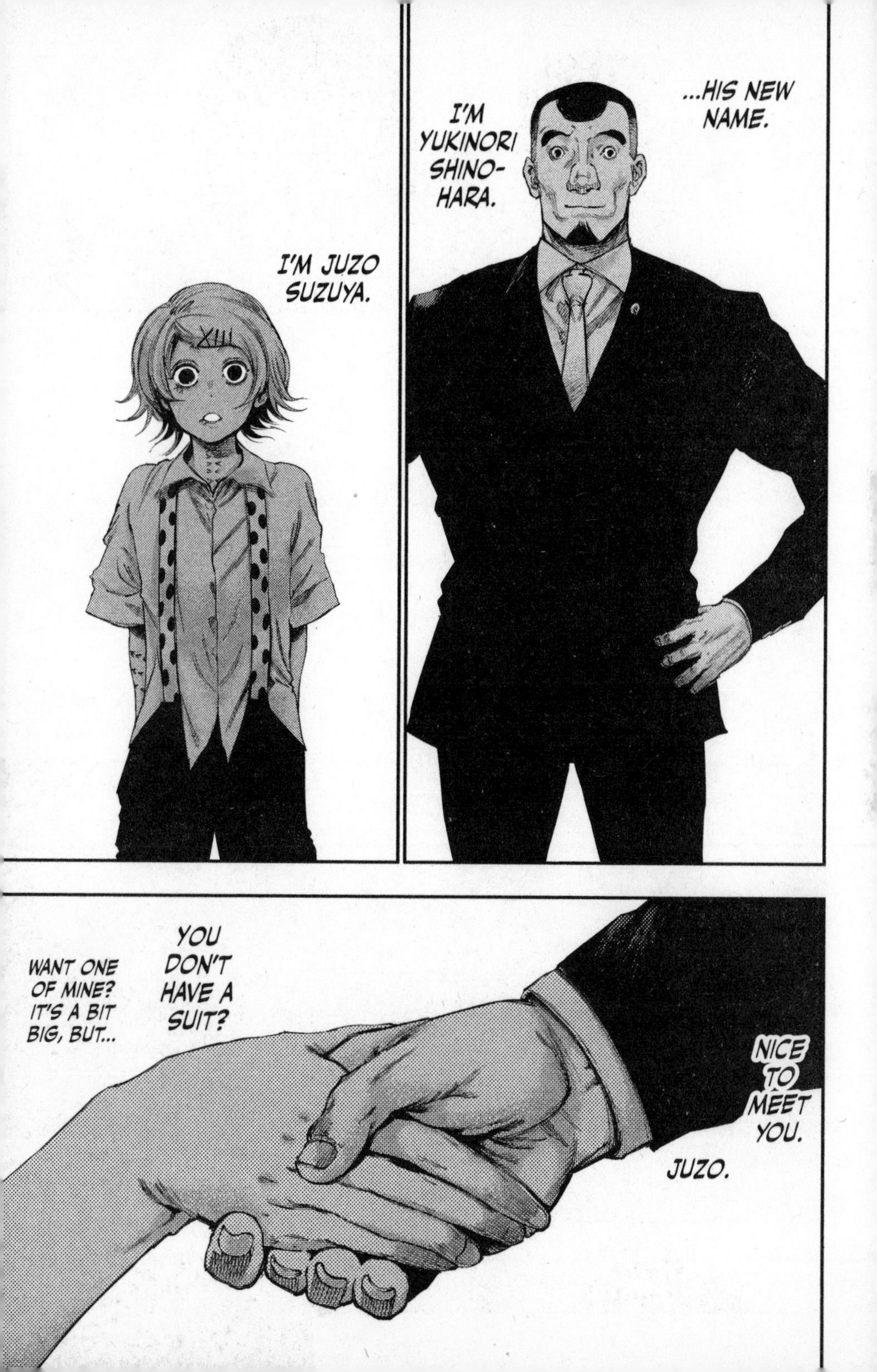
...HIS NEW NAME.
I'M YUKINORI SHINO-HARA.
I'M JUZO SUZUYA.
NICE TO MEET YOU.
JUZO.
YOU DON'T HAVE A SUIT?
WANT ONE OF MINE? IT'S A BIT BIG, BUT...

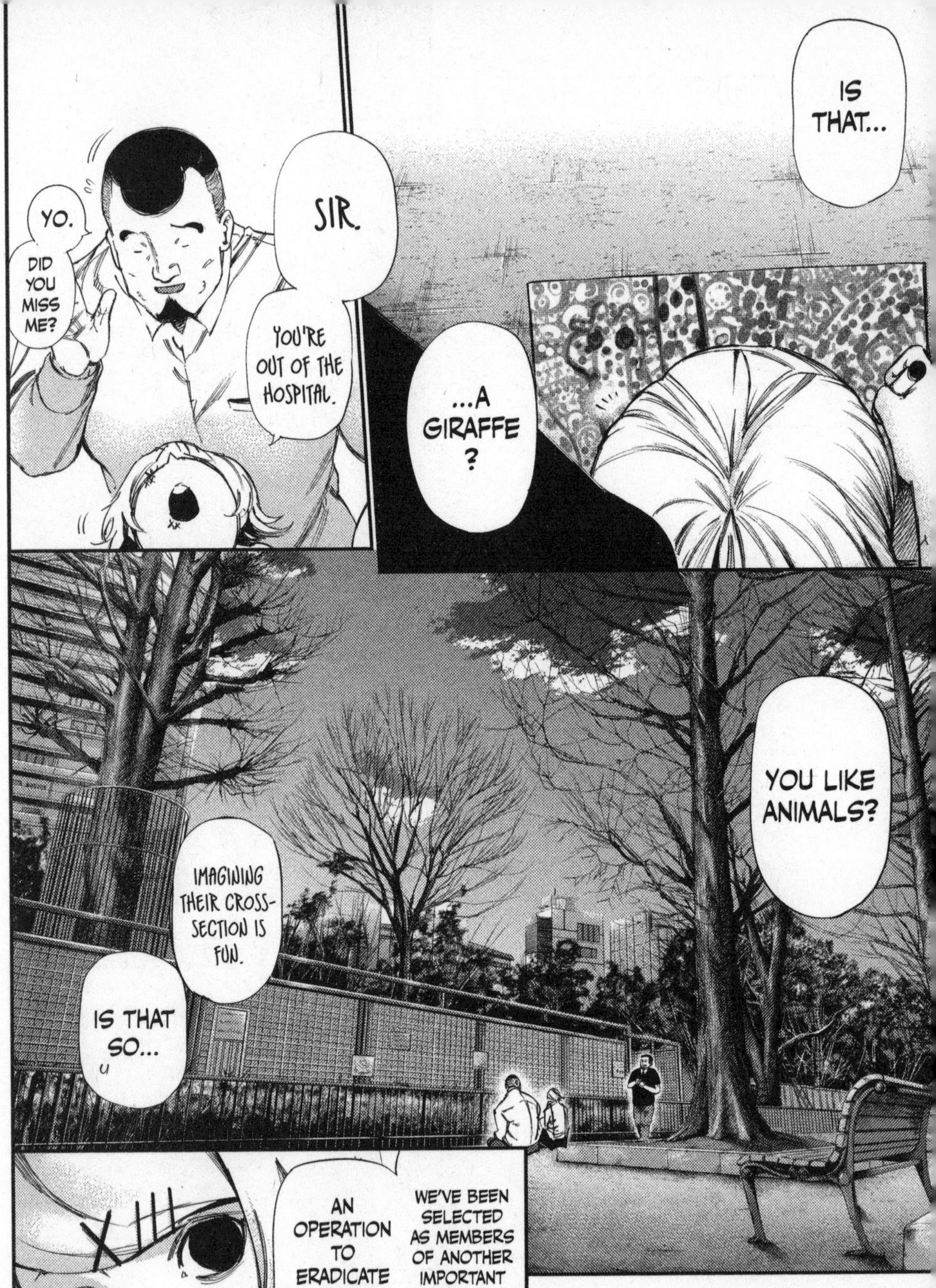
IS THAT...
...A GIRAFFE?
SIR.
YOU'RE OUT OF THE HOSPITAL.
YO.
DID YOU MISS ME?
YOU LIKE ANIMALS?
IMAGINING THEIR CROSS-SECTION IS FUN.
IS THAT SO...
WE'VE BEEN SELECTED AS MEMBERS OF ANOTHER IMPORTANT OPERATION...
AN OPERATION TO ERADICATE A CERTAIN GHOUL.

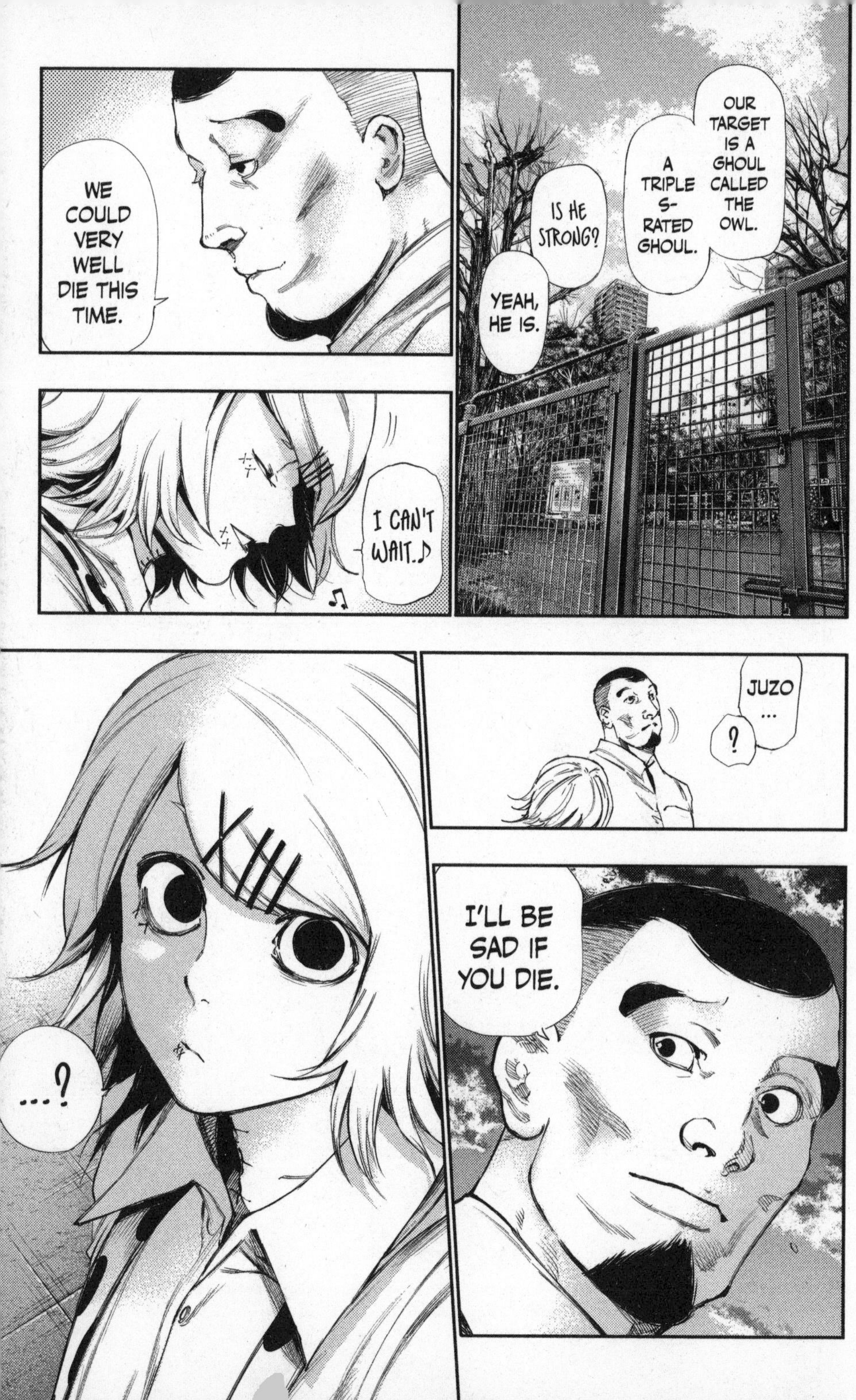
OUR TARGET IS A GHOUL CALLED THE OWL.
A TRIPLE S-RATED GHOUL.
IS HE STRONG?
YEAH, HE IS.
WE COULD VERY WELL DIE THIS TIME.
I CAN'T WAIT.♪
JUZO...
?
I'LL BE SAD IF YOU DIE.
...?

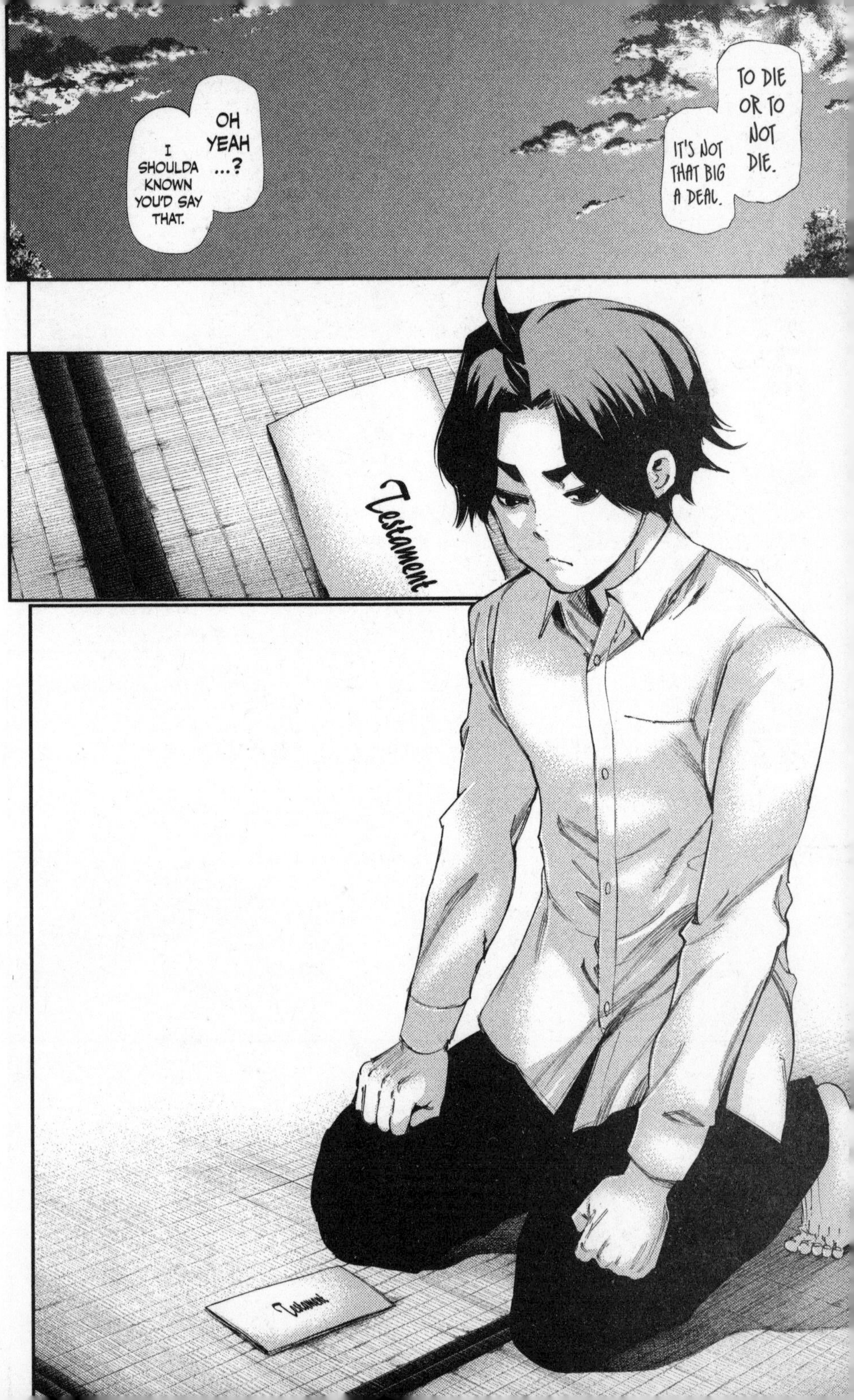
TO DIE OR TO NOT DIE.
IT'S NOT THAT BIG A DEAL.
OH YEAH ...?
I SHOULDA KNOWN YOU'D SAY THAT.
Testament

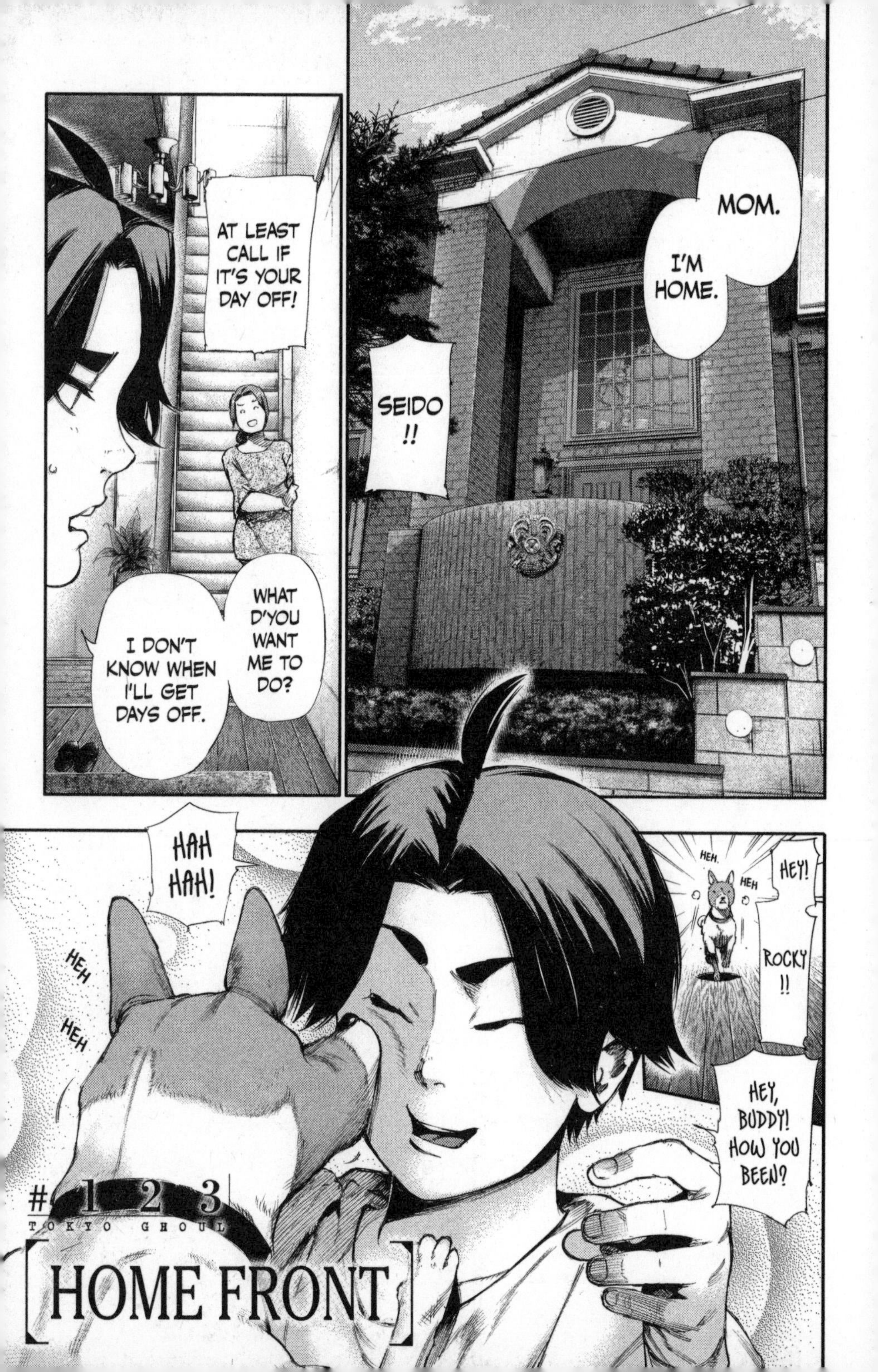
MOM.
I'M HOME.
SEIDO !!
AT LEAST CALL IF IT'S YOUR DAY OFF!
WHAT D'YOU WANT ME TO DO?
I DON'T KNOW WHEN I'LL GET DAYS OFF.
HEY!
ROCKY !!
HEH. HEH
HAH HAH!
HEH HEH
HEY, BUDDY! HOW YOU BEEN?
#123 TOKYO GHOUL
[HOME FRONT]

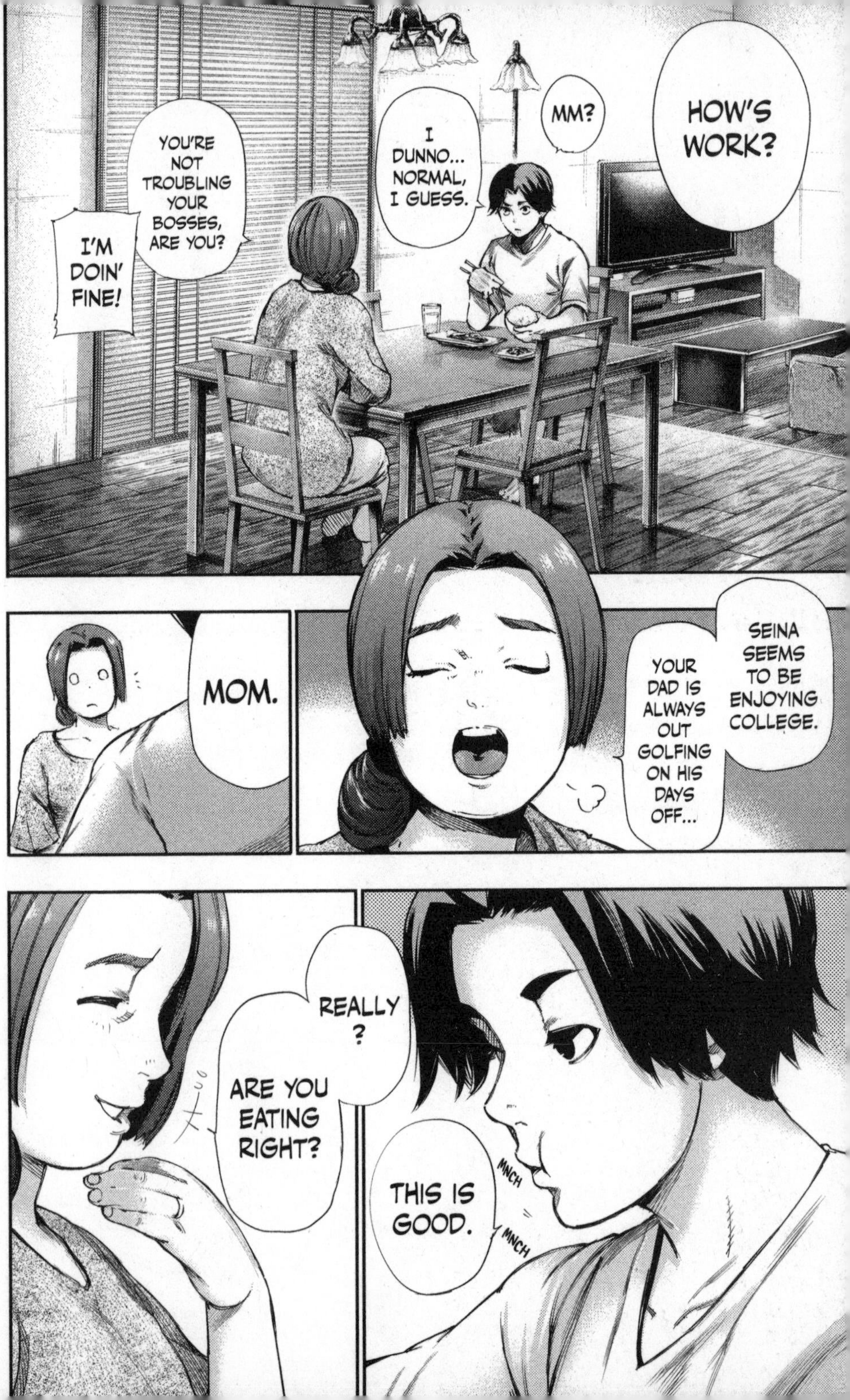
HOW'S WORK?
MM?
I DUNNO... NORMAL, I GUESS.
YOU'RE NOT TROUBLING YOUR BOSSES, ARE YOU?
I'M DOIN' FINE!
SEINA SEEMS TO BE ENJOYING COLLEGE.
YOUR DAD IS ALWAYS OUT GOLFING ON HIS DAYS OFF...
MOM.
MNCH
THIS IS GOOD.
MNCH
REALLY?
ARE YOU EATING RIGHT?

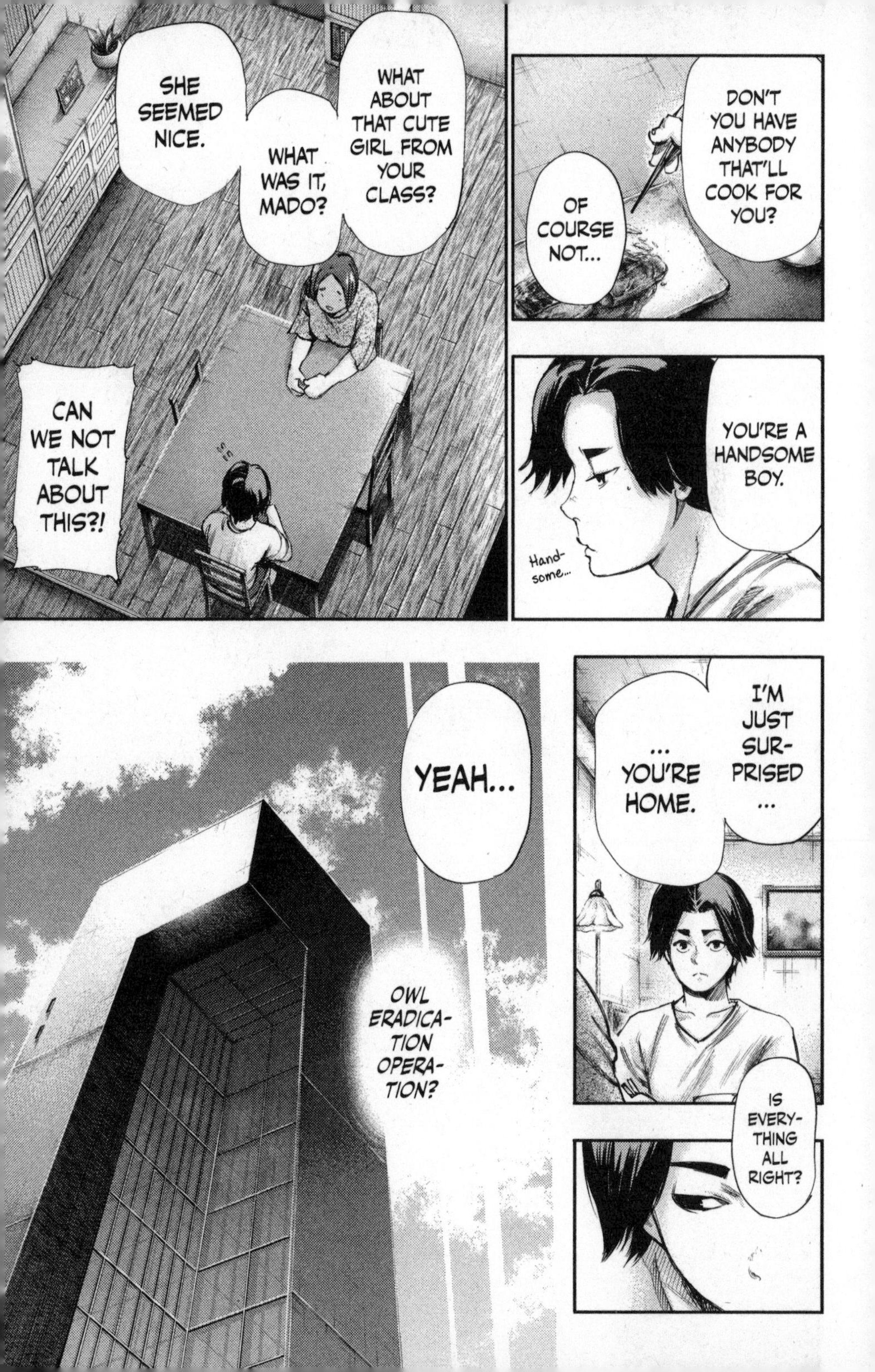
DON'T YOU HAVE ANYBODY THAT'LL COOK FOR YOU?
OF COURSE NOT...
YOU'RE A HANDSOME BOY.
Handsome...
WHAT ABOUT THAT CUTE GIRL FROM YOUR CLASS?
WHAT WAS IT, MADO?
SHE SEEMED NICE.
CAN WE NOT TALK ABOUT THIS?!
I'M JUST SURPRISED...
...YOU'RE HOME.
IS EVERYTHING ALL RIGHT?
YEAH...
OWL ERADICATION OPERATION?

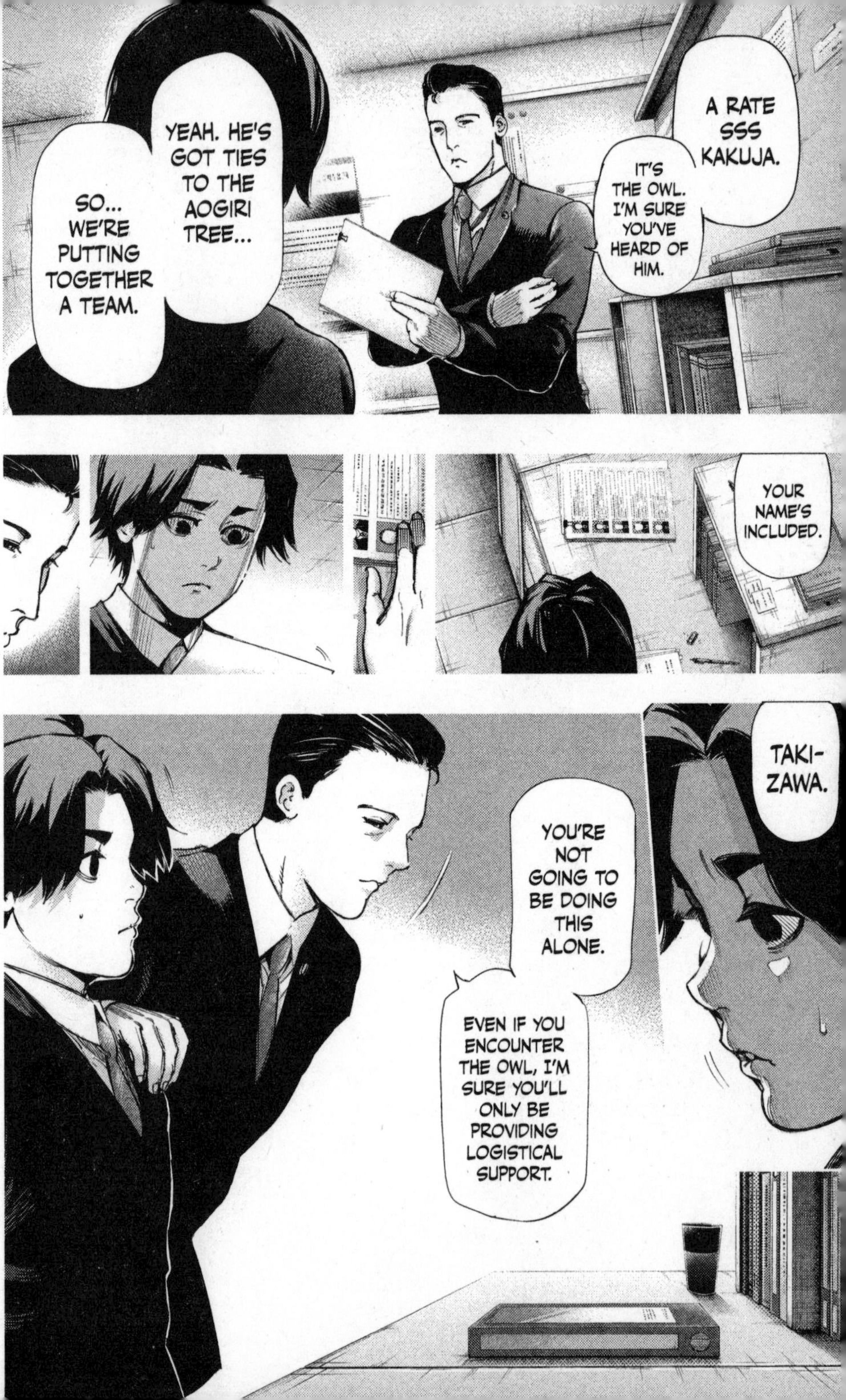
A RATE SSS KAKUJA.
IT'S THE OWL. I'M SURE YOU'VE HEARD OF HIM.
YEAH. HE'S GOT TIES TO THE AOGIRI TREE...
SO... WE'RE PUTTING TOGETHER A TEAM.
YOUR NAME'S INCLUDED.
TAKI-ZAWA.
YOU'RE NOT GOING TO BE DOING THIS ALONE.
EVEN IF YOU ENCOUNTER THE OWL, I'M SURE YOU'LL ONLY BE PROVIDING LOGISTICAL SUPPORT.

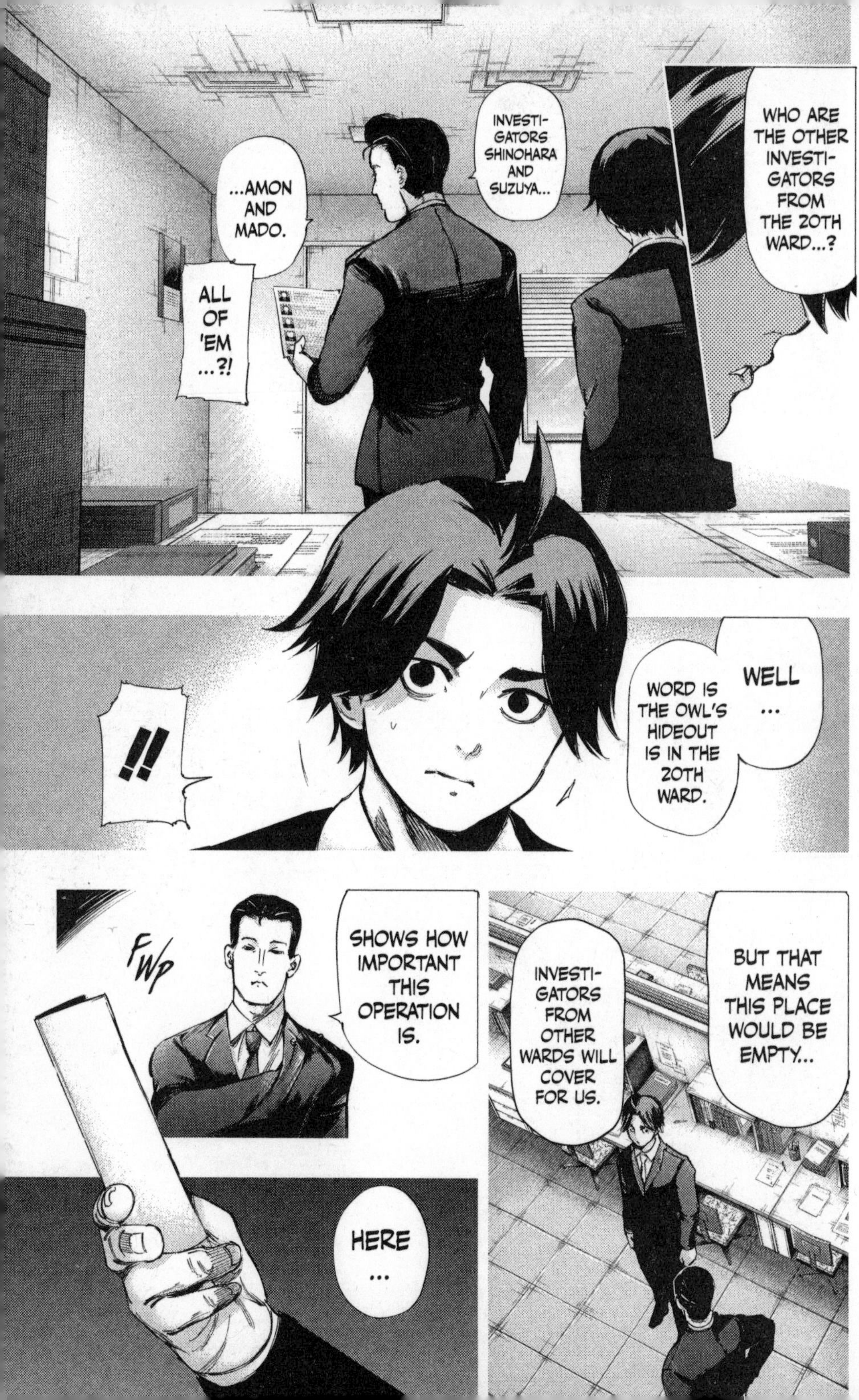
WHO ARE THE OTHER INVESTIGATORS FROM THE 20TH WARD...?
INVESTIGATORS SHINOHARA AND SUZUYA...
...AMON AND MADO.
ALL OF 'EM...?!
WELL...
WORD IS THE OWL'S HIDEOUT IS IN THE 20TH WARD.
!!
BUT THAT MEANS THIS PLACE WOULD BE EMPTY...
INVESTIGATORS FROM OTHER WARDS WILL COVER FOR US.
SHOWS HOW IMPORTANT THIS OPERATION IS.
FWP
HERE...

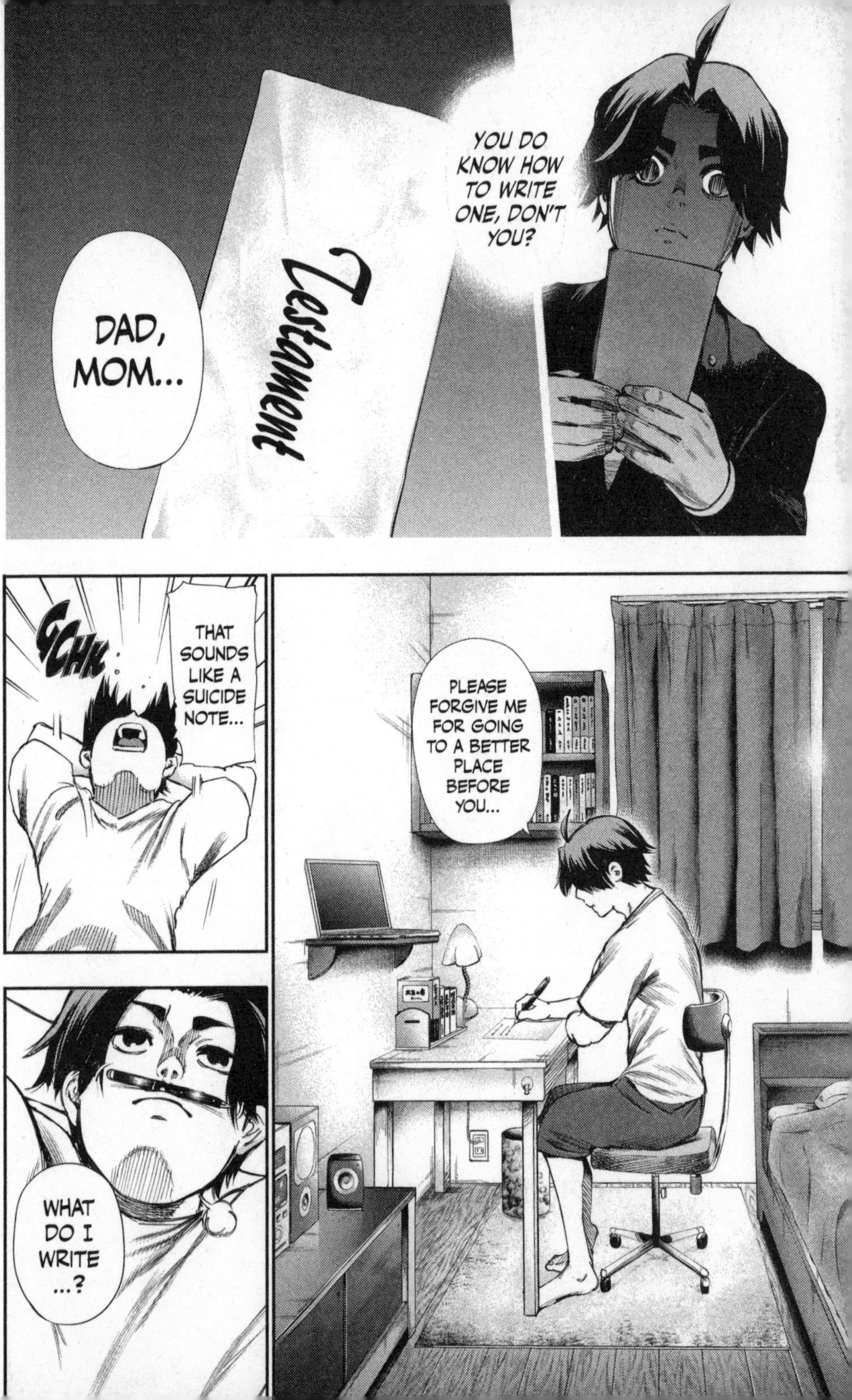
YOU DO KNOW HOW TO WRITE ONE, DON'T YOU?
Testament
DAD, MOM...
PLEASE FORGIVE ME FOR GOING TO A BETTER PLACE BEFORE YOU...
GCHK
THAT SOUNDS LIKE A SUICIDE NOTE...
WHAT DO I WRITE ...?

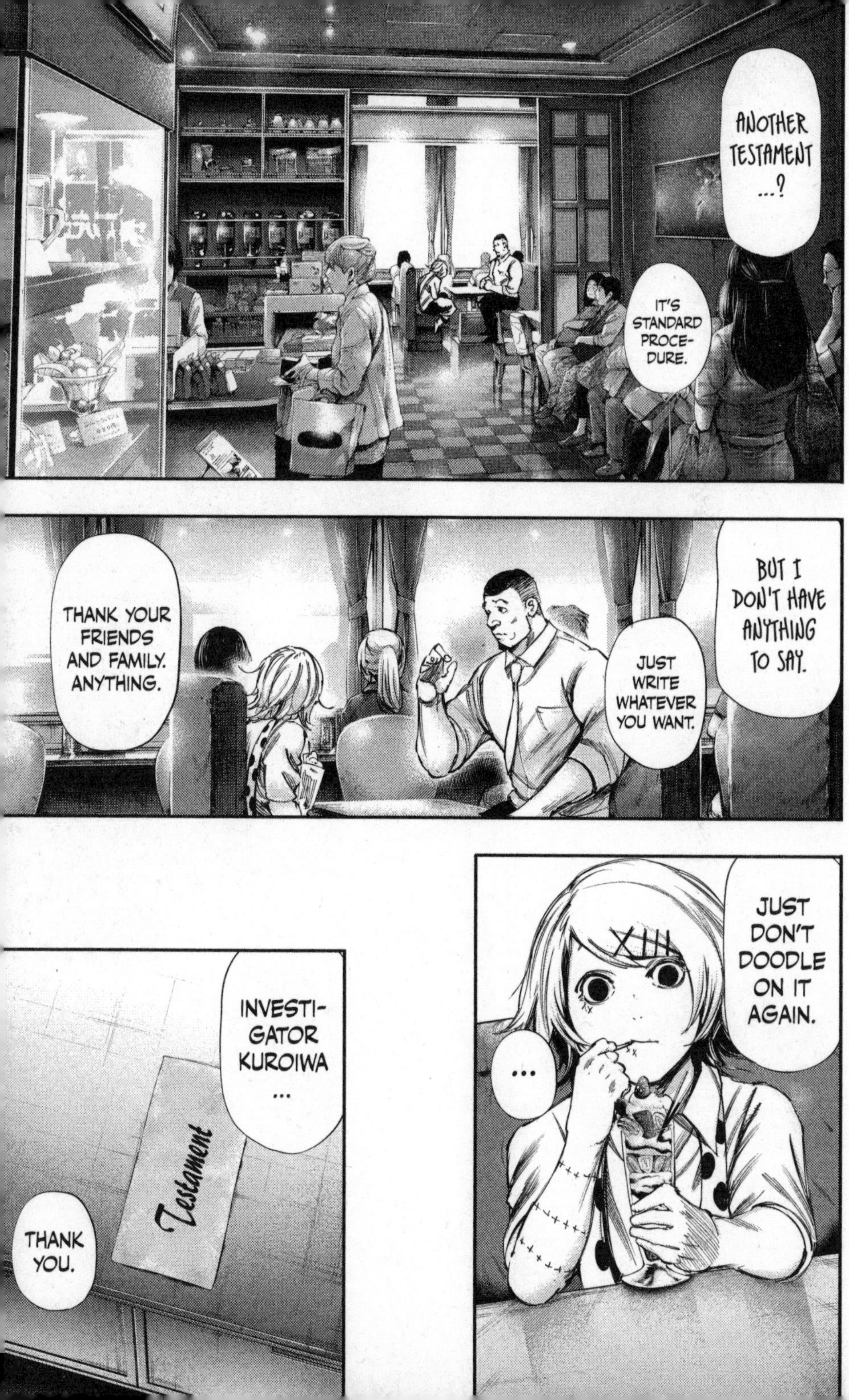
ANOTHER TESTAMENT ...?
IT'S STANDARD PROCE-DURE.
BUT I DON'T HAVE ANYTHING TO SAY.
JUST WRITE WHATEVER YOU WANT.
THANK YOUR FRIENDS AND FAMILY. ANYTHING.
JUST DON'T DOODLE ON IT AGAIN.
...
INVESTI-GATOR KUROIWA ...
Testament
THANK YOU.

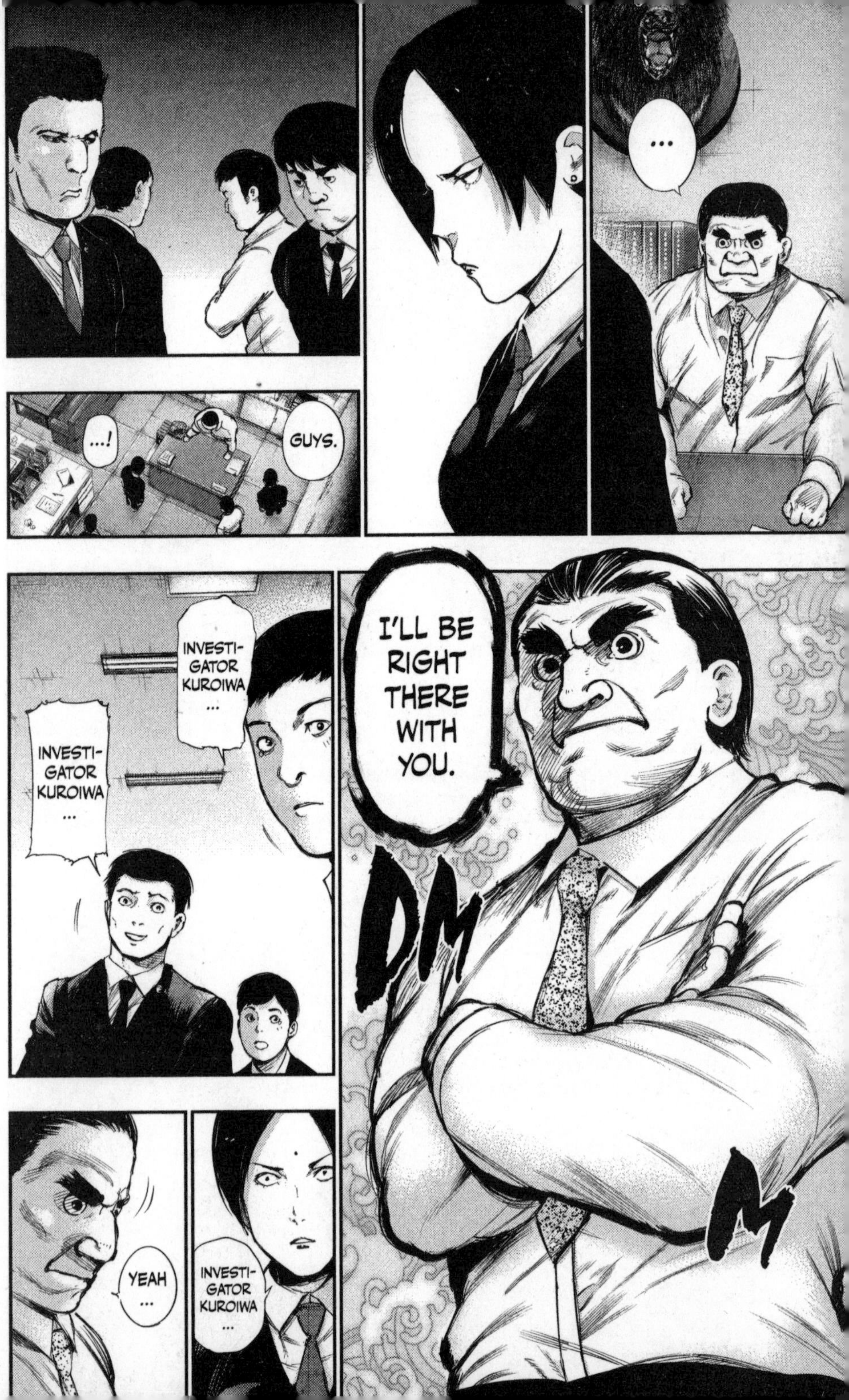
...
GUYS.
...!
I'LL BE RIGHT THERE WITH YOU.
DM
M
INVESTI-GATOR KUROIWA ...
INVESTI-GATOR KUROIWA ...
INVESTI-GATOR KUROIWA ...
YEAH ...

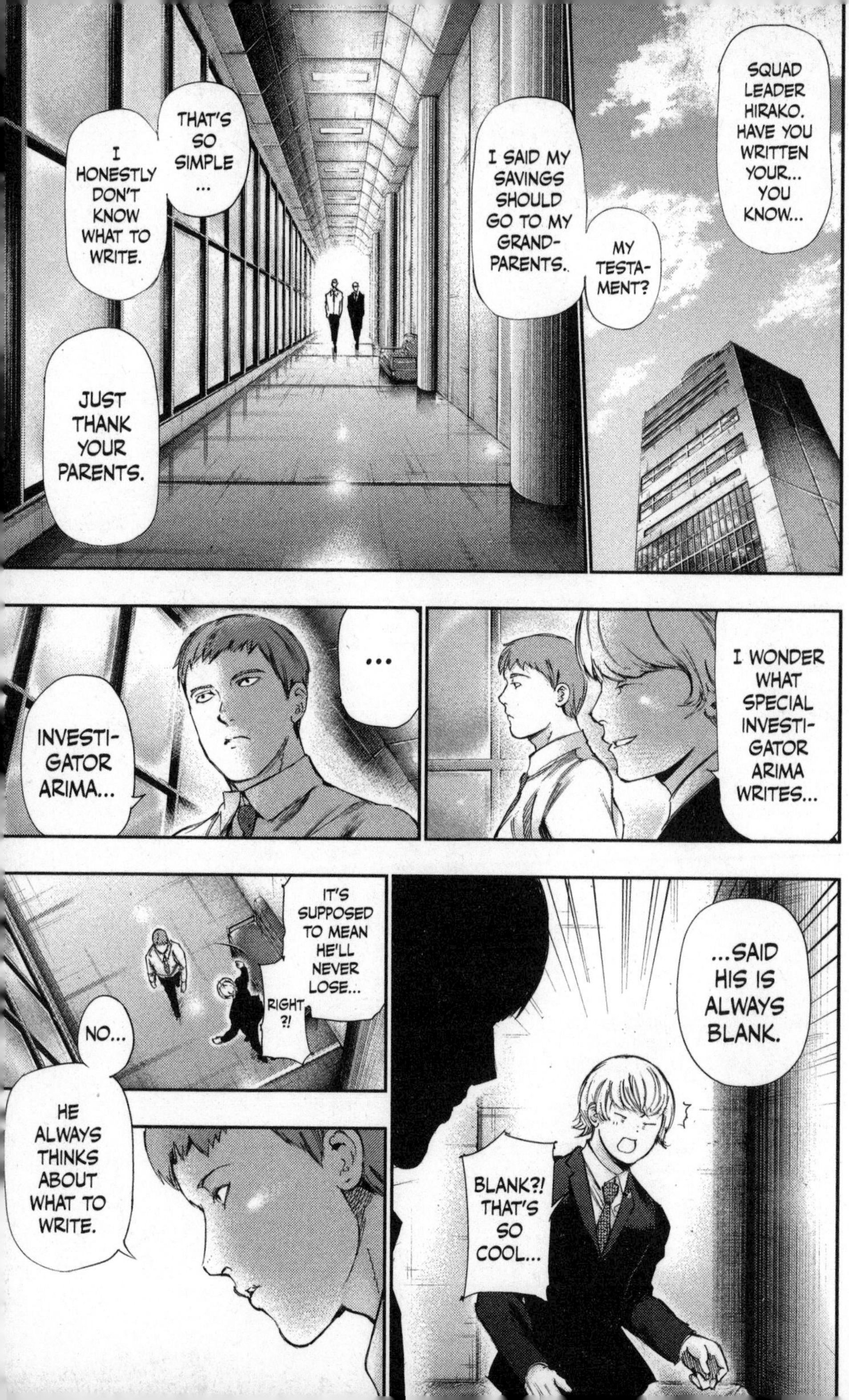
SQUAD LEADER HIRAKO. HAVE YOU WRITTEN YOUR... YOU KNOW...
MY TESTAMENT?
I SAID MY SAVINGS SHOULD GO TO MY GRANDPARENTS.
THAT'S SO SIMPLE ...
I HONESTLY DON'T KNOW WHAT TO WRITE.
JUST THANK YOUR PARENTS.
I WONDER WHAT SPECIAL INVESTIGATOR ARIMA WRITES...
...
INVESTIGATOR ARIMA...
...SAID HIS IS ALWAYS BLANK.
BLANK?! THAT'S SO COOL...
IT'S SUPPOSED TO MEAN HE'LL NEVER LOSE...
RIGHT?!
NO...
HE ALWAYS THINKS ABOUT WHAT TO WRITE.

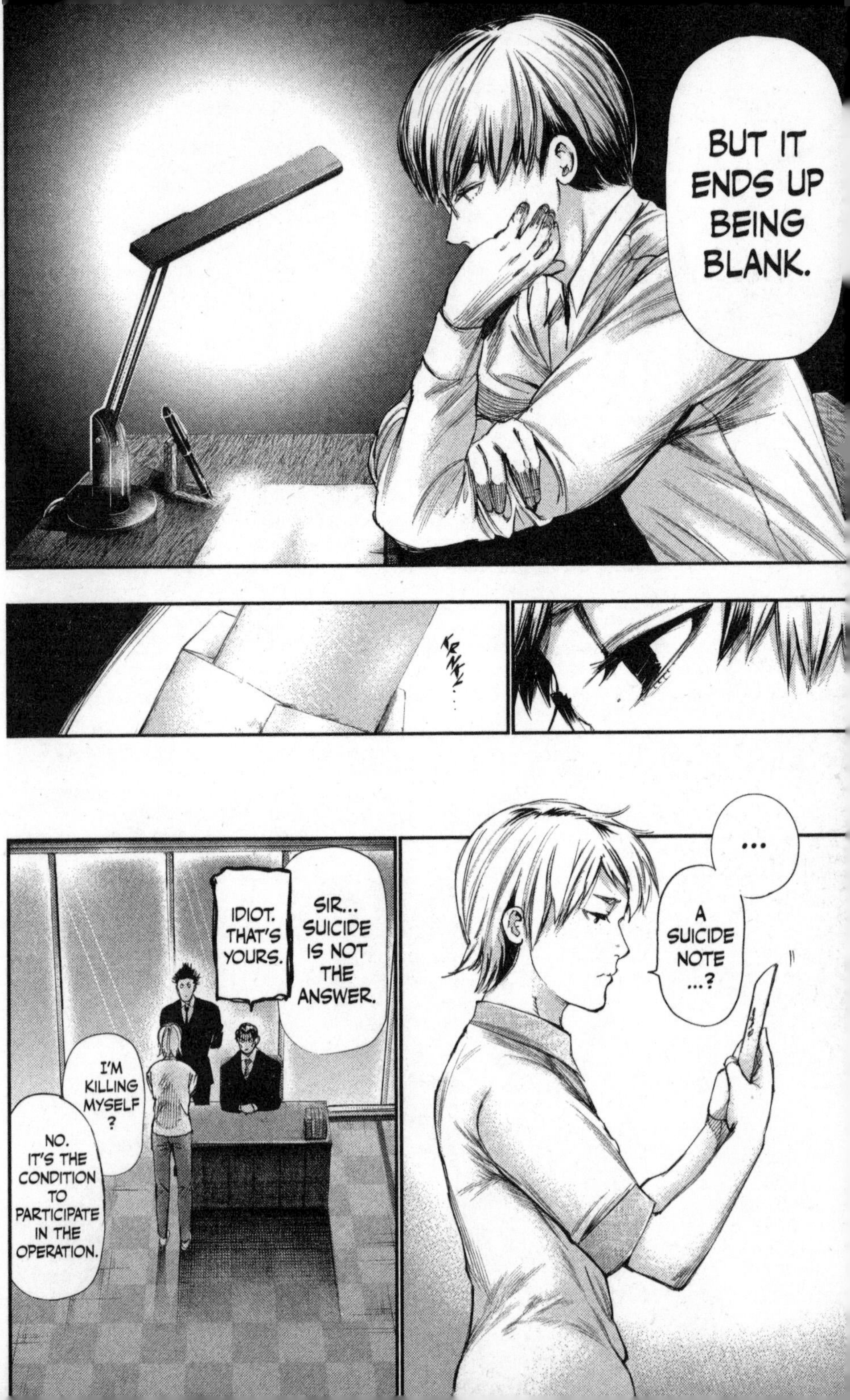
BUT IT ENDS UP BEING BLANK.
KRNKL...
...
A SUICIDE NOTE ...?
SIR... SUICIDE IS NOT THE ANSWER.
IDIOT. THAT'S YOURS.
I'M KILLING MYSELF ?
NO. IT'S THE CONDITION TO PARTICIPATE IN THE OPERATION.

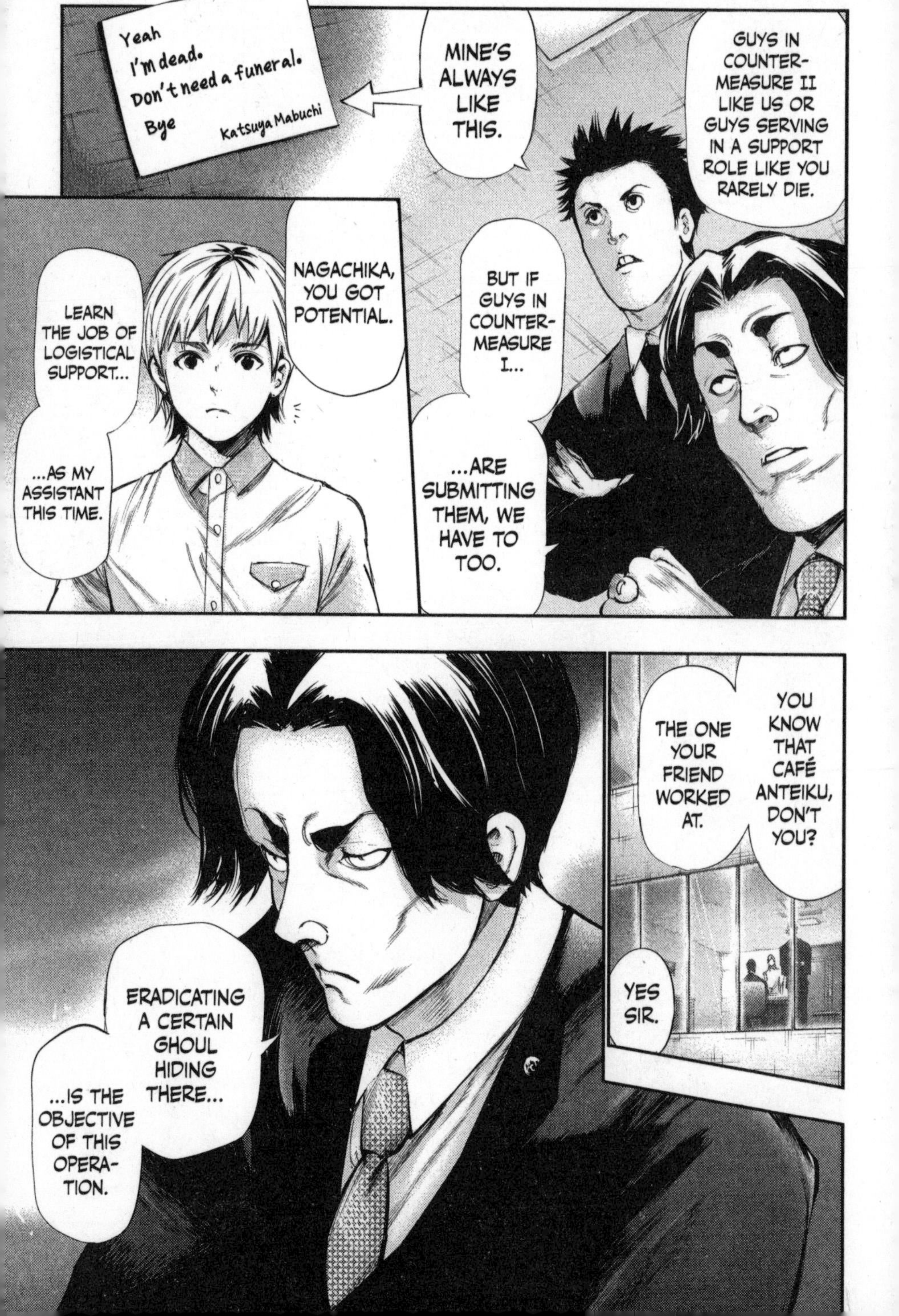
GUYS IN COUNTER-MEASURE II LIKE US OR GUYS SERVING IN A SUPPORT ROLE LIKE YOU RARELY DIE.
BUT IF GUYS IN COUNTER-MEASURE I...
...ARE SUBMITTING THEM, WE HAVE TO TOO.
MINE'S ALWAYS LIKE THIS.
Yeah
I'm dead.
Don't need a funeral.
Bye
Katsuya Mabuchi
NAGACHIKA, YOU GOT POTENTIAL.
LEARN THE JOB OF LOGISTICAL SUPPORT...
...AS MY ASSISTANT THIS TIME.
YOU KNOW THAT CAFÉ ANTEIKU, DON'T YOU?
THE ONE YOUR FRIEND WORKED AT.
YES SIR.
ERADICATING A CERTAIN GHOUL HIDING THERE...
...IS THE OBJECTIVE OF THIS OPERA-TION.

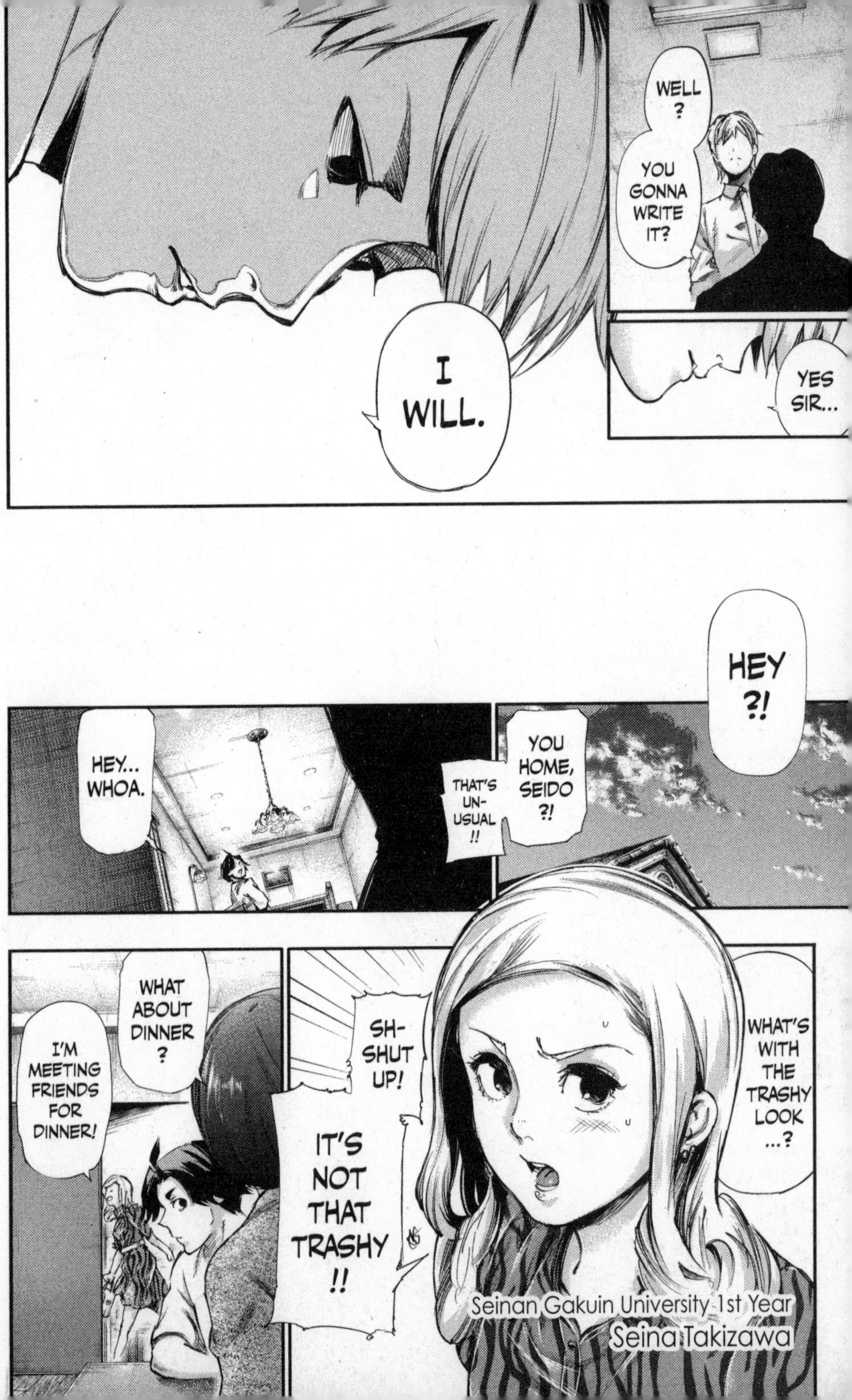
WELL?
YOU GONNA WRITE IT?
YES SIR...
I WILL.
HEY?!
YOU HOME, SEIDO?!
THAT'S UN-USUAL!!
HEY... WHOA.
WHAT'S WITH THE TRASHY LOOK...?
SH-SHUT UP!
IT'S NOT THAT TRASHY!!
Seinan Gakuin University 1st Year
Seina Takizawa
WHAT ABOUT DINNER?
I'M MEETING FRIENDS FOR DINNER!

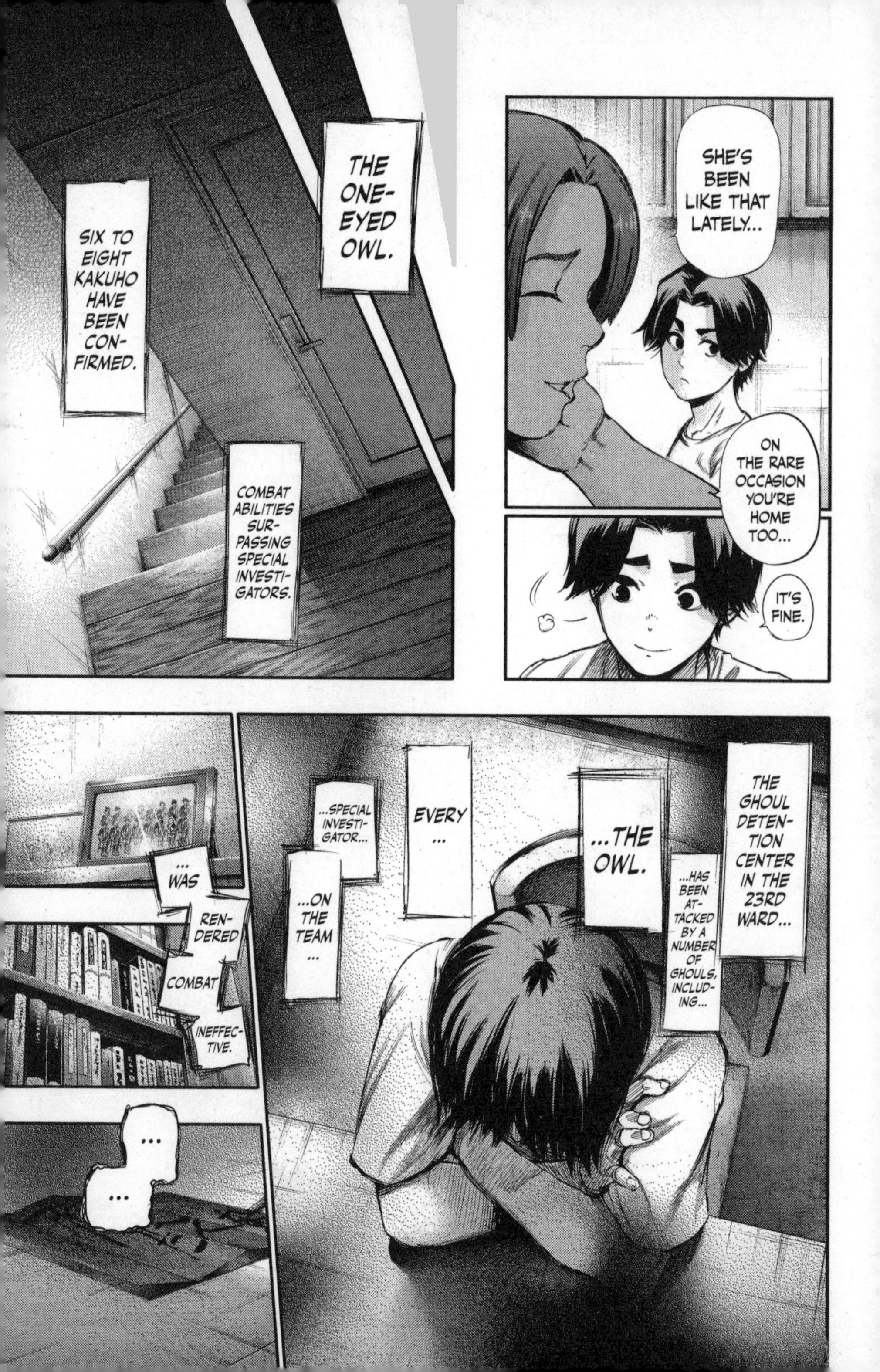
SHE'S BEEN LIKE THAT LATELY...
ON THE RARE OCCASION YOU'RE HOME TOO...
IT'S FINE.
THE ONE-EYED OWL.
SIX TO EIGHT KAKUHO HAVE BEEN CONFIRMED.
COMBAT ABILITIES SURPASSING SPECIAL INVESTIGATORS.
THE GHOUL DETENTION CENTER IN THE 23RD WARD...
...HAS BEEN ATTACKED BY A NUMBER OF GHOULS, INCLUDING...
...THE OWL.
EVERY...
...SPECIAL INVESTIGATOR...
...ON THE TEAM...
...WAS
RENDERED
COMBAT
INEFFECTIVE.
...
...

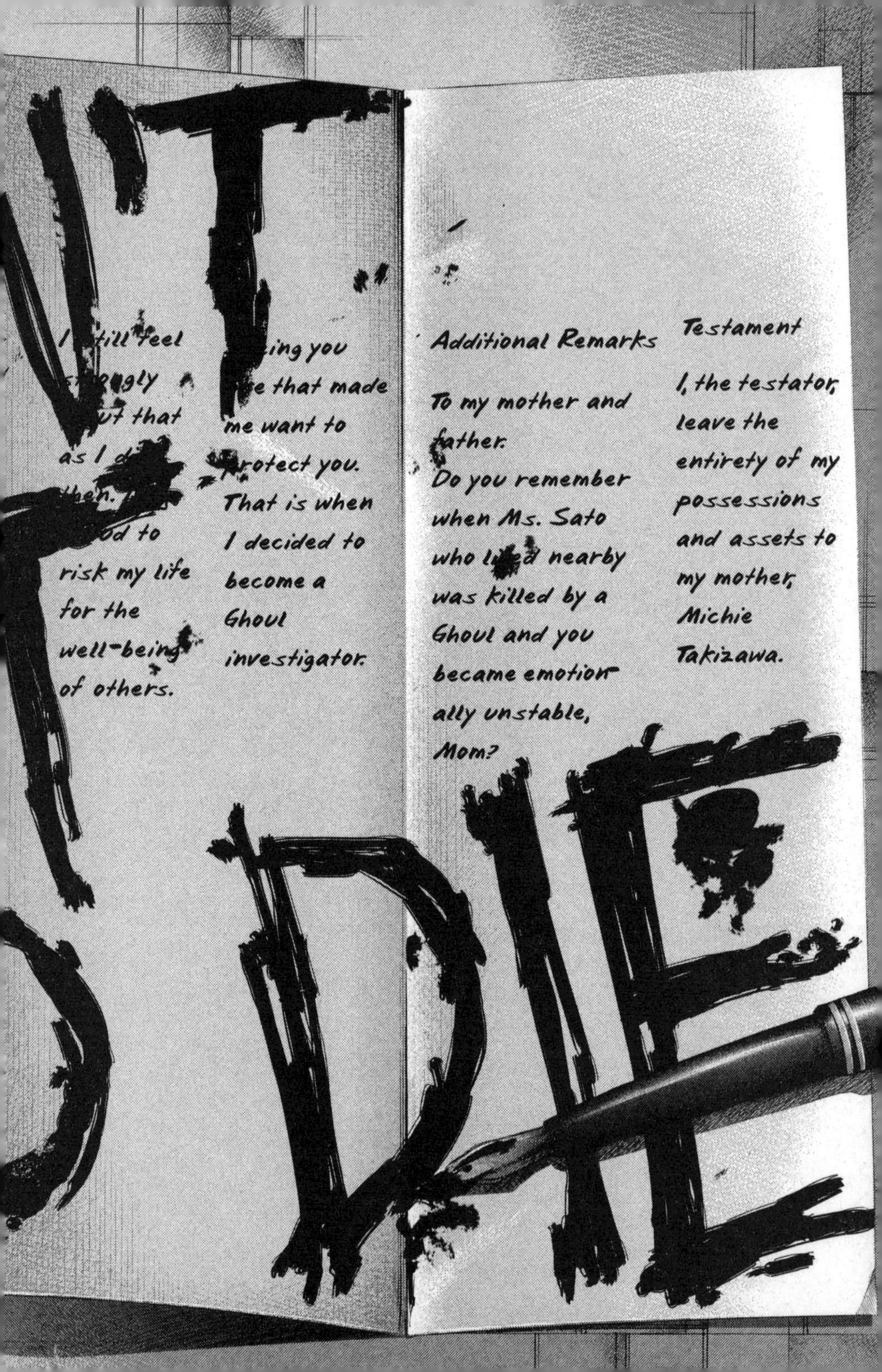
Testament
I, the testator, leave the entirety of my possessions and assets to my mother, Michie Takizawa.
Additional Remarks
To my mother and father.
Do you remember when Ms. Sato who lived nearby was killed by a Ghoul and you became emotionally unstable, Mom?
ing you
e that made me want to
rotect you.
That is when I decided to become a Ghoul investigator.
I
till feel
ut that
as I
then.
od to risk my life for the well-being of others.
DIE

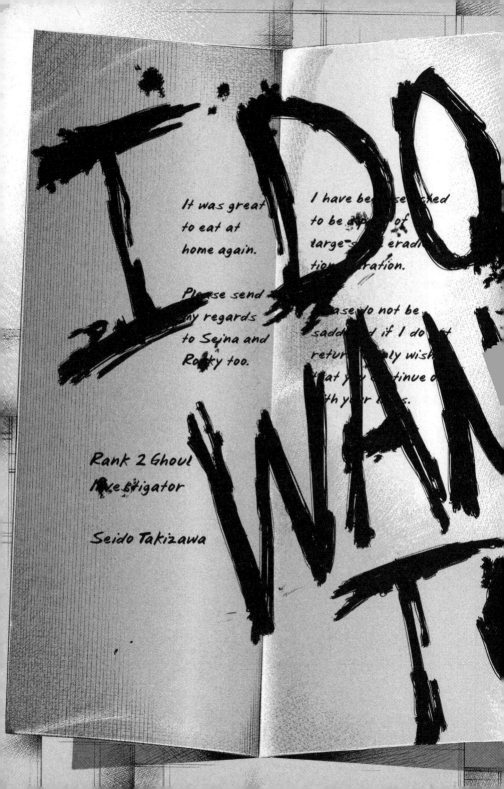

It was great to eat at home again.

Please send my regards to Sejna and Rocky too.

I have be~~~ ~~~~ ~ked to be ~ ~ ~ of large-s~~ ~ eradi~~~ tion ~ration.

~~ase to not be sadd~~ ~d if I do ~~t retur~~ ~nly wish ~at y~~ ~~tinue ~ ~h y~~r ~~~s.

Rank 2 Ghoul Investigator

Seido Takizawa

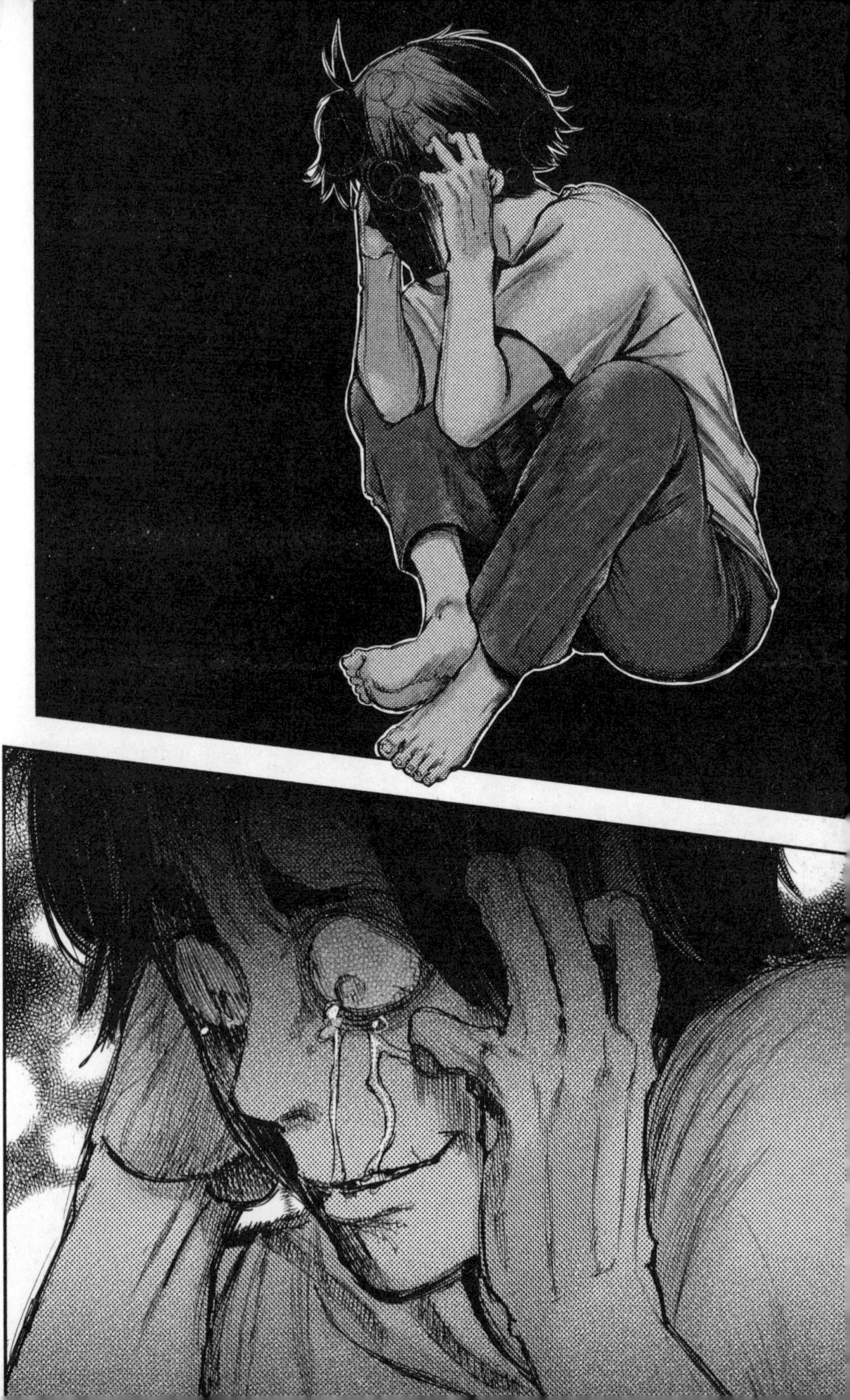

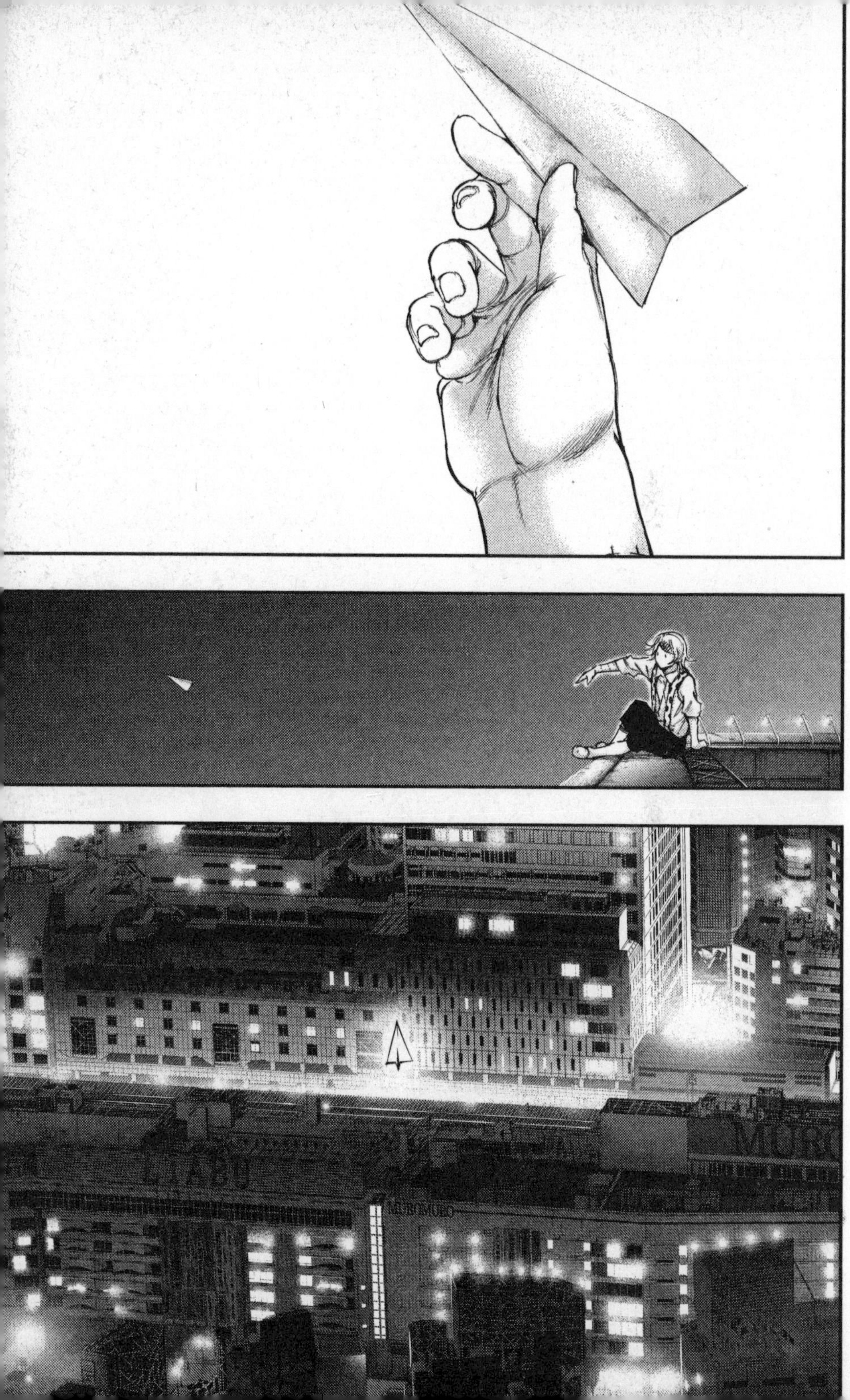
MURO
MUROMURO

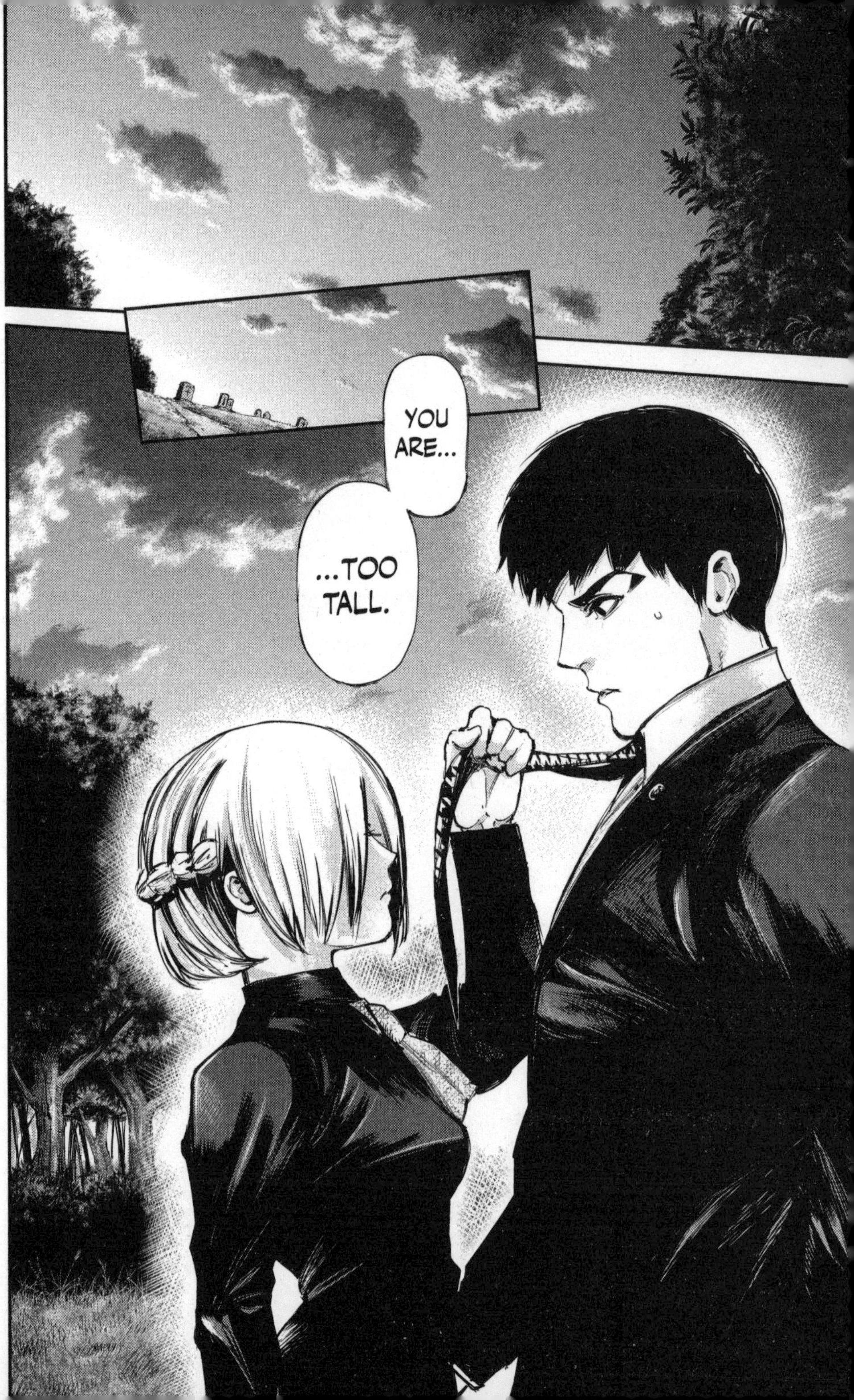
YOU ARE...
...TOO TALL.

東京喰種
トーキョーグール
Tokyo Ghoul

Poetry Time. (4)

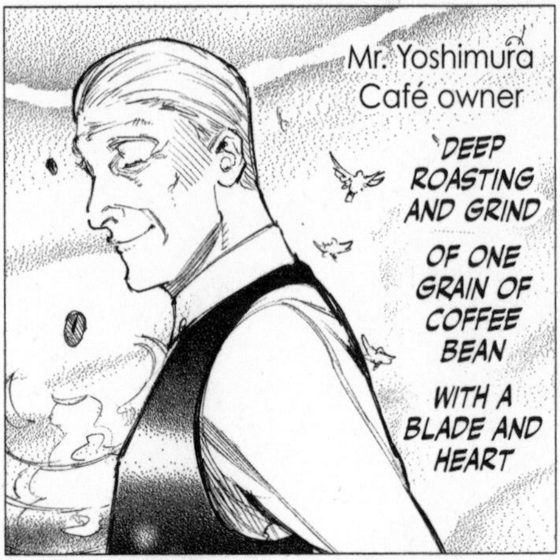
Mr. Yoshimura
Café owner
DEEP ROASTING AND GRIND
OF ONE GRAIN OF COFFEE BEAN
WITH A BLADE AND HEART

IT'S VERY MR. YOSHIMURA. IT'S WONDERFUL... (KANEKI)

SIMPLY GOOD. I FEEL IT SPEAKS TO THE HEART. (YOMO)

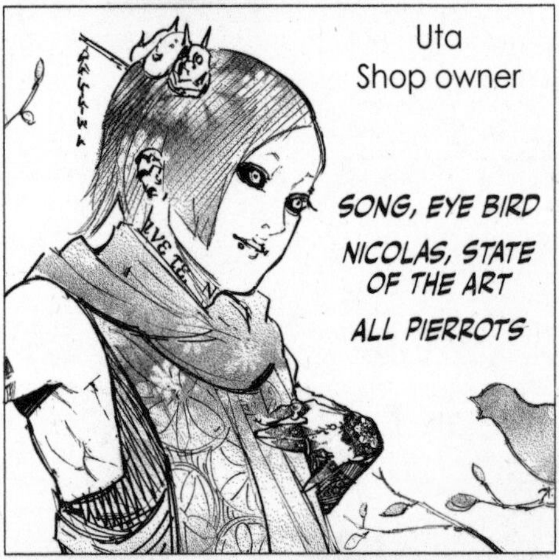
Uta
Shop owner
SONG, EYE BIRD
NICOLAS, STATE OF THE ART
ALL PIERROTS

I'M INTERESTED IN YOUR POETIC SENSIBILITIES. (SHU TSUKIYAMA - MOONLIGHT OF SADNESS)

VERY NICE. UNLIKE TSUKI-YAMA'S. (TOUKA)

I DON'T GET IT!!! (YOMO)

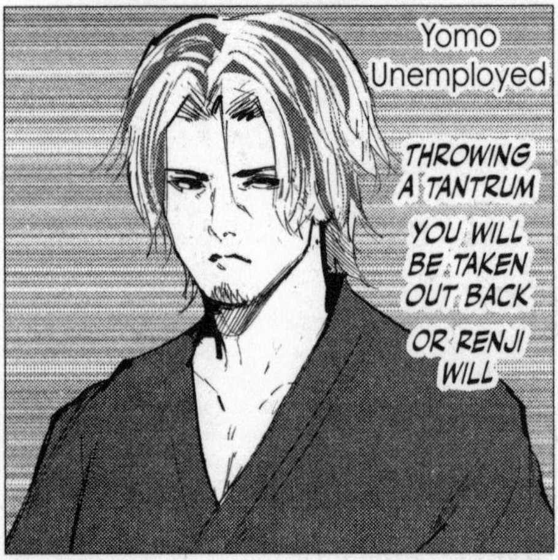
Yomo
Unemployed
THROWING A TANTRUM
YOU WILL BE TAKEN OUT BACK
OR RENJI WILL

THE LEVEL JUST SUD-DENLY... (KANEKI)

'OR RENJI'! (LAUGH) (ITORI)

THOUGHT HE SAID ORANGE. (UTA)

I KINDA LIKE IT. EASY TO UNDER-STAND... (TOUKA)

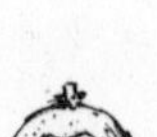
Mr. Orange

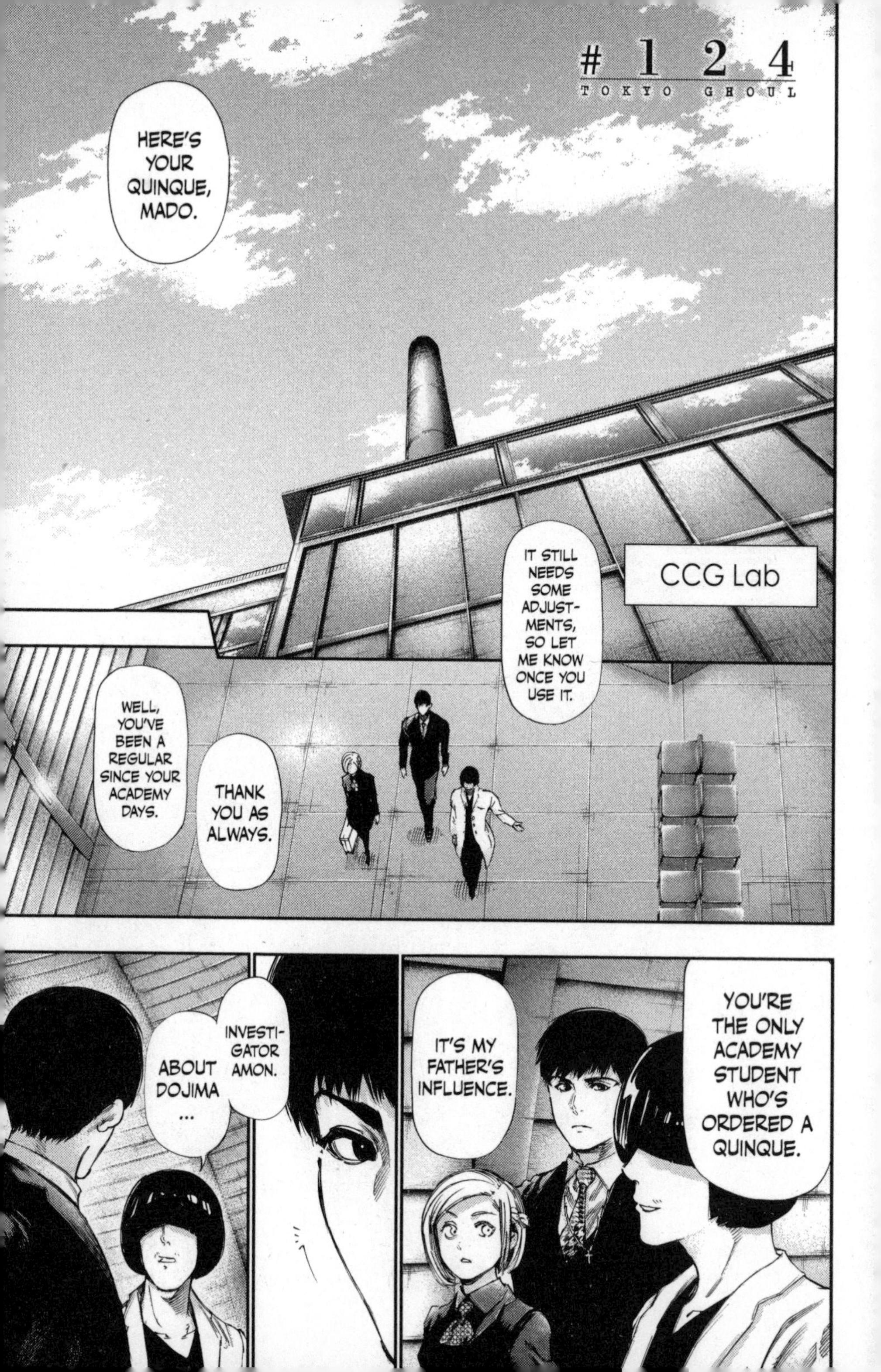
#124
TOKYO GHOUL
HERE'S YOUR QUINQUE, MADO.
CCG Lab
IT STILL NEEDS SOME ADJUST-MENTS, SO LET ME KNOW ONCE YOU USE IT.
THANK YOU AS ALWAYS.
WELL, YOU'VE BEEN A REGULAR SINCE YOUR ACADEMY DAYS.
YOU'RE THE ONLY ACADEMY STUDENT WHO'S ORDERED A QUINQUE.
IT'S MY FATHER'S INFLUENCE.
INVESTI-GATOR AMON.
ABOUT DOJIMA ...

#124 PUBLIC

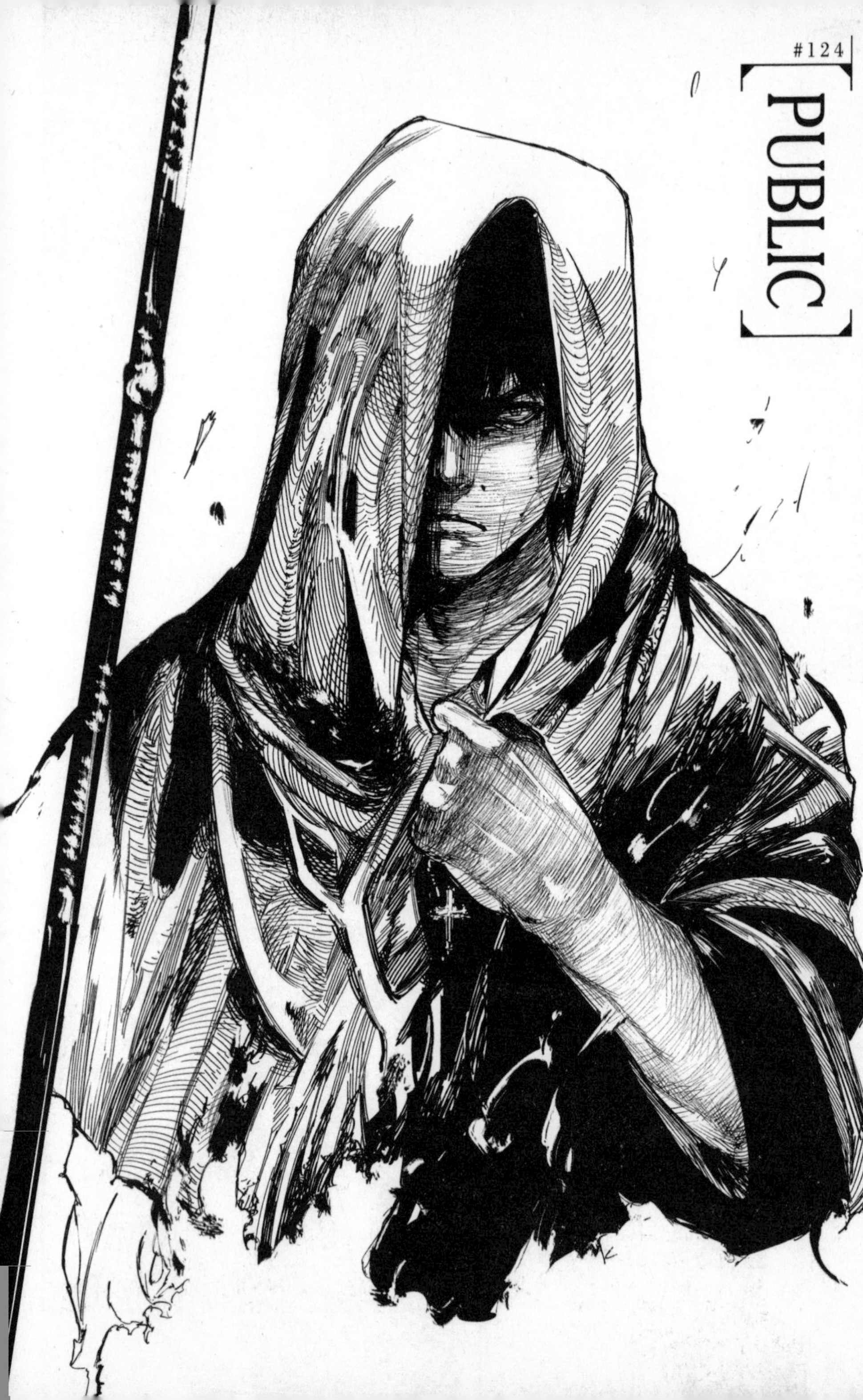

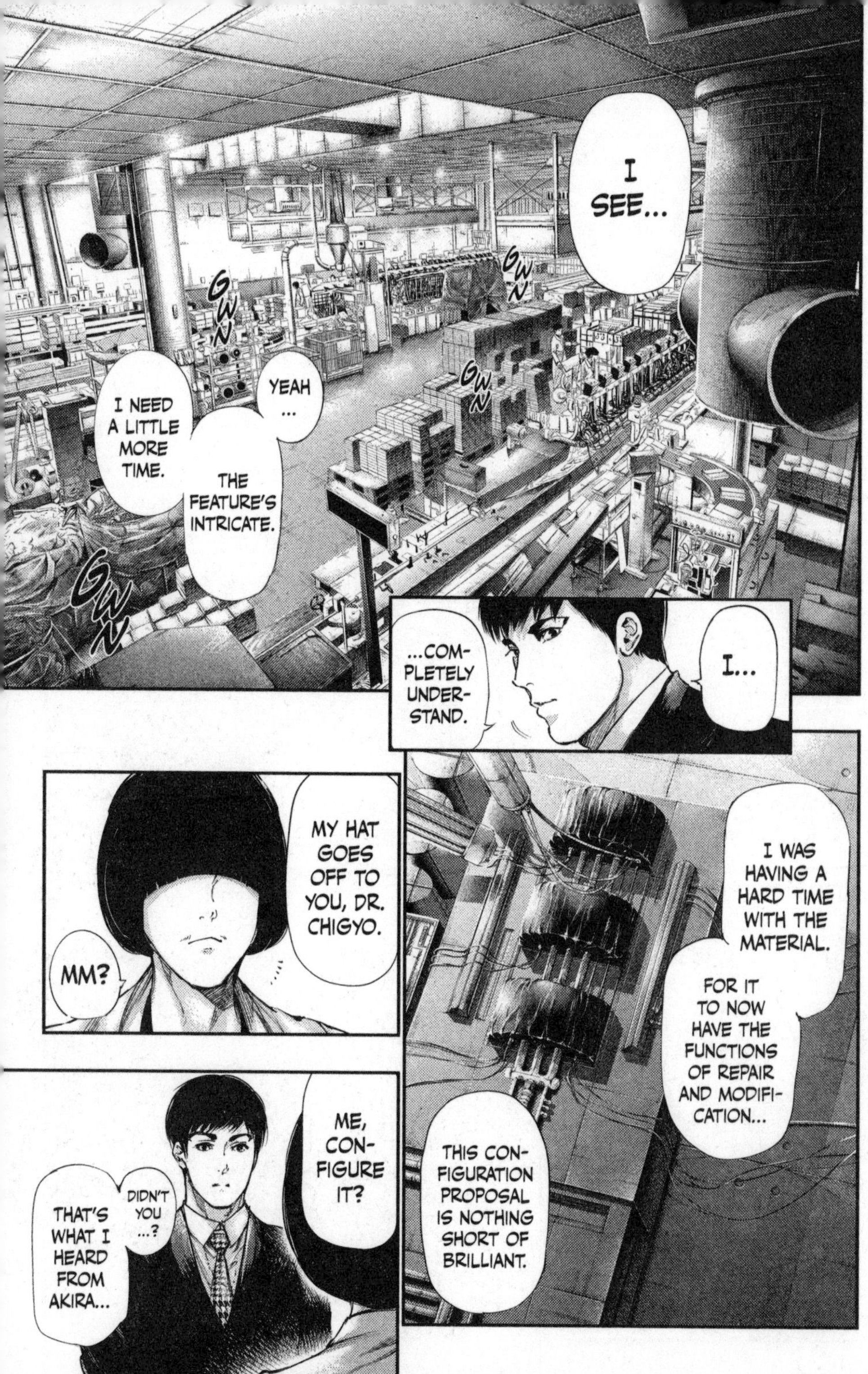
I SEE...
GWN
GWN
GWN
GWN
YEAH ...
THE FEATURE'S INTRICATE.
I NEED A LITTLE MORE TIME.
GWN
I...
...COMPLETELY UNDERSTAND.
I WAS HAVING A HARD TIME WITH THE MATERIAL.
FOR IT TO NOW HAVE THE FUNCTIONS OF REPAIR AND MODIFICATION...
THIS CONFIGURATION PROPOSAL IS NOTHING SHORT OF BRILLIANT.
MY HAT GOES OFF TO YOU, DR. CHIGYO.
MM?
ME, CONFIGURE IT?
DIDN'T YOU ...?
THAT'S WHAT I HEARD FROM AKIRA...

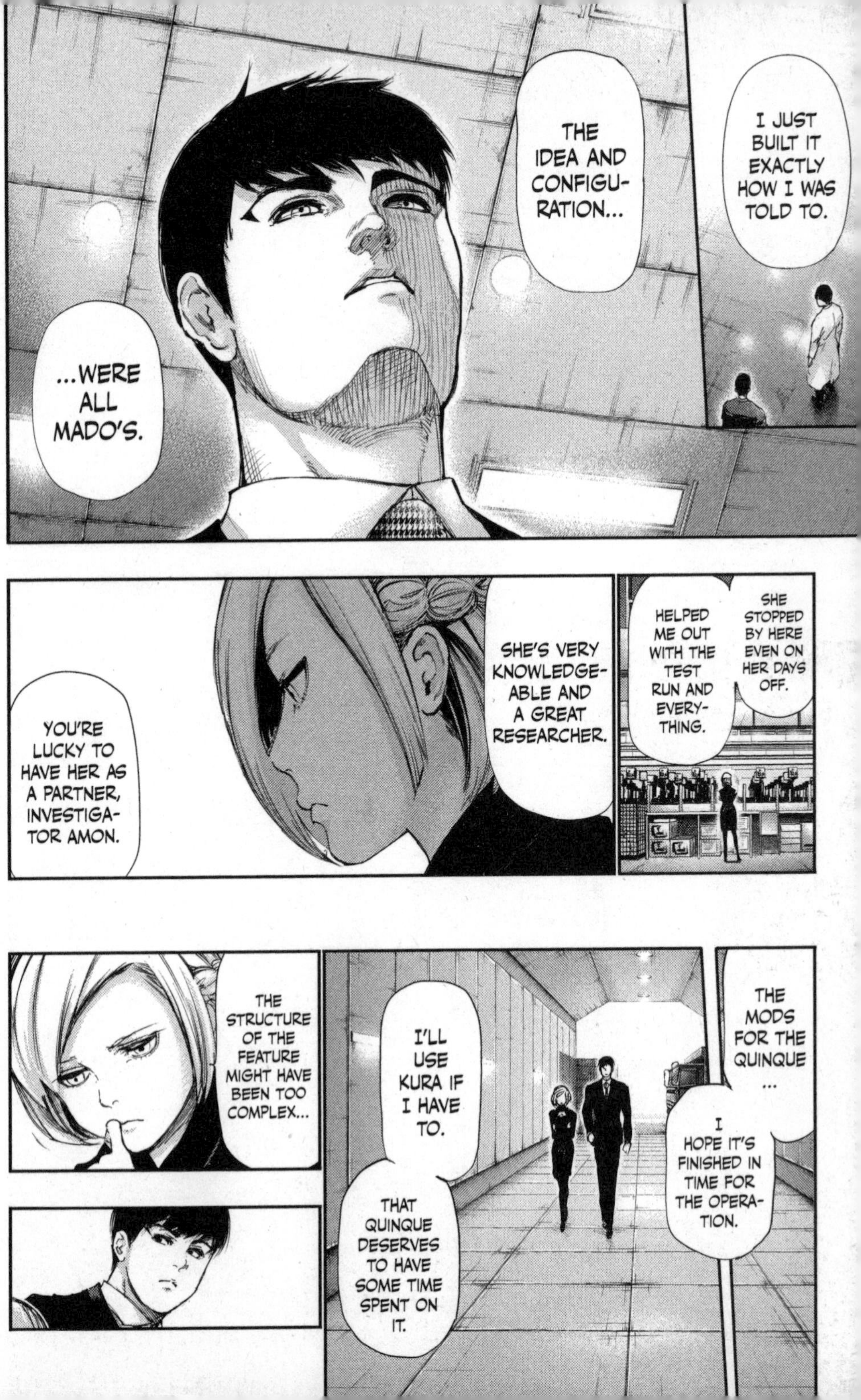
I JUST BUILT IT EXACTLY HOW I WAS TOLD TO.
THE IDEA AND CONFIGURATION...
...WERE ALL MADO'S.
SHE STOPPED BY HERE EVEN ON HER DAYS OFF.
HELPED ME OUT WITH THE TEST RUN AND EVERYTHING.
SHE'S VERY KNOWLEDGEABLE AND A GREAT RESEARCHER.
YOU'RE LUCKY TO HAVE HER AS A PARTNER, INVESTIGATOR AMON.
THE MODS FOR THE QUINQUE ...
I HOPE IT'S FINISHED IN TIME FOR THE OPERATION.
I'LL USE KURA IF I HAVE TO.
THAT QUINQUE DESERVES TO HAVE SOME TIME SPENT ON IT.
THE STRUCTURE OF THE FEATURE MIGHT HAVE BEEN TOO COMPLEX...

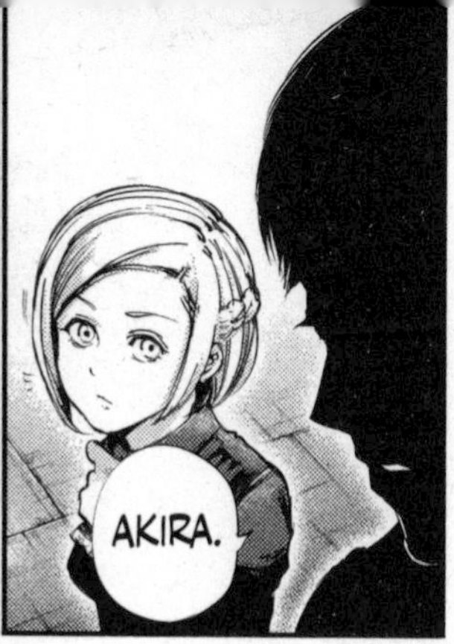
AKIRA.
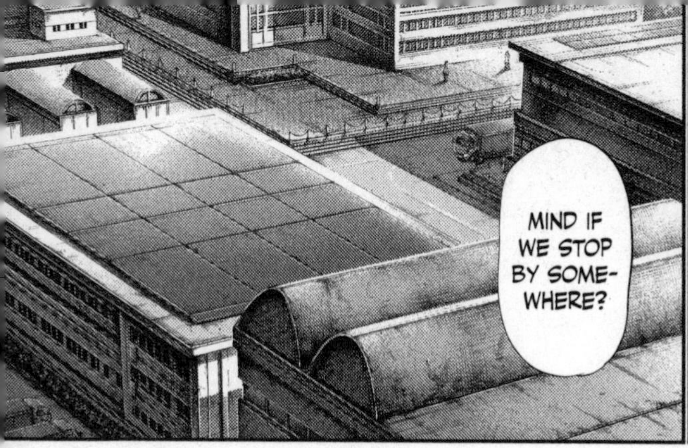
MIND IF WE STOP BY SOME-WHERE?
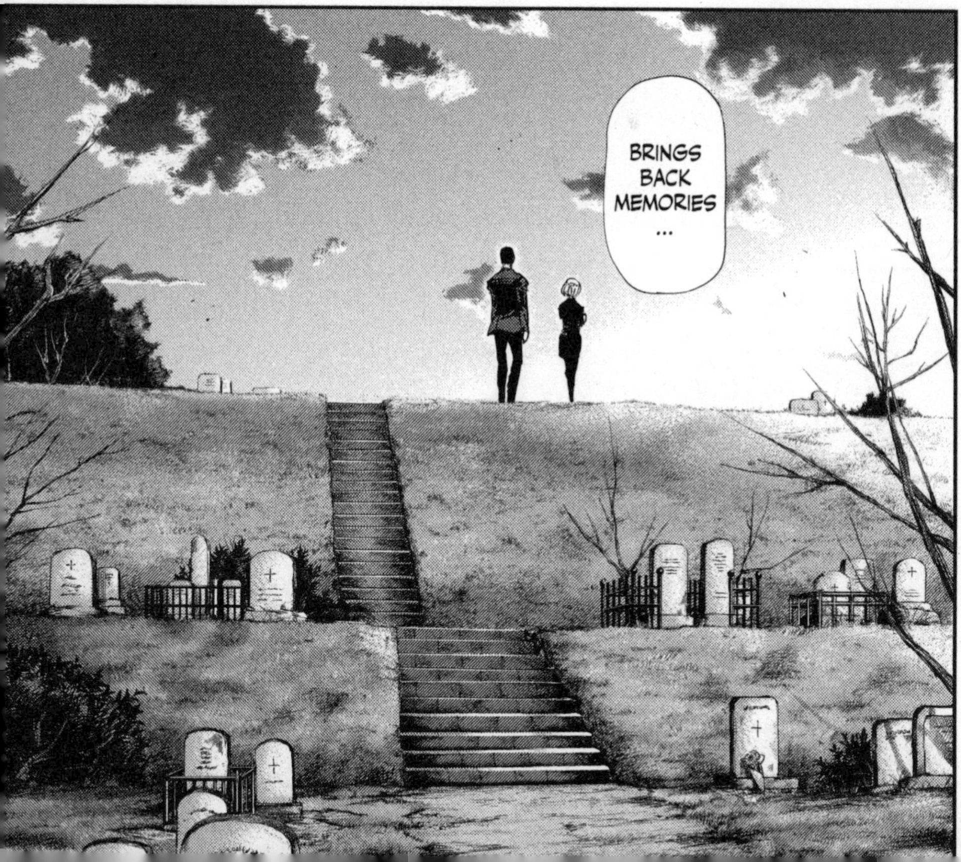
BRINGS BACK MEMORIES ...

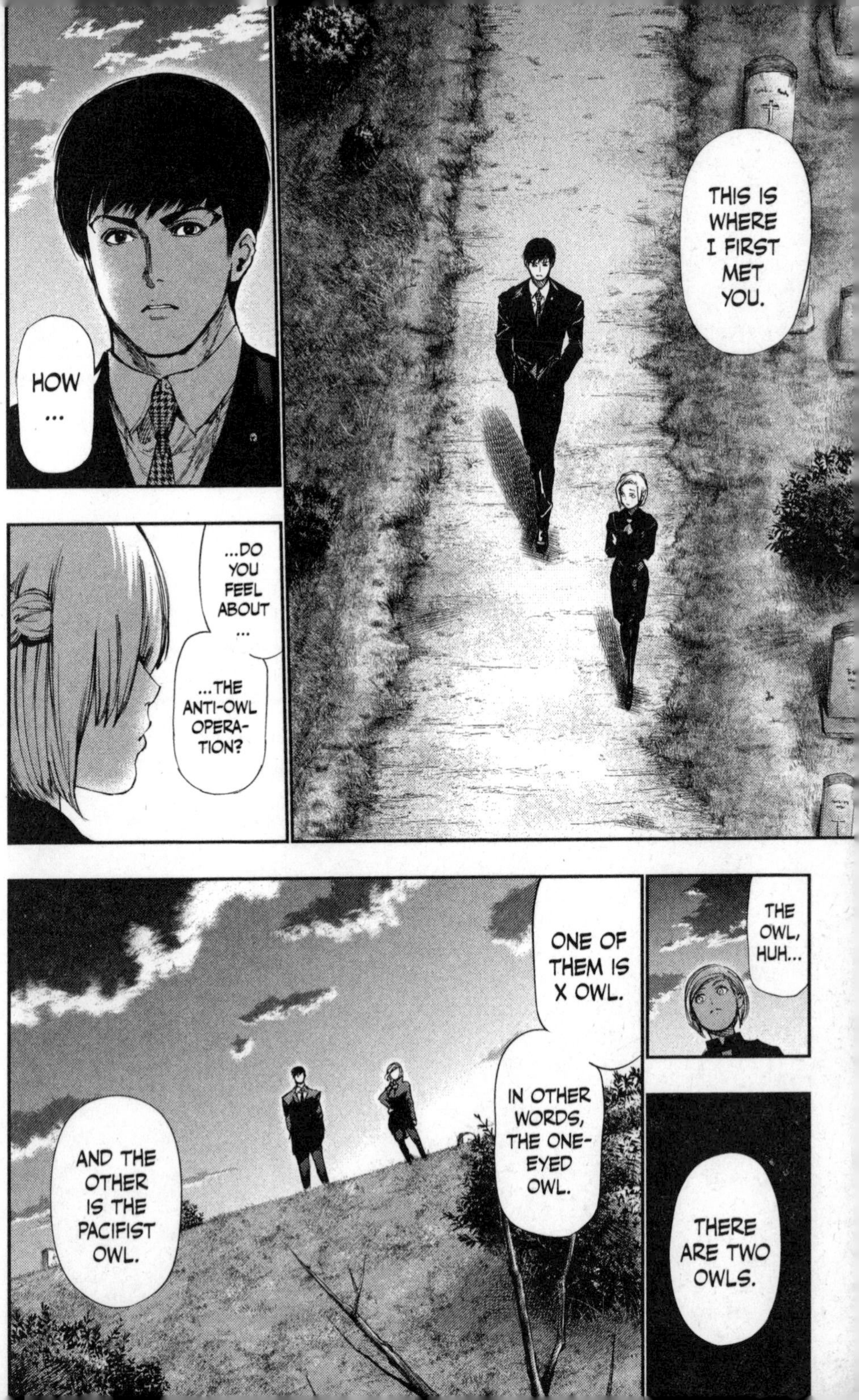
THIS IS WHERE I FIRST MET YOU.
HOW ...
...DO YOU FEEL ABOUT ...
...THE ANTI-OWL OPERATION?
THE OWL, HUH...
THERE ARE TWO OWLS.
ONE OF THEM IS X OWL.
IN OTHER WORDS, THE ONE-EYED OWL.
AND THE OTHER IS THE PACIFIST OWL.

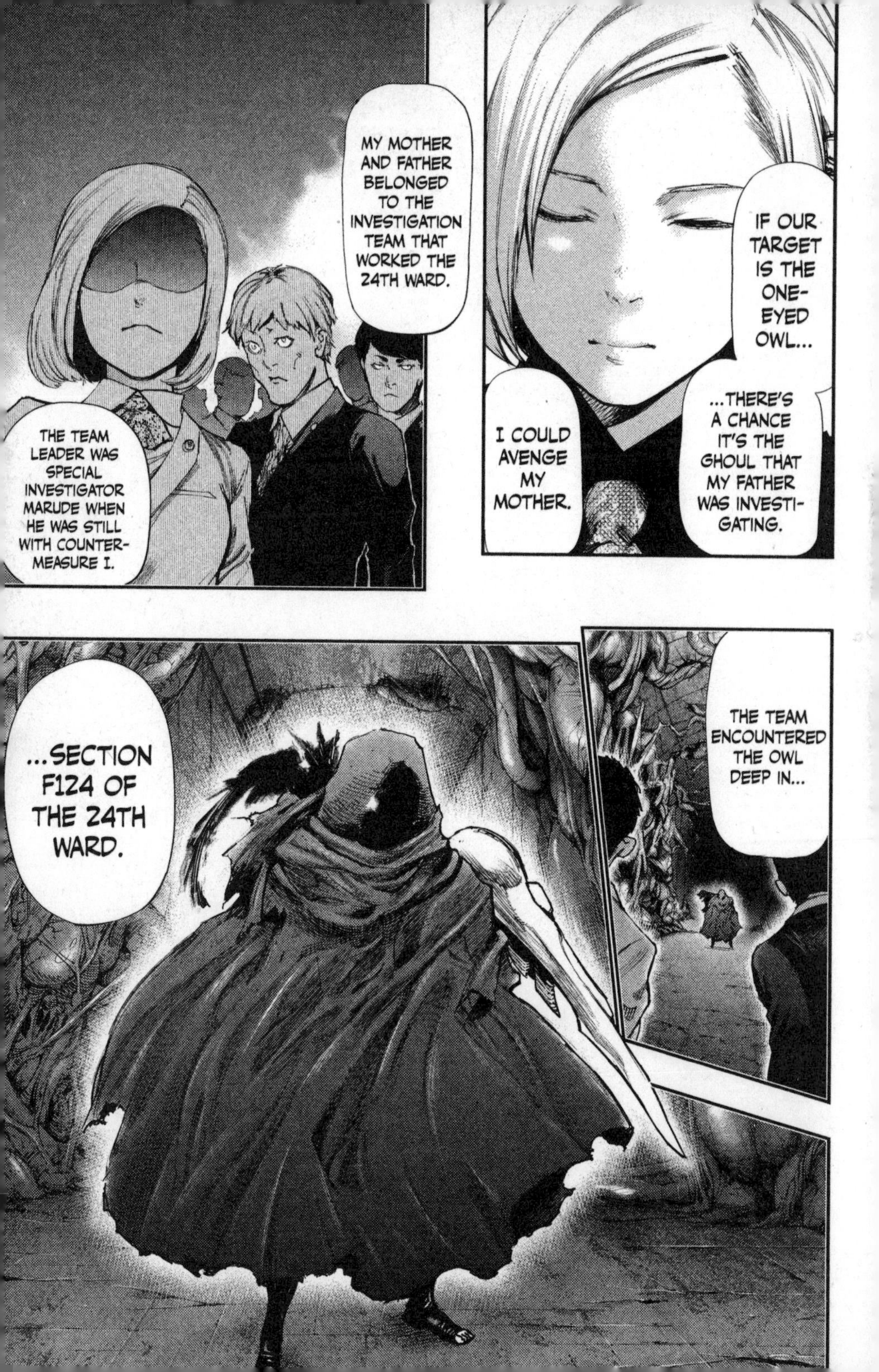
IF OUR TARGET IS THE ONE-EYED OWL...
...THERE'S A CHANCE IT'S THE GHOUL THAT MY FATHER WAS INVESTIGATING.
I COULD AVENGE MY MOTHER.
MY MOTHER AND FATHER BELONGED TO THE INVESTIGATION TEAM THAT WORKED THE 24TH WARD.
THE TEAM LEADER WAS SPECIAL INVESTIGATOR MARUDE WHEN HE WAS STILL WITH COUNTER-MEASURE I.
THE TEAM ENCOUNTERED THE OWL DEEP IN...
...SECTION F124 OF THE 24TH WARD.

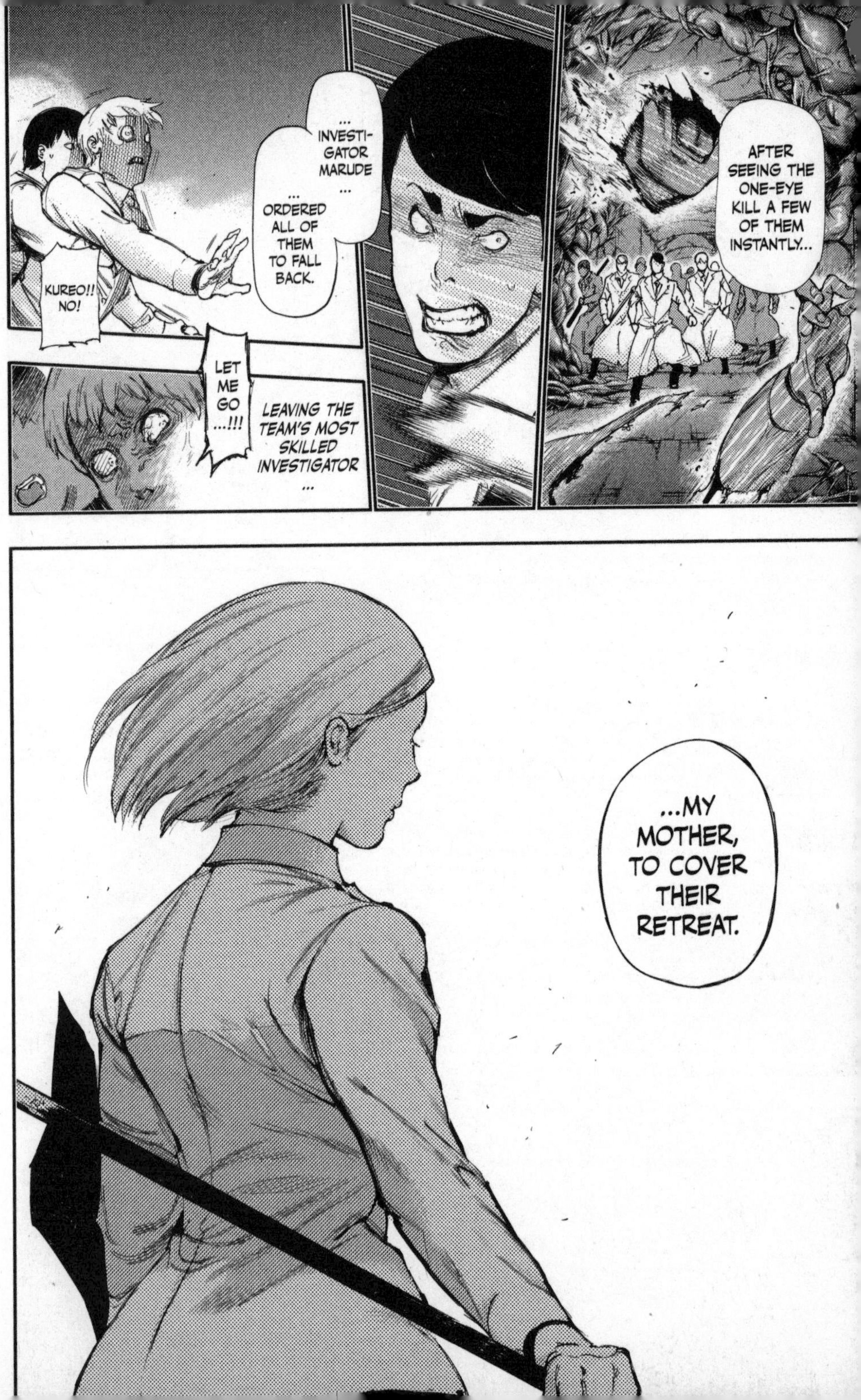
AFTER SEEING THE ONE-EYE KILL A FEW OF THEM INSTANTLY...
... INVESTIGATOR MARUDE ... ORDERED ALL OF THEM TO FALL BACK.
KUREO!! NO!
LET ME GO ...!!!
LEAVING THE TEAM'S MOST SKILLED INVESTIGATOR ...
...MY MOTHER, TO COVER THEIR RETREAT.

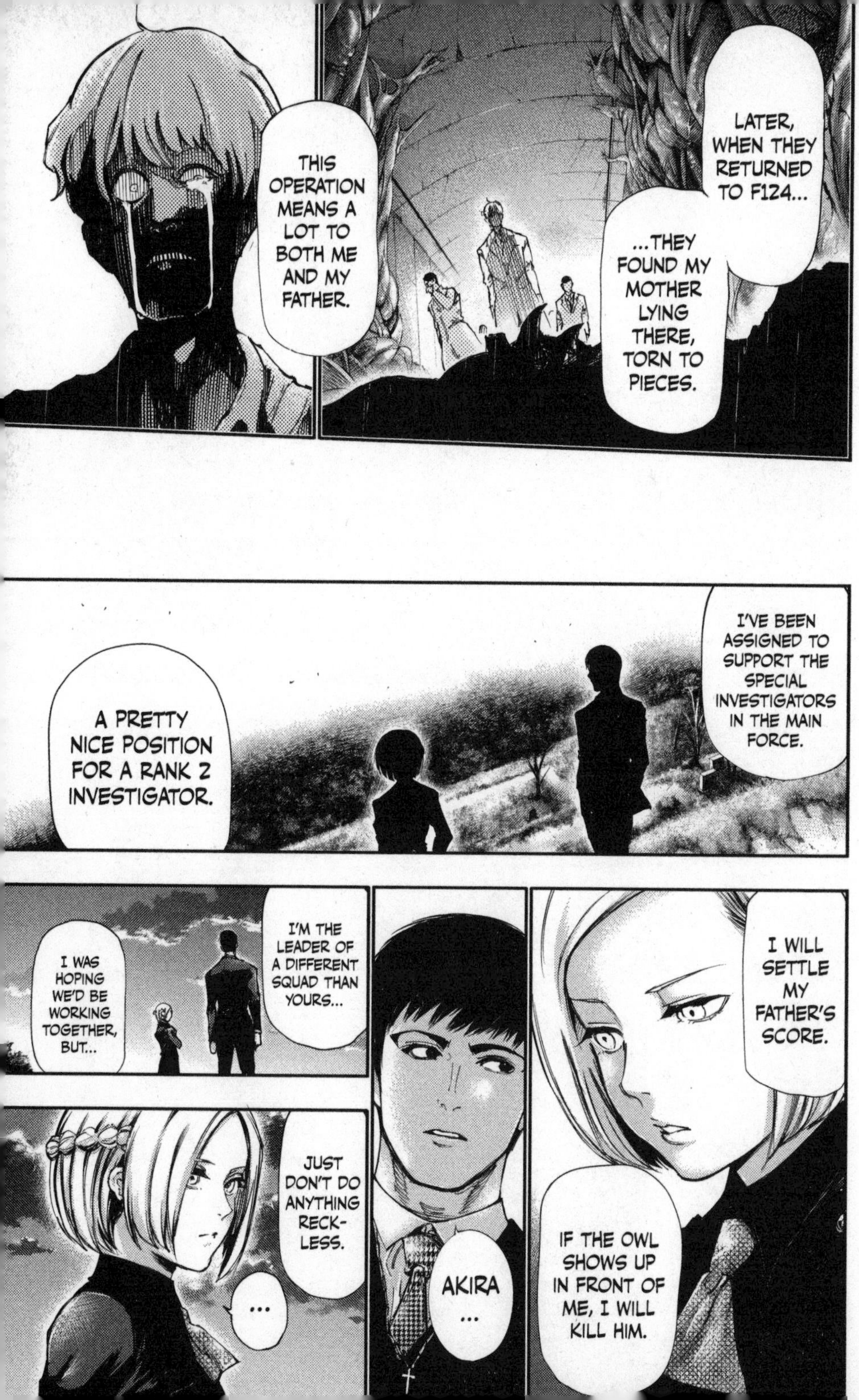
LATER, WHEN THEY RETURNED TO F124...
...THEY FOUND MY MOTHER LYING THERE, TORN TO PIECES.
THIS OPERATION MEANS A LOT TO BOTH ME AND MY FATHER.
I'VE BEEN ASSIGNED TO SUPPORT THE SPECIAL INVESTIGATORS IN THE MAIN FORCE.
A PRETTY NICE POSITION FOR A RANK 2 INVESTIGATOR.
I WILL SETTLE MY FATHER'S SCORE.
IF THE OWL SHOWS UP IN FRONT OF ME, I WILL KILL HIM.
AKIRA ...
I'M THE LEADER OF A DIFFERENT SQUAD THAN YOURS...
I WAS HOPING WE'D BE WORKING TOGETHER, BUT...
JUST DON'T DO ANYTHING RECK-LESS.
...

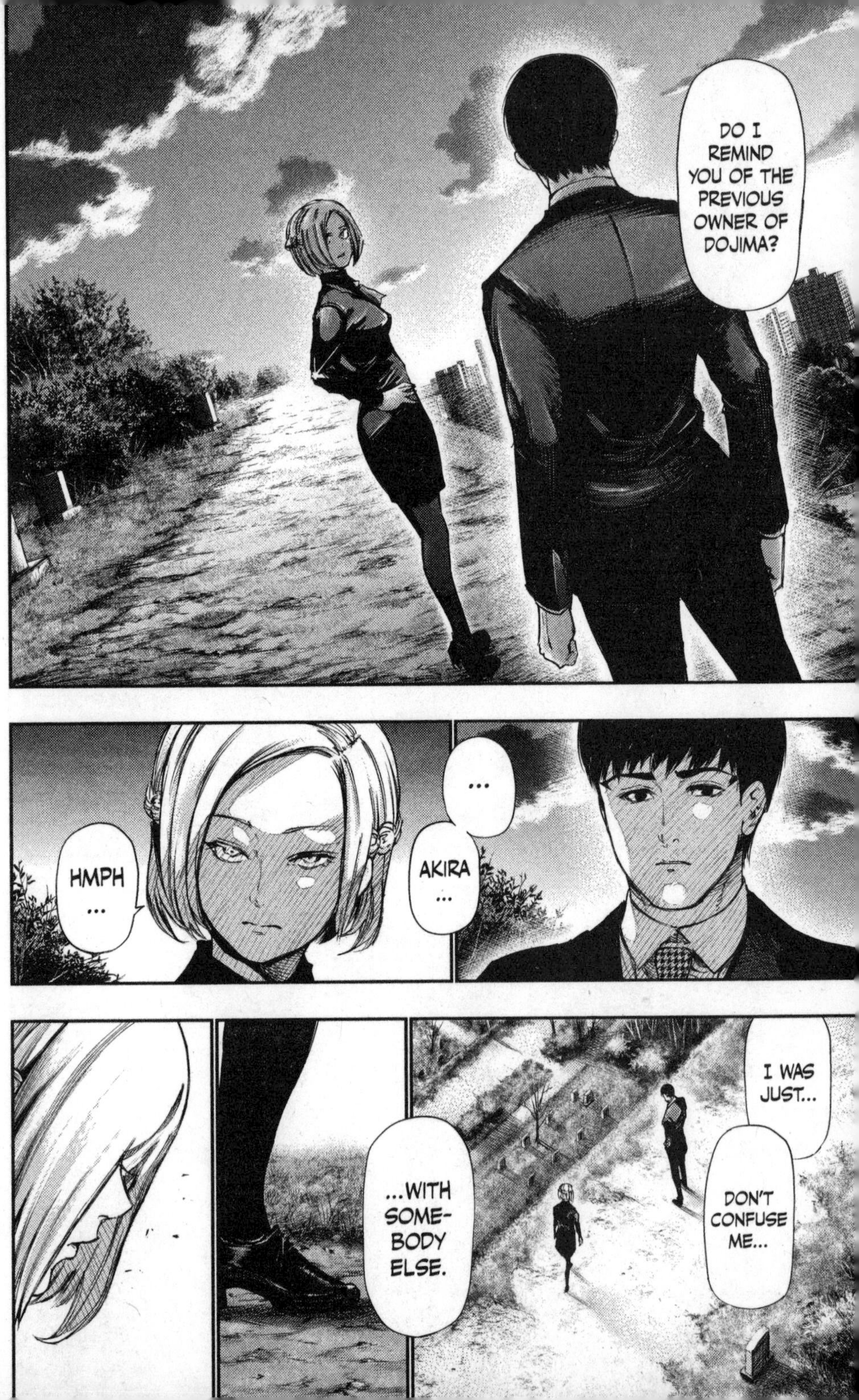
DO I REMIND YOU OF THE PREVIOUS OWNER OF DOJIMA?
...
AKIRA ...
HMPH ...
I WAS JUST...
DON'T CONFUSE ME...
...WITH SOMEBODY ELSE.

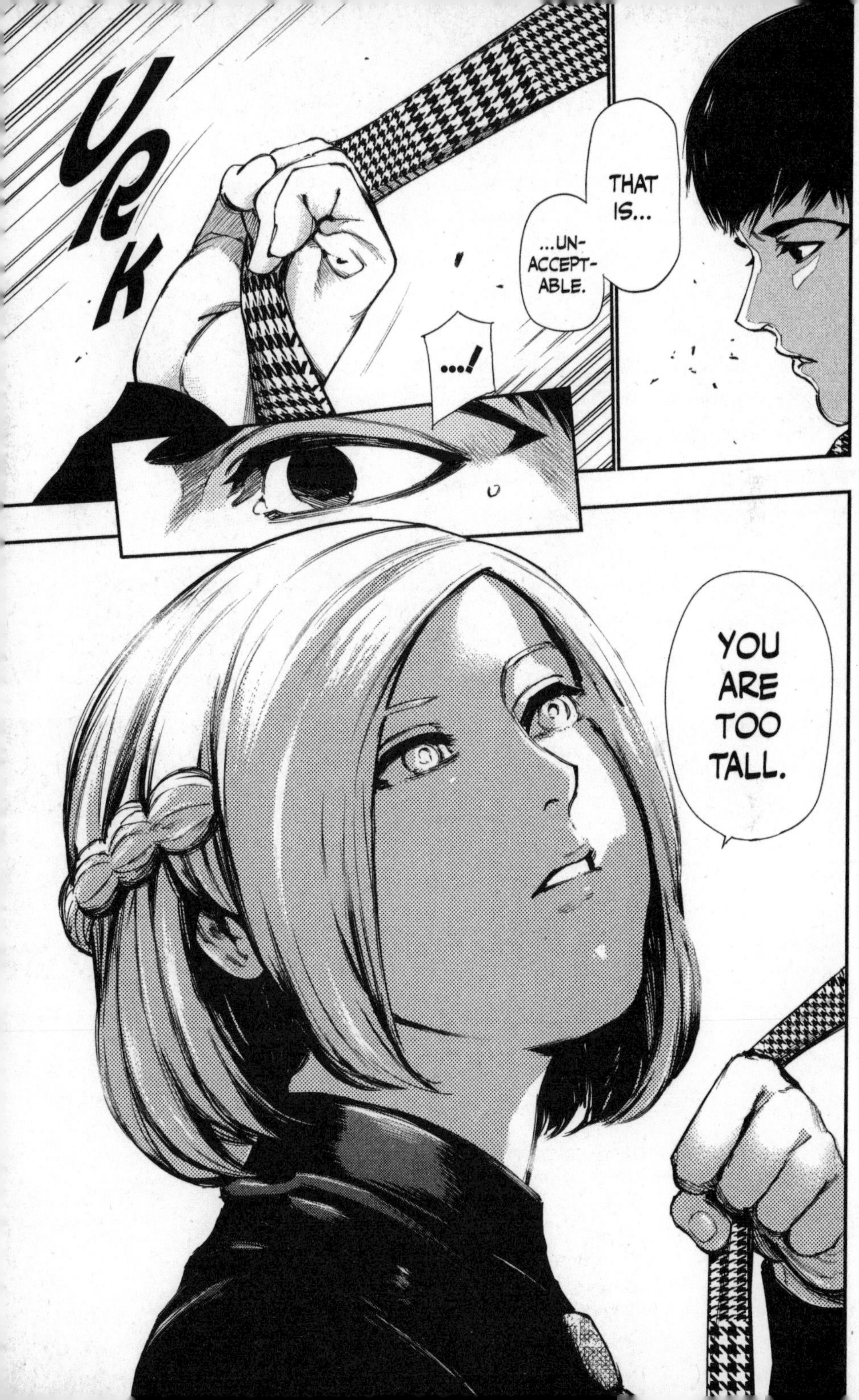
THAT IS...
...UN-ACCEPTABLE.
URK
...!
YOU ARE TOO TALL.

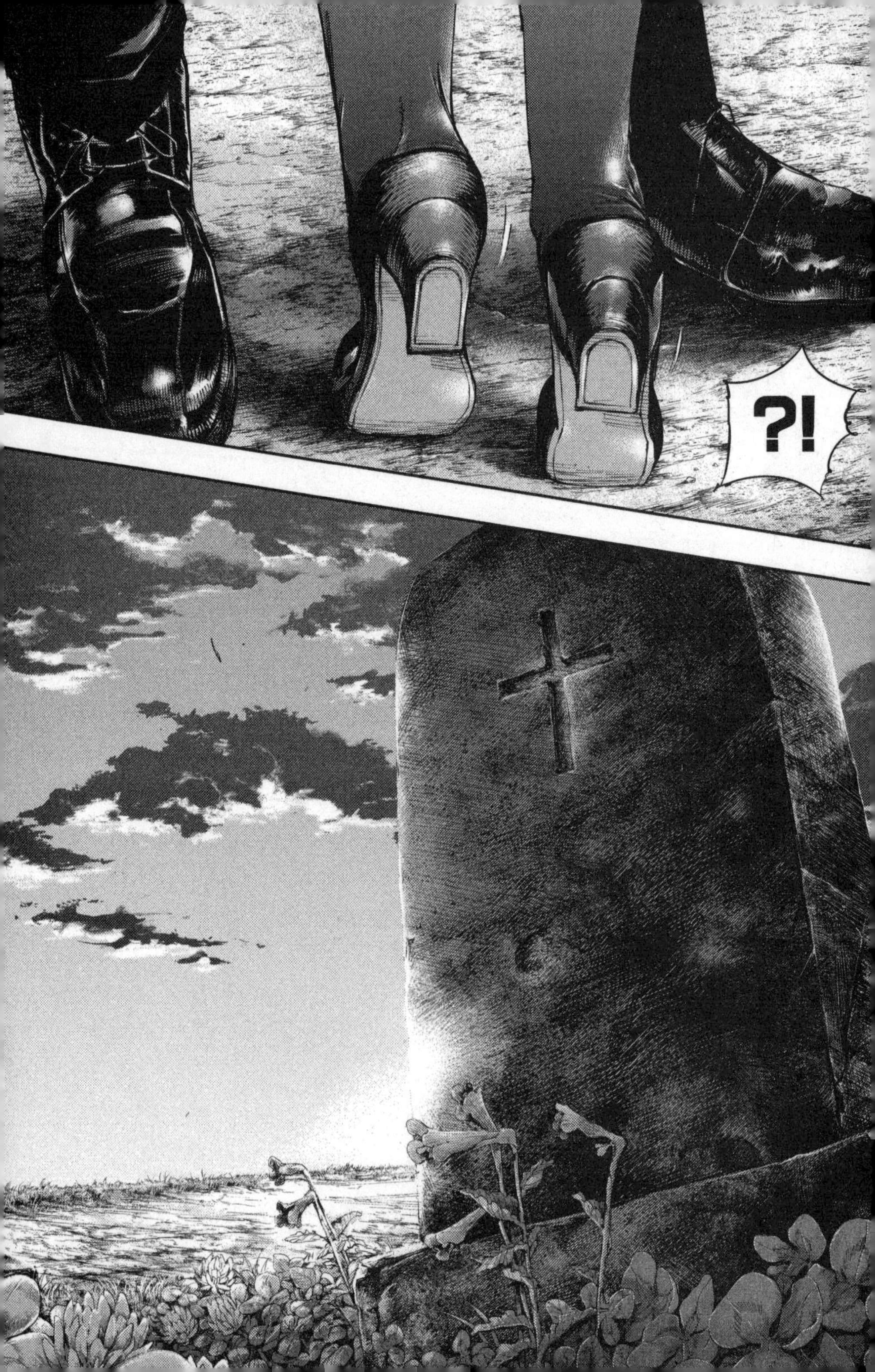
?!

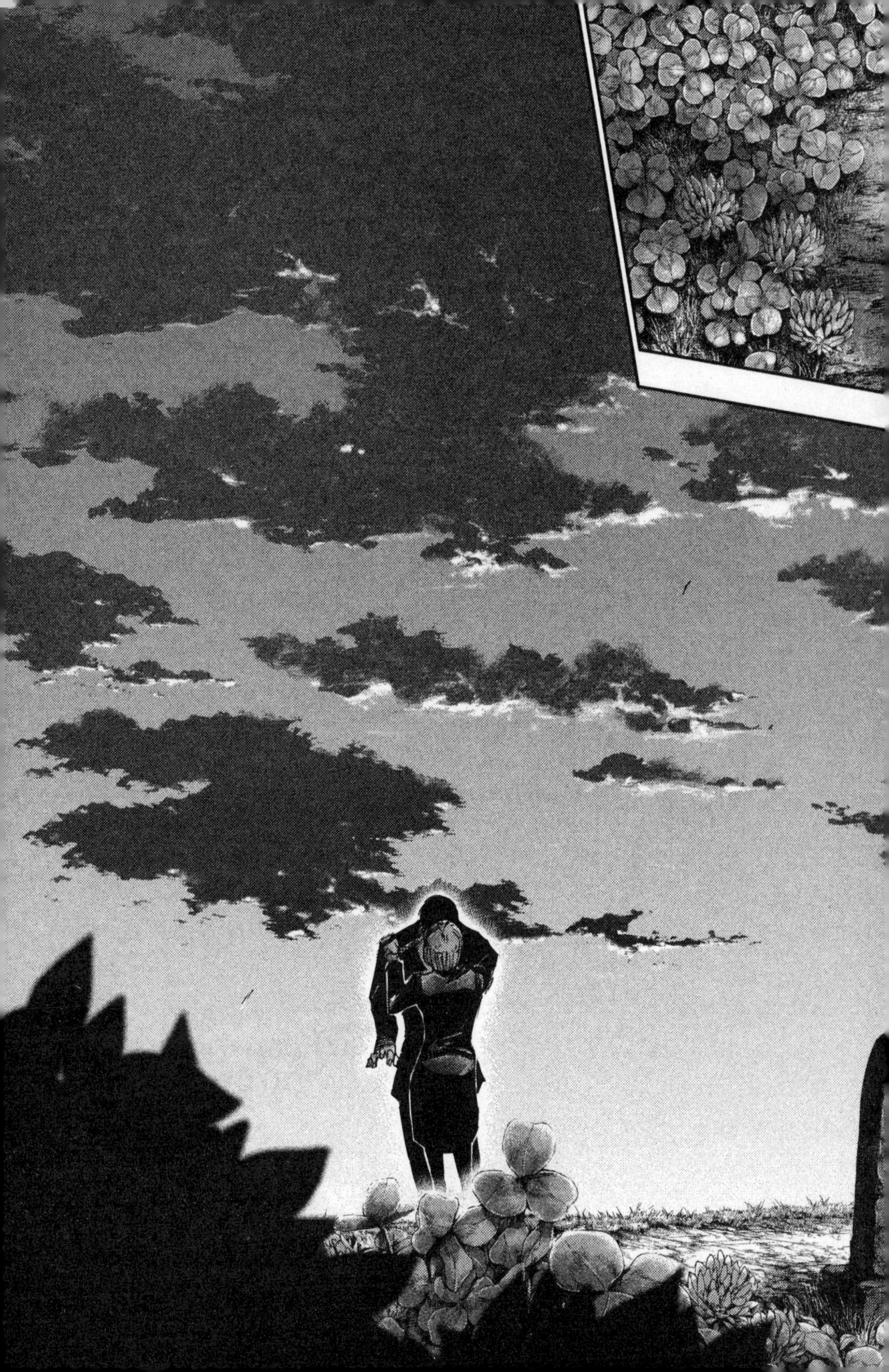

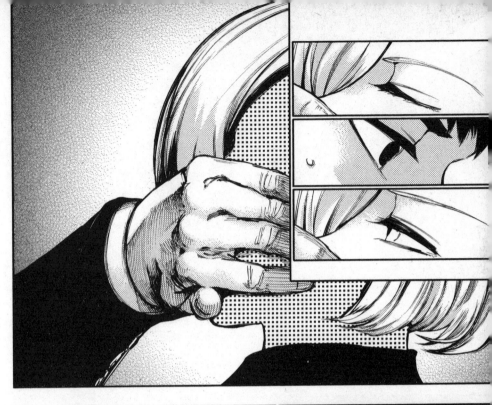

SO VERY ...

IT'S SO YOU...

... YOU.

LET'S GO.

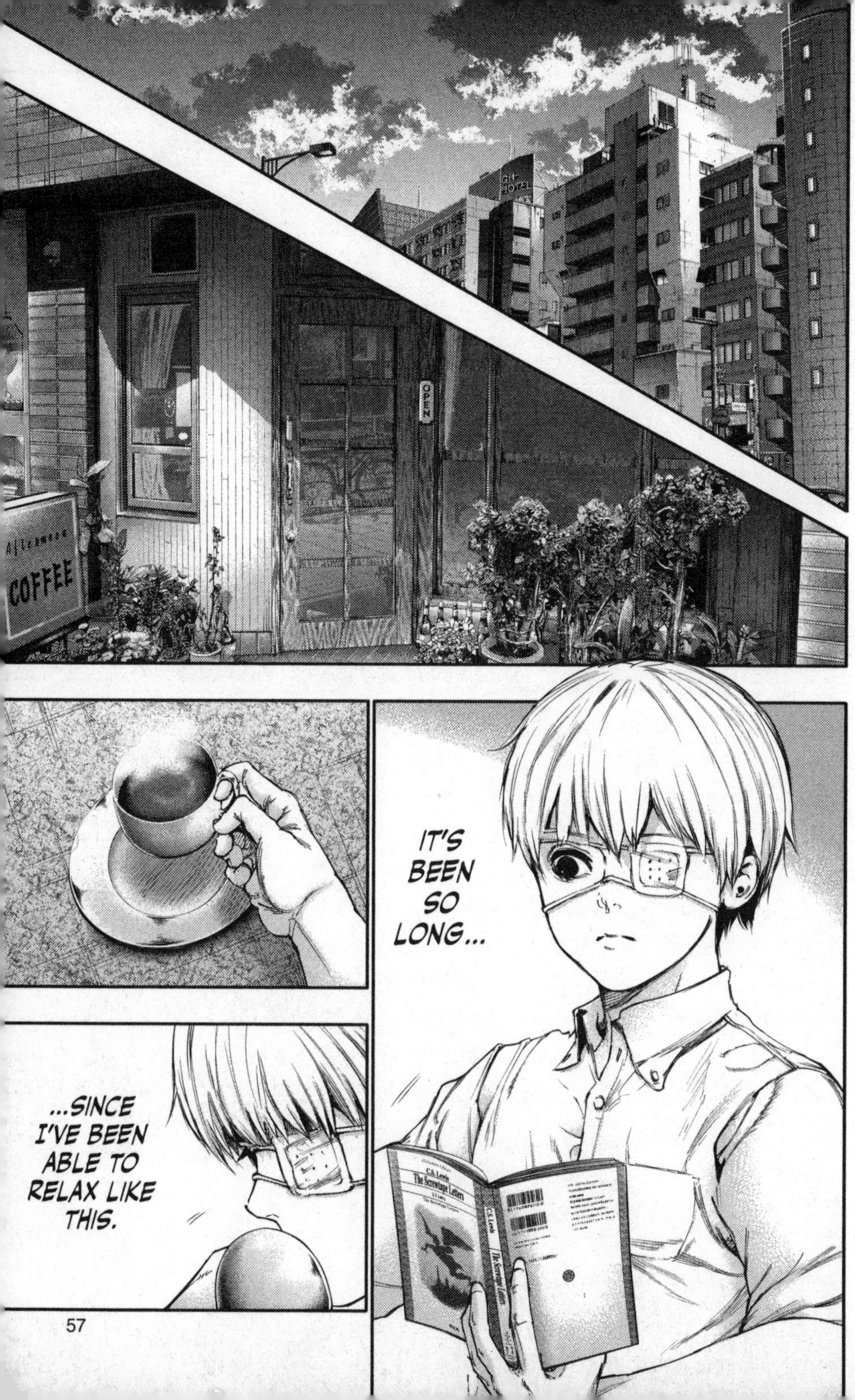
OPEN
COFFEE
IT'S BEEN SO LONG...
C.S. Lewis
The Screwtape Letters
...SINCE I'VE BEEN ABLE TO RELAX LIKE THIS.

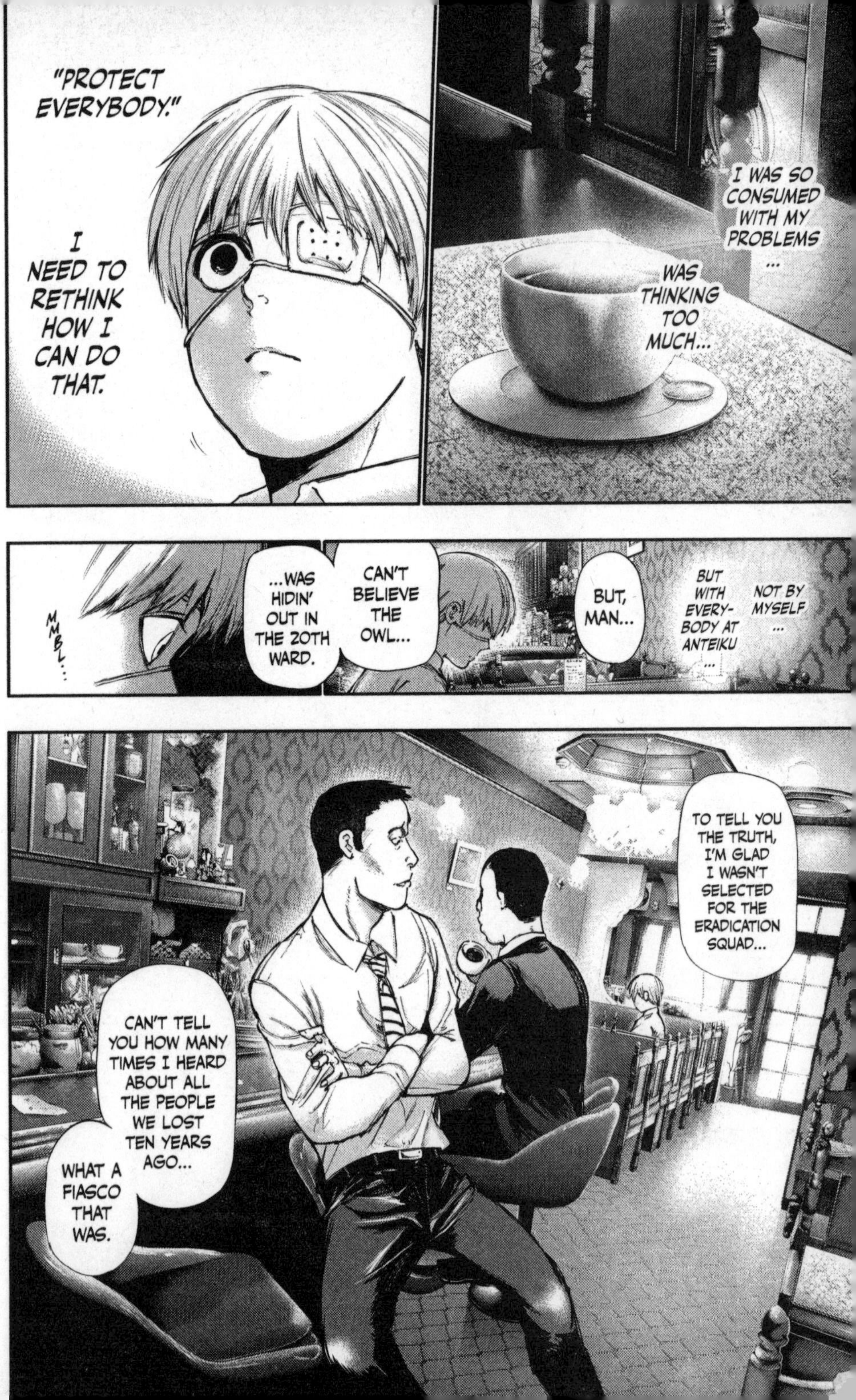
I WAS SO CONSUMED WITH MY PROBLEMS...
WAS THINKING TOO MUCH...
"PROTECT EVERYBODY."
I NEED TO RETHINK HOW I CAN DO THAT.
NOT BY MYSELF...
BUT WITH EVERY-BODY AT ANTEIKU...
BUT, MAN...
CAN'T BELIEVE THE OWL...
...WAS HIDIN' OUT IN THE 20TH WARD.
MMBL...
TO TELL YOU THE TRUTH, I'M GLAD I WASN'T SELECTED FOR THE ERADICATION SQUAD...
CAN'T TELL YOU HOW MANY TIMES I HEARD ABOUT ALL THE PEOPLE WE LOST TEN YEARS AGO...
WHAT A FIASCO THAT WAS.

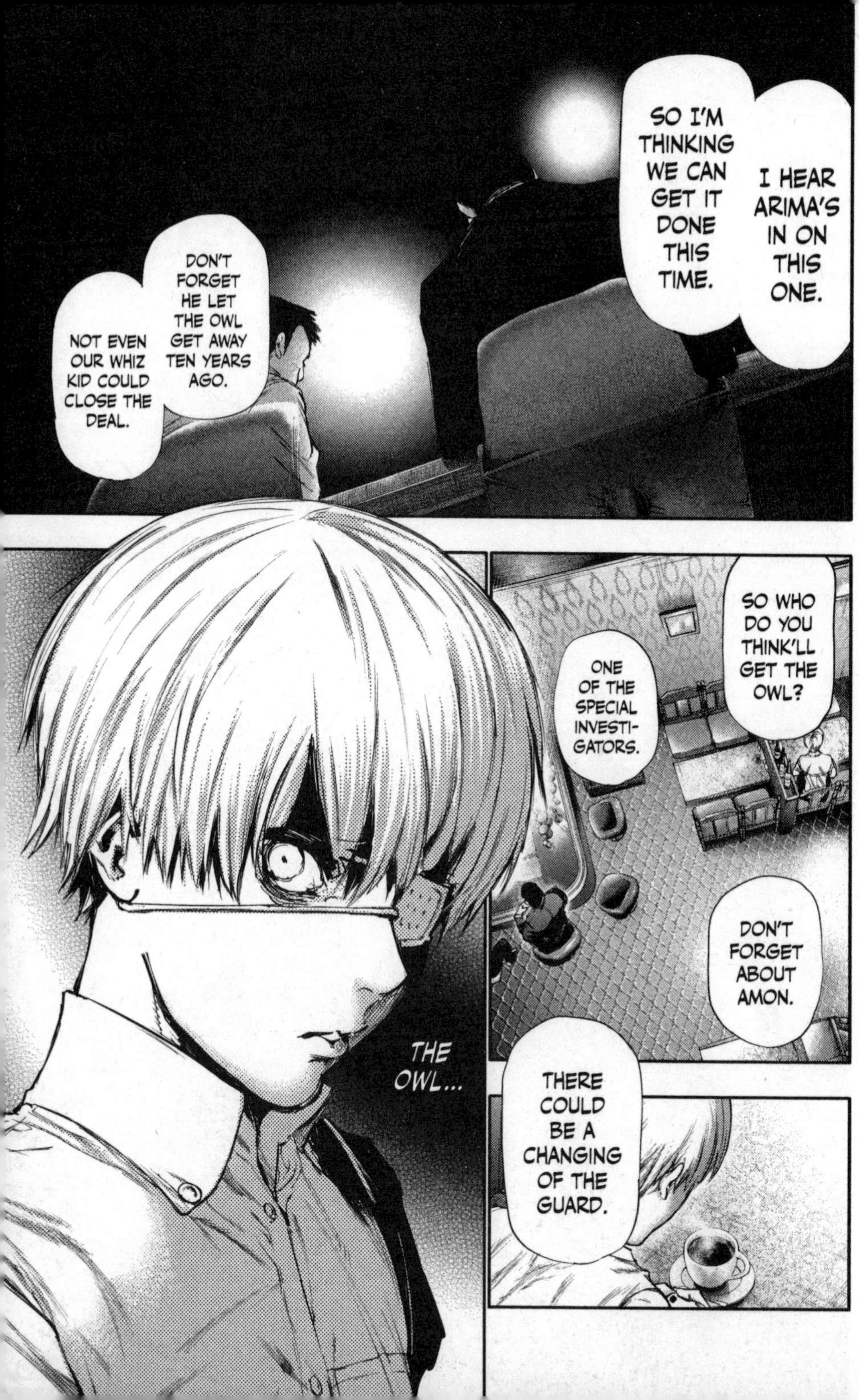
I HEAR ARIMA'S IN ON THIS ONE.
SO I'M THINKING WE CAN GET IT DONE THIS TIME.
DON'T FORGET HE LET THE OWL GET AWAY TEN YEARS AGO.
NOT EVEN OUR WHIZ KID COULD CLOSE THE DEAL.
SO WHO DO YOU THINK'LL GET THE OWL?
ONE OF THE SPECIAL INVESTI-GATORS.
DON'T FORGET ABOUT AMON.
THERE COULD BE A CHANGING OF THE GUARD.
THE OWL...

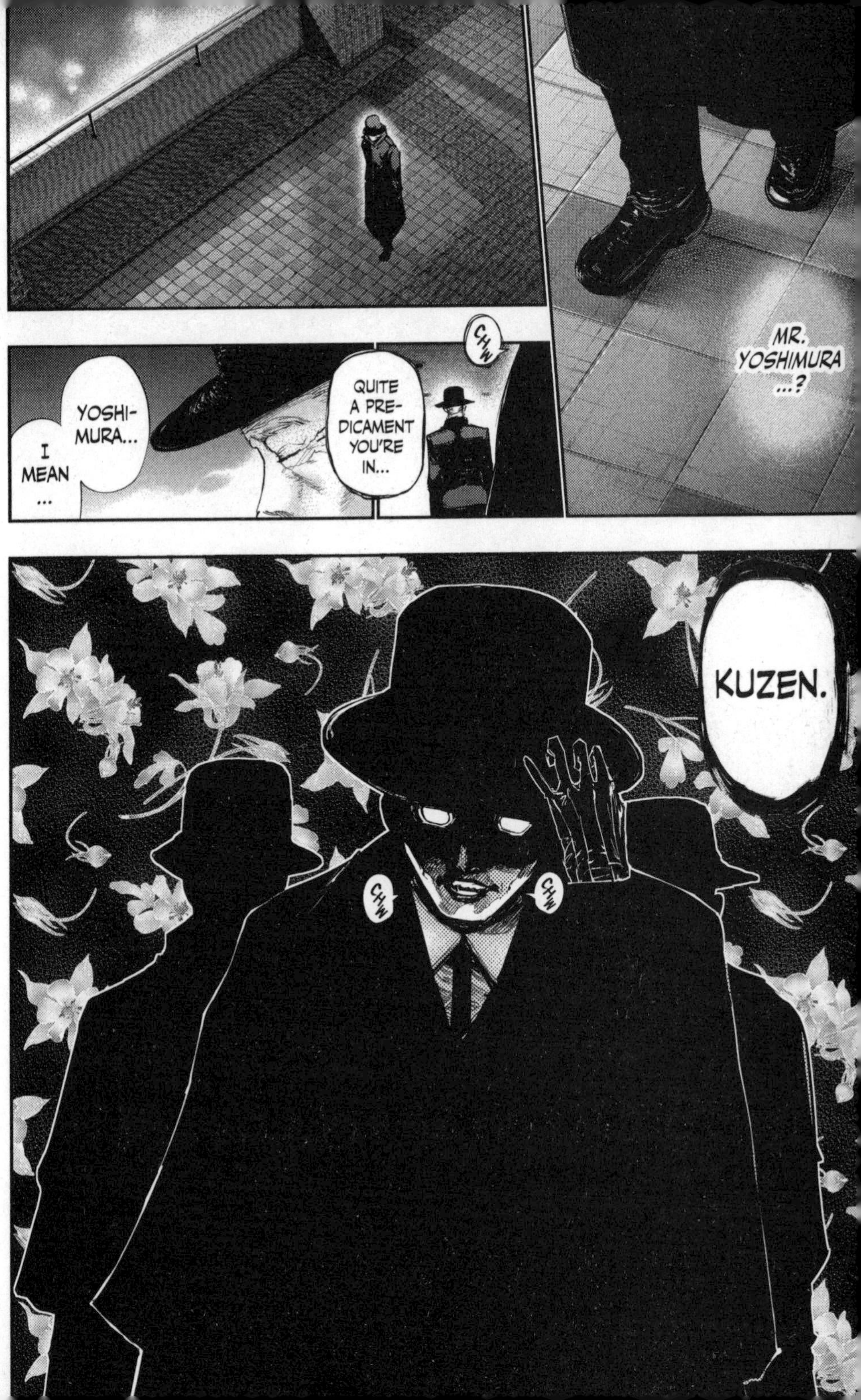
MR. YOSHIMURA ...?
CHW
QUITE A PRE-DICAMENT YOU'RE IN...
YOSHI-MURA...
I MEAN ...
KUZEN.
CHW
CHW

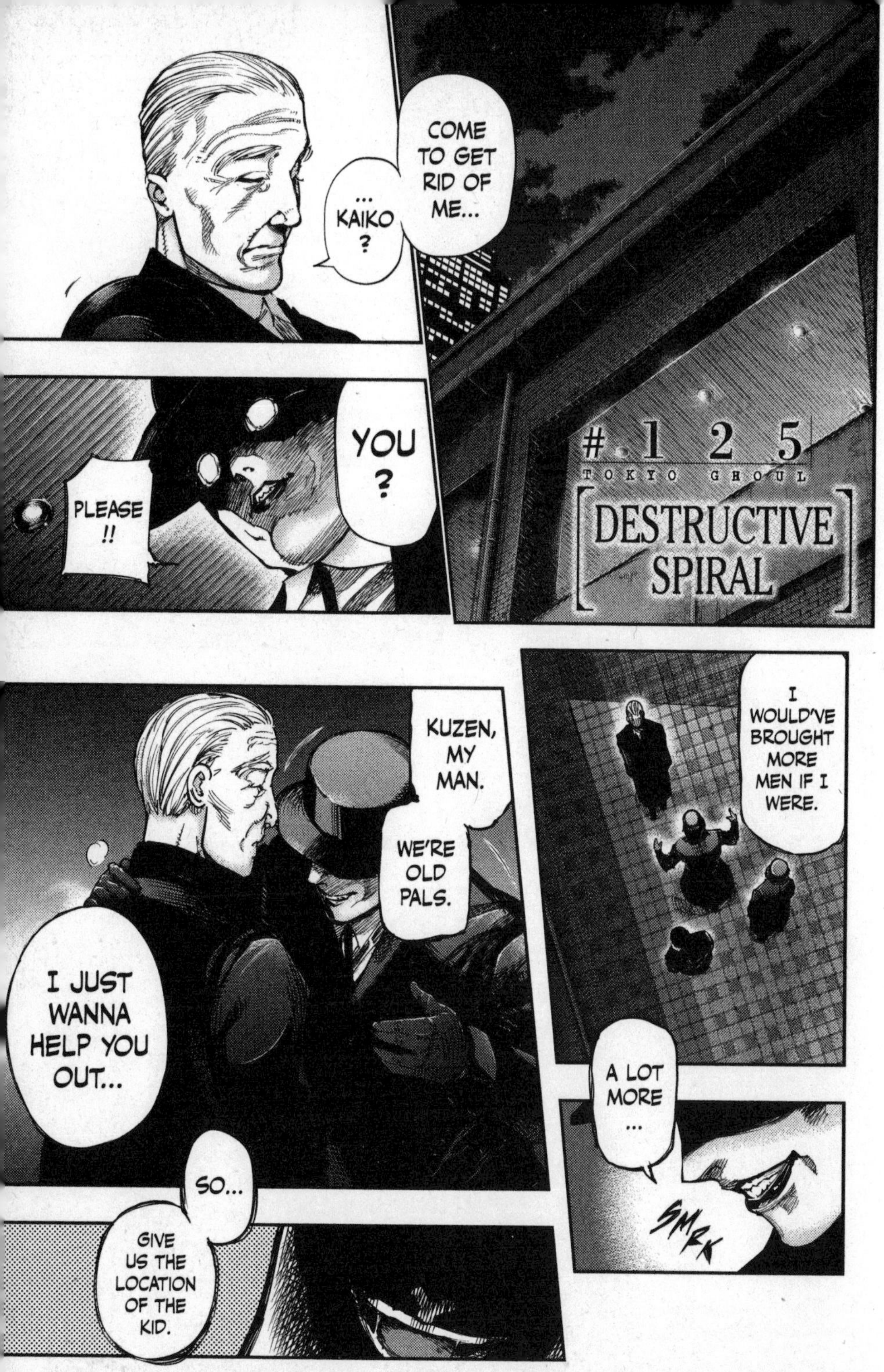

#125
TOKYO GHOUL
DESTRUCTIVE SPIRAL
COME TO GET RID OF ME...
...KAIKO?
YOU?
PLEASE!!
I WOULD'VE BROUGHT MORE MEN IF I WERE.
A LOT MORE...
SMRK
KUZEN, MY MAN.
WE'RE OLD PALS.
I JUST WANNA HELP YOU OUT...
SO...
GIVE US THE LOCATION OF THE KID.

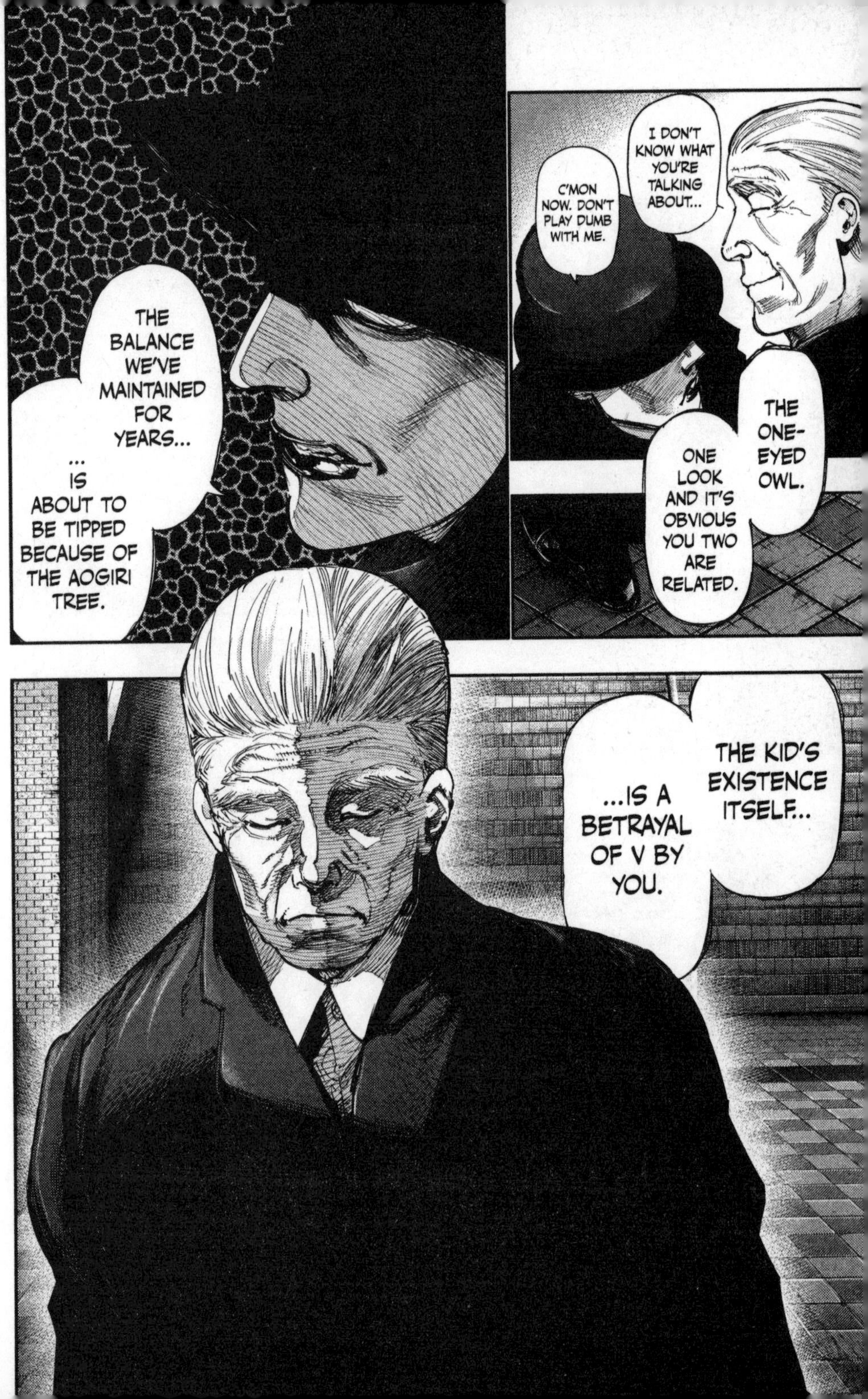
I DON'T KNOW WHAT YOU'RE TALKING ABOUT...
C'MON NOW. DON'T PLAY DUMB WITH ME.
THE ONE-EYED OWL.
ONE LOOK AND IT'S OBVIOUS YOU TWO ARE RELATED.
THE BALANCE WE'VE MAINTAINED FOR YEARS...
...IS ABOUT TO BE TIPPED BECAUSE OF THE AOGIRI TREE.
THE KID'S EXISTENCE ITSELF...
...IS A BETRAYAL OF V BY YOU.

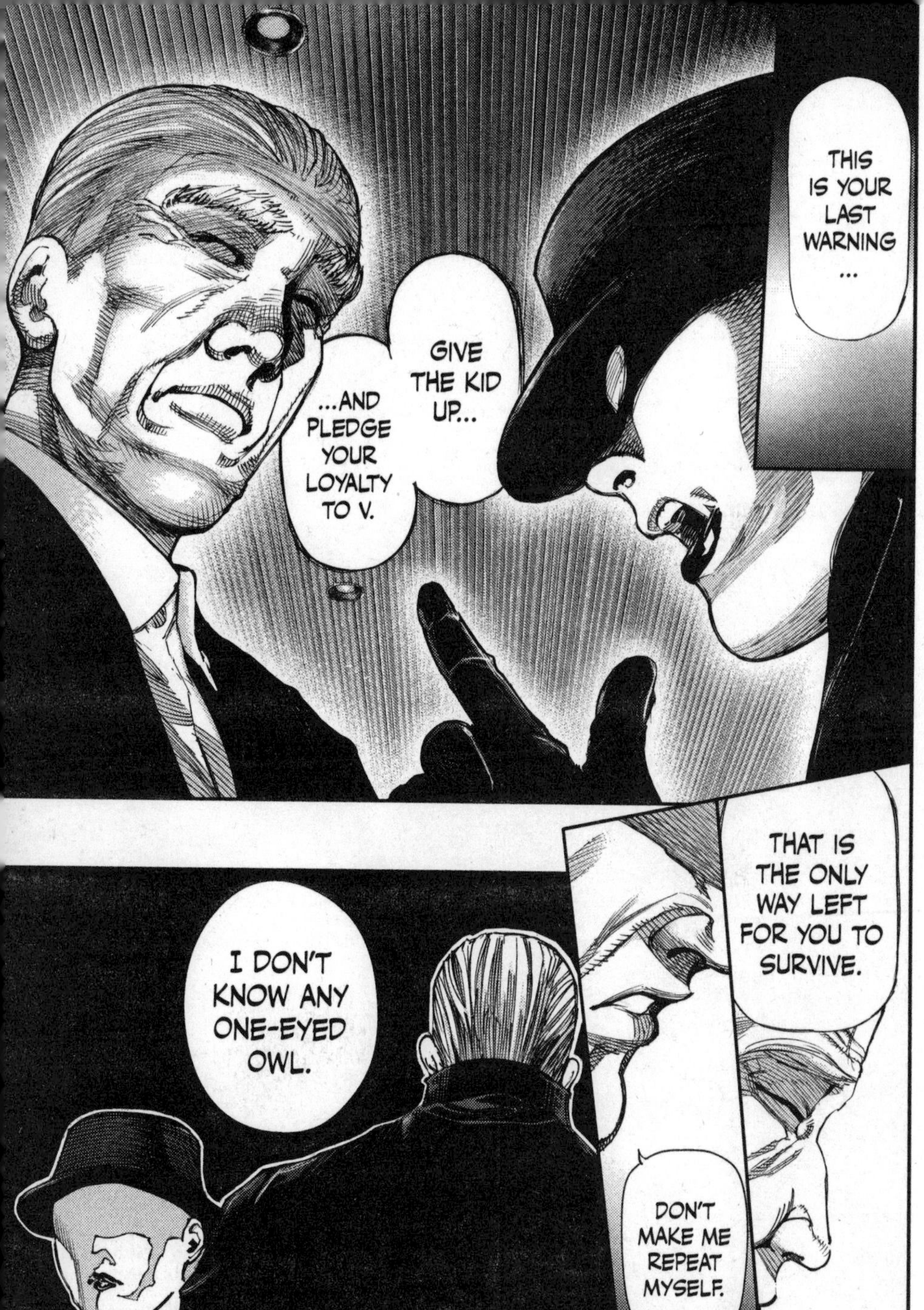
THIS IS YOUR LAST WARNING...
GIVE THE KID UP...
...AND PLEDGE YOUR LOYALTY TO V.
THAT IS THE ONLY WAY LEFT FOR YOU TO SURVIVE.
DON'T MAKE ME REPEAT MYSELF.
I DON'T KNOW ANY ONE-EYED OWL.

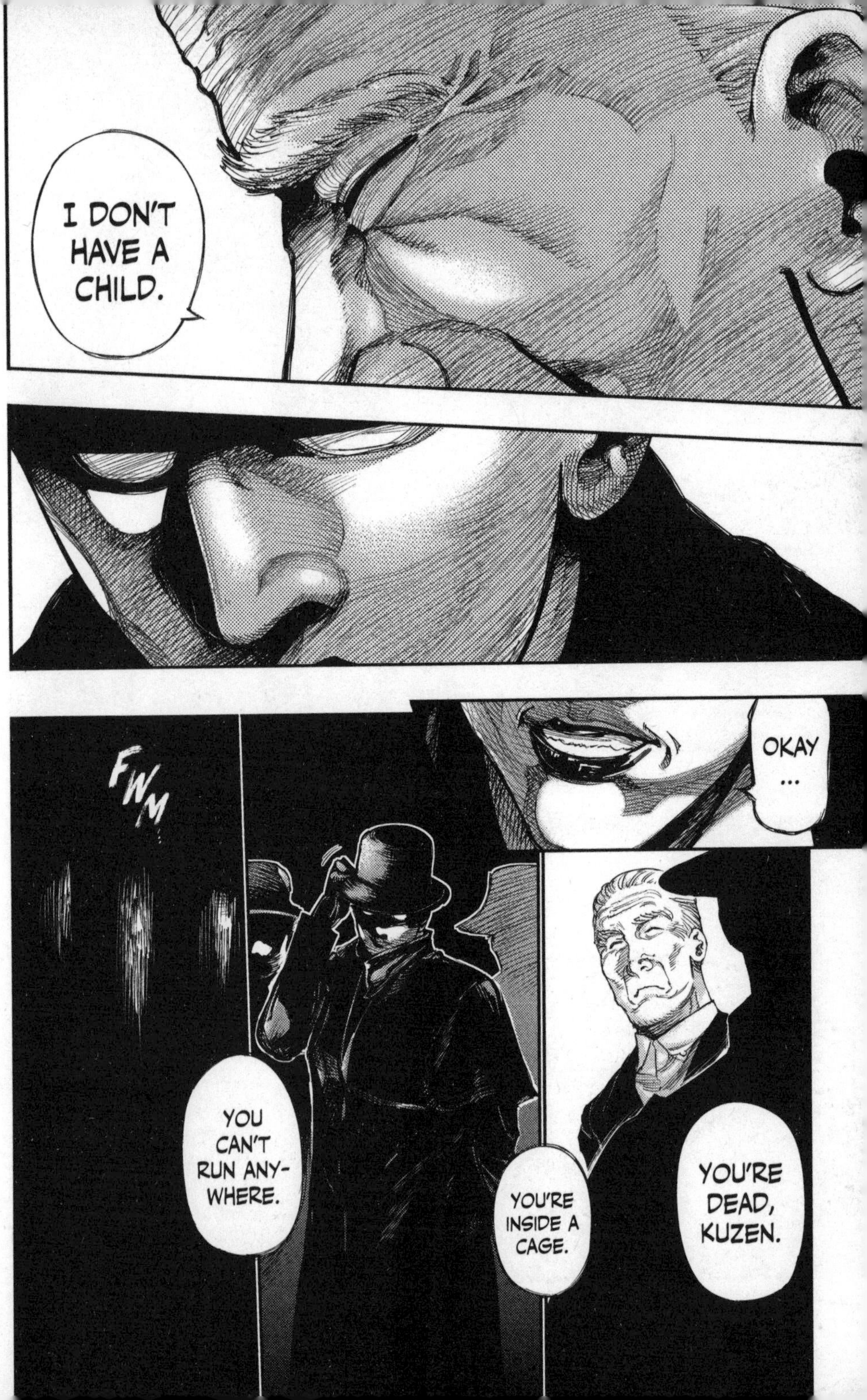
I DON'T HAVE A CHILD.
OKAY ...
YOU'RE DEAD, KUZEN.
YOU'RE INSIDE A CAGE.
FWM
YOU CAN'T RUN ANY-WHERE.

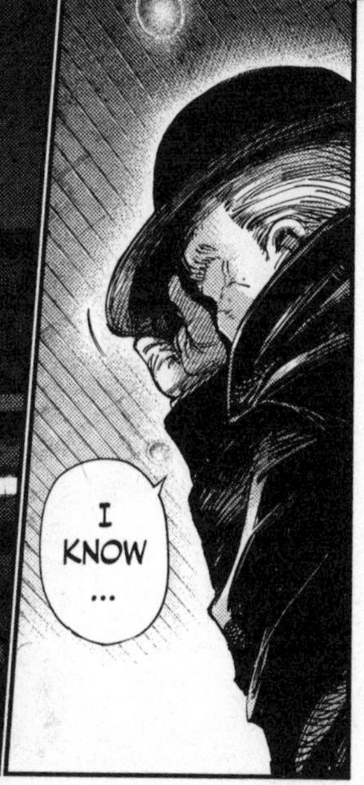
I KNOW ...

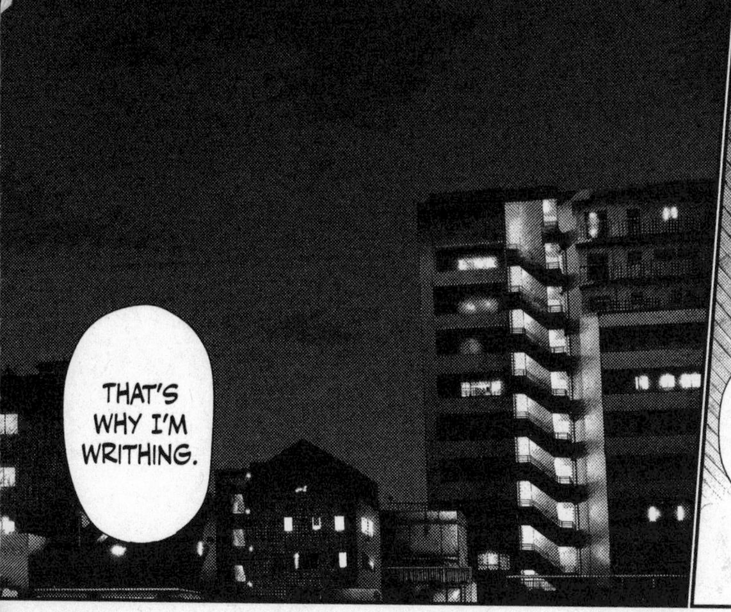
THAT'S WHY I'M WRITHING.

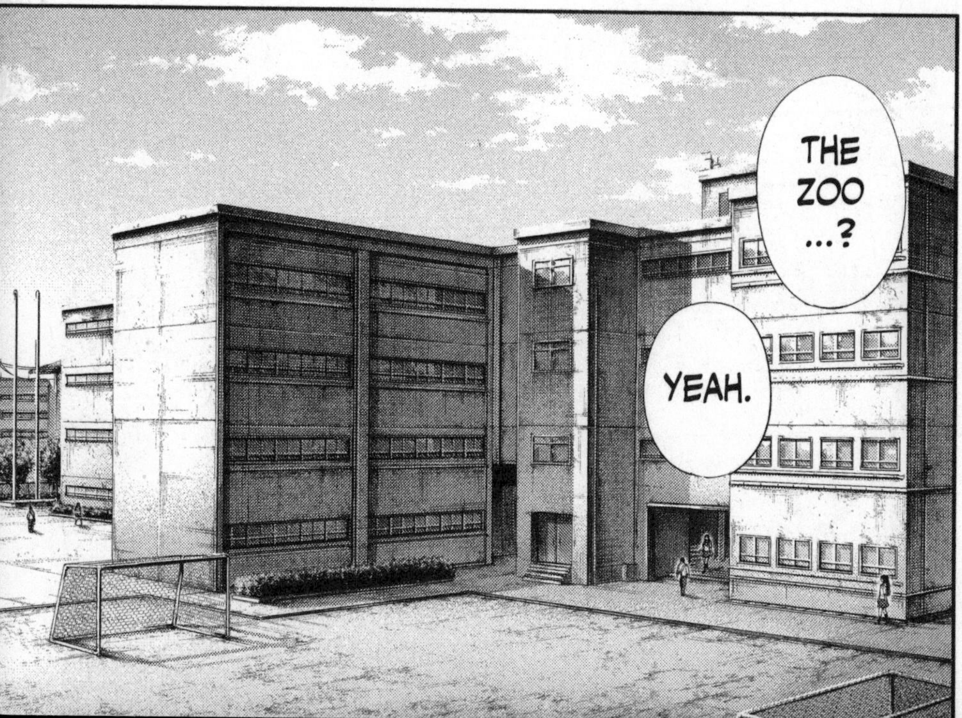
THE ZOO ...?
YEAH.

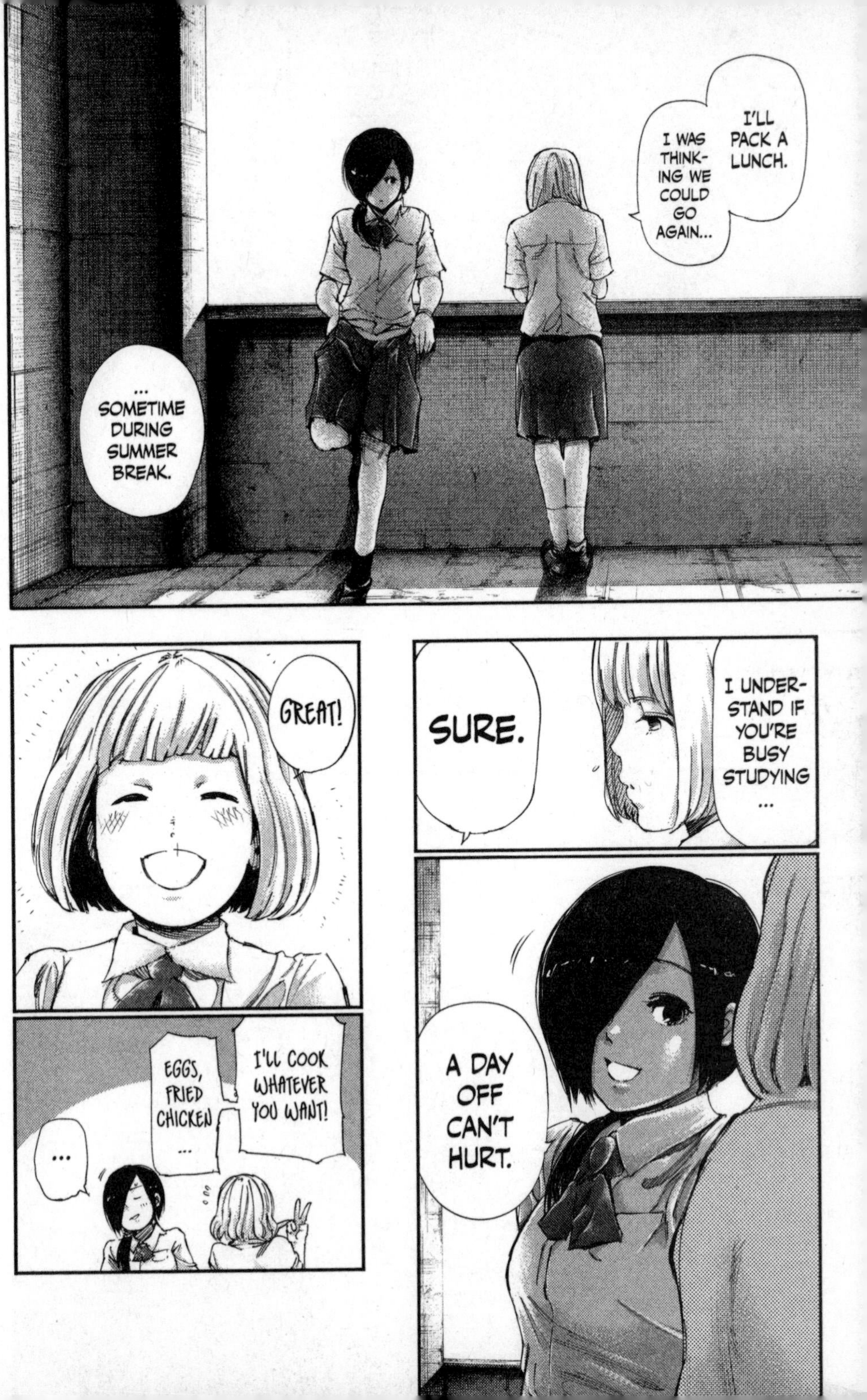
I'LL PACK A LUNCH.
I WAS THINKING WE COULD GO AGAIN...
... SOMETIME DURING SUMMER BREAK.
I UNDERSTAND IF YOU'RE BUSY STUDYING ...
SURE.
A DAY OFF CAN'T HURT.
GREAT!
I'LL COOK WHATEVER YOU WANT!
EGGS, FRIED CHICKEN ...
...

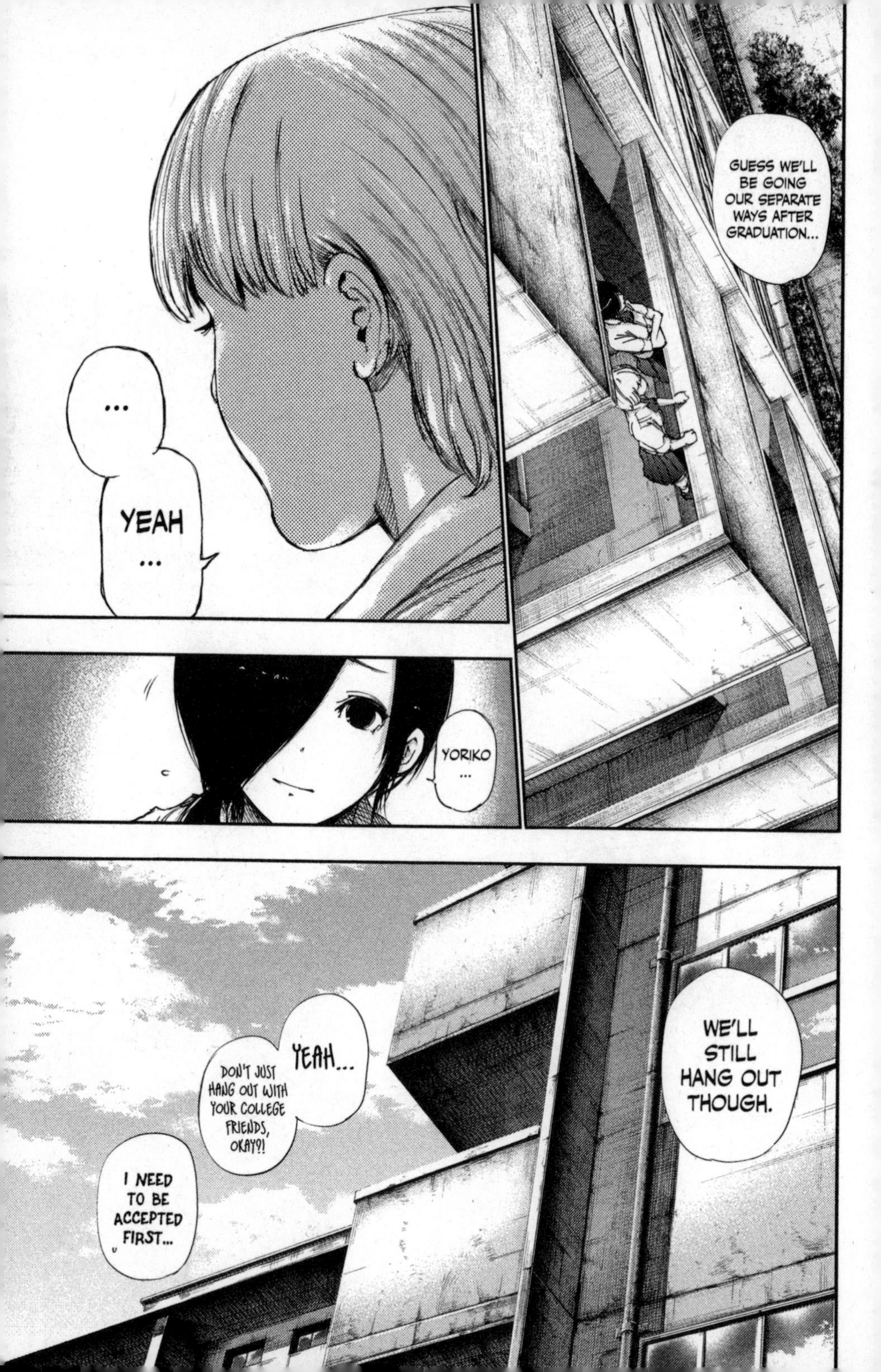
GUESS WE'LL BE GOING OUR SEPARATE WAYS AFTER GRADUATION...
... YEAH ...
YORIKO ...
WE'LL STILL HANG OUT THOUGH.
YEAH...
DON'T JUST HANG OUT WITH YOUR COLLEGE FRIENDS, OKAY?!
I NEED TO BE ACCEPTED FIRST...

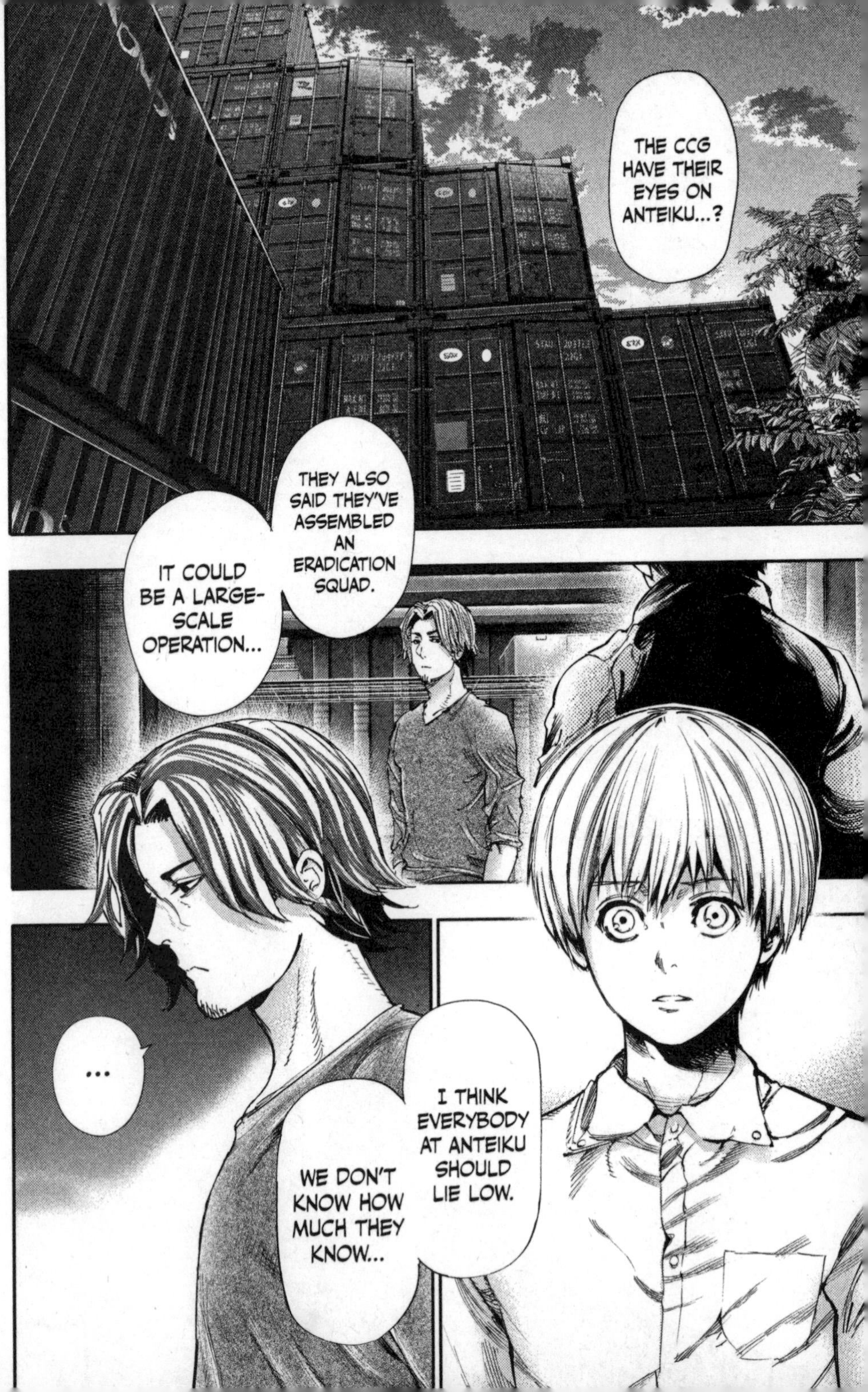
THE CCG HAVE THEIR EYES ON ANTEIKU...?
THEY ALSO SAID THEY'VE ASSEMBLED AN ERADICATION SQUAD.
IT COULD BE A LARGE-SCALE OPERATION...
I THINK EVERYBODY AT ANTEIKU SHOULD LIE LOW.
WE DON'T KNOW HOW MUCH THEY KNOW...
...

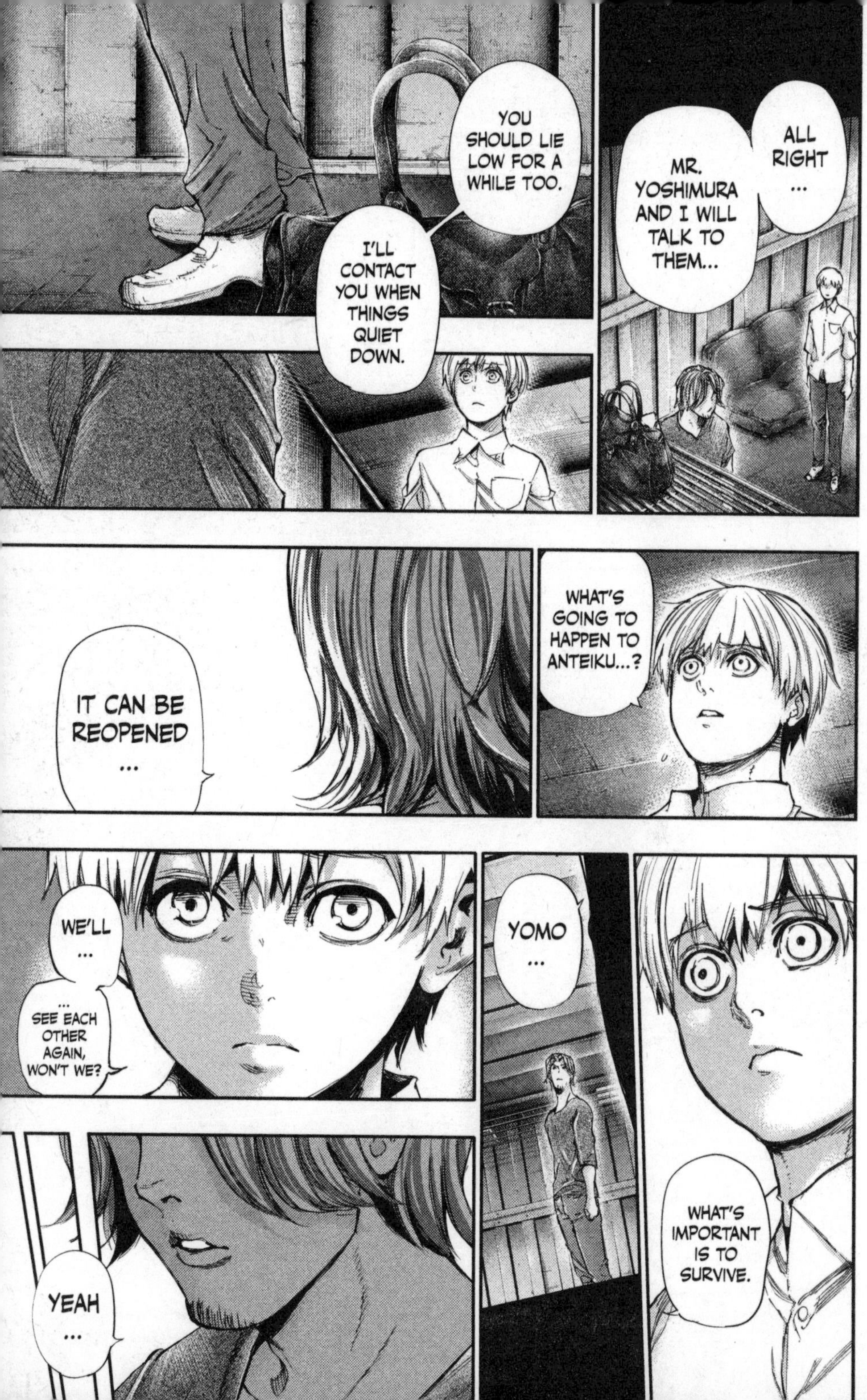
ALL RIGHT ...
MR. YOSHIMURA AND I WILL TALK TO THEM...
YOU SHOULD LIE LOW FOR A WHILE TOO.
I'LL CONTACT YOU WHEN THINGS QUIET DOWN.
WHAT'S GOING TO HAPPEN TO ANTEIKU...?
IT CAN BE REOPENED ...
WHAT'S IMPORTANT IS TO SURVIVE.
YOMO ...
WE'LL ...
... SEE EACH OTHER AGAIN, WON'T WE?
YEAH ...

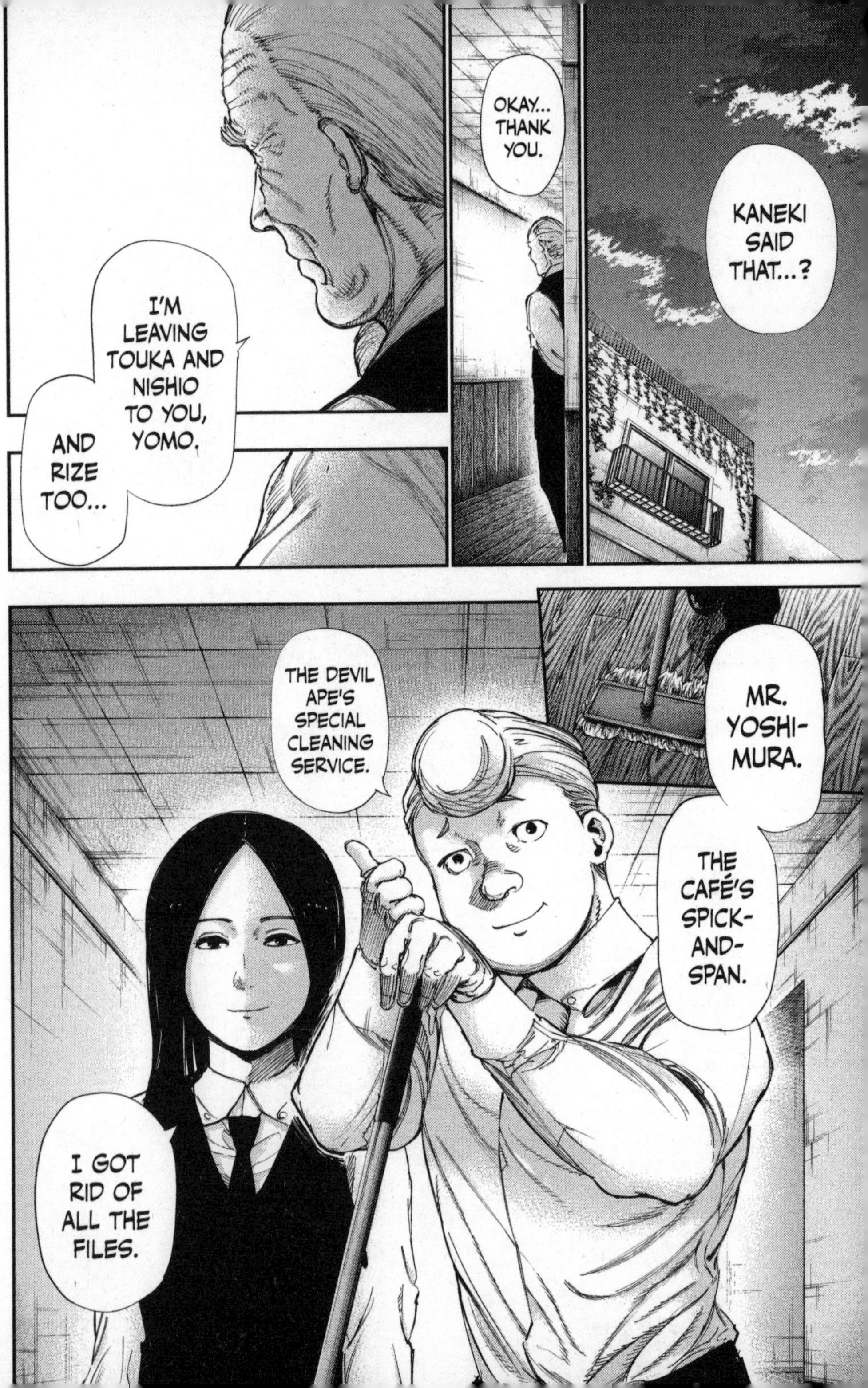
KANEKI SAID THAT...?
OKAY... THANK YOU.
I'M LEAVING TOUKA AND NISHIO TO YOU, YOMO.
AND RIZE TOO...
MR. YOSHI-MURA.
THE CAFÉ'S SPICK-AND-SPAN.
THE DEVIL APE'S SPECIAL CLEANING SERVICE.
I GOT RID OF ALL THE FILES.

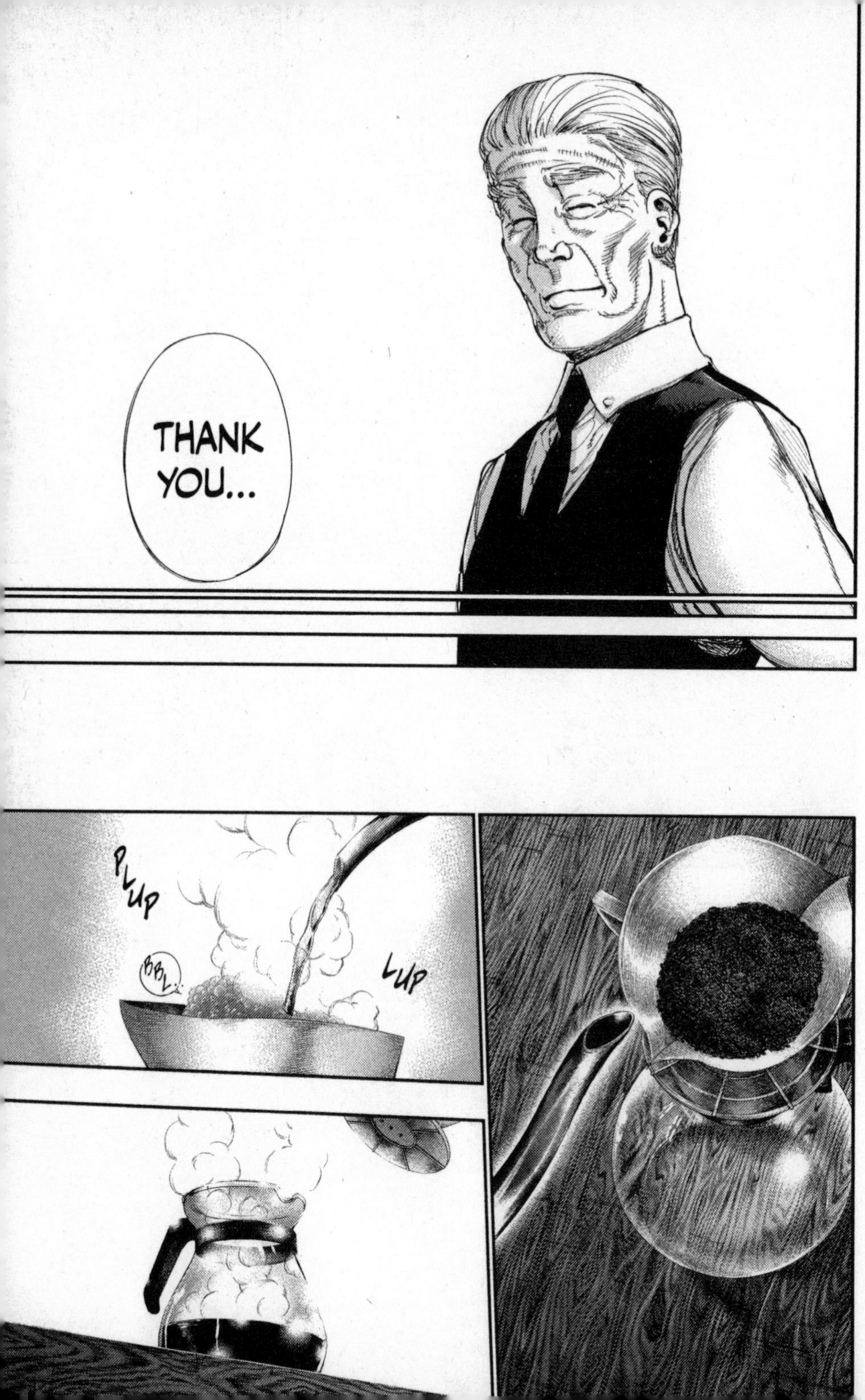
THANK YOU...
PLUP
BBL...
LUP

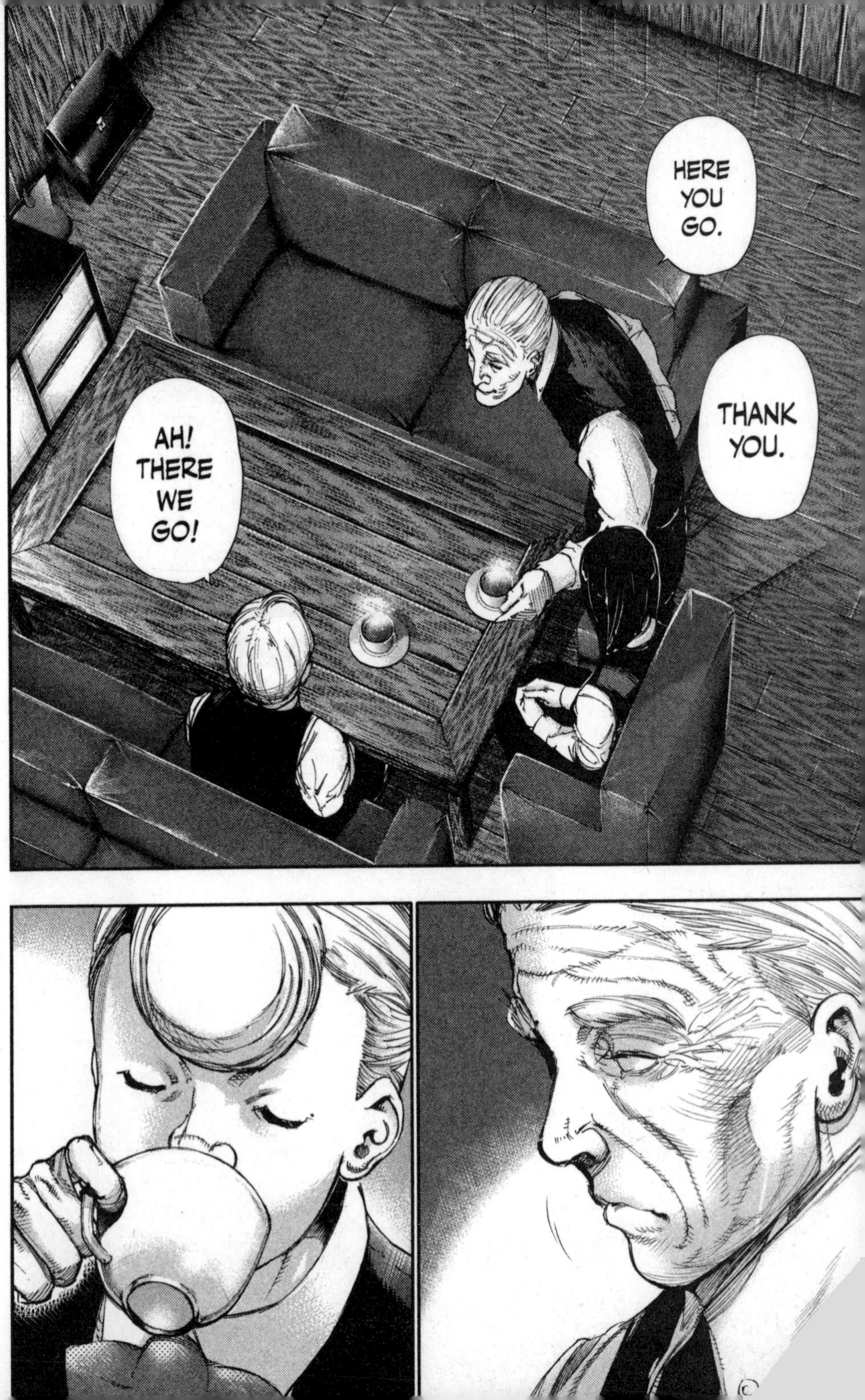
HERE YOU GO.
THANK YOU.
AH! THERE WE GO!

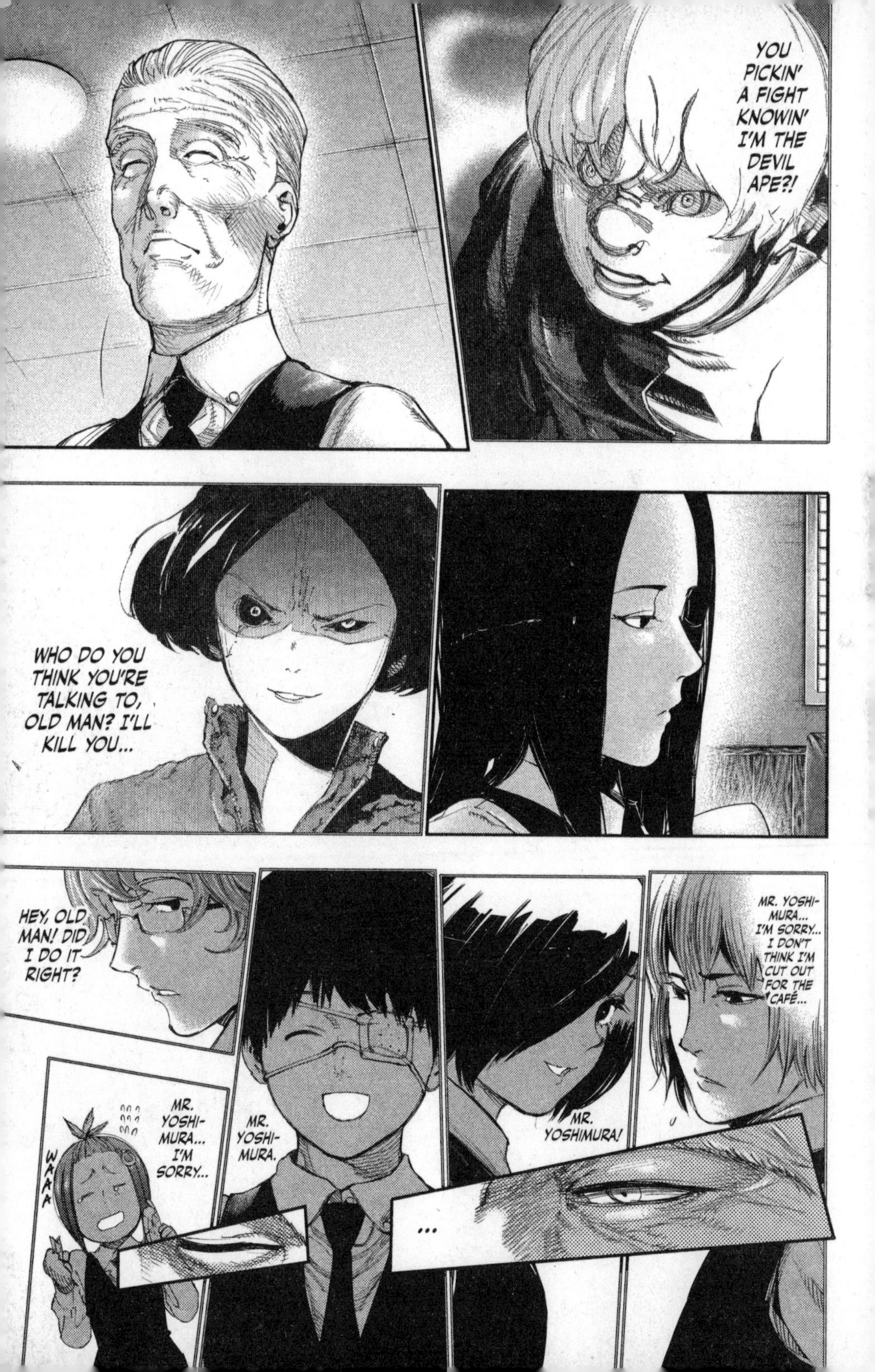
YOU PICKIN' A FIGHT KNOWIN' I'M THE DEVIL APE?!
WHO DO YOU THINK YOU'RE TALKING TO, OLD MAN? I'LL KILL YOU...
MR. YOSHIMURA... I'M SORRY... I DON'T THINK I'M CUT OUT FOR THE CAFÉ...
MR. YOSHIMURA!
MR. YOSHIMURA.
HEY, OLD MAN! DID I DO IT RIGHT?
MR. YOSHIMURA... I'M SORRY...
WAAA
...

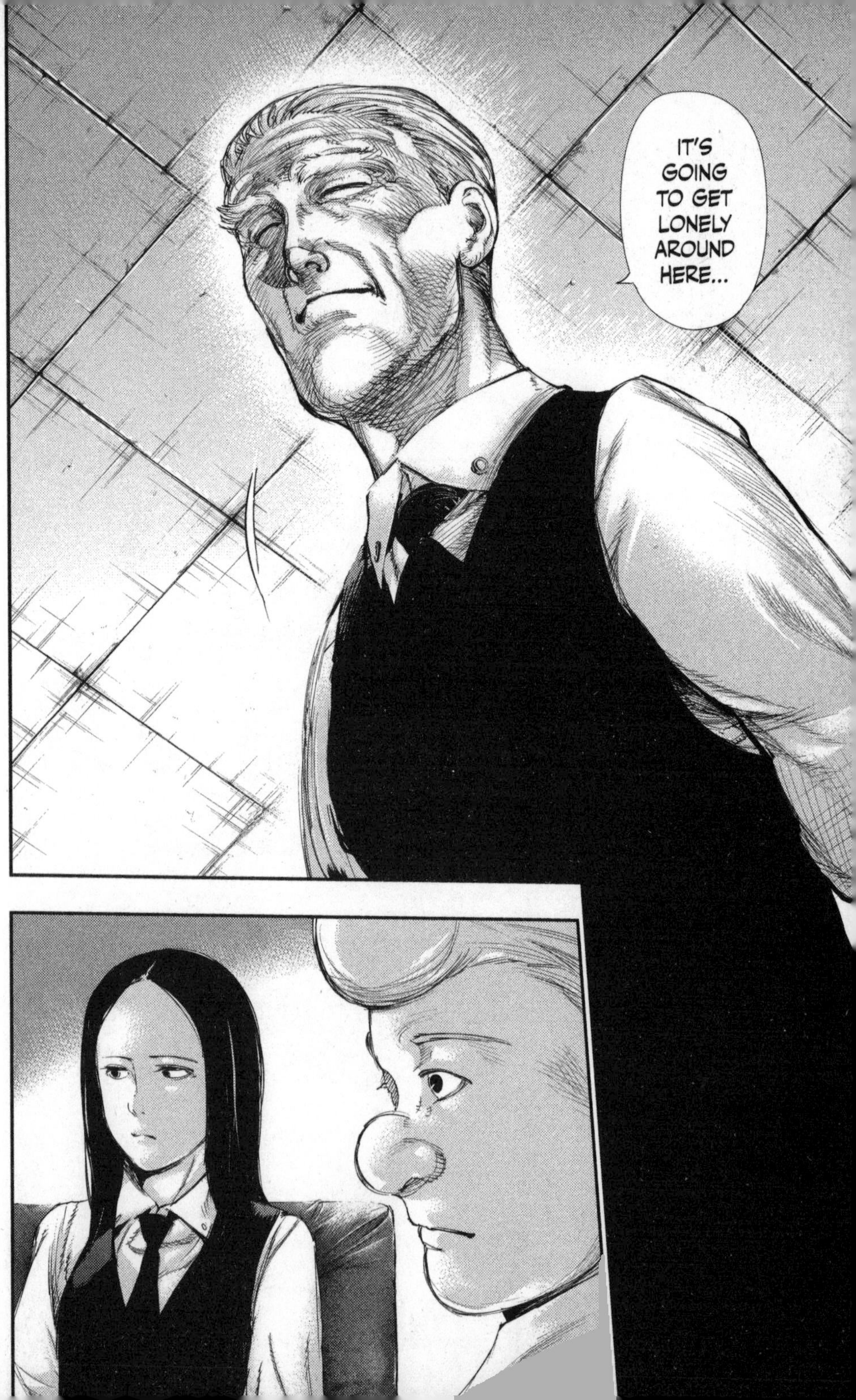
IT'S GOING TO GET LONELY AROUND HERE...

MR. YOSHI-MURA.

KAYA AND I ARE WITH YOU TILL THE END.

ISN'T THAT ENOUGH?

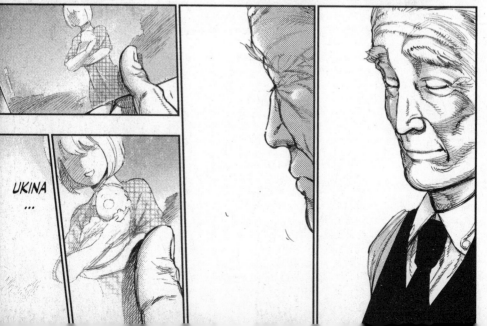

UKINA ...

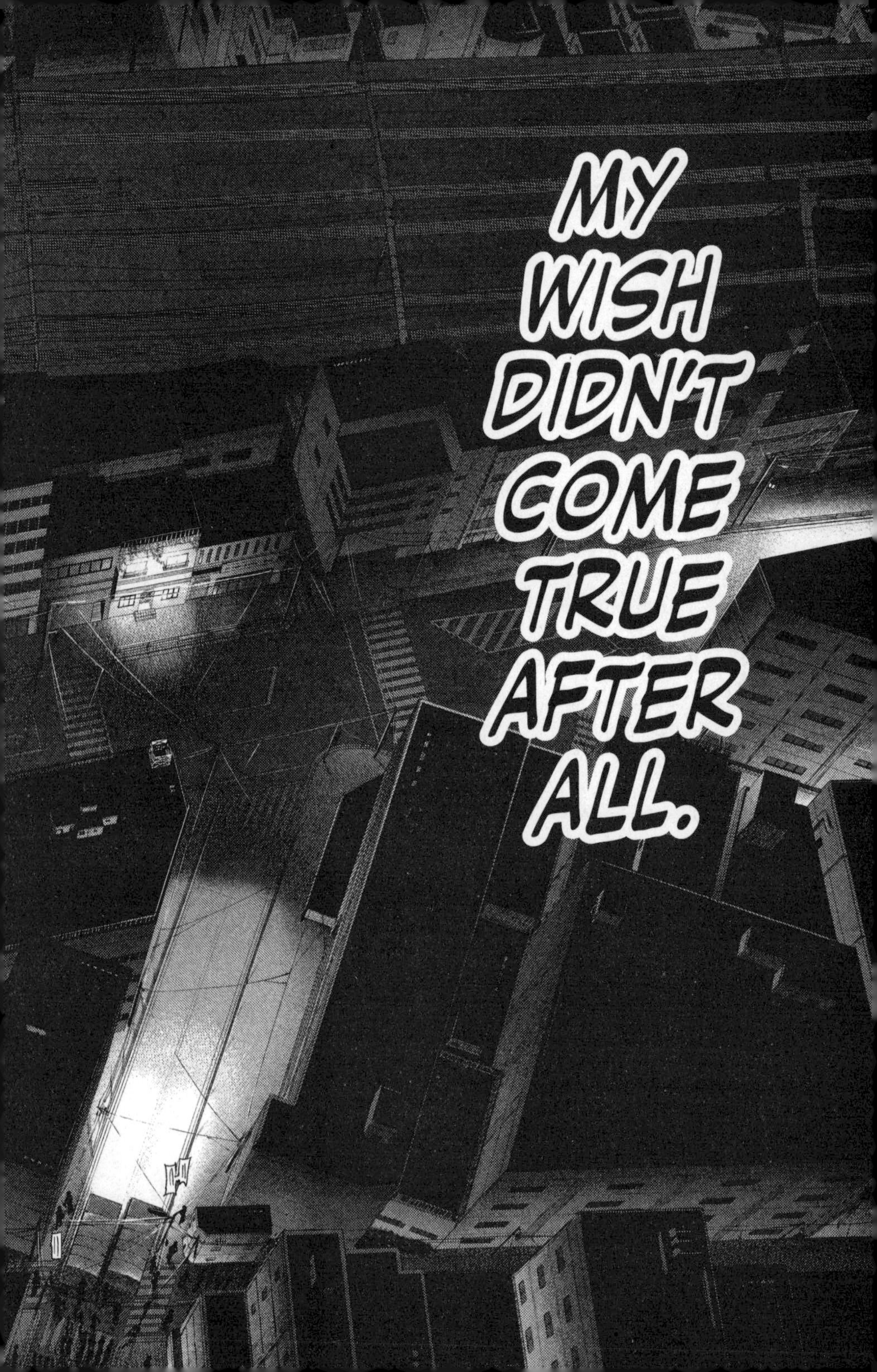
MY WISH DIDN'T COME TRUE AFTER ALL.

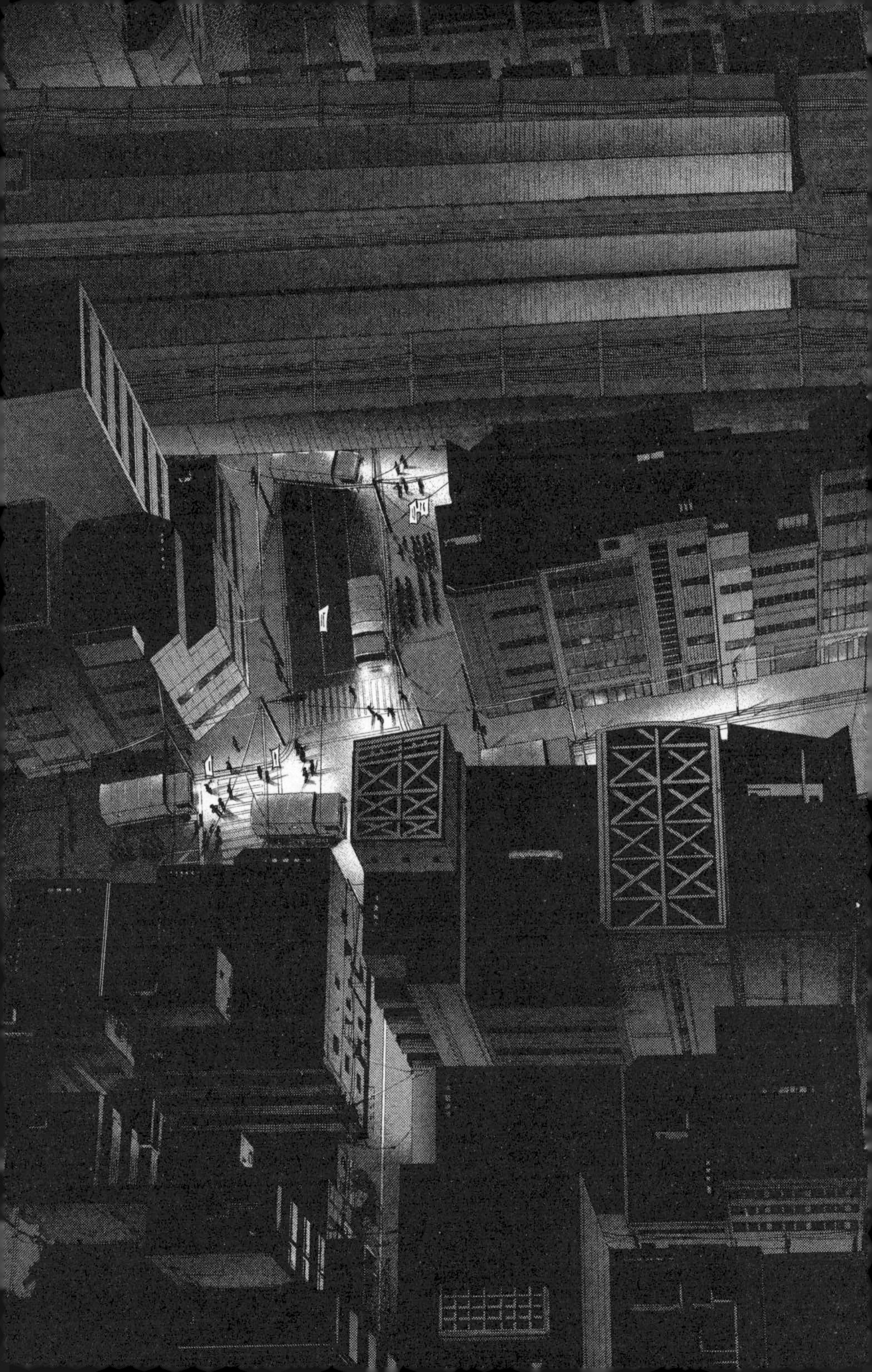

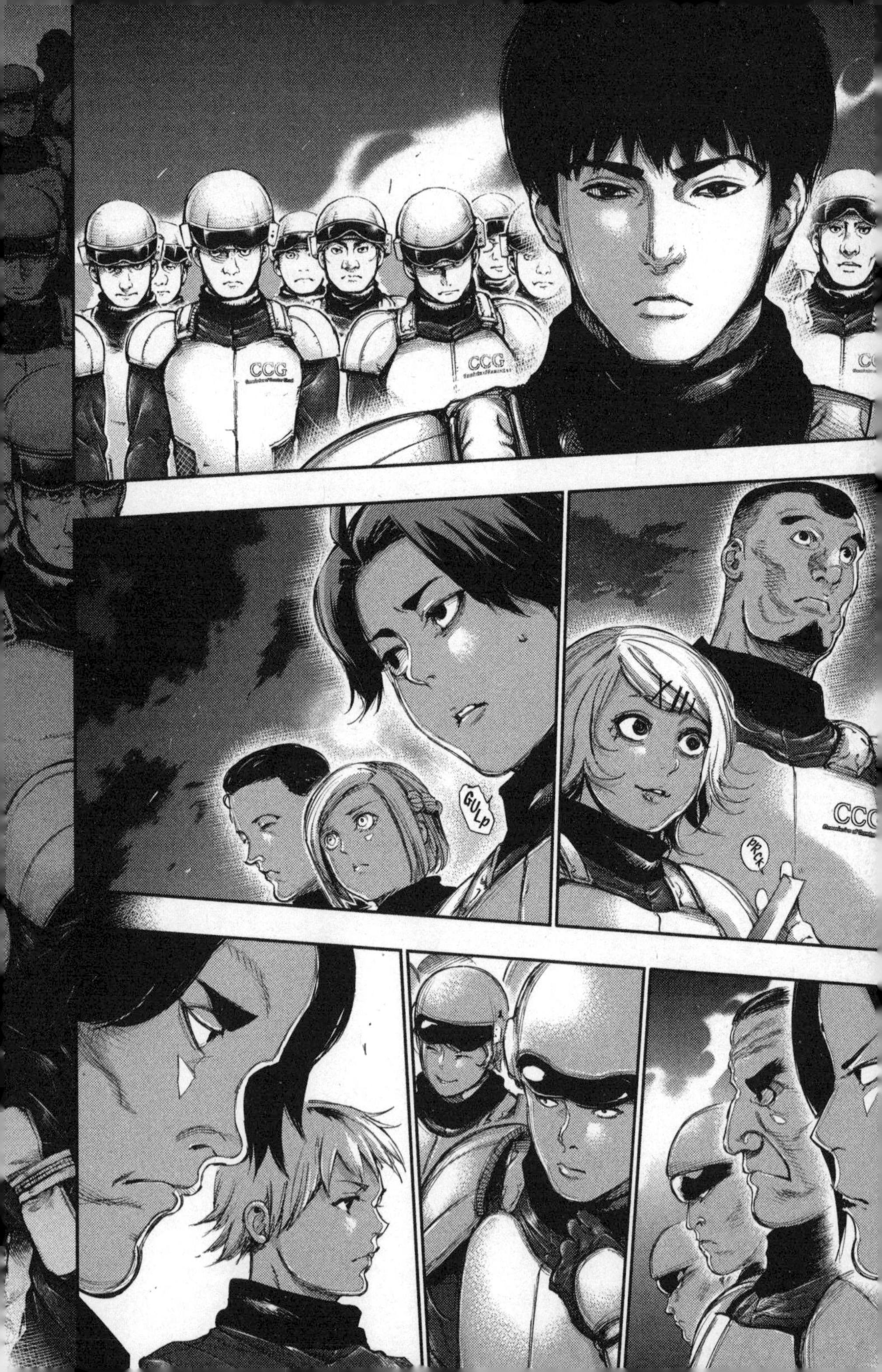
CCG
CCG
PRCK
GULP

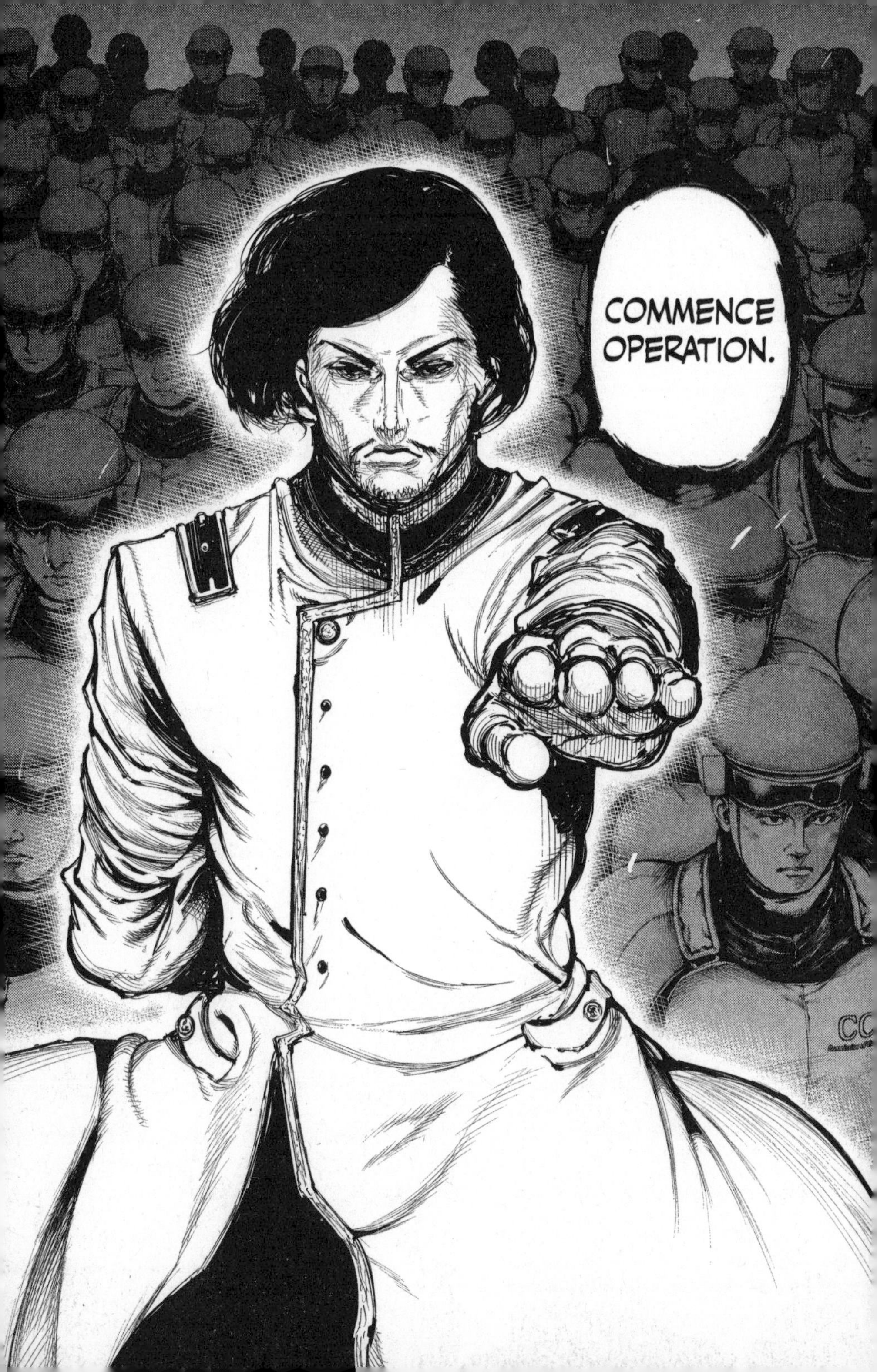
COMMENCE OPERATION.

TESTAMENT
SPECIAL GHOUL INVESTIGATOR KISHO ARIMA

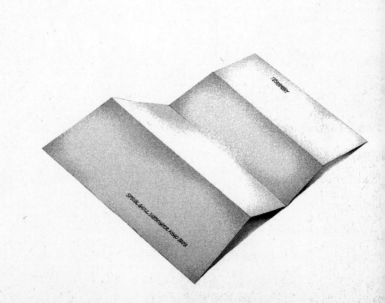

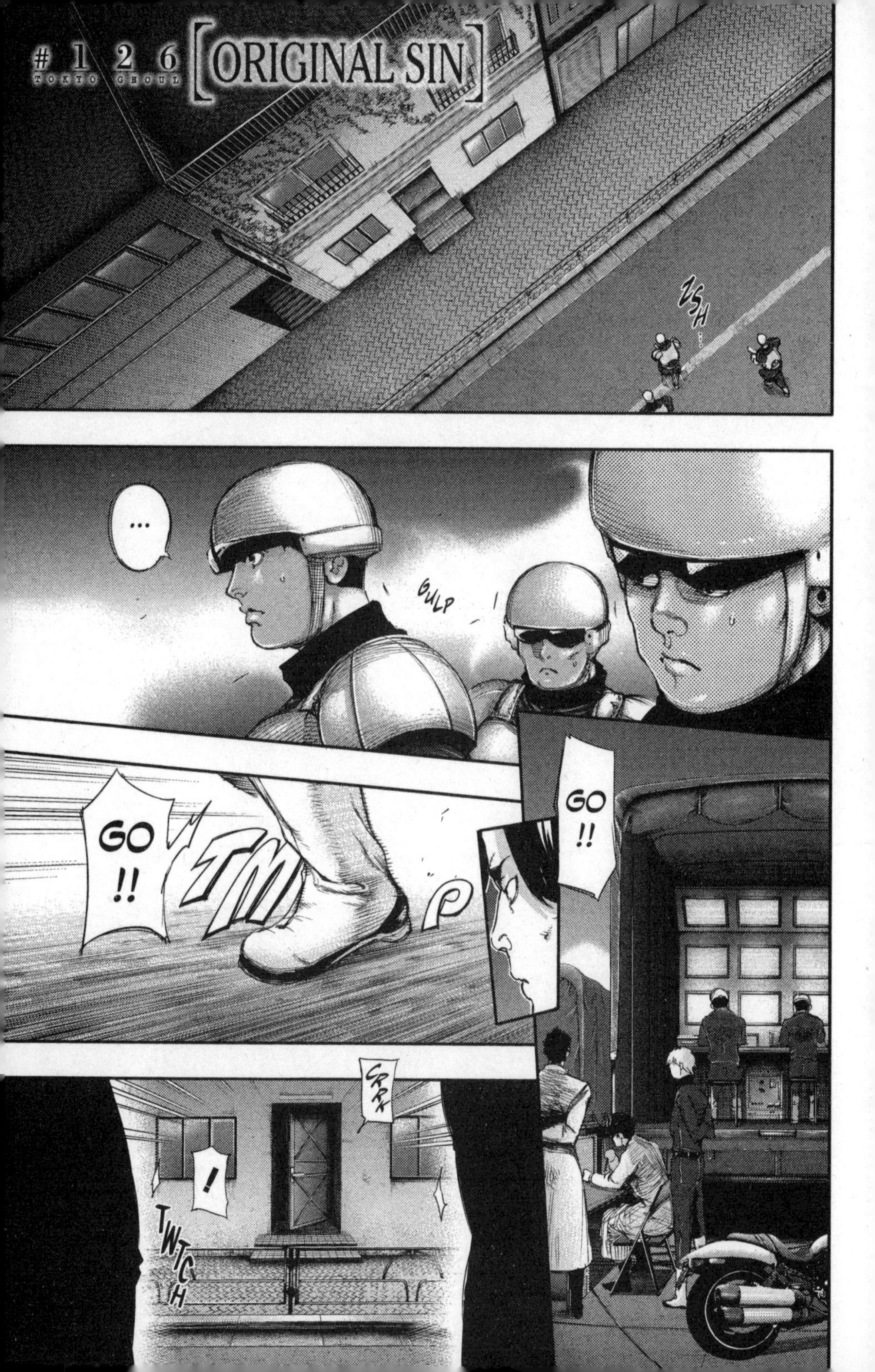
#126
TOKYO GHOUL
[ORIGINAL SIN]
VSH
...
GULP
GO !!
GO !!
TMP
CRRK
!
TWITCH

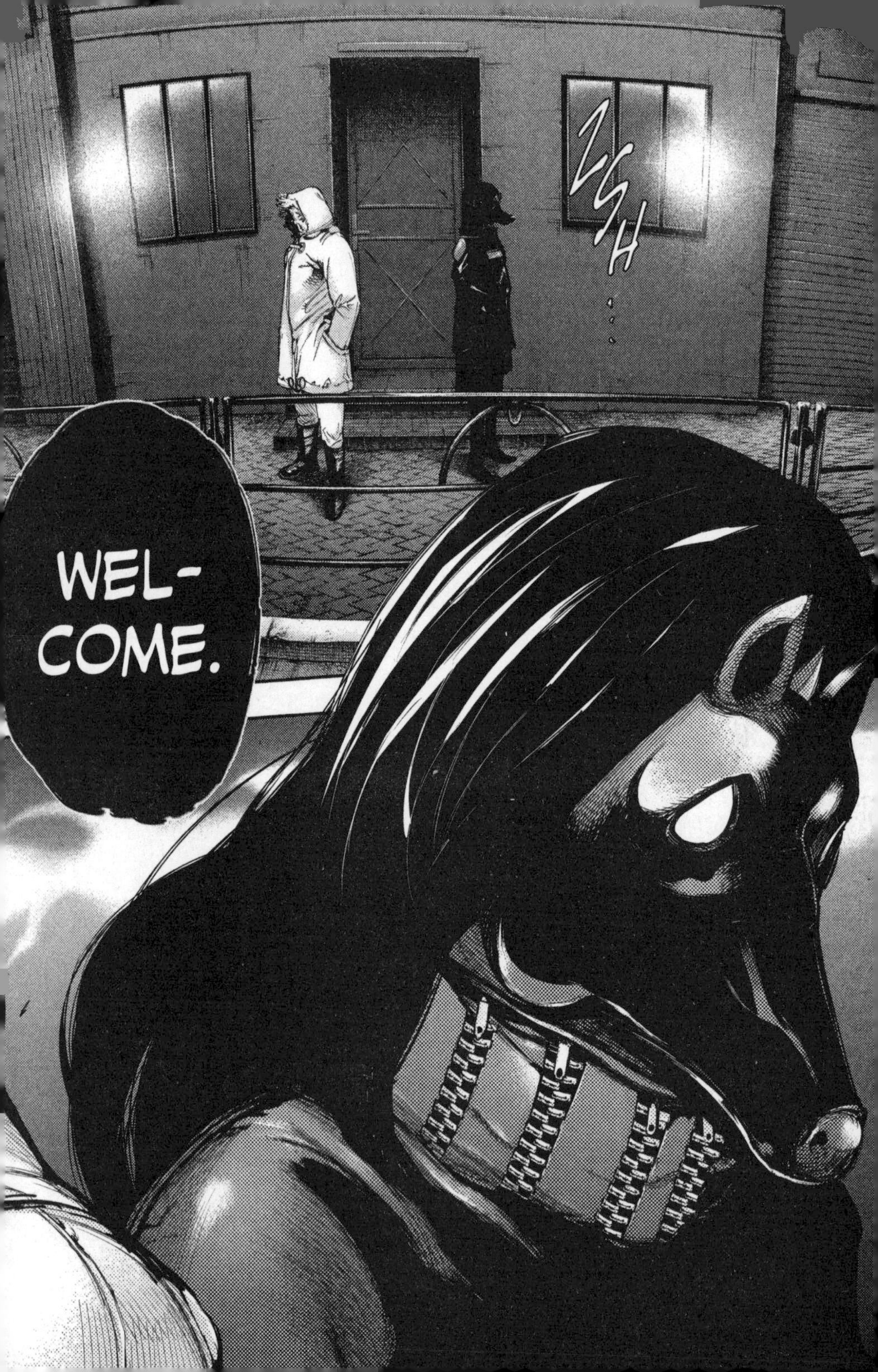
ZSH...
WEL-
COME.

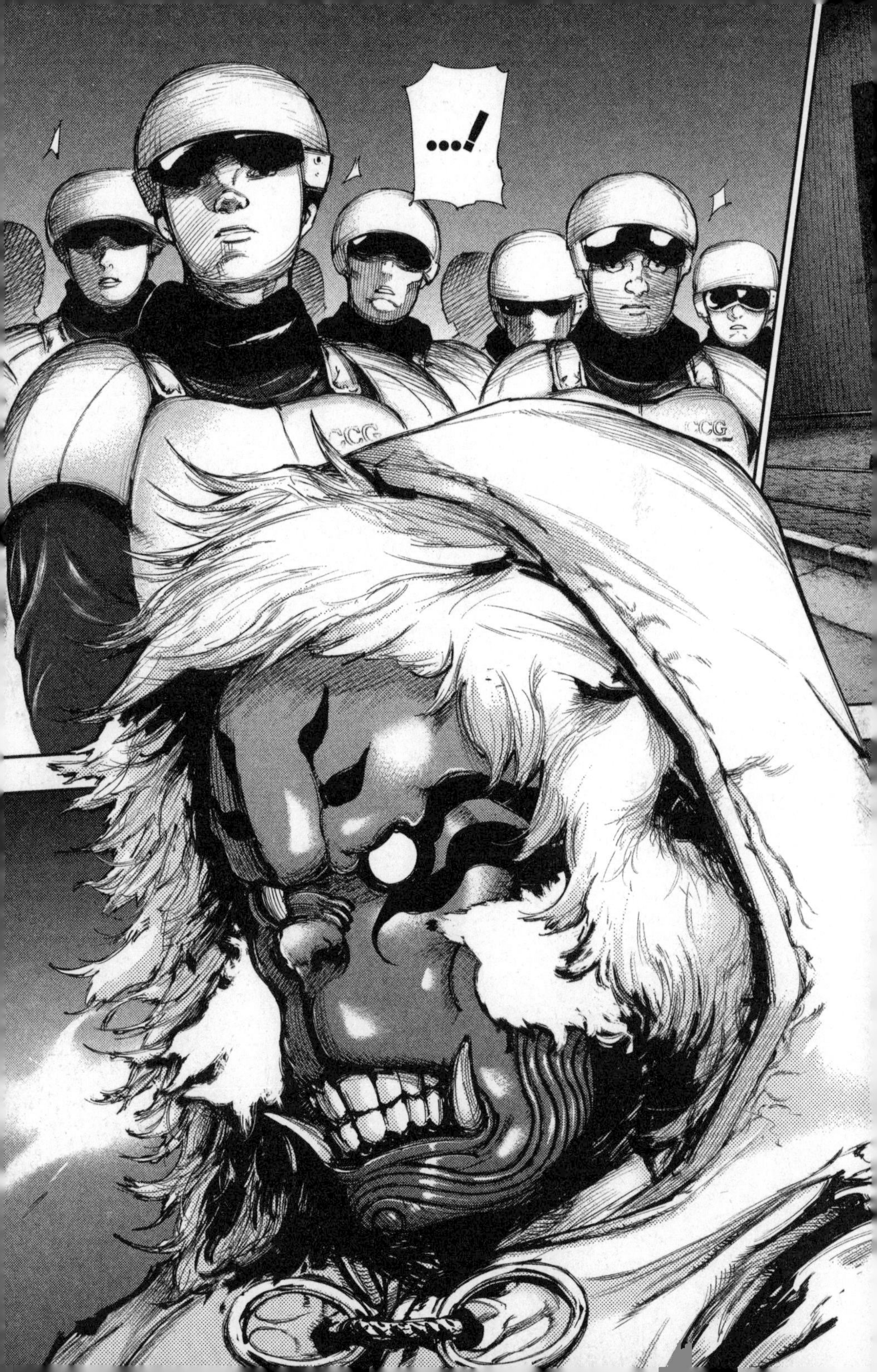
...!
CCG
CCG

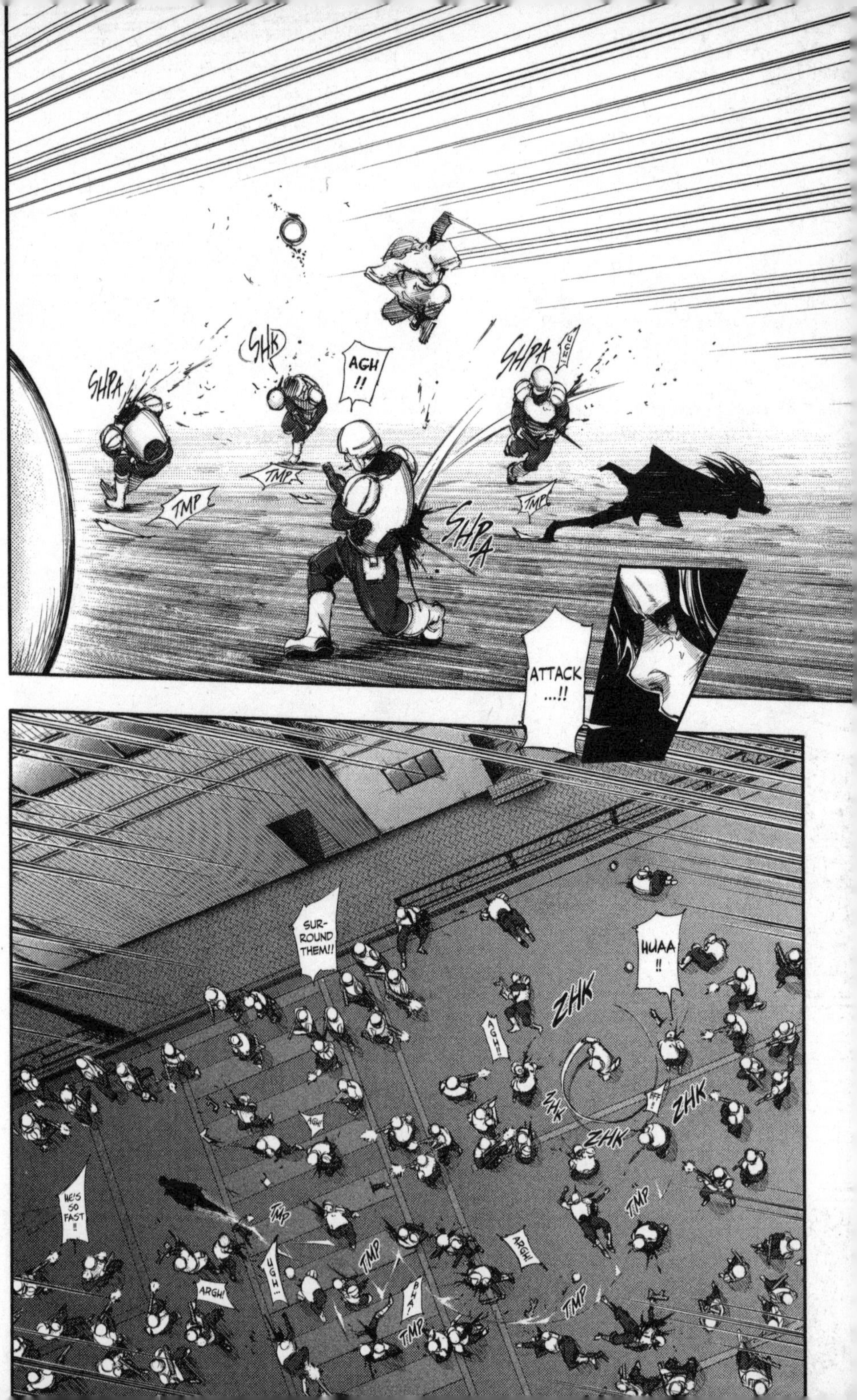
SHPA
UGH!
AGH!!
SHK
SHPA
TMP
TMP
TMP
SHPA
ATTACK ...!!
HUAA!!
ZHK
SUR-ROUND THEM!!
AGH!!
ZHK
ZHK
ZHK
AGH!
TMP
HE'S SO FAST!!
ARGH!
TMP
UGH..!
TMP
BHA!
TMP
ARGH!
TMP

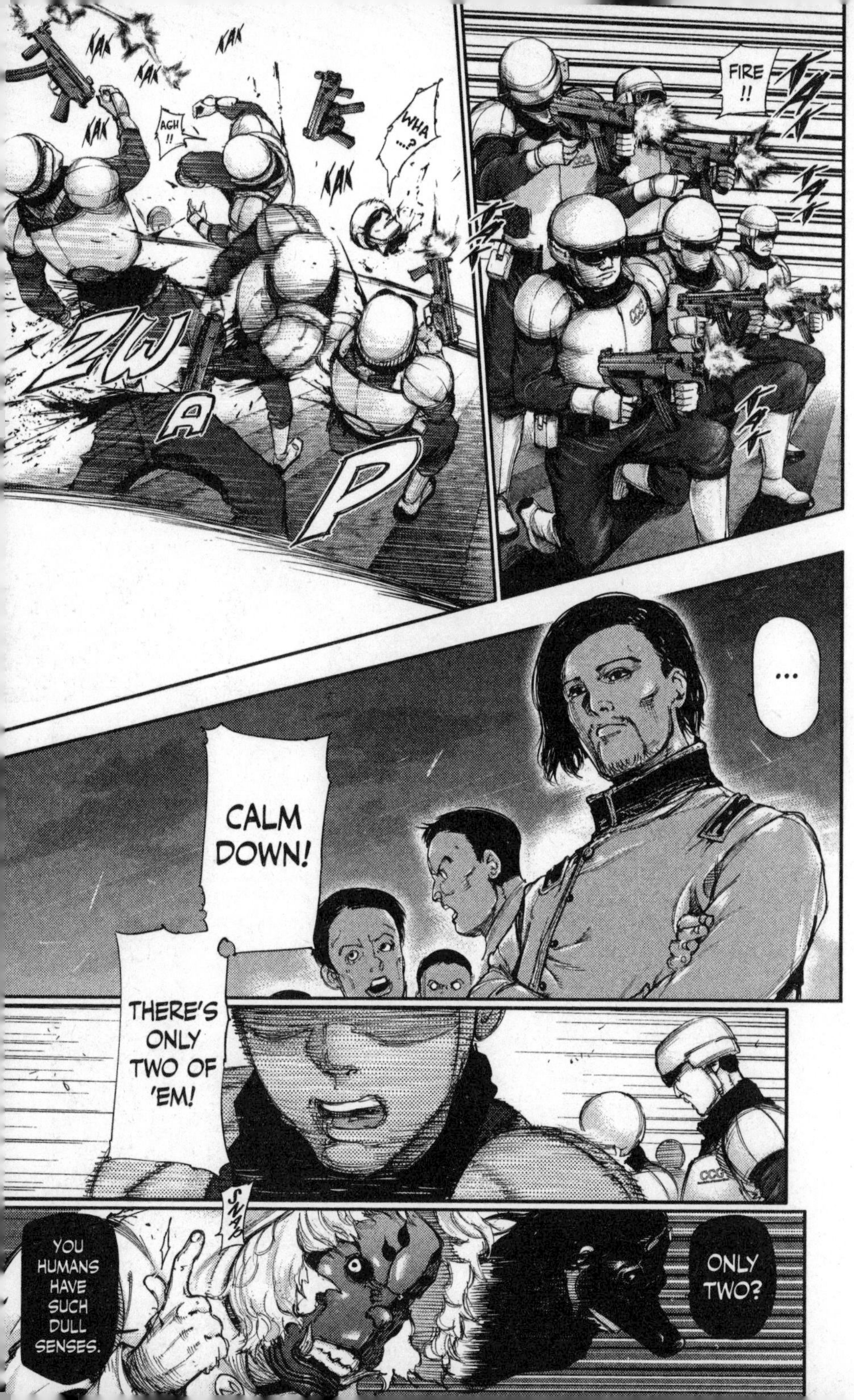
FIRE!!
KAK
KAK
KAK
KAK
KAK
KAK
AGH!!
WHA...?
KAK
ZWAP
...
CALM DOWN!
THERE'S ONLY TWO OF 'EM!
ONLY TWO?
SNAP
YOU HUMANS HAVE SUCH DULL SENSES.

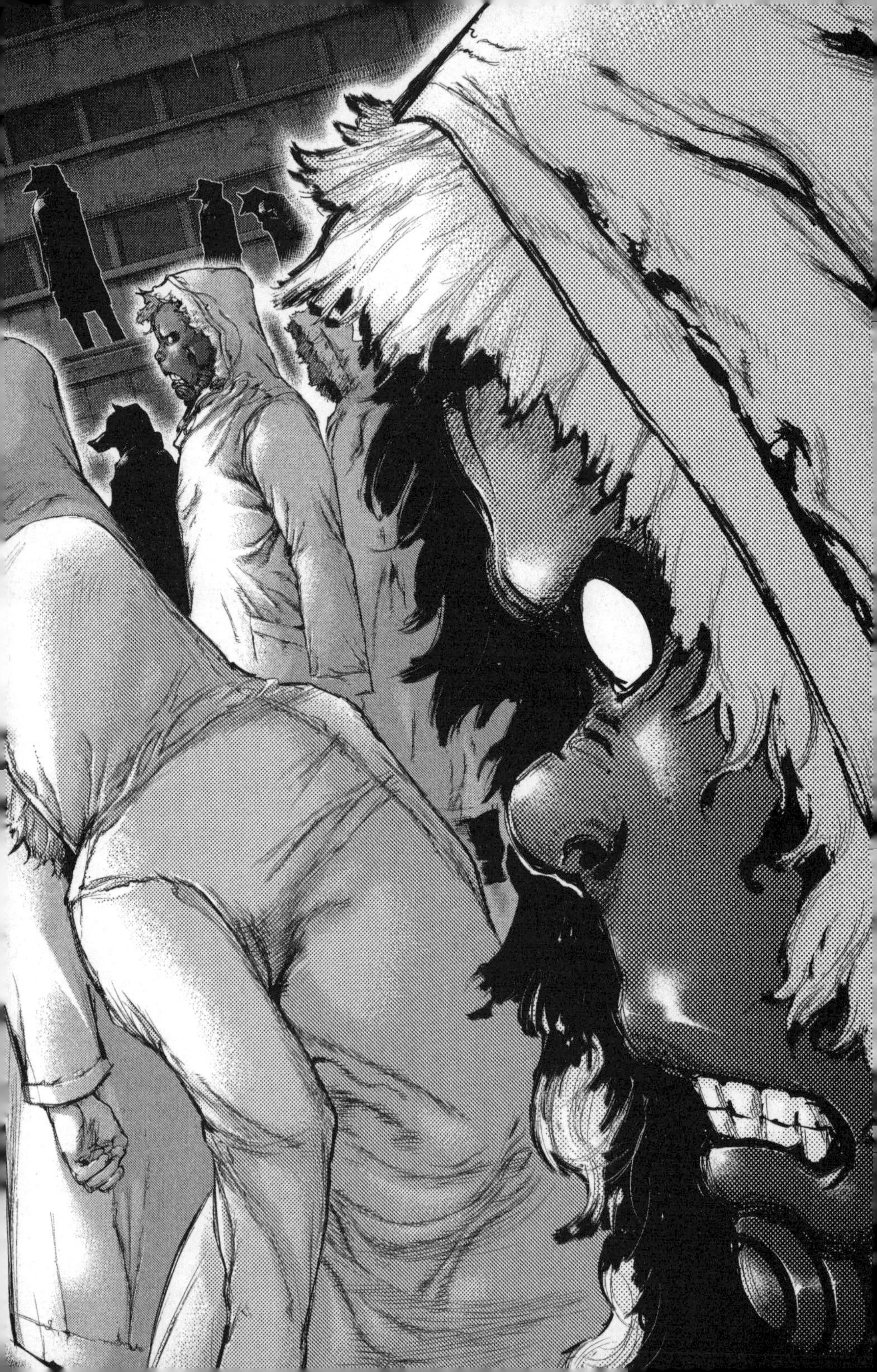

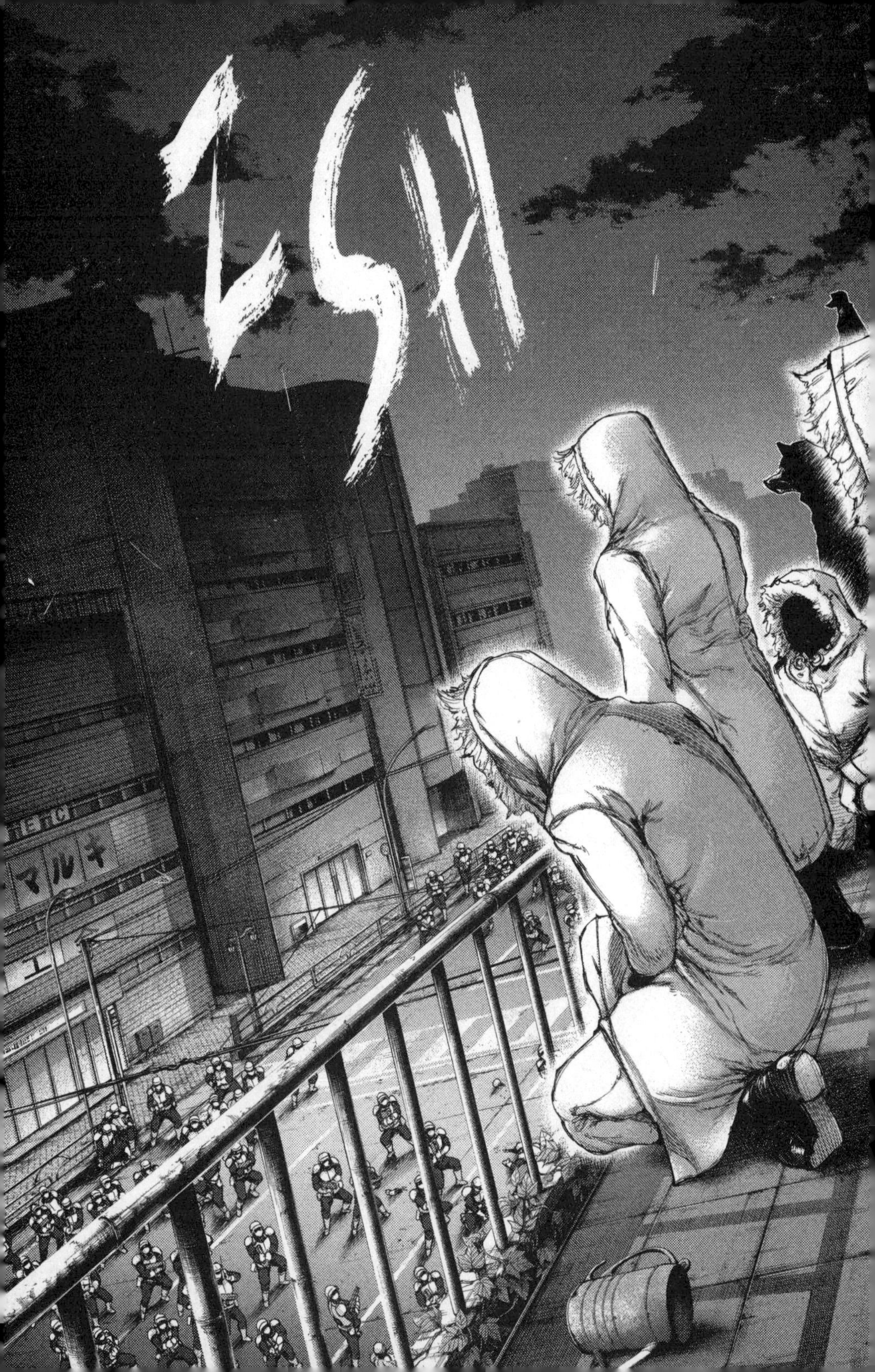
ZSH
マルキ

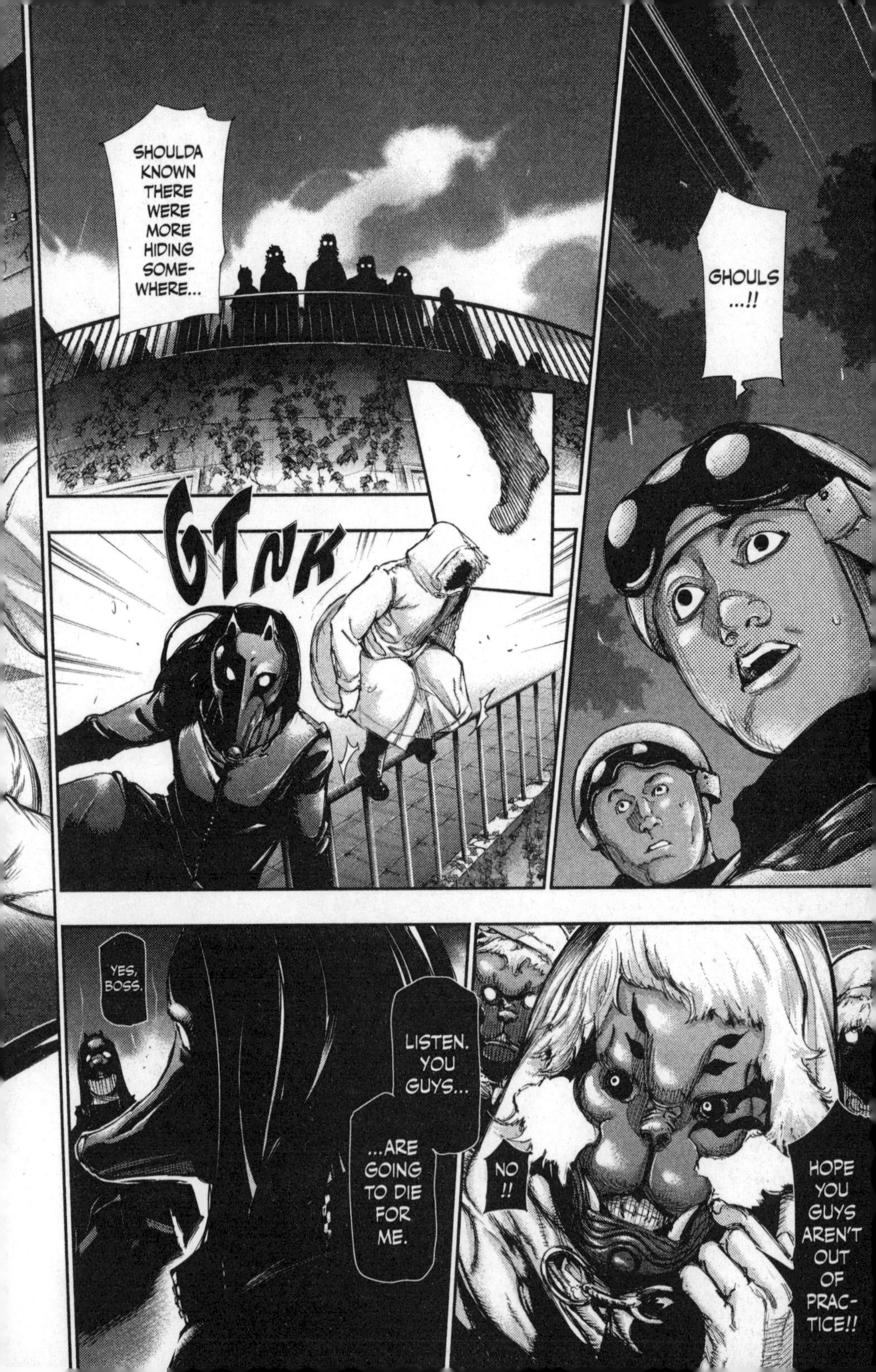
GHOULS ...!!
SHOULDA KNOWN THERE WERE MORE HIDING SOME-WHERE...
GTNK
HOPE YOU GUYS AREN'T OUT OF PRAC-TICE!!
NO !!
LISTEN. YOU GUYS...
...ARE GOING TO DIE FOR ME.
YES, BOSS.

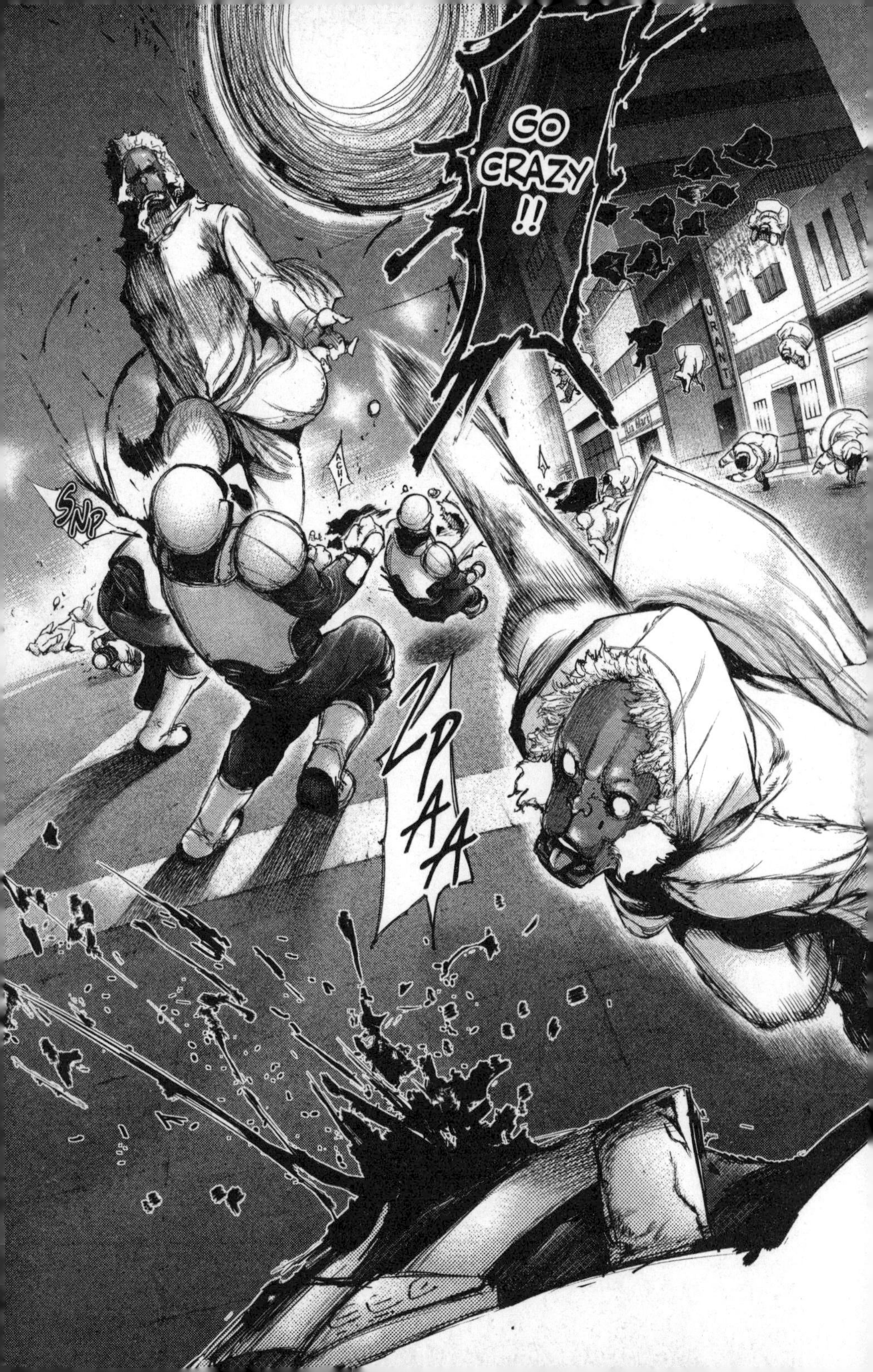
GO CRAZY !!
URANT
SNP
ACH!
ZPAA

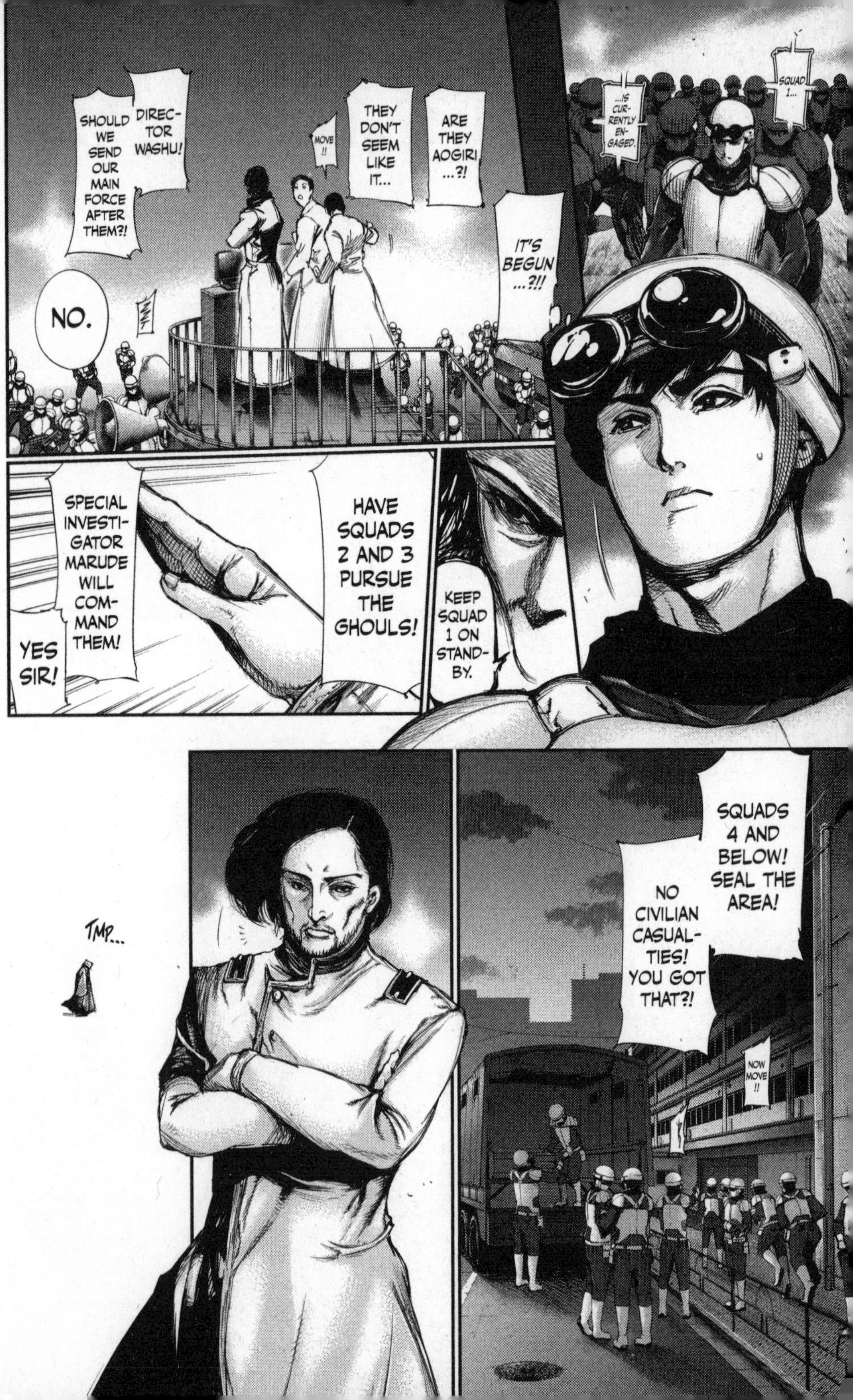
SQUAD 1...
...IS CURRENTLY ENGAGED.
IT'S BEGUN...?!!
ARE THEY AOGIRI...?!
THEY DON'T SEEM LIKE IT...
MOVE!!
DIRECTOR WASHU!
SHOULD WE SEND OUR MAIN FORCE AFTER THEM?!
NO.
KEEP SQUAD 1 ON STANDBY.
HAVE SQUADS 2 AND 3 PURSUE THE GHOULS!
SPECIAL INVESTIGATOR MARUDE WILL COMMAND THEM!
YES SIR!
SQUADS 4 AND BELOW! SEAL THE AREA!
NO CIVILIAN CASUALTIES! YOU GOT THAT?!
NOW MOVE!!
TMP...

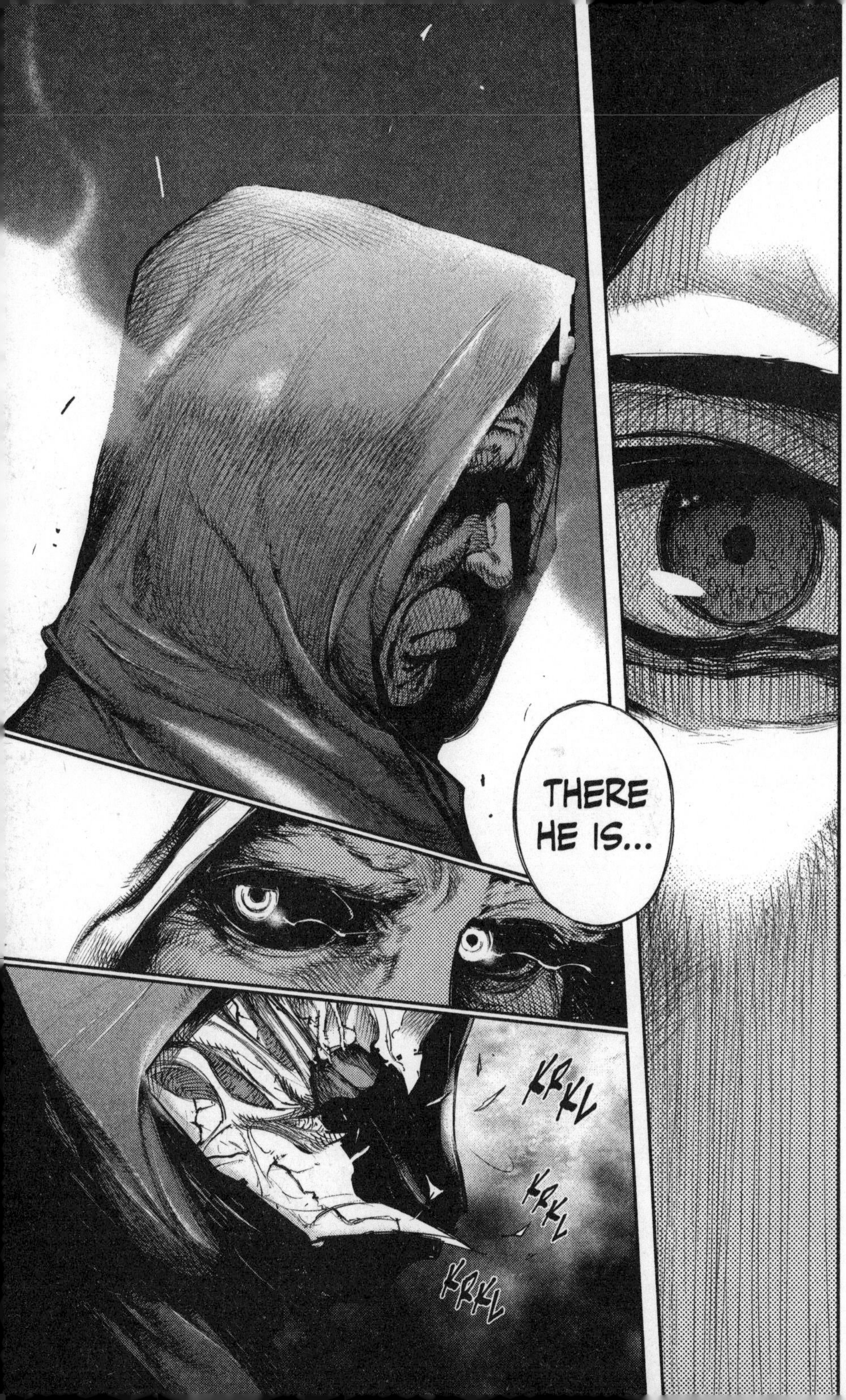
THERE HE IS...
KRKL
KRKL
KRKL

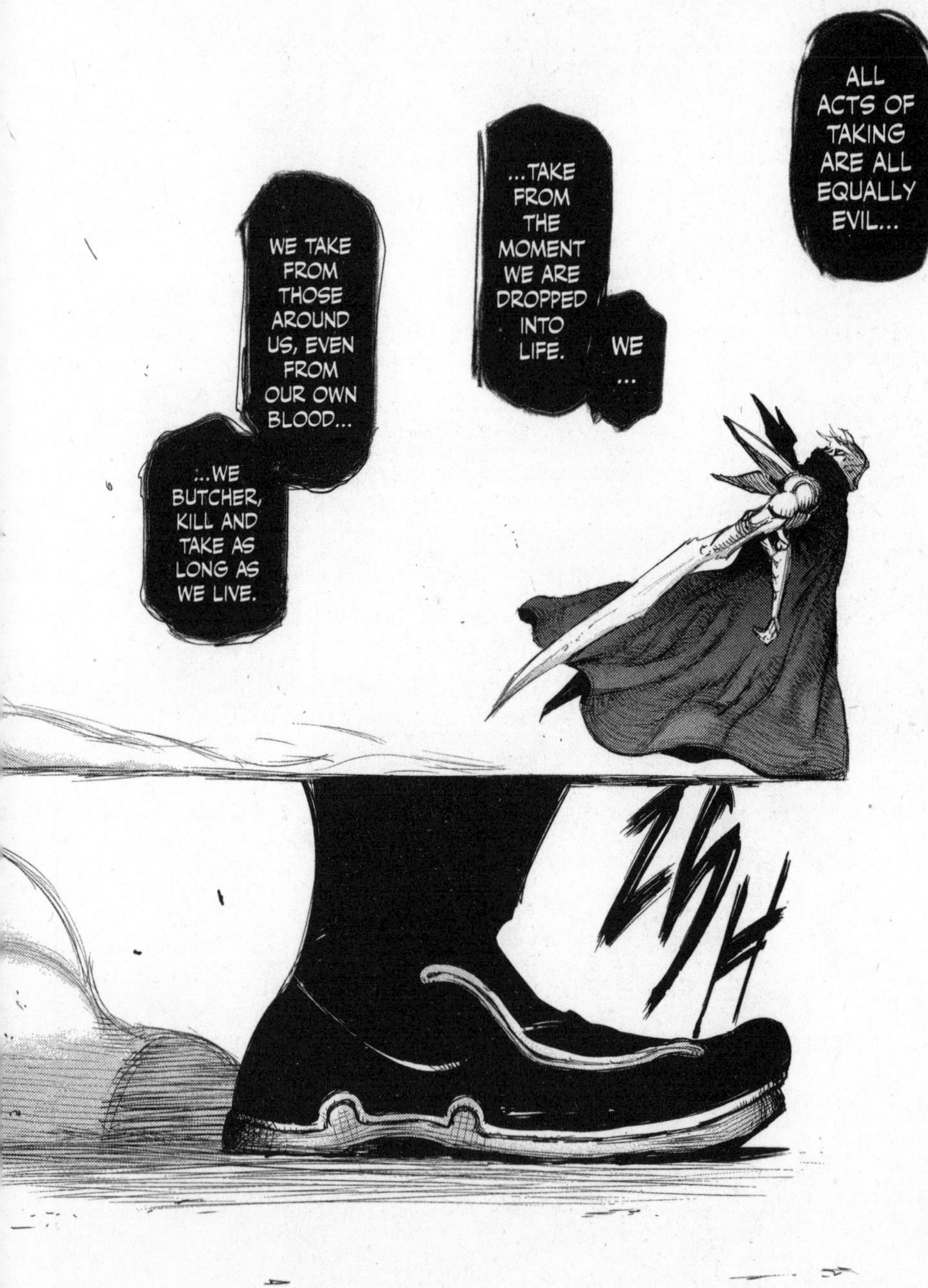
ALL ACTS OF TAKING ARE ALL EQUALLY EVIL...
WE ...
...TAKE FROM THE MOMENT WE ARE DROPPED INTO LIFE.
WE TAKE FROM THOSE AROUND US, EVEN FROM OUR OWN BLOOD...
...WE BUTCHER, KILL AND TAKE AS LONG AS WE LIVE.
ZSH

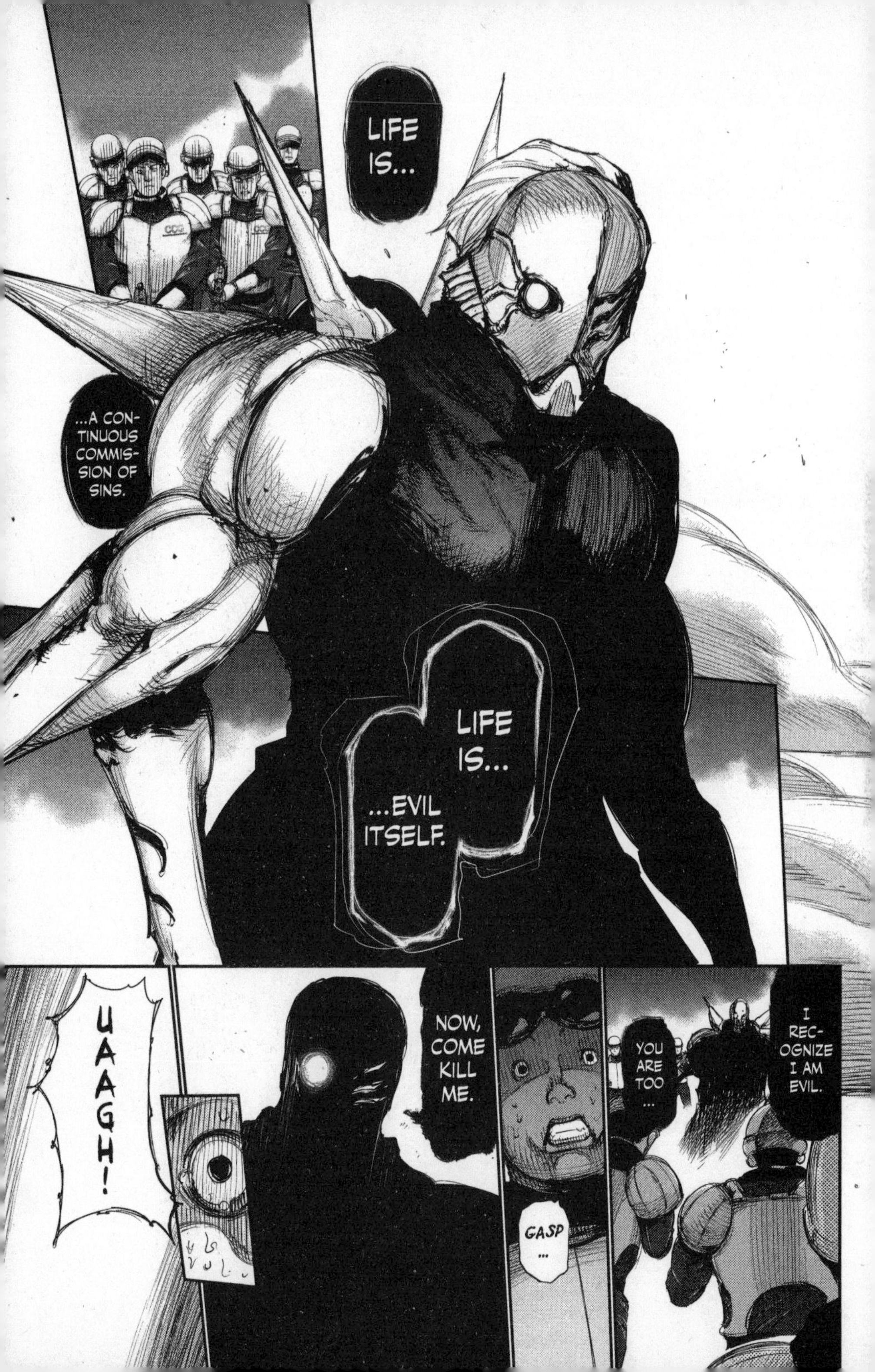
LIFE IS...
...A CONTINUOUS COMMISSION OF SINS.
LIFE IS...
...EVIL ITSELF.
I RECOGNIZE I AM EVIL.
YOU ARE TOO...
NOW, COME KILL ME.
GASP...
UAAGH!

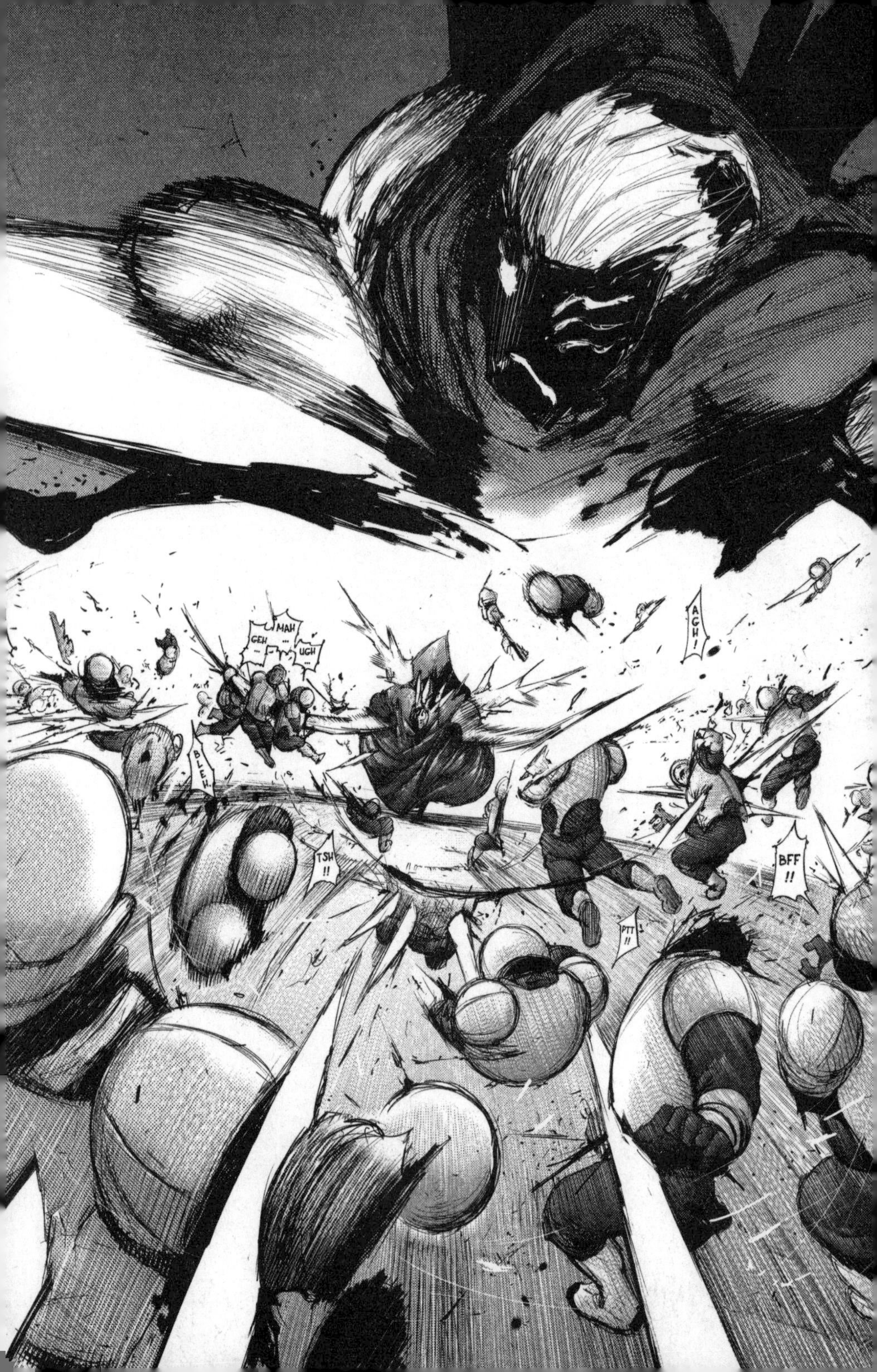
AGH!
UGH...
MAH...
GEH...
BLEH.
BFF!!
PTT!!
TSH!!

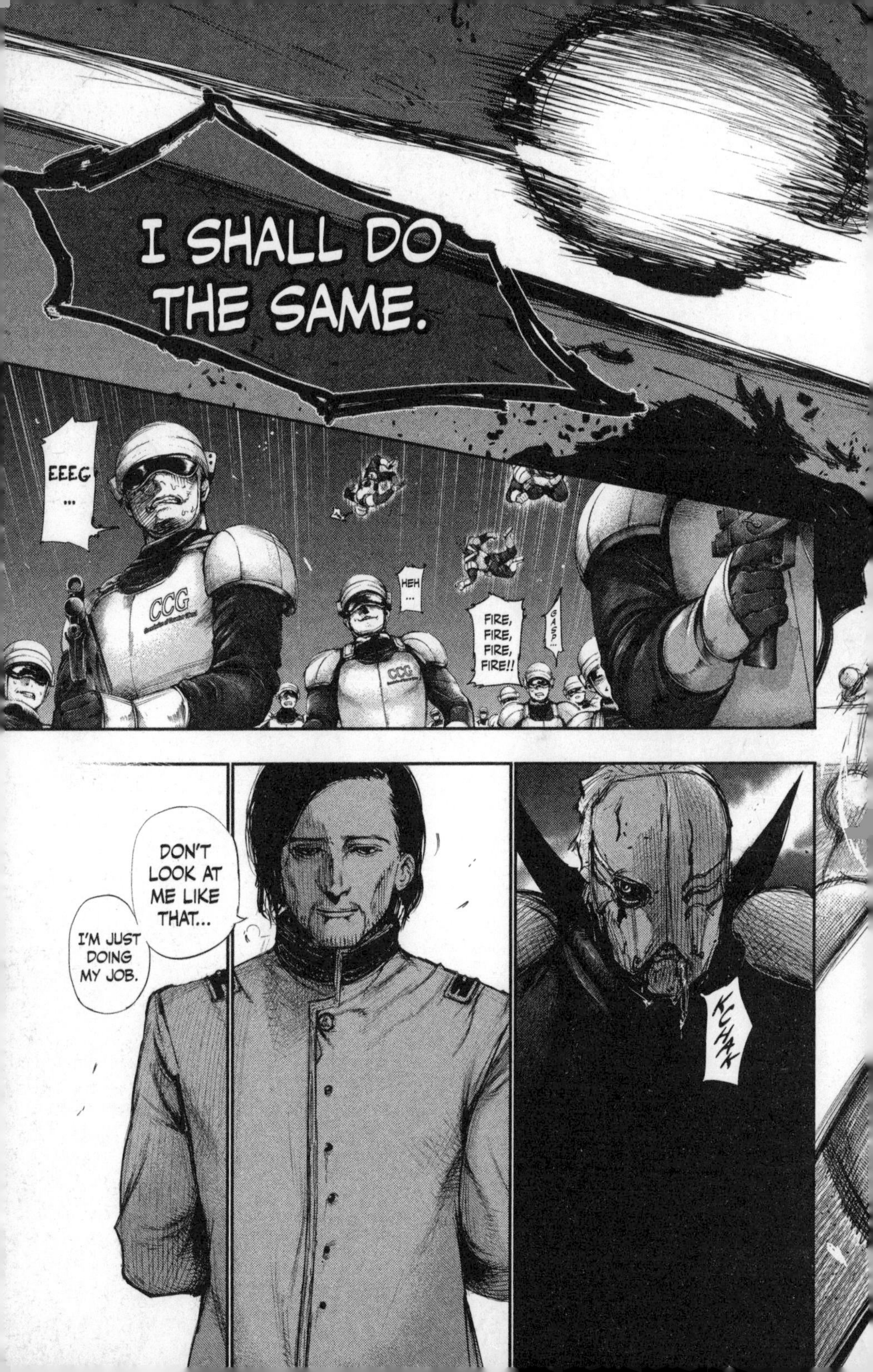
I SHALL DO THE SAME.
GASP...
FIRE, FIRE, FIRE, FIRE!!
HEH...
EEEG...
KCHAK
DON'T LOOK AT ME LIKE THAT...
I'M JUST DOING MY JOB.

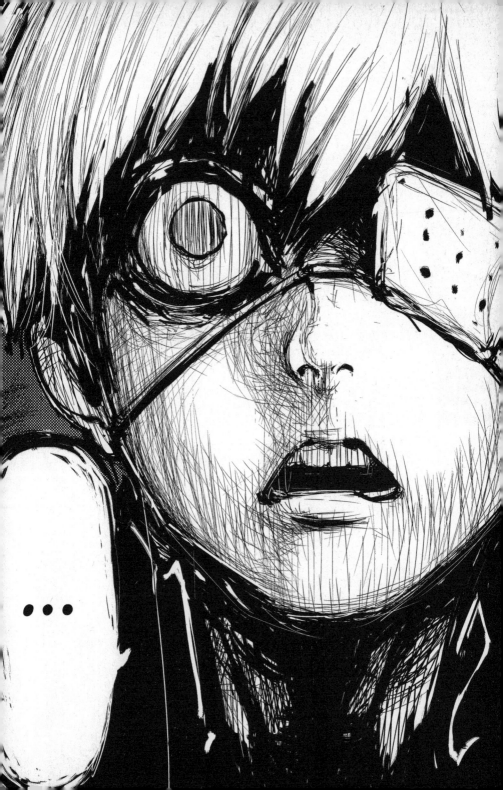

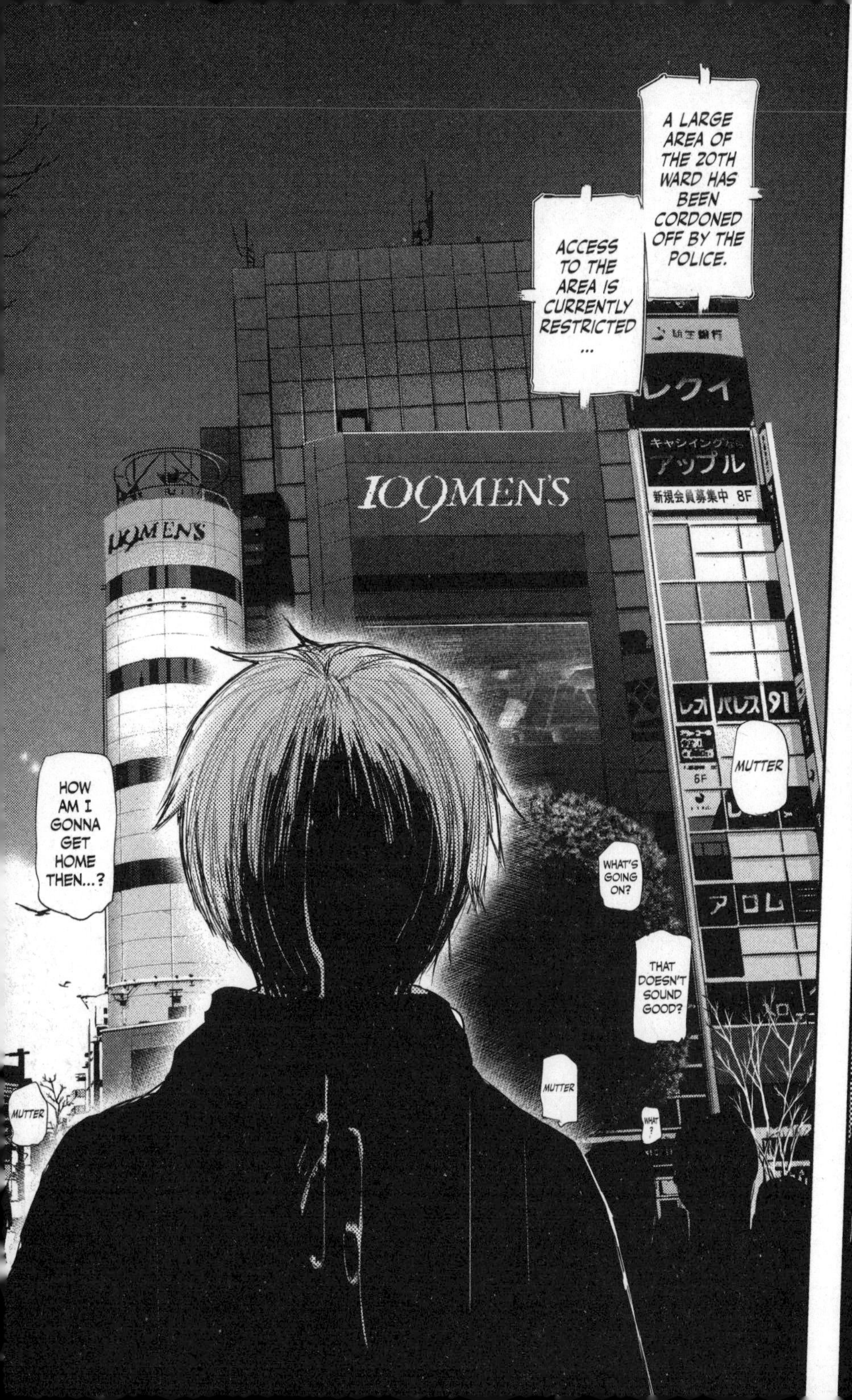
A LARGE AREA OF THE 20TH WARD HAS BEEN CORDONED OFF BY THE POLICE.
ACCESS TO THE AREA IS CURRENTLY RESTRICTED ...
レクイ
キャシングなら
アップル
新規会員募集中 8F
109MEN'S
109MEN'S
レオパレス91
アロム
MUTTER
HOW AM I GONNA GET HOME THEN...?
WHAT'S GOING ON?
THAT DOESN'T SOUND GOOD?
MUTTER
WHAT?
MUTTER

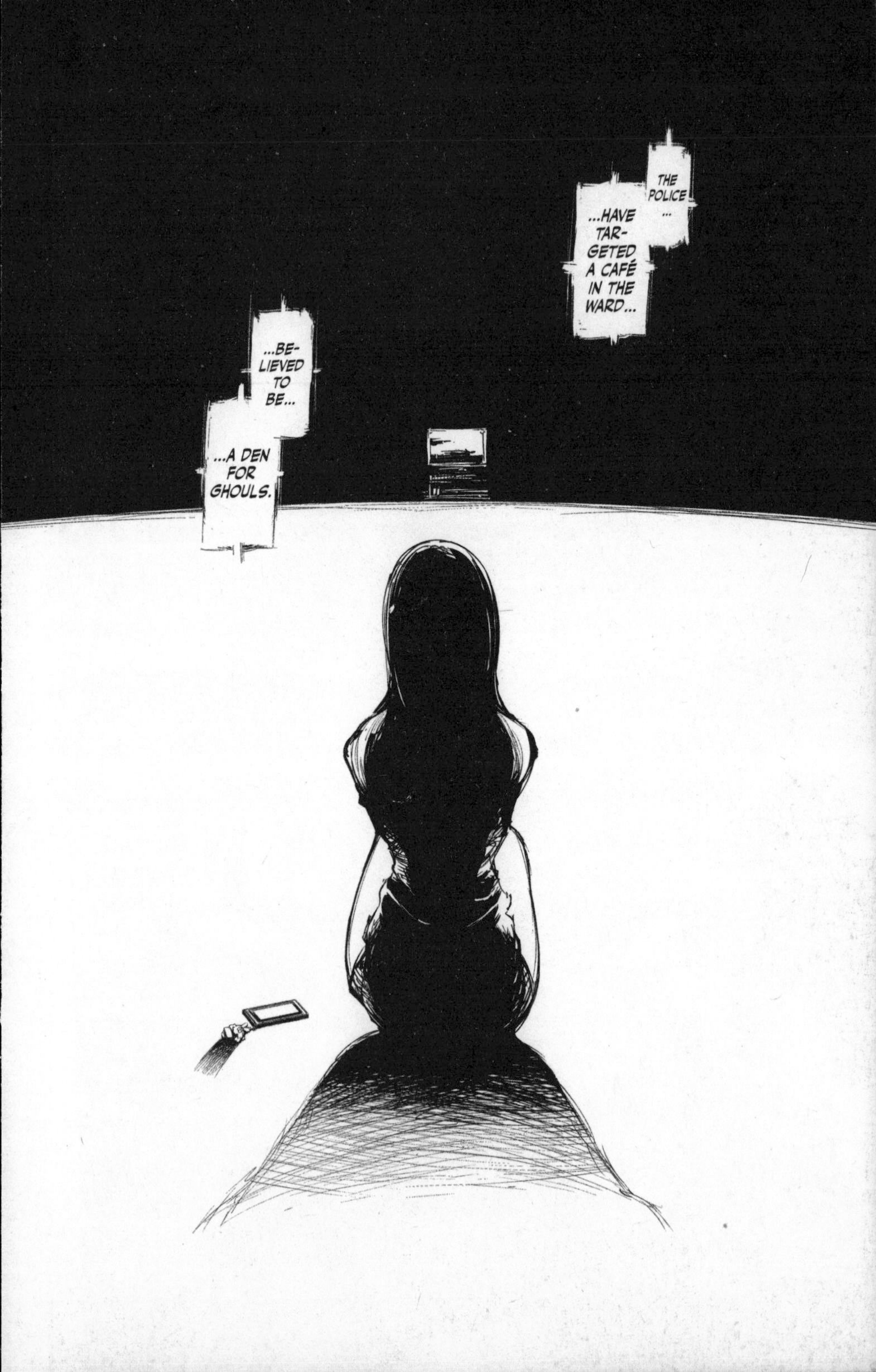
THE POLICE...
...HAVE TARGETED A CAFÉ IN THE WARD...
...BELIEVED TO BE...
...A DEN FOR GHOULS.

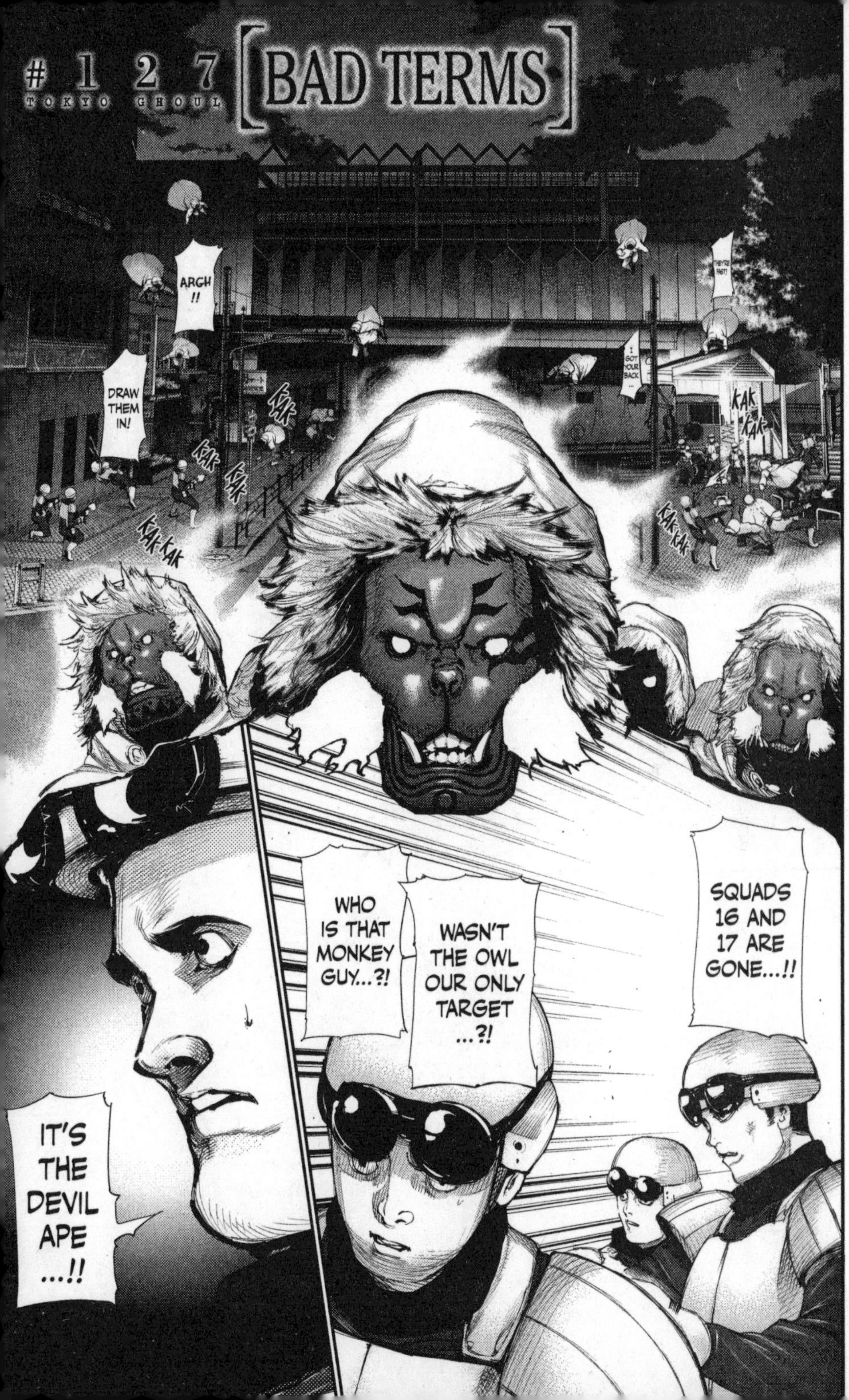
#127 TOKYO GHOUL
BAD TERMS
THEY'RE FAST!
I GOT YOUR BACK...
ARGH!!
DRAW THEM IN!
KAK KAK
KAK KAK
KAK KAK
KAK KAK
KAK KAK
SQUADS 16 AND 17 ARE GONE...!!
WASN'T THE OWL OUR ONLY TARGET...?!
WHO IS THAT MONKEY GUY...?!
IT'S THE DEVIL APE...!!

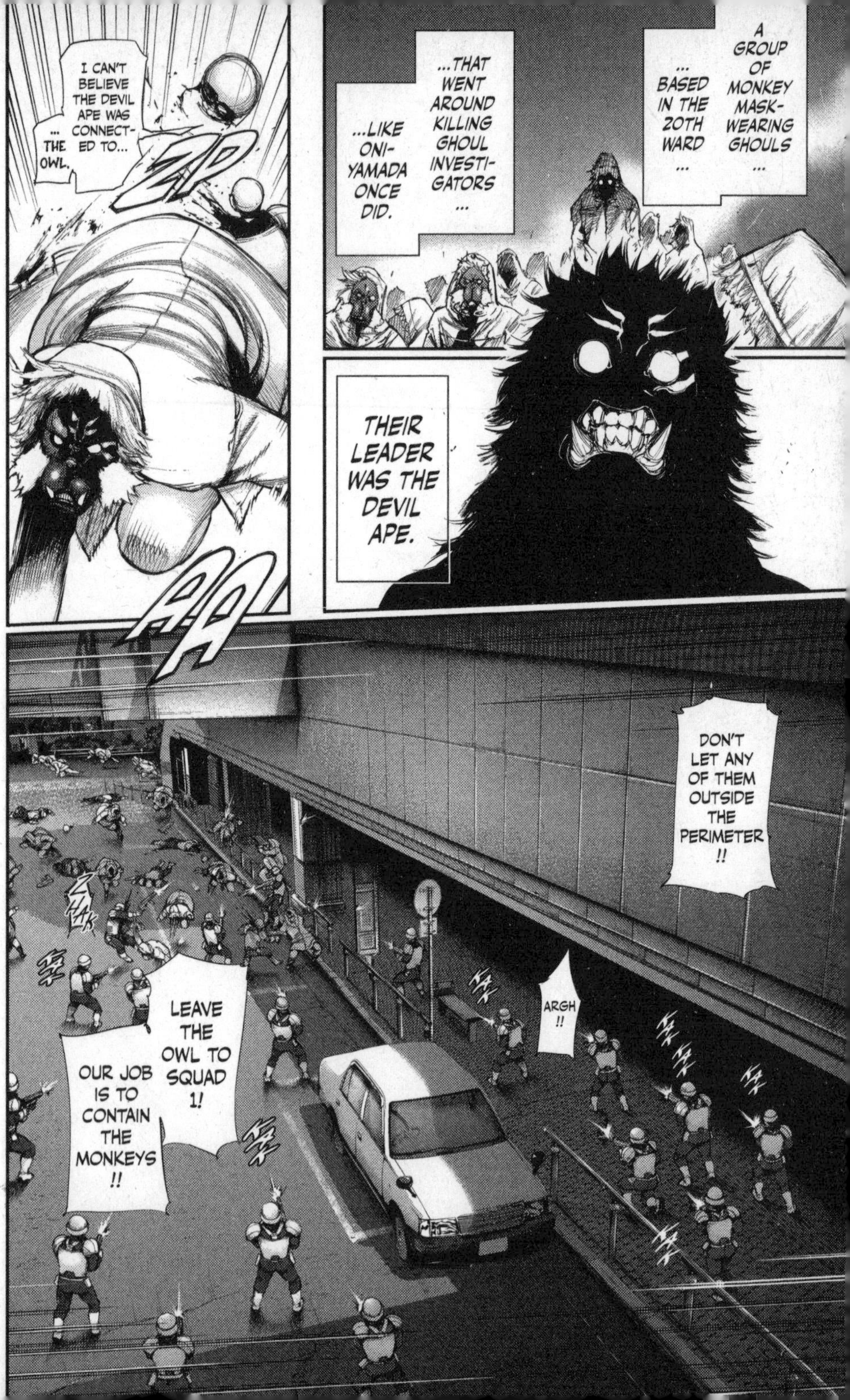
A GROUP OF MONKEY MASK-WEARING GHOULS...
...BASED IN THE 20TH WARD...
...THAT WENT AROUND KILLING GHOUL INVESTIGATORS...
...LIKE ONI-YAMADA ONCE DID.
THEIR LEADER WAS THE DEVIL APE.
I CAN'T BELIEVE THE DEVIL APE WAS CONNECTED TO...
...THE OWL.
ZAP
DON'T LET ANY OF THEM OUTSIDE THE PERIMETER!!
ARGH!!
KAK
LEAVE THE OWL TO SQUAD 1!
OUR JOB IS TO CONTAIN THE MONKEYS!!

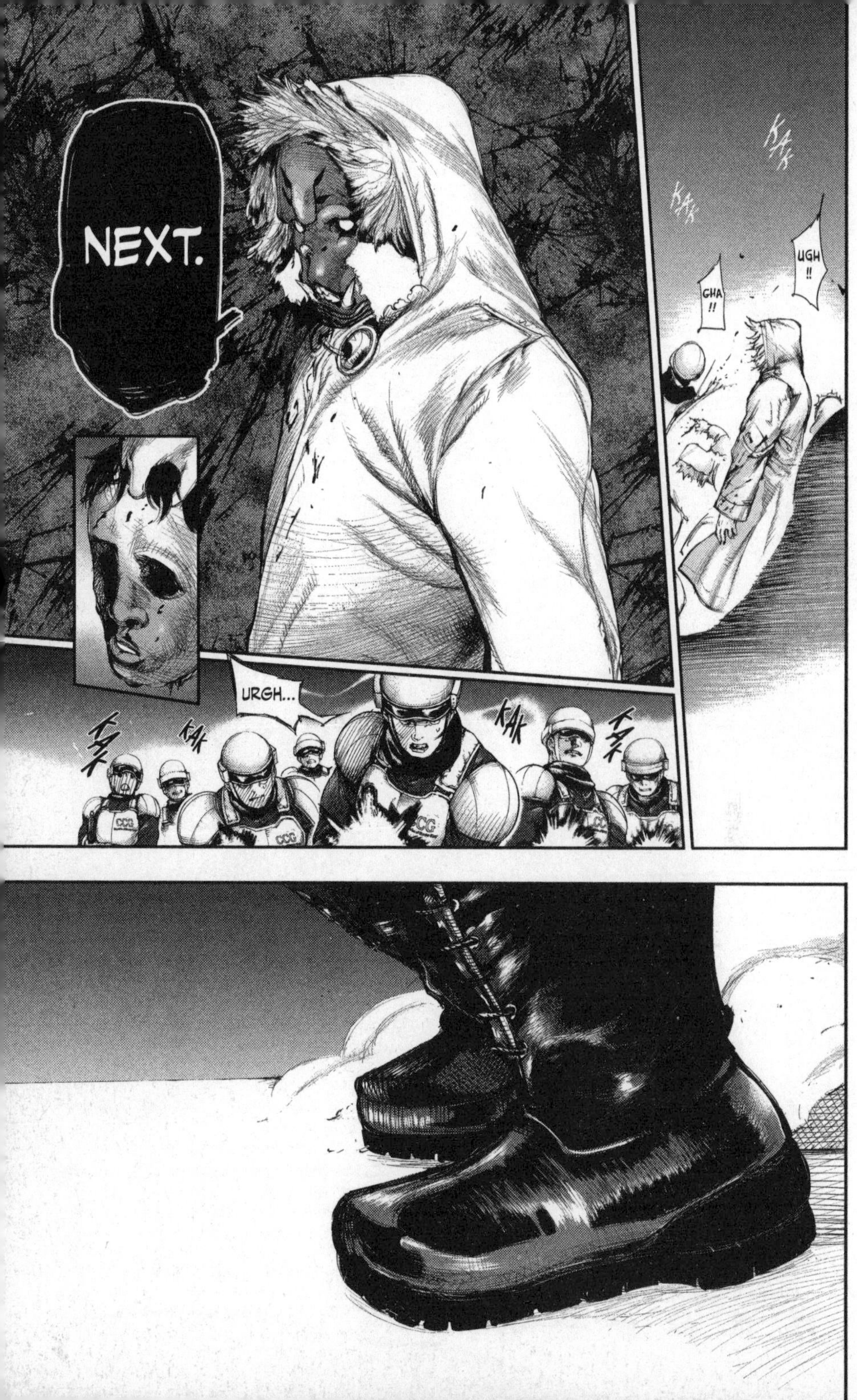
KAK
KAK
UGH!!
GHA!!
NEXT.
KAK
KAK
URGH...
KAK
KAK

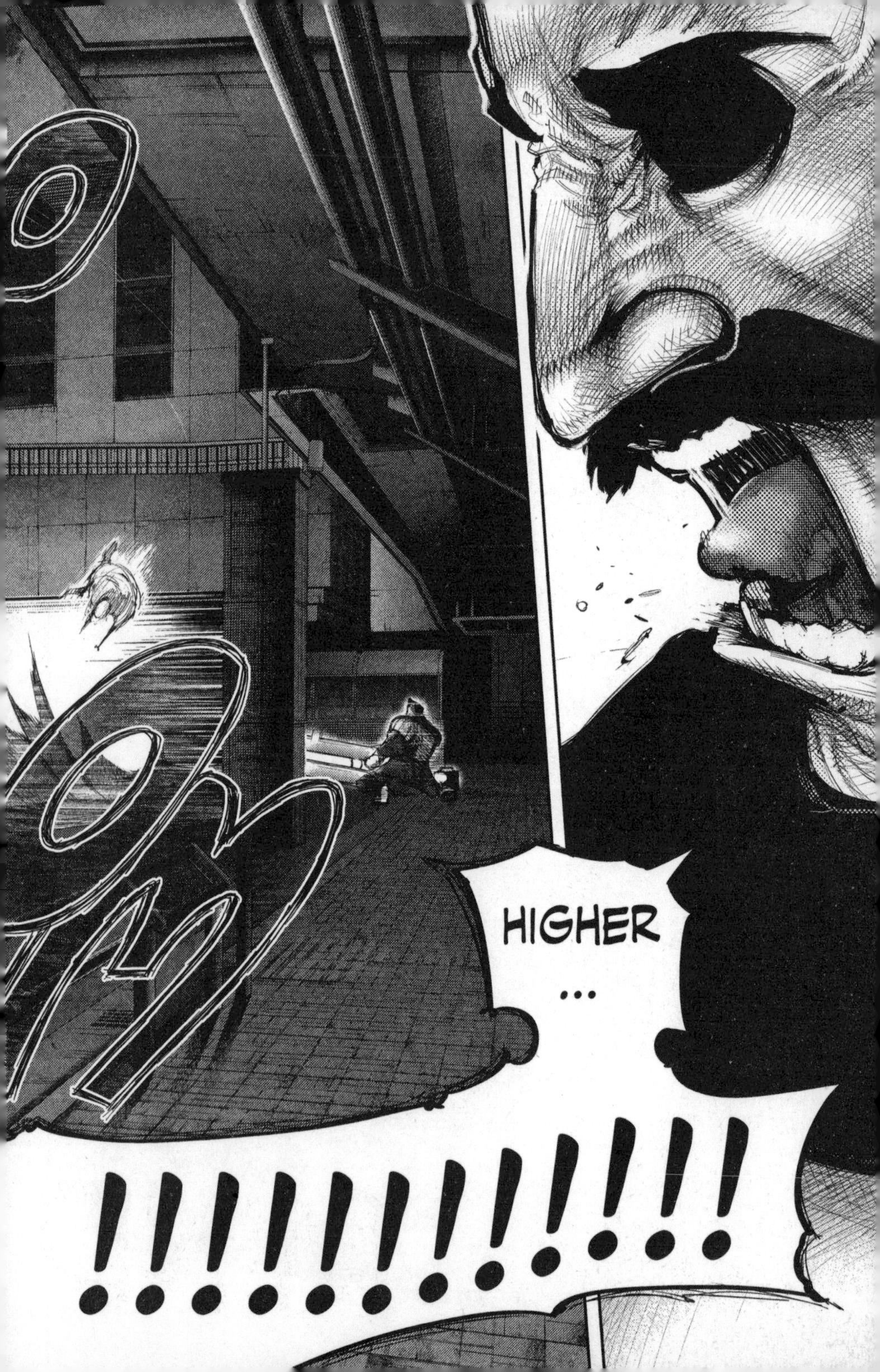
HIGHER
...
!!!!!!!!!!!!!

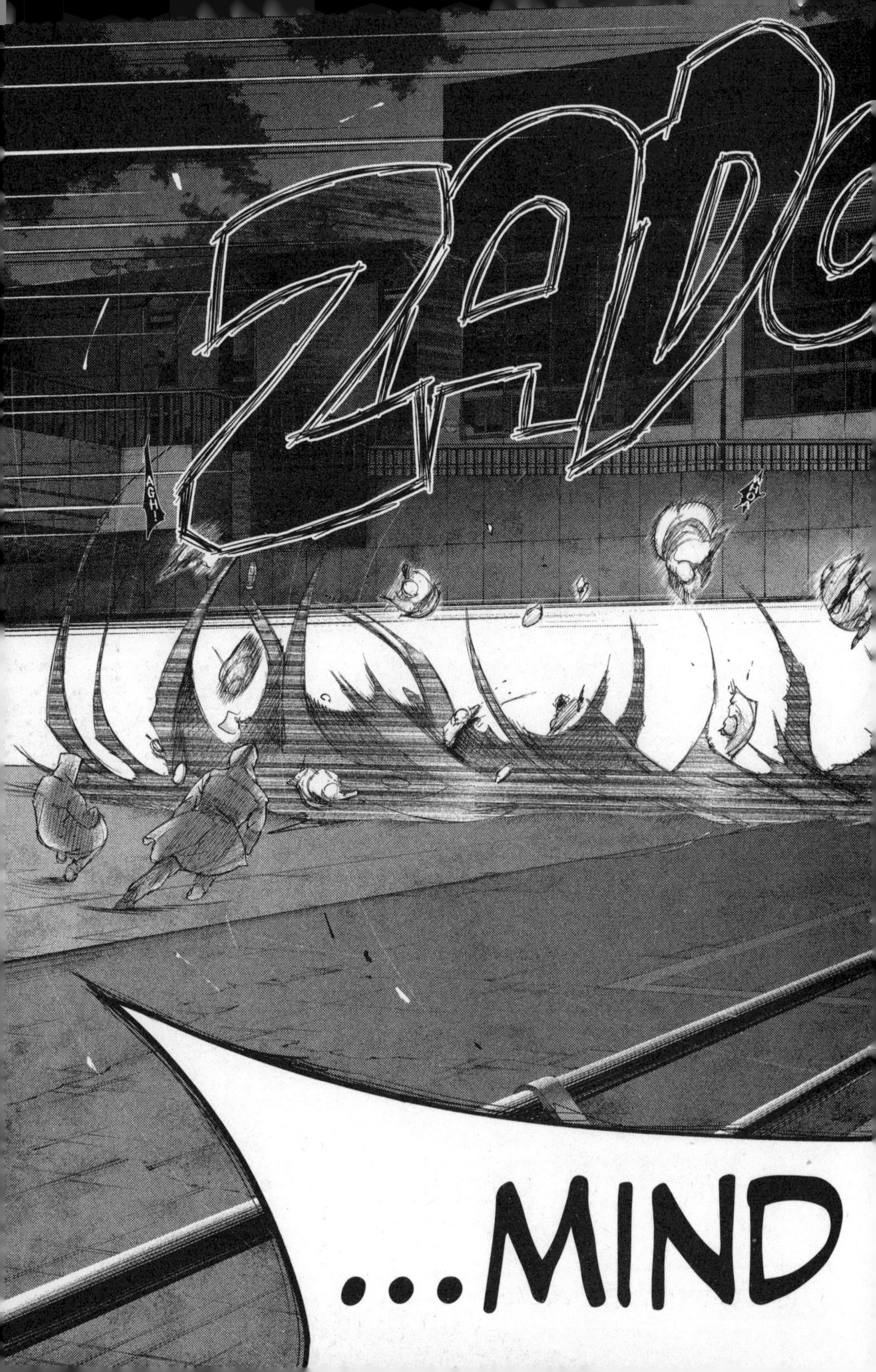
WHOA
AGH!
...MIND

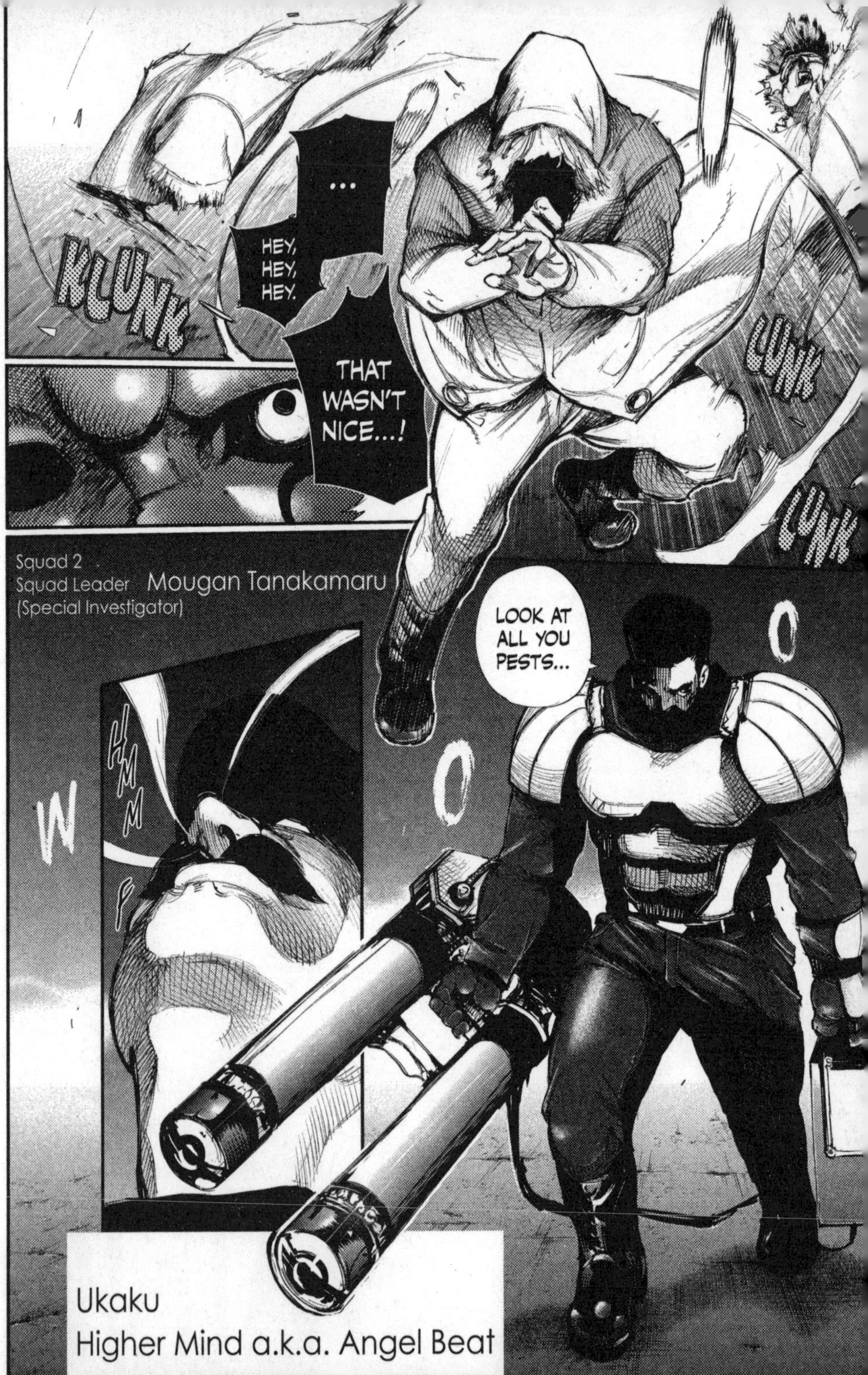
LUNK
LUNK
...
HEY, HEY, HEY.
THAT WASN'T NICE...!
KLUNK
Squad 2
Squad Leader Mougan Tanakamaru
(Special Investigator)
LOOK AT ALL YOU PESTS...
Ukaku
Higher Mind a.k.a. Angel Beat

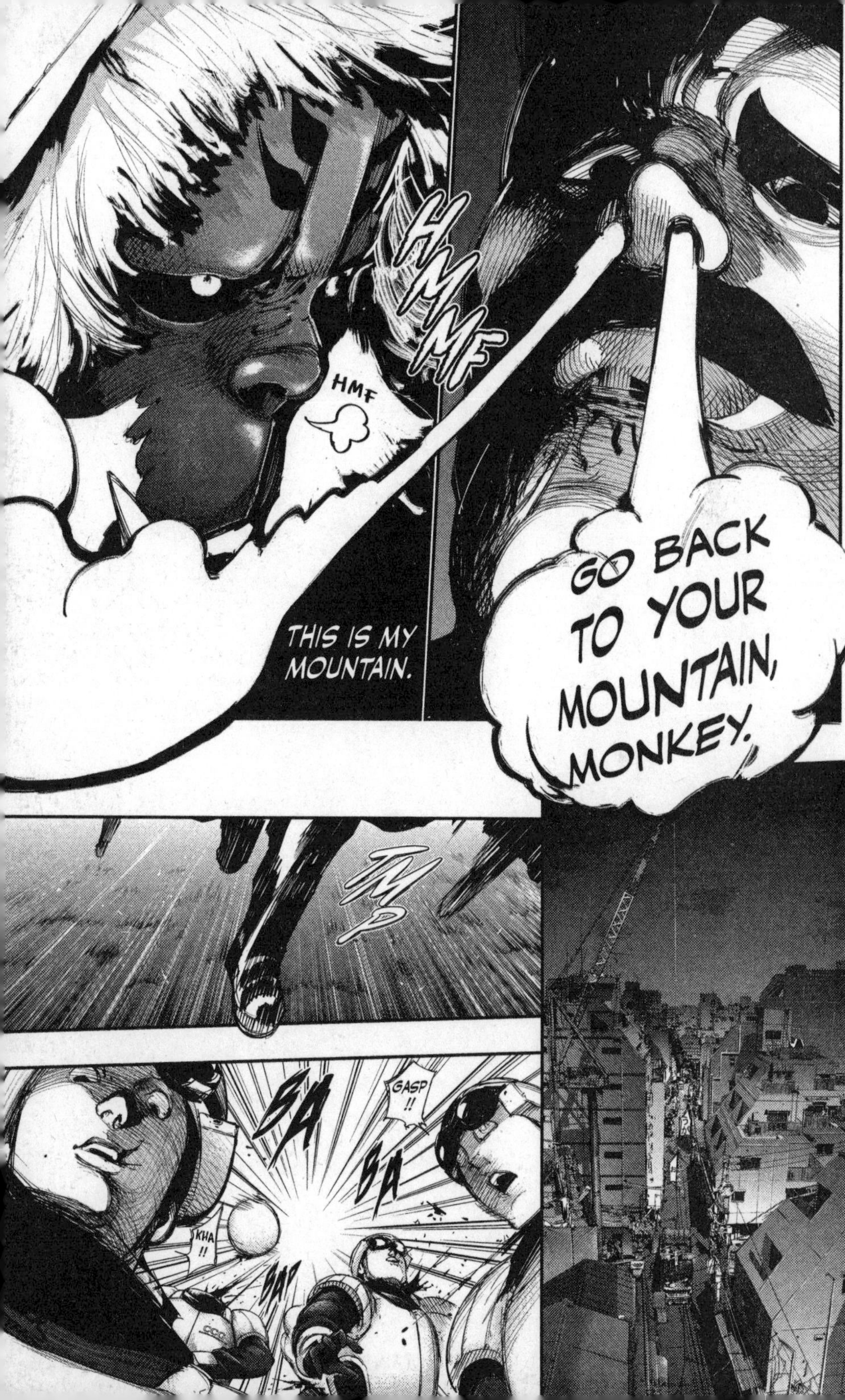
GO BACK TO YOUR MOUNTAIN, MONKEY.
HMMMF
HMF
THIS IS MY MOUNTAIN.
TMP
GASP!!
BA BA
BA
KHA!!
BAP

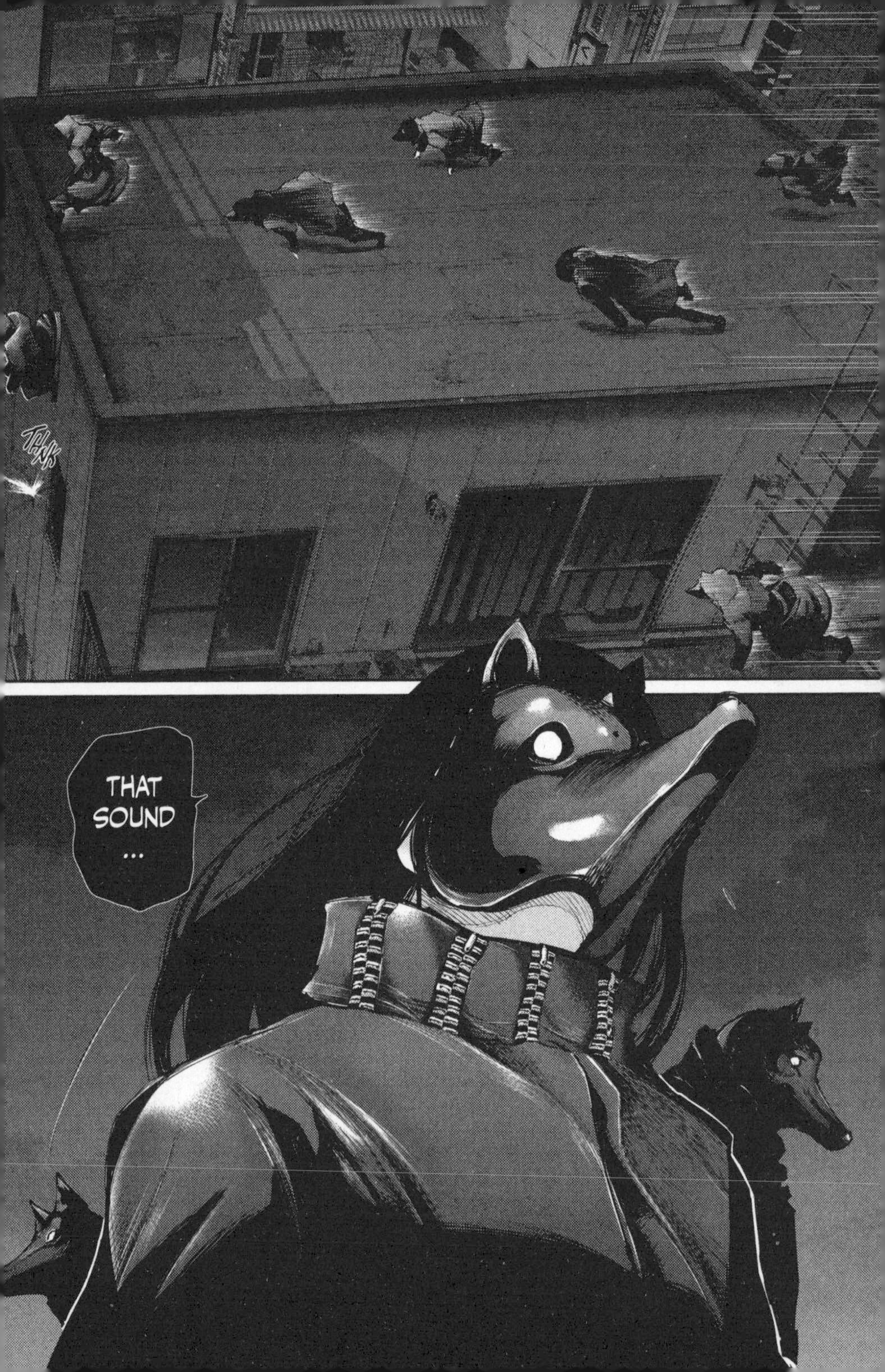
TINK
THAT SOUND ...

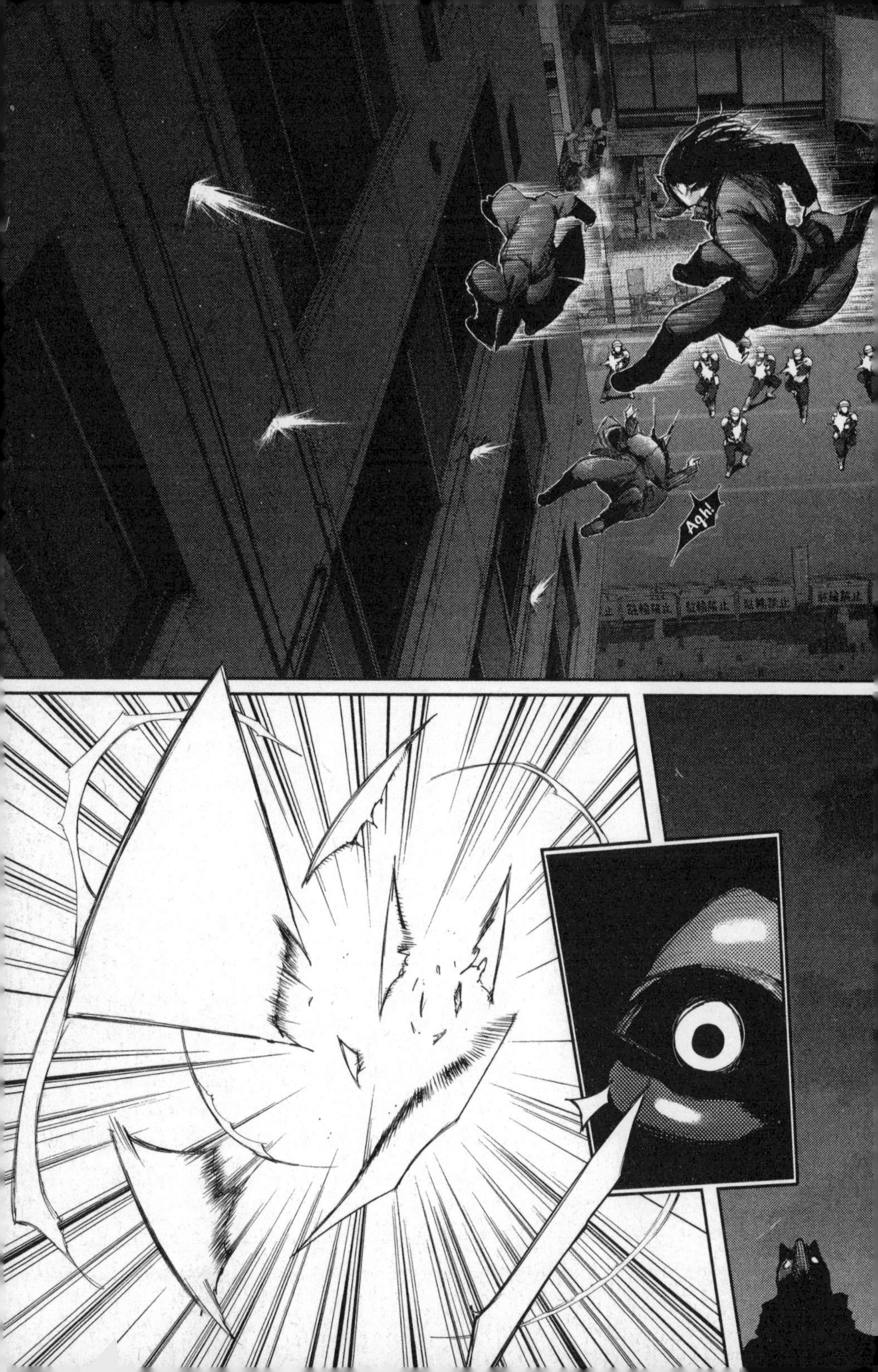
Agh!

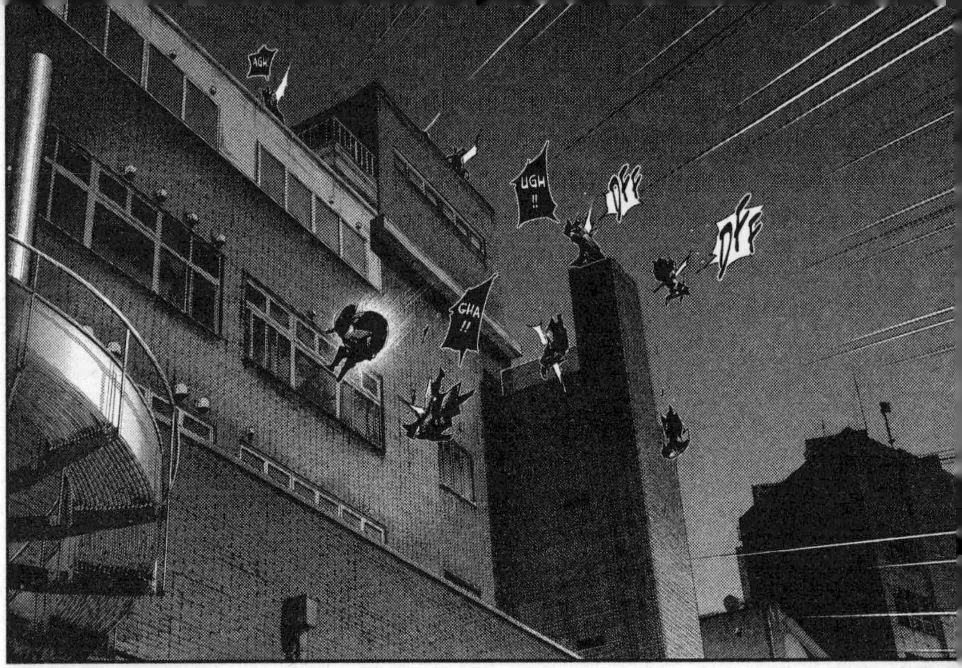
DFF
DFF
UGH!!
GHA!!
AGW

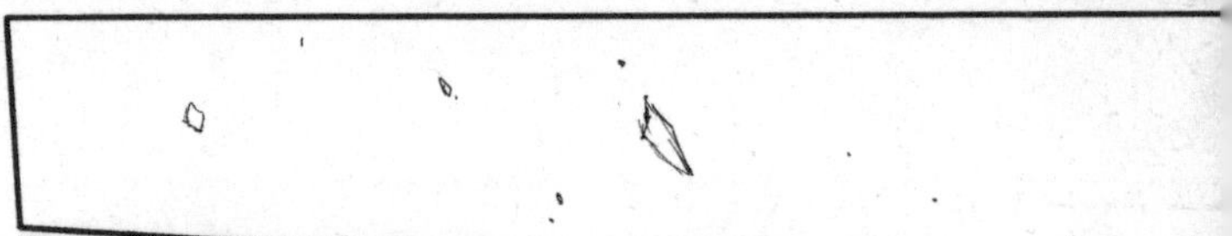

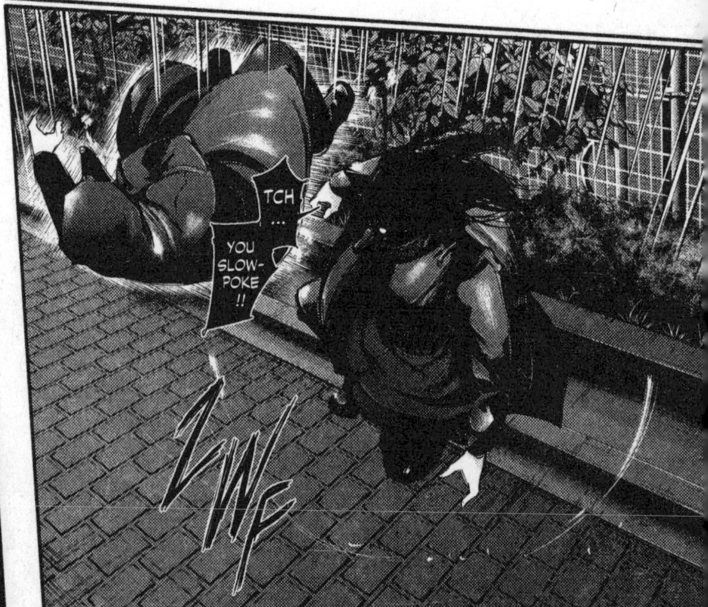
TCH...
YOU SLOW-POKE!!
ZWF

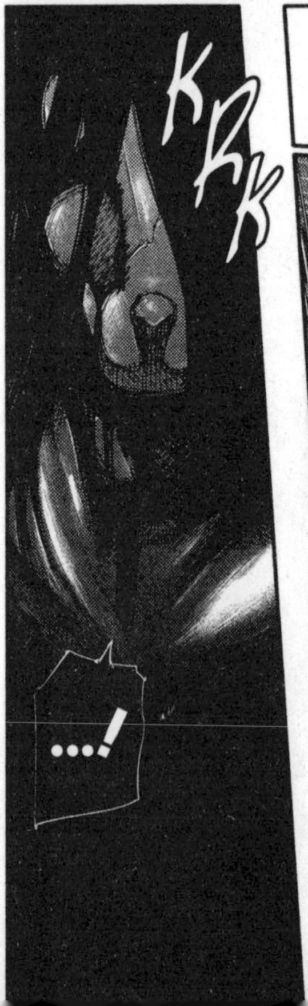
KRK
...!

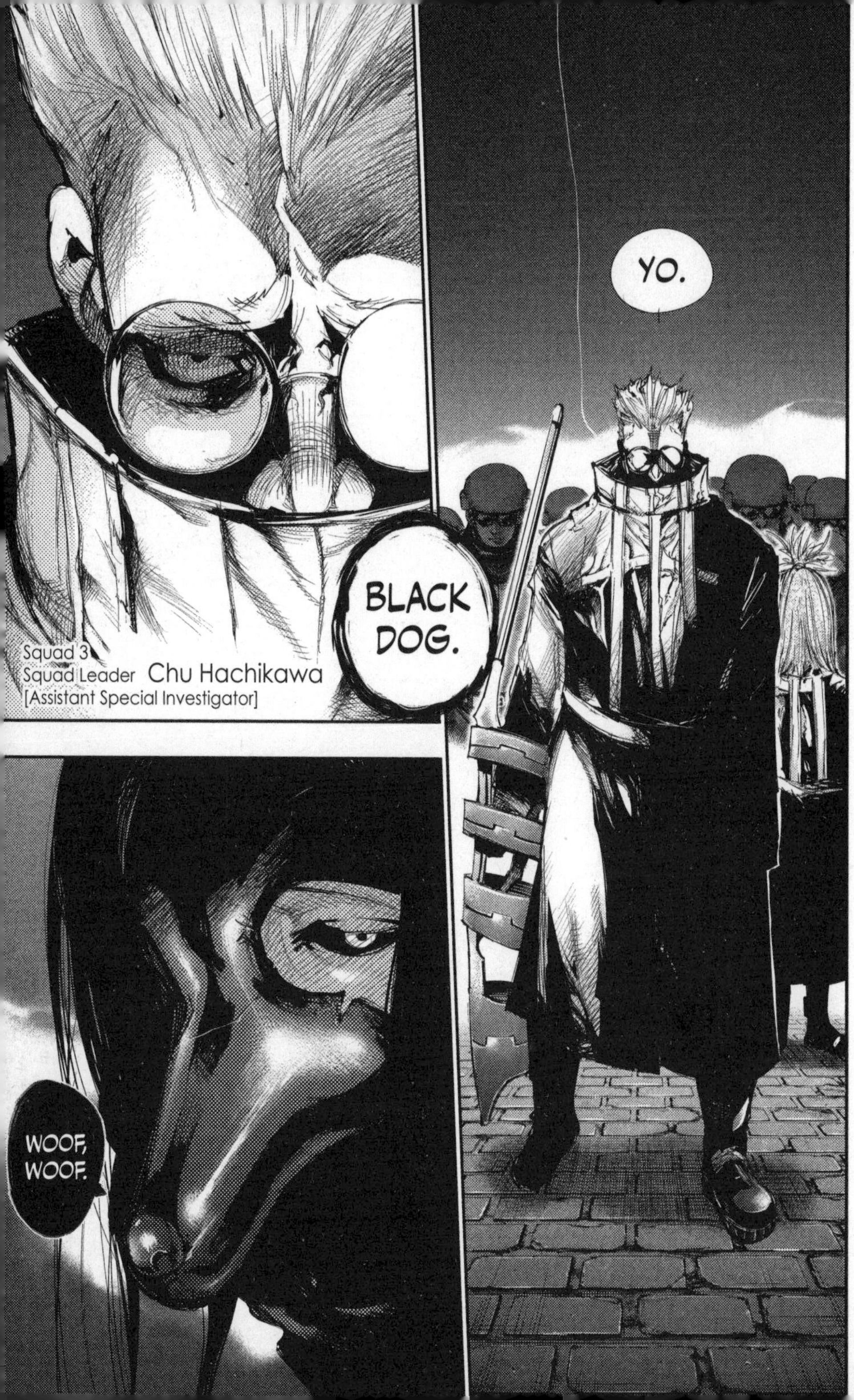
YO.
BLACK DOG.
Squad 3
Squad Leader Chu Hachikawa
[Assistant Special Investigator]
WOOF, WOOF.

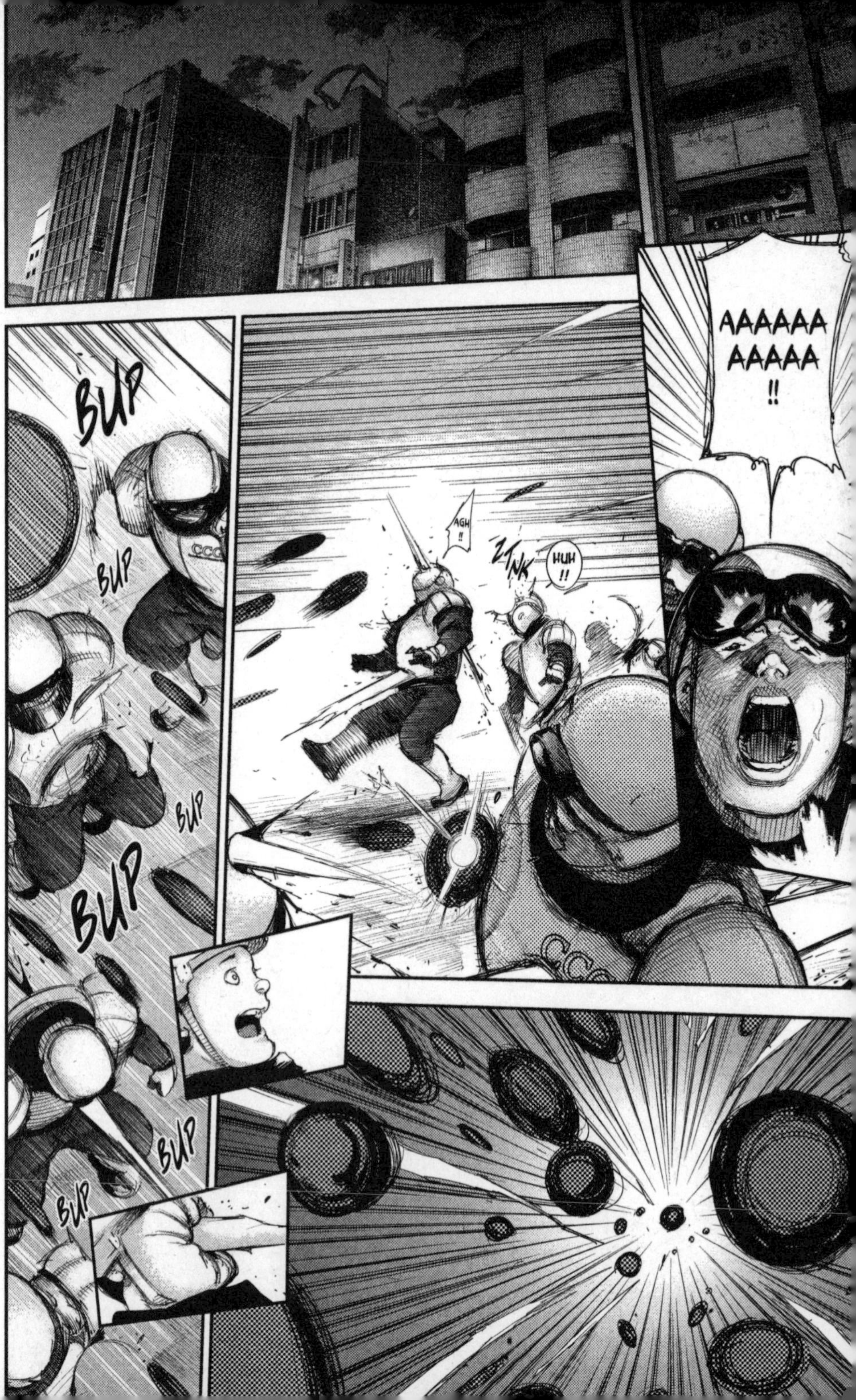
AAAAAA AAAAA !!
HUH !!
ZTINK
AGH !!
BUP
BUP
BUP
BUP
BUP
BUP

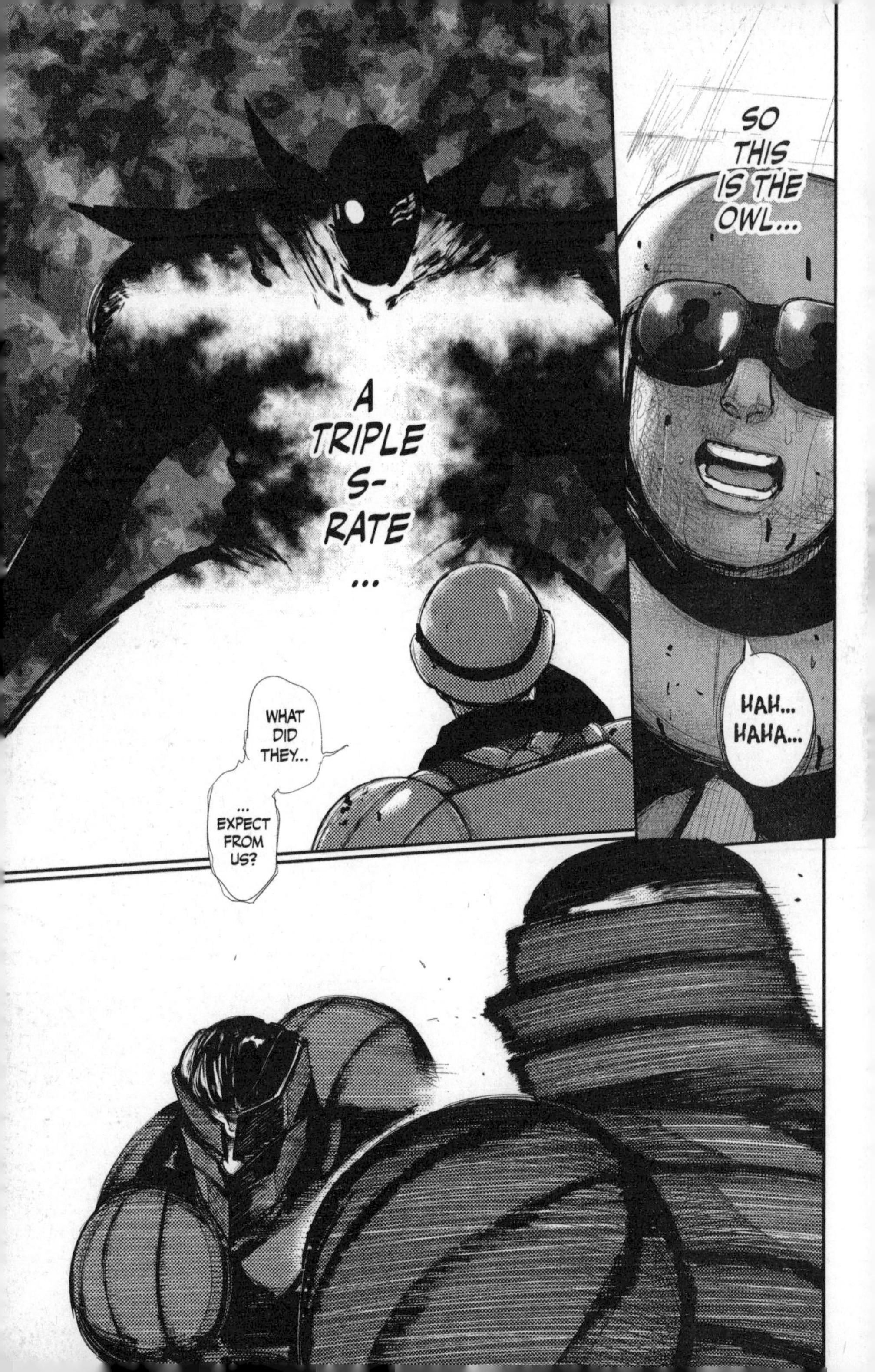
SO THIS IS THE OWL...
HAH... HAHA...
A TRIPLE S-RATE...
WHAT DID THEY...
...EXPECT FROM US?

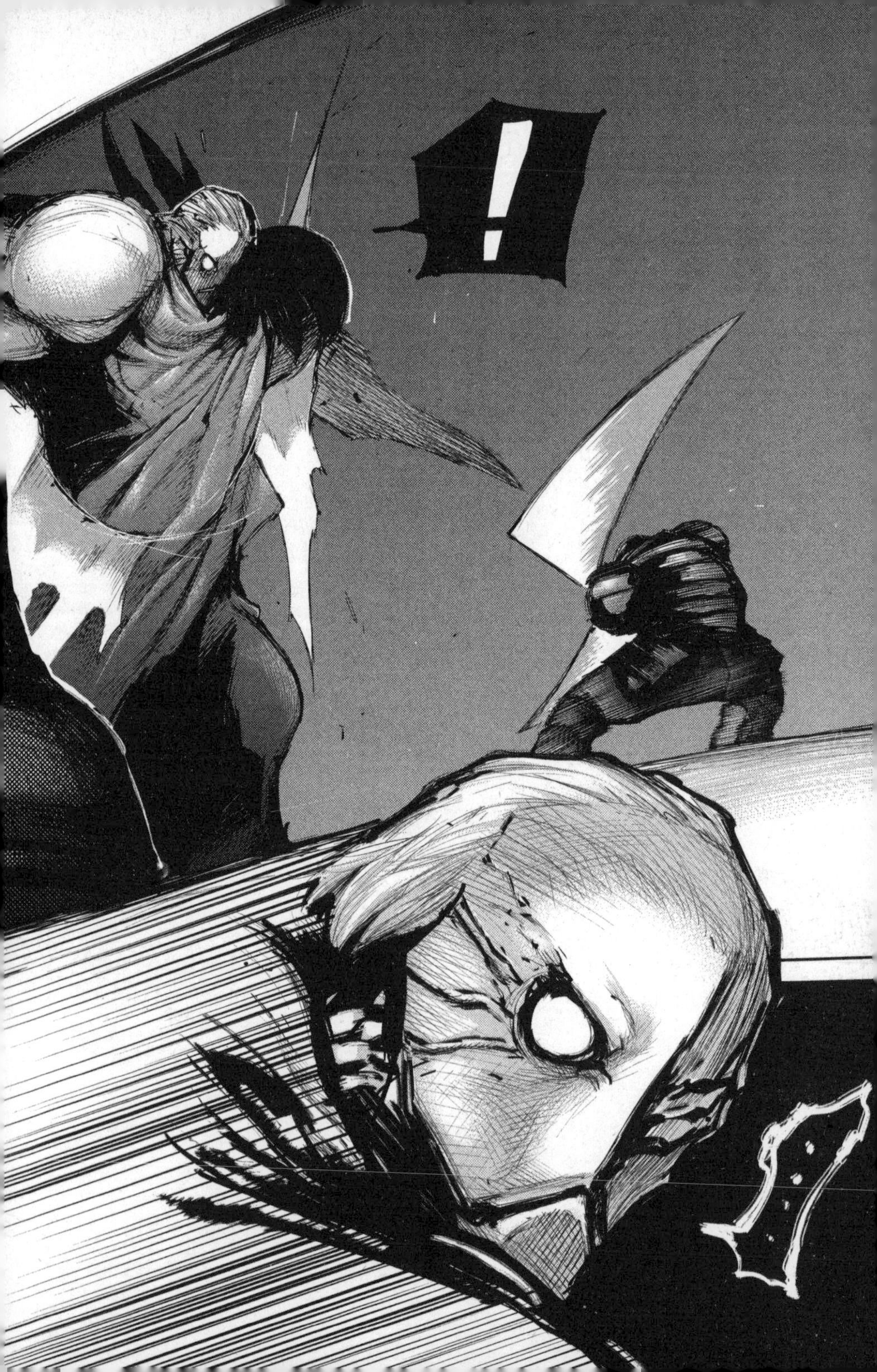
!

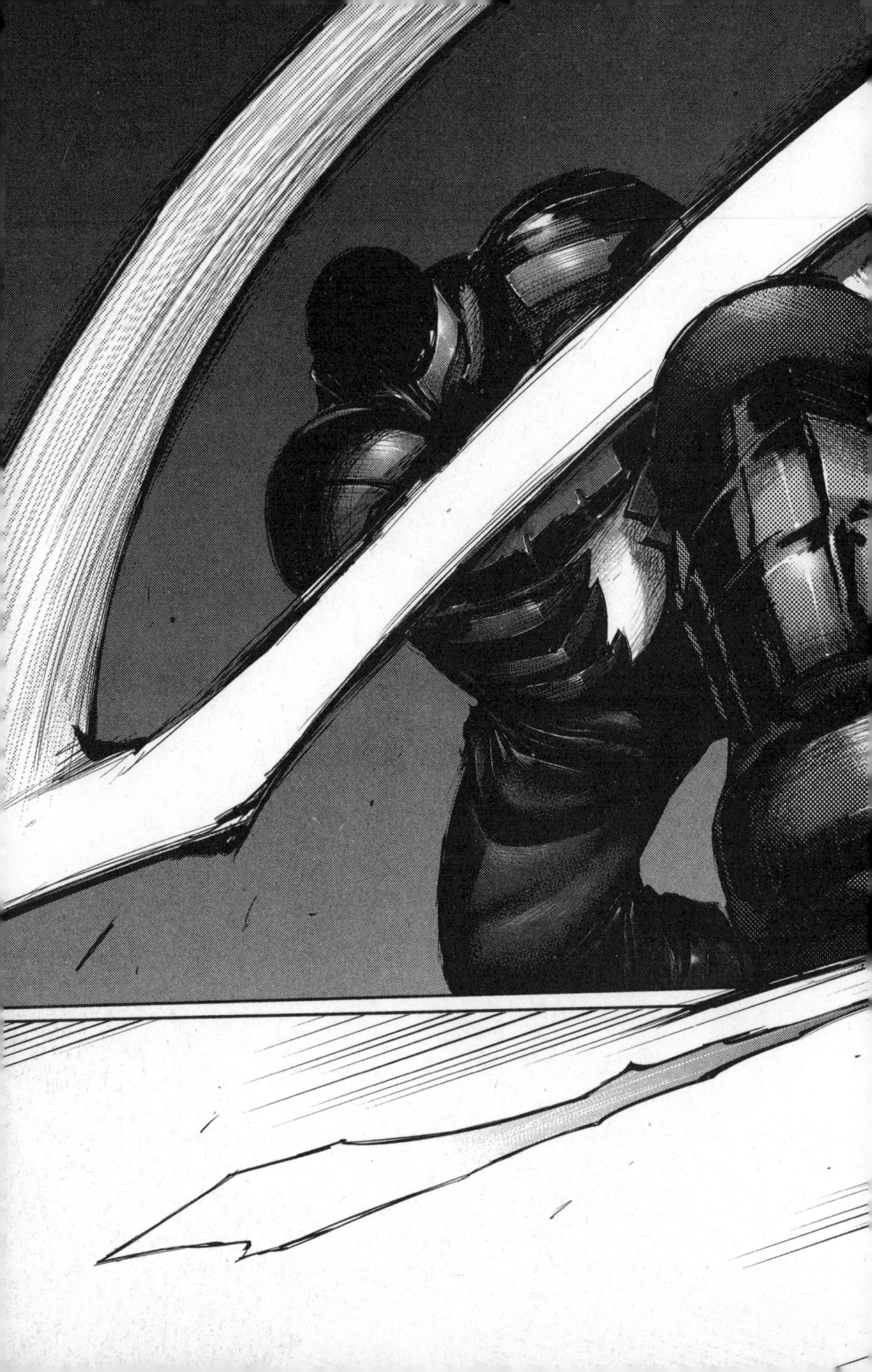

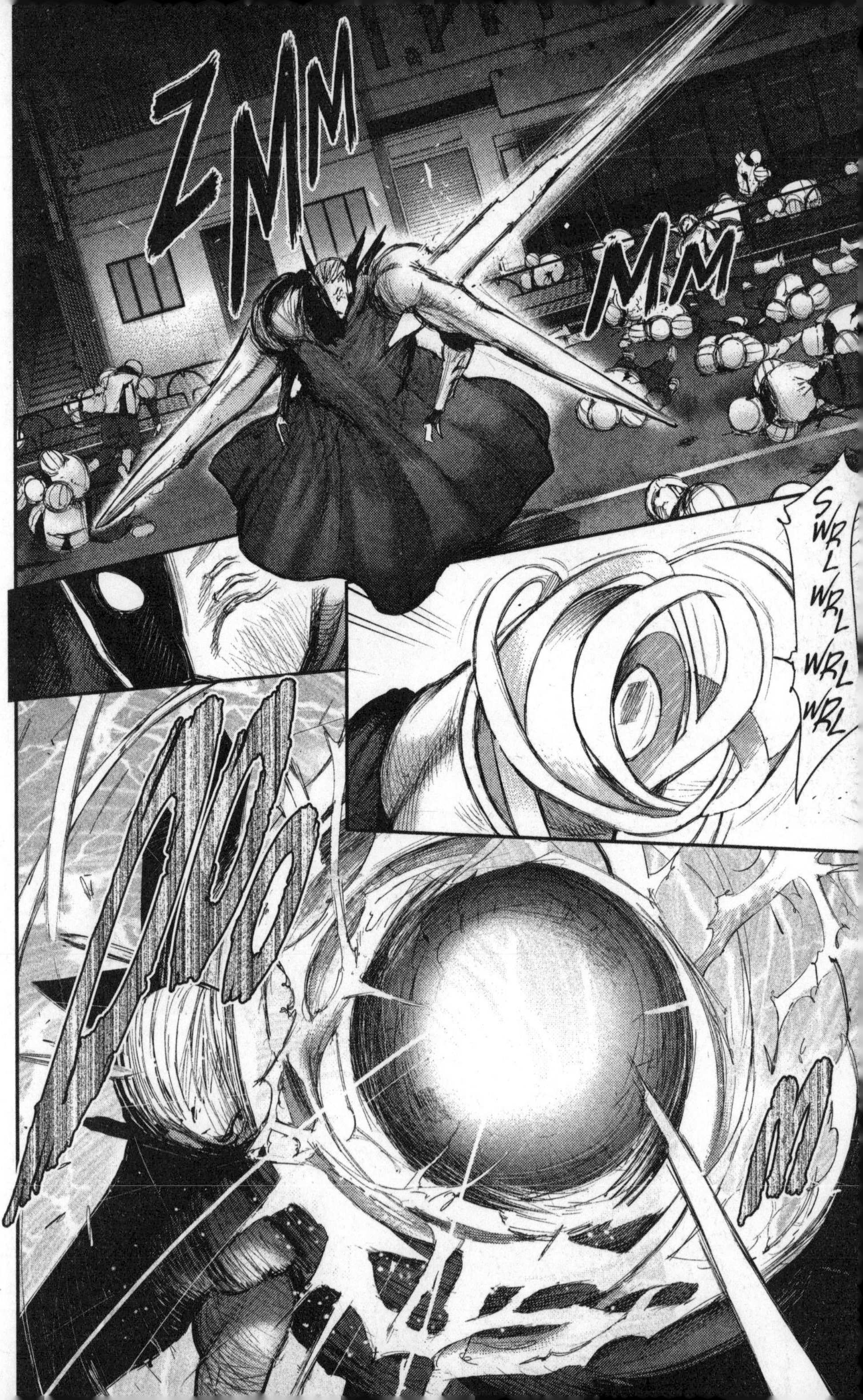
ZMM
MM
SWRL WRL WRL WRL WRL

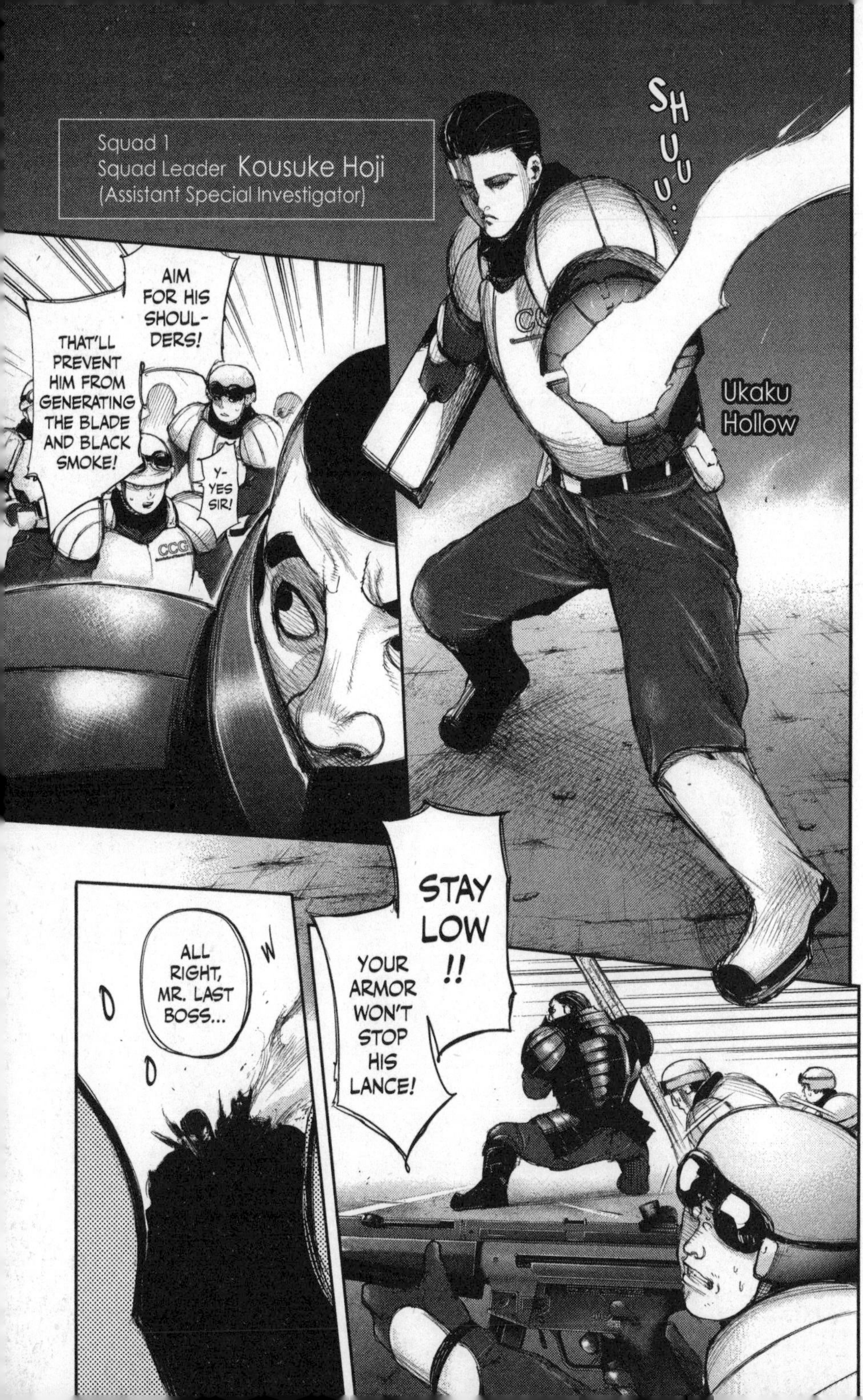
Squad 1
Squad Leader Kousuke Hoji
(Assistant Special Investigator)
SHUUU...
Ukaku Hollow
AIM FOR HIS SHOULDERS!
THAT'LL PREVENT HIM FROM GENERATING THE BLADE AND BLACK SMOKE!
Y-YES SIR!
STAY LOW!!
YOUR ARMOR WON'T STOP HIS LANCE!
ALL RIGHT, MR. LAST BOSS...

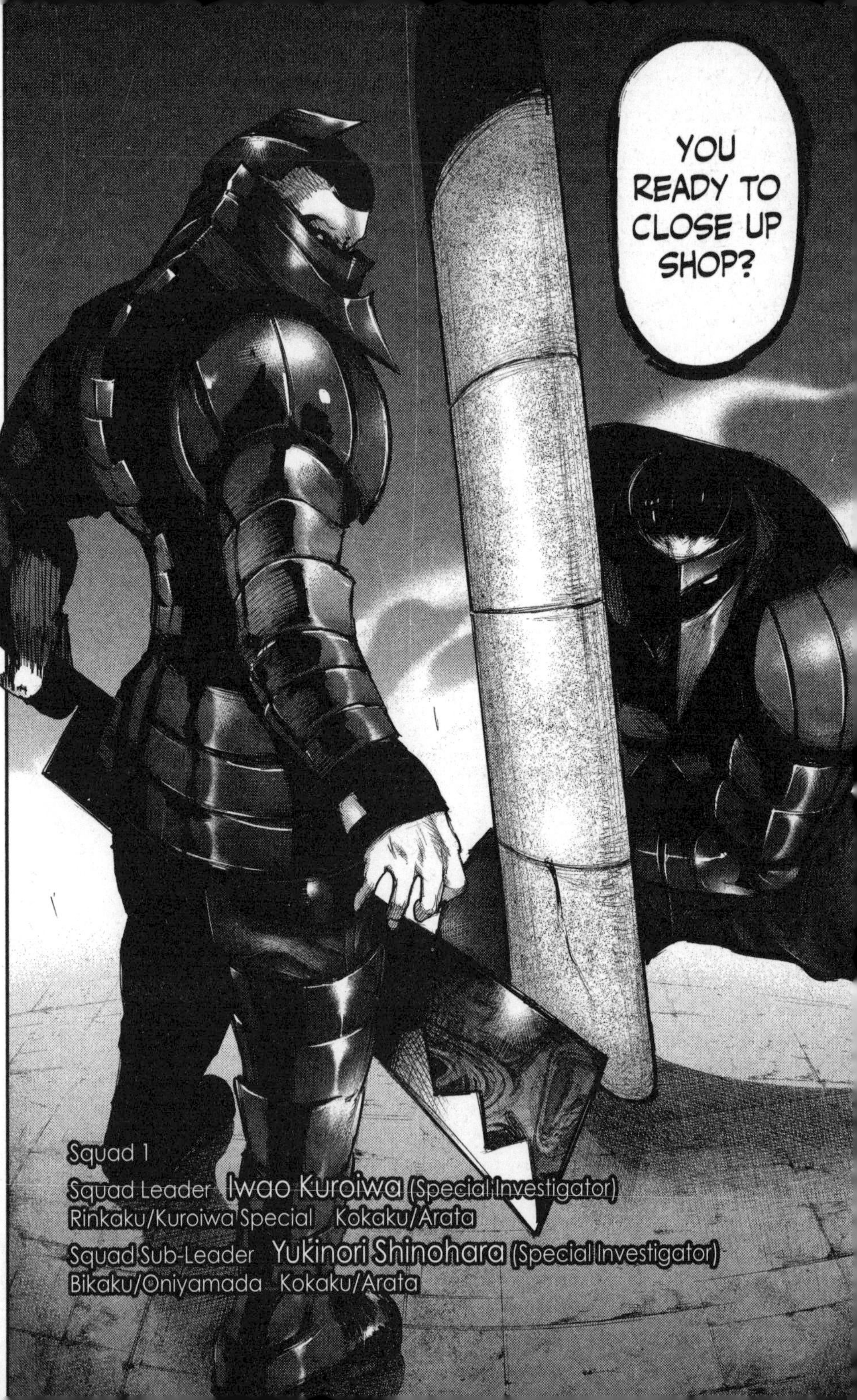
YOU READY TO CLOSE UP SHOP?
Squad 1
Squad Leader Iwao Kuroiwa (Special Investigator)
Rinkaku/Kuroiwa Special Kokaku/Arata
Squad Sub-Leader Yukinori Shinohara (Special Investigator)
Bikaku/Oniyamada Kokaku/Arata

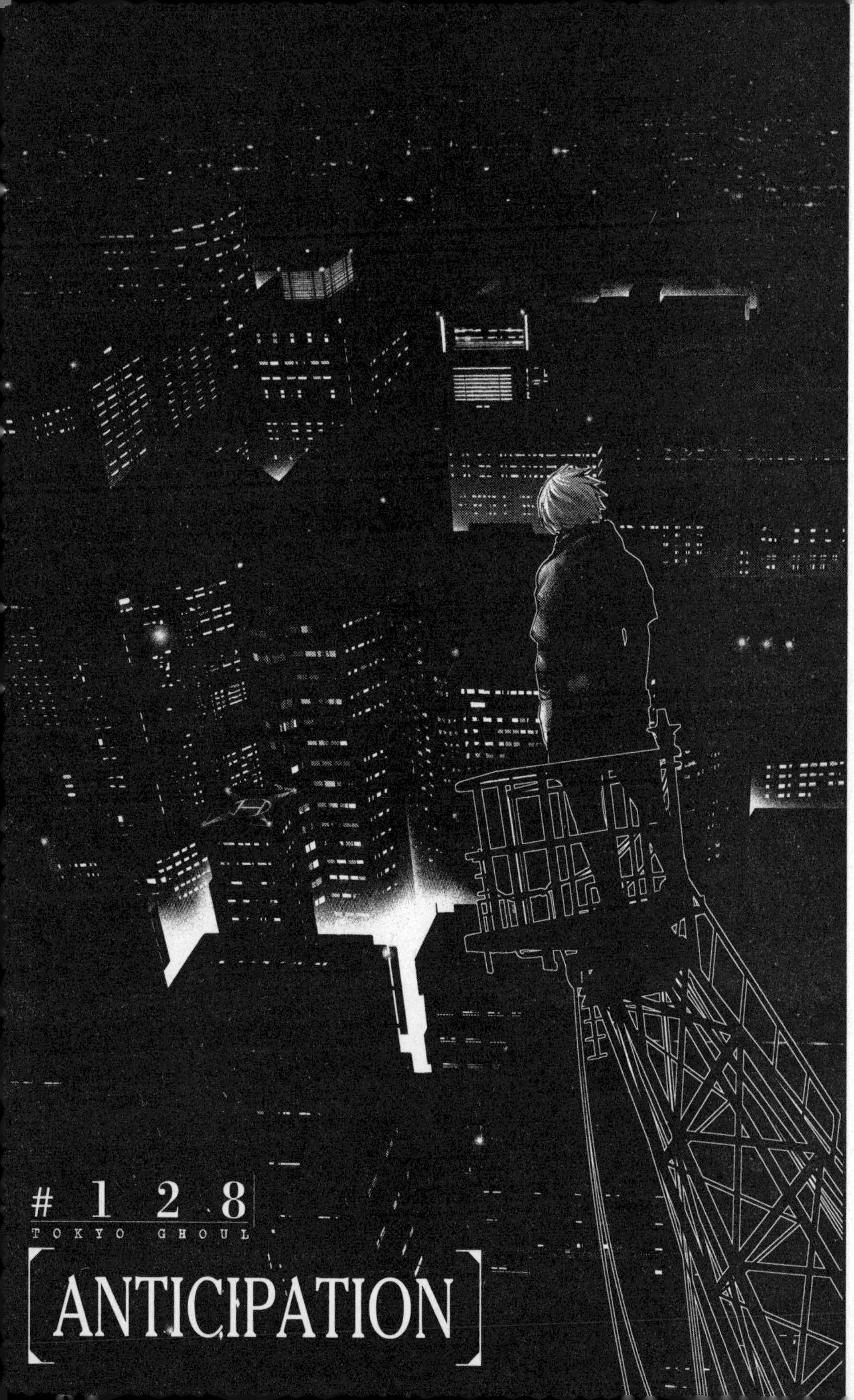
#128
TOKYO GHOUL
ANTICIPATION

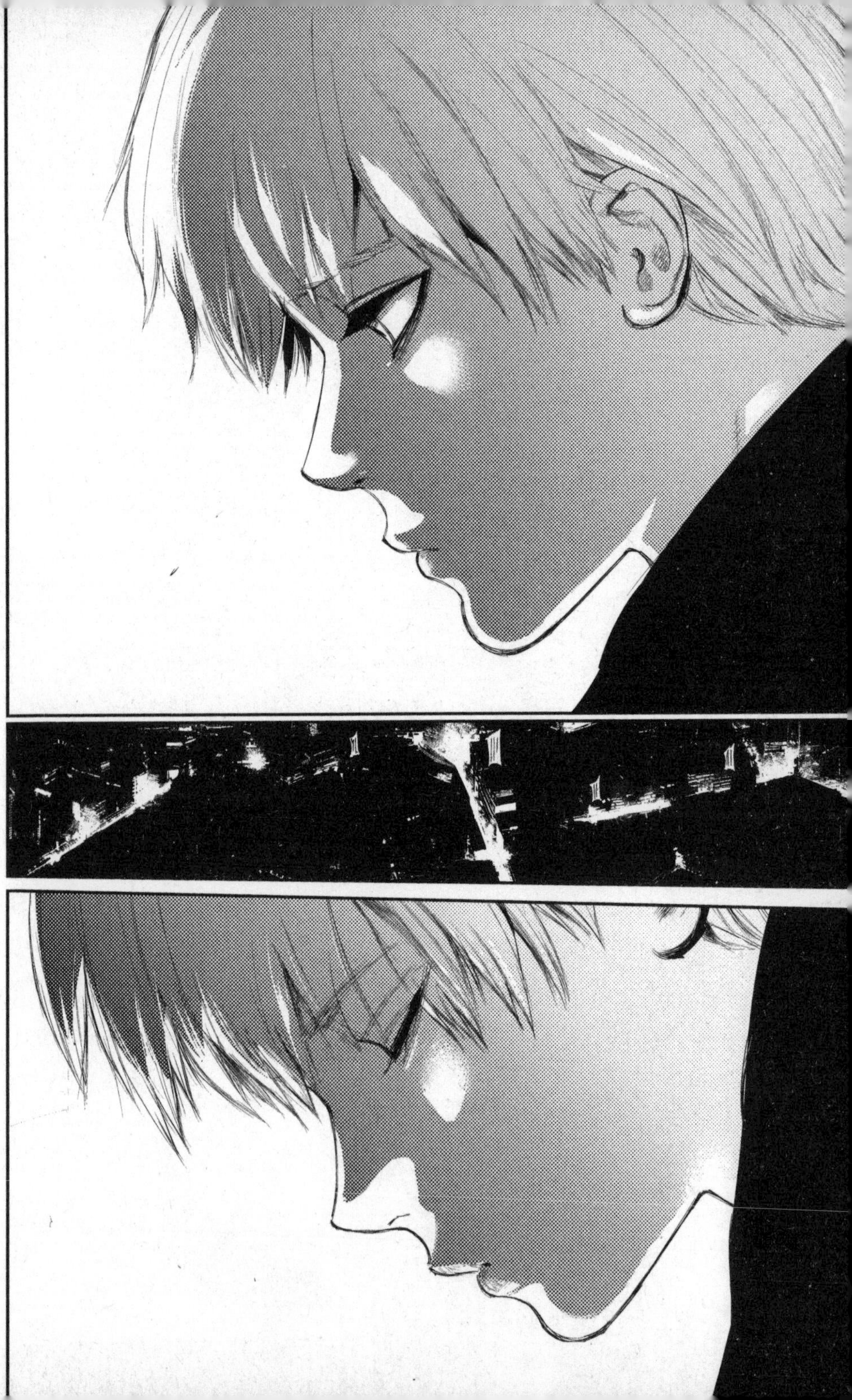

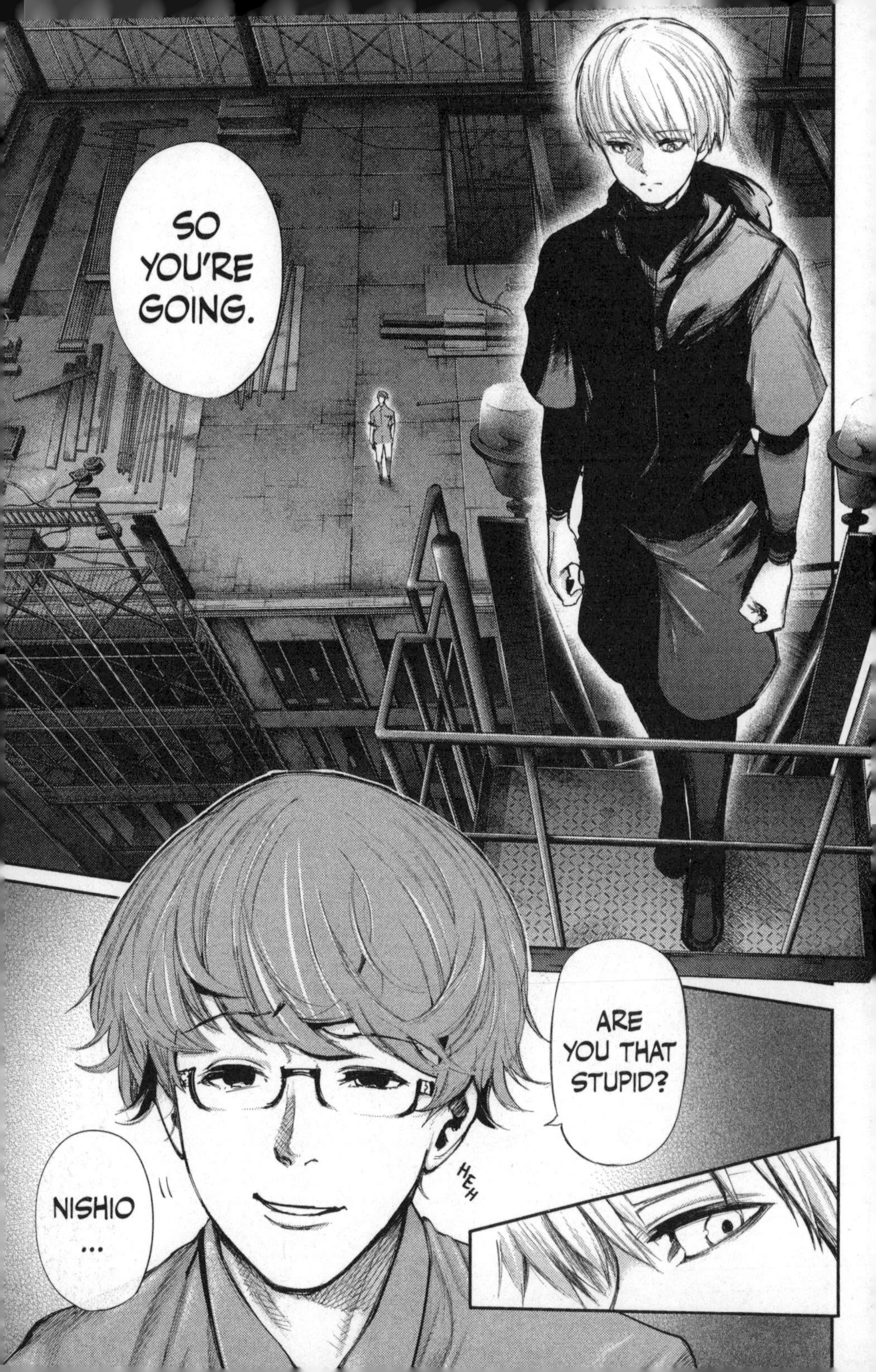
SO YOU'RE GOING.
ARE YOU THAT STUPID?
HEH
NISHIO ...

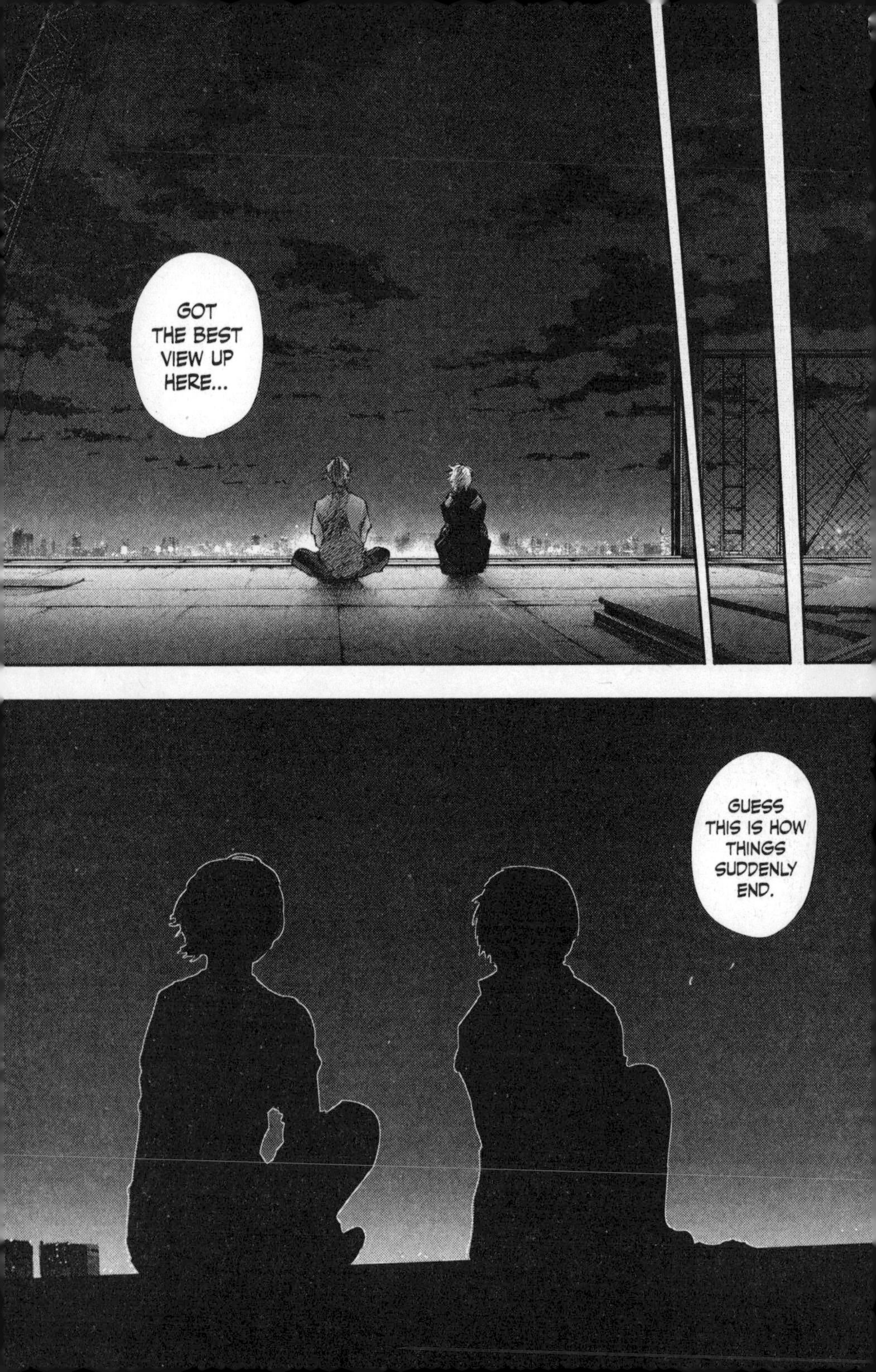
GOT THE BEST VIEW UP HERE...
GUESS THIS IS HOW THINGS SUDDENLY END.

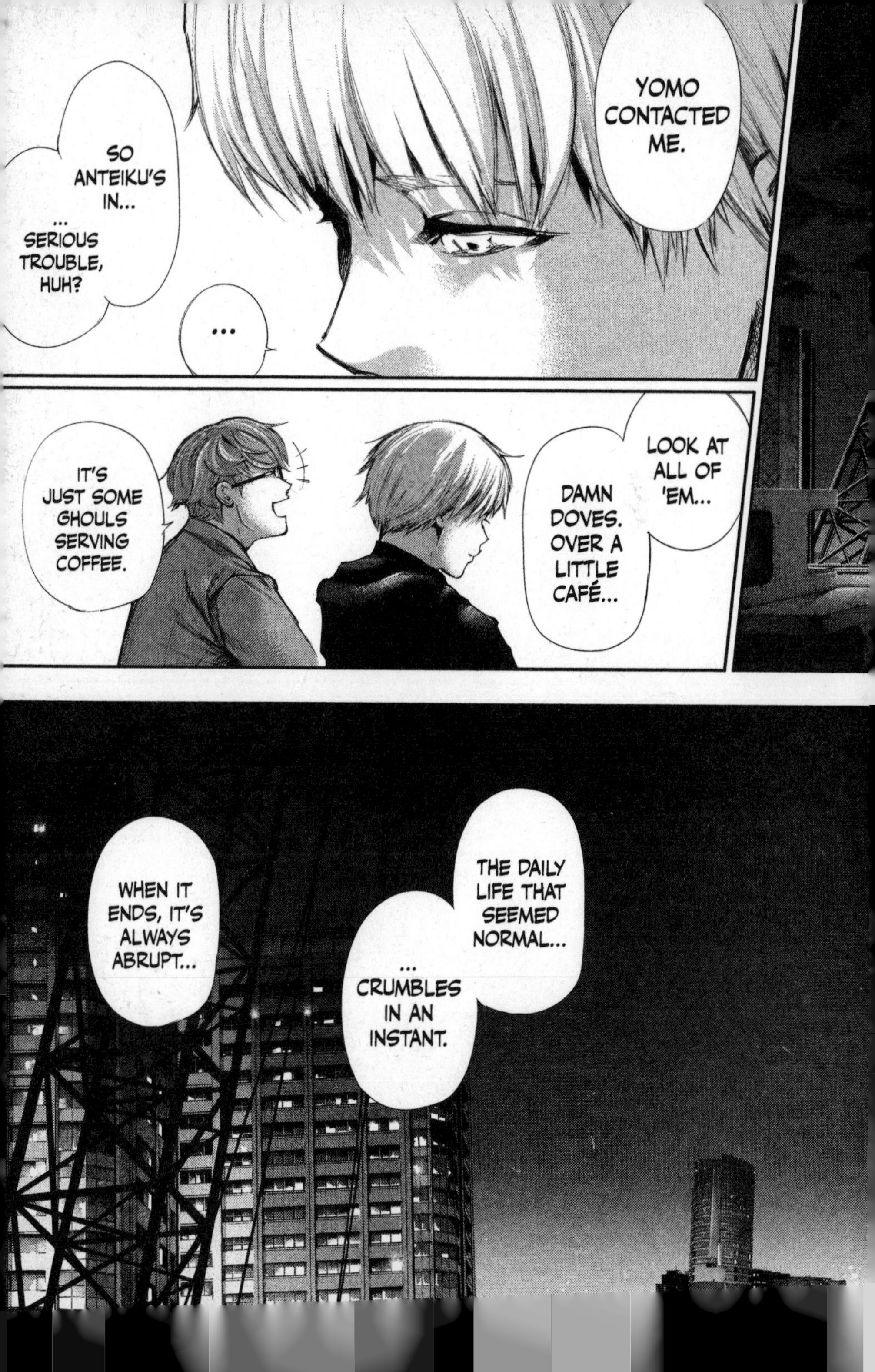
YOMO CONTACTED ME.
SO ANTEIKU'S IN... ...SERIOUS TROUBLE, HUH?
...
LOOK AT ALL OF 'EM...
DAMN DOVES. OVER A LITTLE CAFÉ...
IT'S JUST SOME GHOULS SERVING COFFEE.
THE DAILY LIFE THAT SEEMED NORMAL...
...CRUMBLES IN AN INSTANT.
WHEN IT ENDS, IT'S ALWAYS ABRUPT...

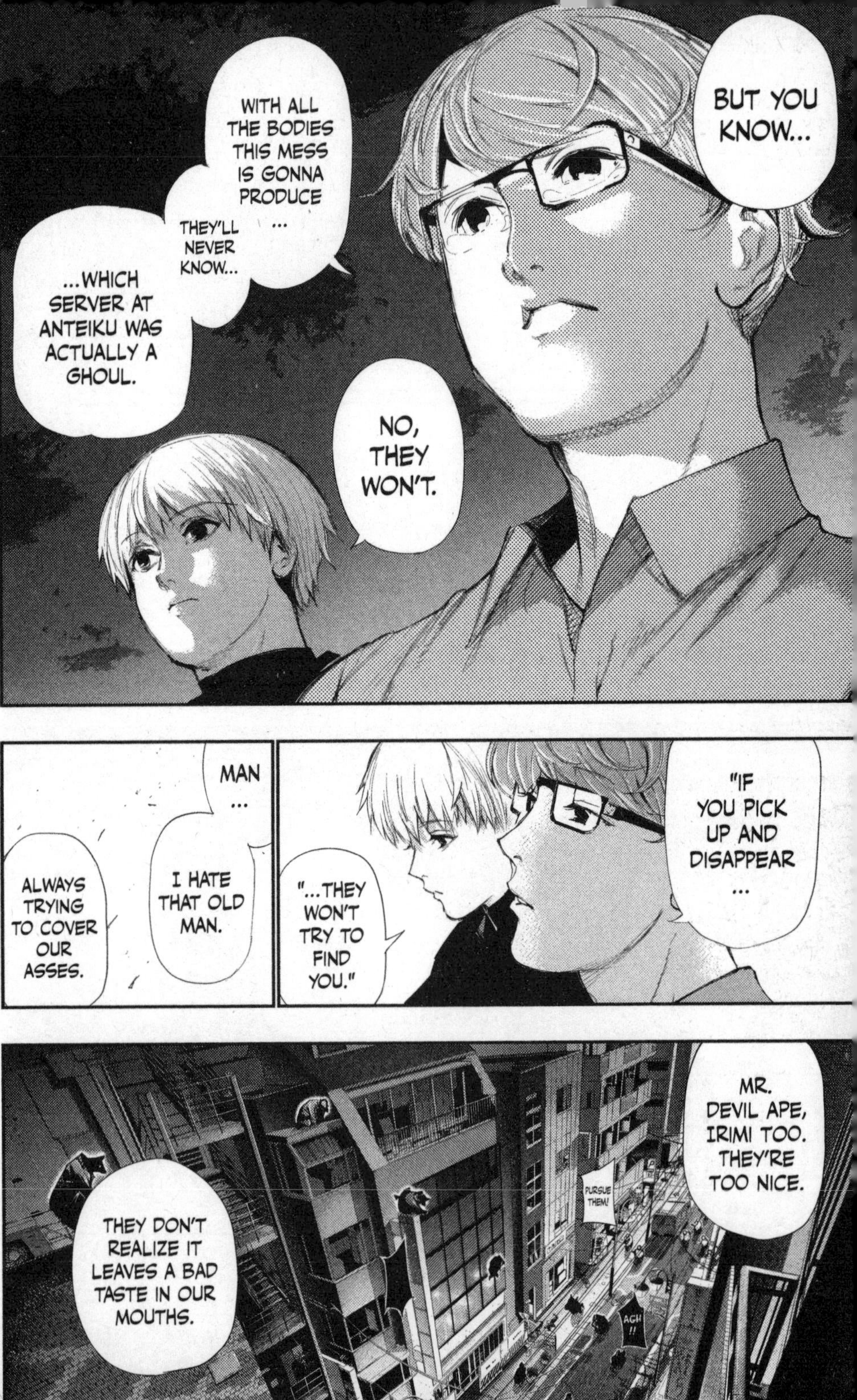
BUT YOU KNOW...
WITH ALL THE BODIES THIS MESS IS GONNA PRODUCE ...
THEY'LL NEVER KNOW...
...WHICH SERVER AT ANTEIKU WAS ACTUALLY A GHOUL.
NO, THEY WON'T.
"IF YOU PICK UP AND DISAPPEAR ...
"...THEY WON'T TRY TO FIND YOU."
MAN ...
I HATE THAT OLD MAN.
ALWAYS TRYING TO COVER OUR ASSES.
MR. DEVIL APE, IRIMI TOO. THEY'RE TOO NICE.
PURSUE THEM!
AGH !!
THEY DON'T REALIZE IT LEAVES A BAD TASTE IN OUR MOUTHS.

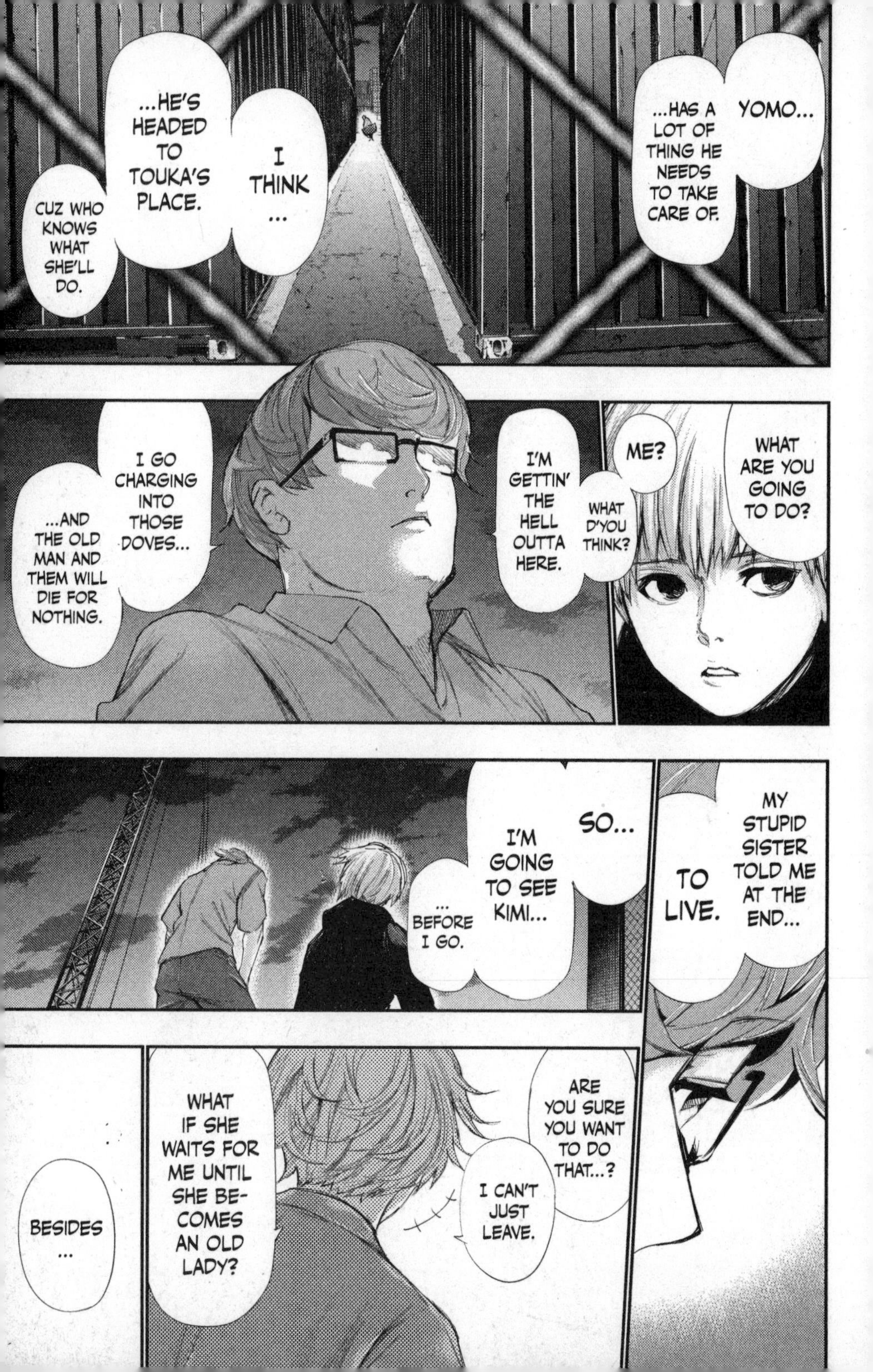
YOMO...
...HAS A LOT OF THING HE NEEDS TO TAKE CARE OF.
I THINK...
...HE'S HEADED TO TOUKA'S PLACE.
CUZ WHO KNOWS WHAT SHE'LL DO.
WHAT ARE YOU GOING TO DO?
ME?
WHAT D'YOU THINK?
I'M GETTIN' THE HELL OUTTA HERE.
I GO CHARGING INTO THOSE DOVES...
...AND THE OLD MAN AND THEM WILL DIE FOR NOTHING.
MY STUPID SISTER TOLD ME AT THE END...
TO LIVE.
SO...
I'M GOING TO SEE KIMI...
...BEFORE I GO.
ARE YOU SURE YOU WANT TO DO THAT...?
I CAN'T JUST LEAVE.
WHAT IF SHE WAITS FOR ME UNTIL SHE BECOMES AN OLD LADY?
BESIDES...

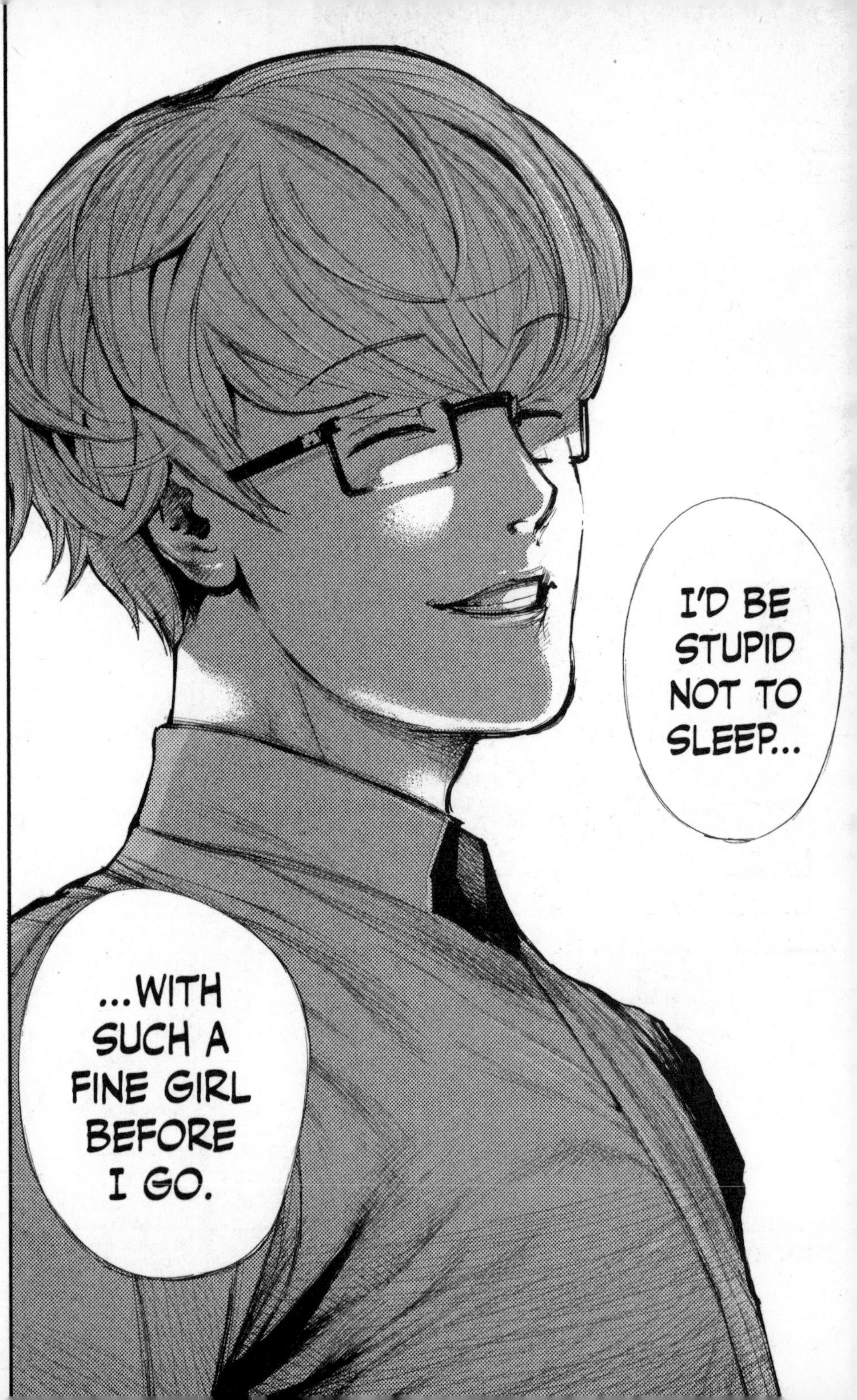
I'D BE STUPID NOT TO SLEEP...
...WITH SUCH A FINE GIRL BEFORE I GO.

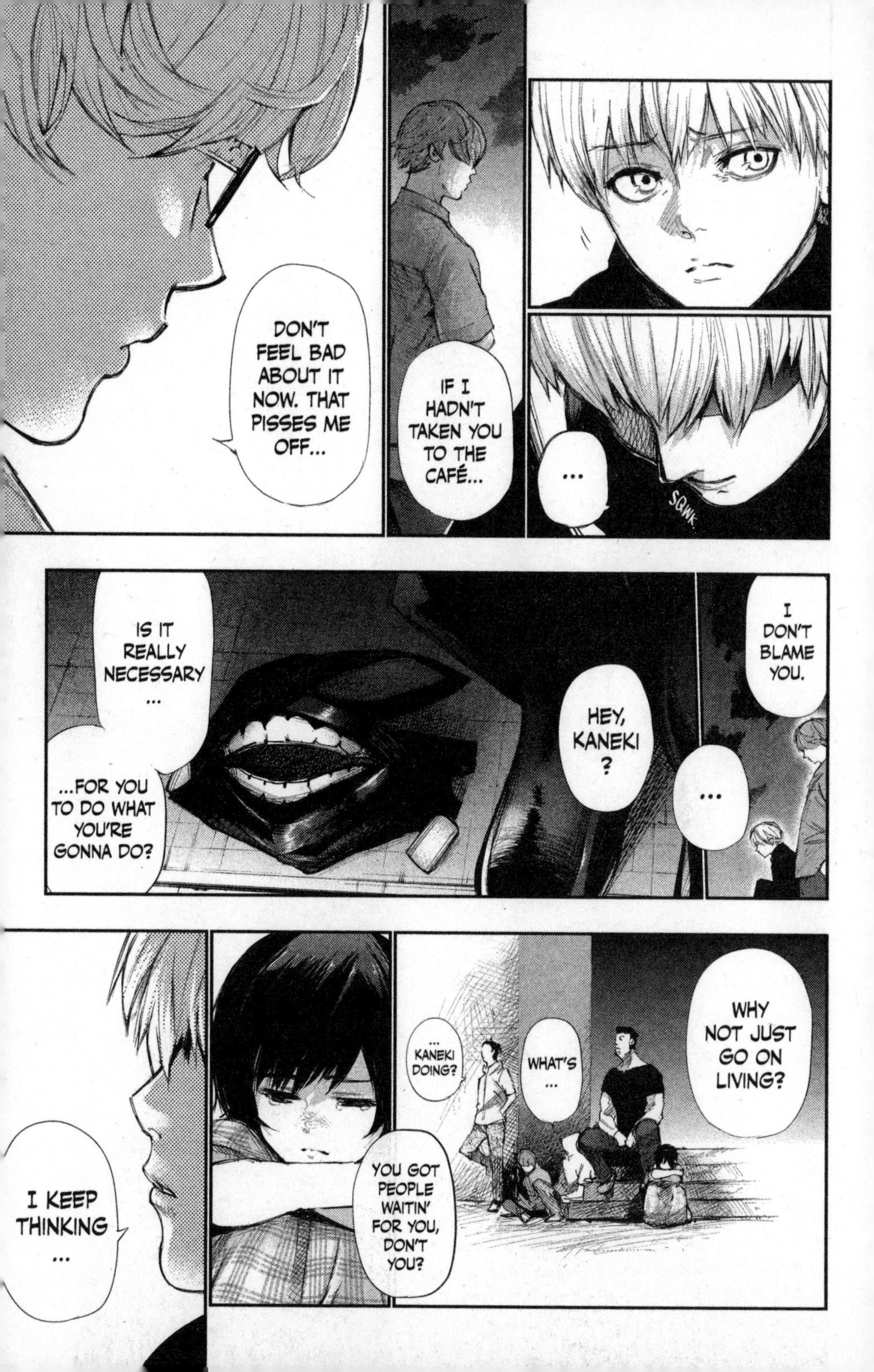
...
SQWK
IF I HADN'T TAKEN YOU TO THE CAFÉ...
DON'T FEEL BAD ABOUT IT NOW. THAT PISSES ME OFF...
I DON'T BLAME YOU.
...
HEY, KANEKI?
IS IT REALLY NECESSARY...
...FOR YOU TO DO WHAT YOU'RE GONNA DO?
WHY NOT JUST GO ON LIVING?
WHAT'S ...
... KANEKI DOING?
YOU GOT PEOPLE WAITIN' FOR YOU, DON'T YOU?
I KEEP THINKING ...

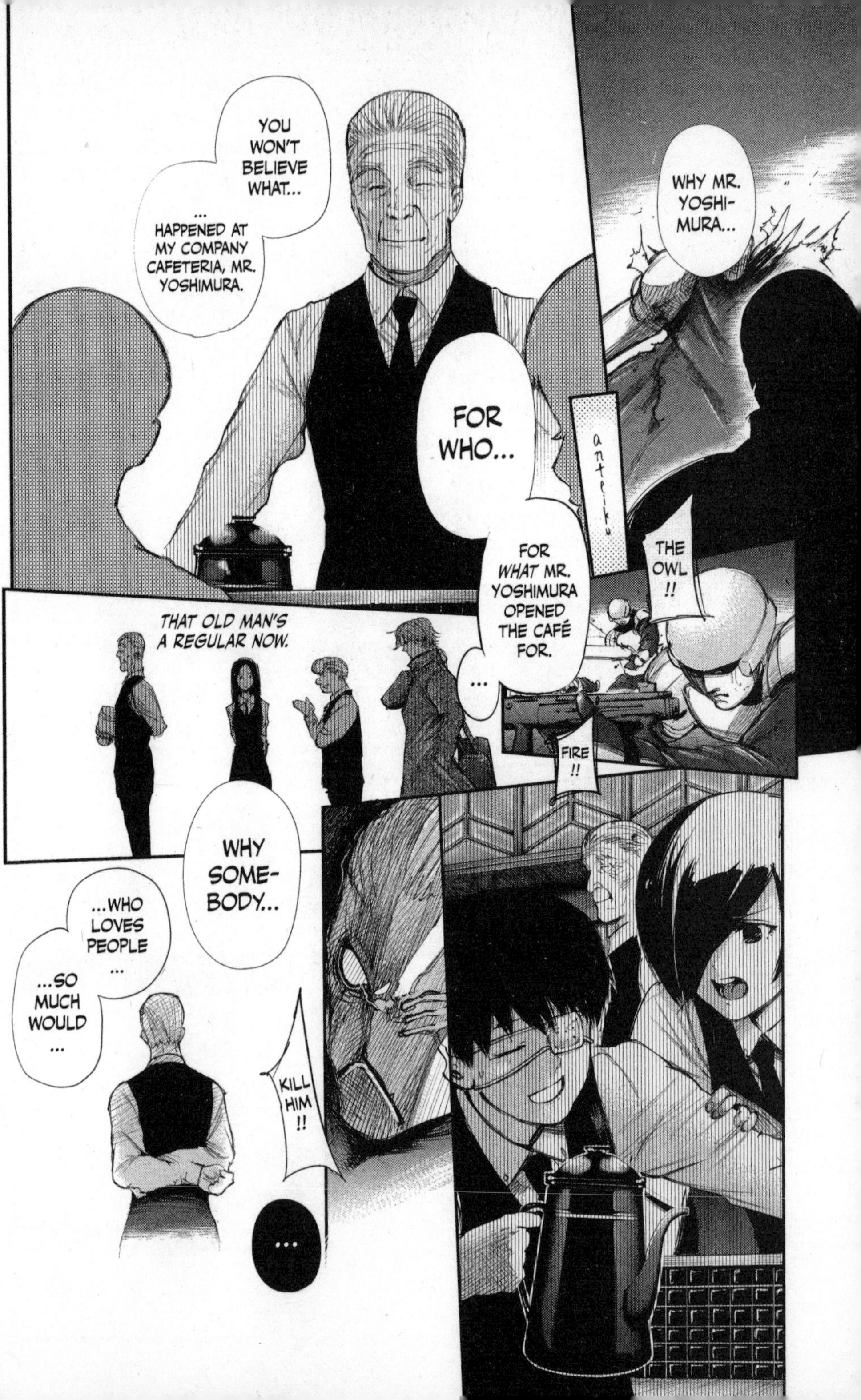
WHY MR. YOSHIMURA...
FOR WHO...
YOU WON'T BELIEVE WHAT...
...HAPPENED AT MY COMPANY CAFETERIA, MR. YOSHIMURA.
anteiku
THE OWL!!
FIRE!!
FOR *WHAT* MR. YOSHIMURA OPENED THE CAFÉ FOR.
...
THAT OLD MAN'S A REGULAR NOW.
KILL HIM!!
WHY SOMEBODY...
...WHO LOVES PEOPLE...
...SO MUCH WOULD...
...

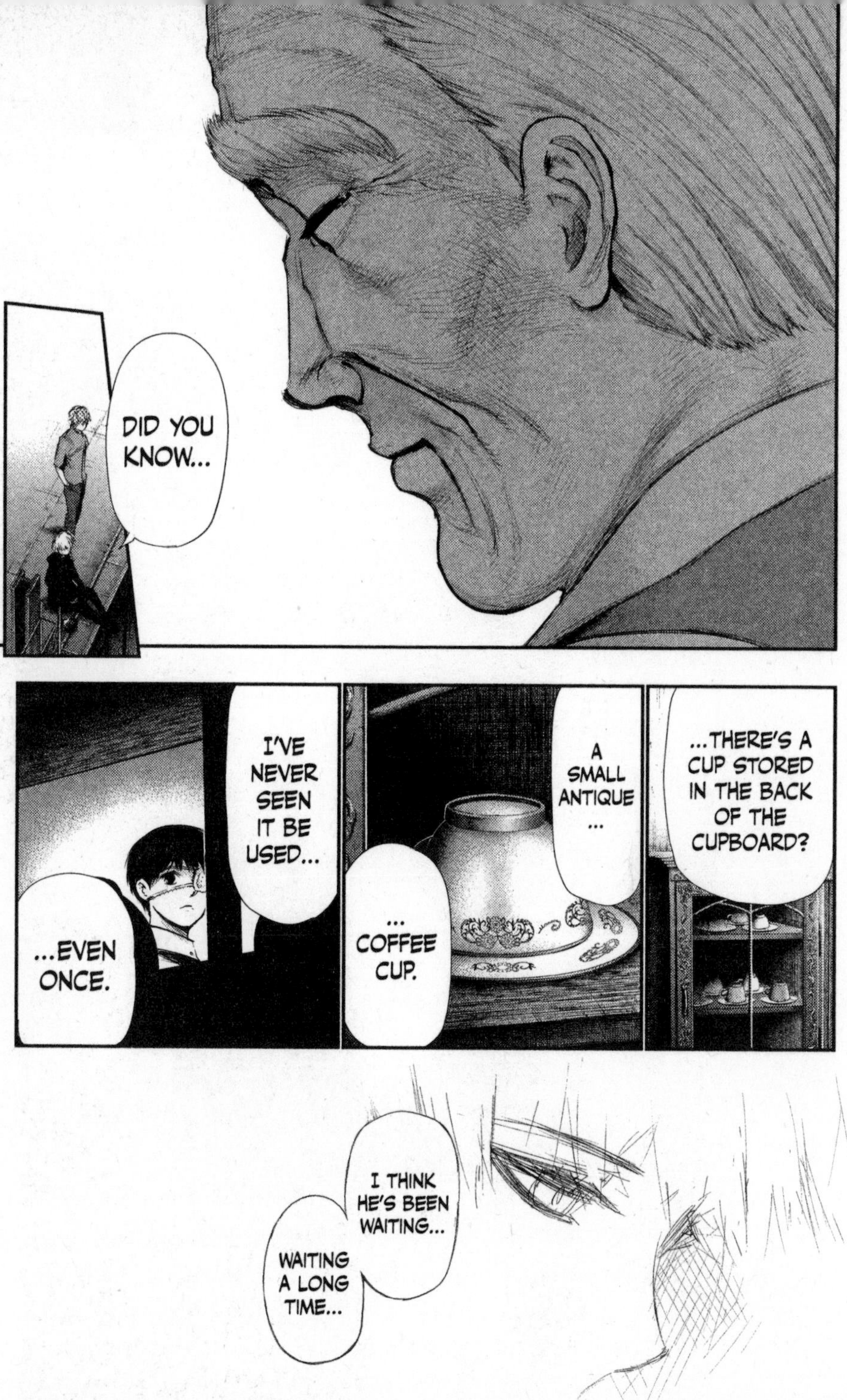
DID YOU KNOW...
...THERE'S A CUP STORED IN THE BACK OF THE CUPBOARD?
A SMALL ANTIQUE ...
... COFFEE CUP.
I'VE NEVER SEEN IT BE USED...
...EVEN ONCE.
I THINK HE'S BEEN WAITING...
WAITING A LONG TIME...

ALL
THIS
TIME.

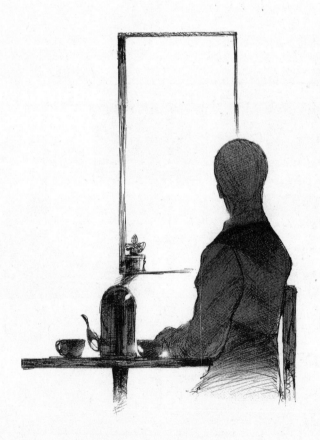

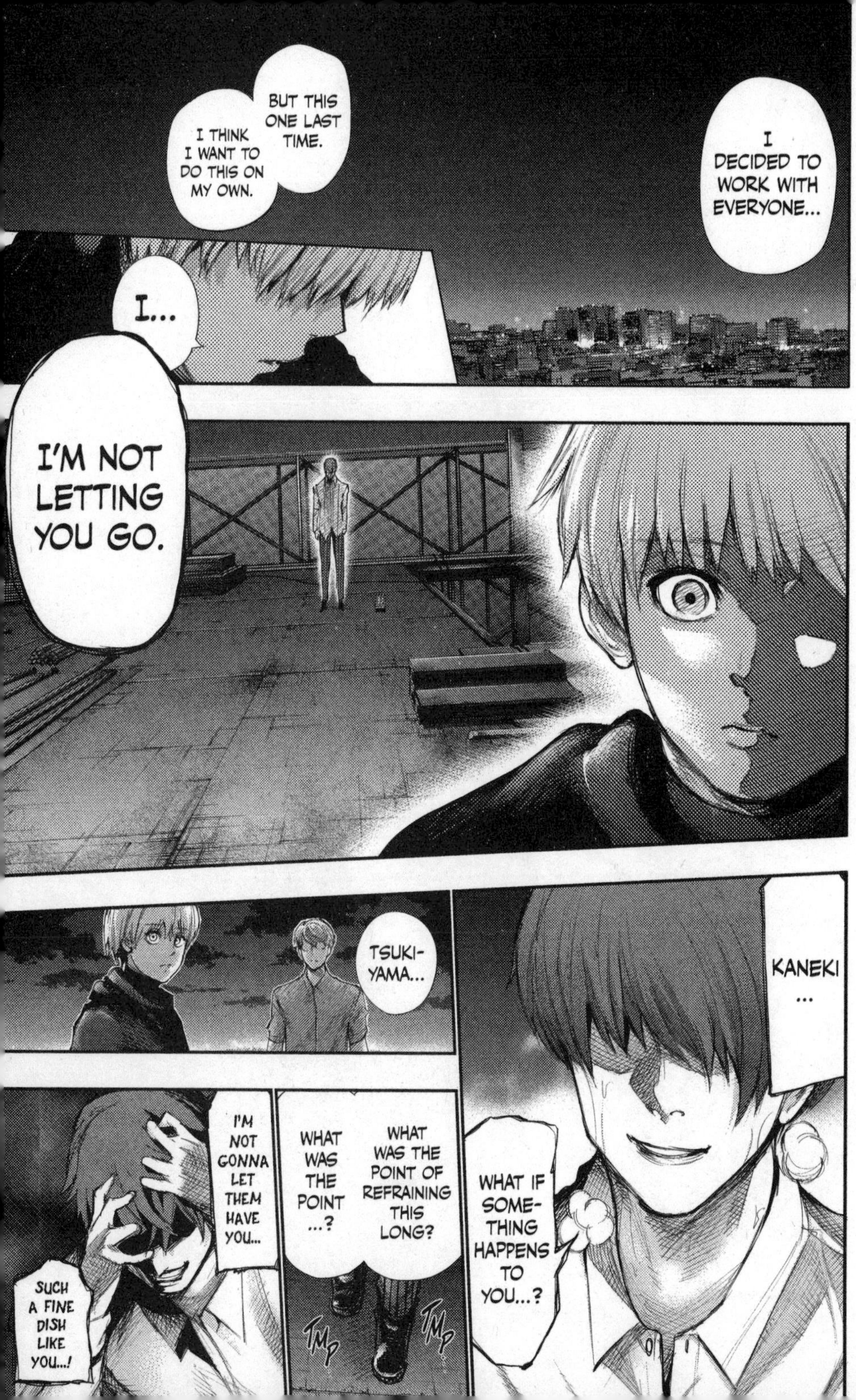
I DECIDED TO WORK WITH EVERYONE...
BUT THIS ONE LAST TIME.
I THINK I WANT TO DO THIS ON MY OWN.
I...
I'M NOT LETTING YOU GO.
KANEKI ...
WHAT IF SOME-THING HAPPENS TO YOU...?
TSUKI-YAMA...
WHAT WAS THE POINT OF REFRAINING THIS LONG?
WHAT WAS THE POINT ...?
TMP
TMP
I'M NOT GONNA LET THEM HAVE YOU...
SUCH A FINE DISH LIKE YOU...!

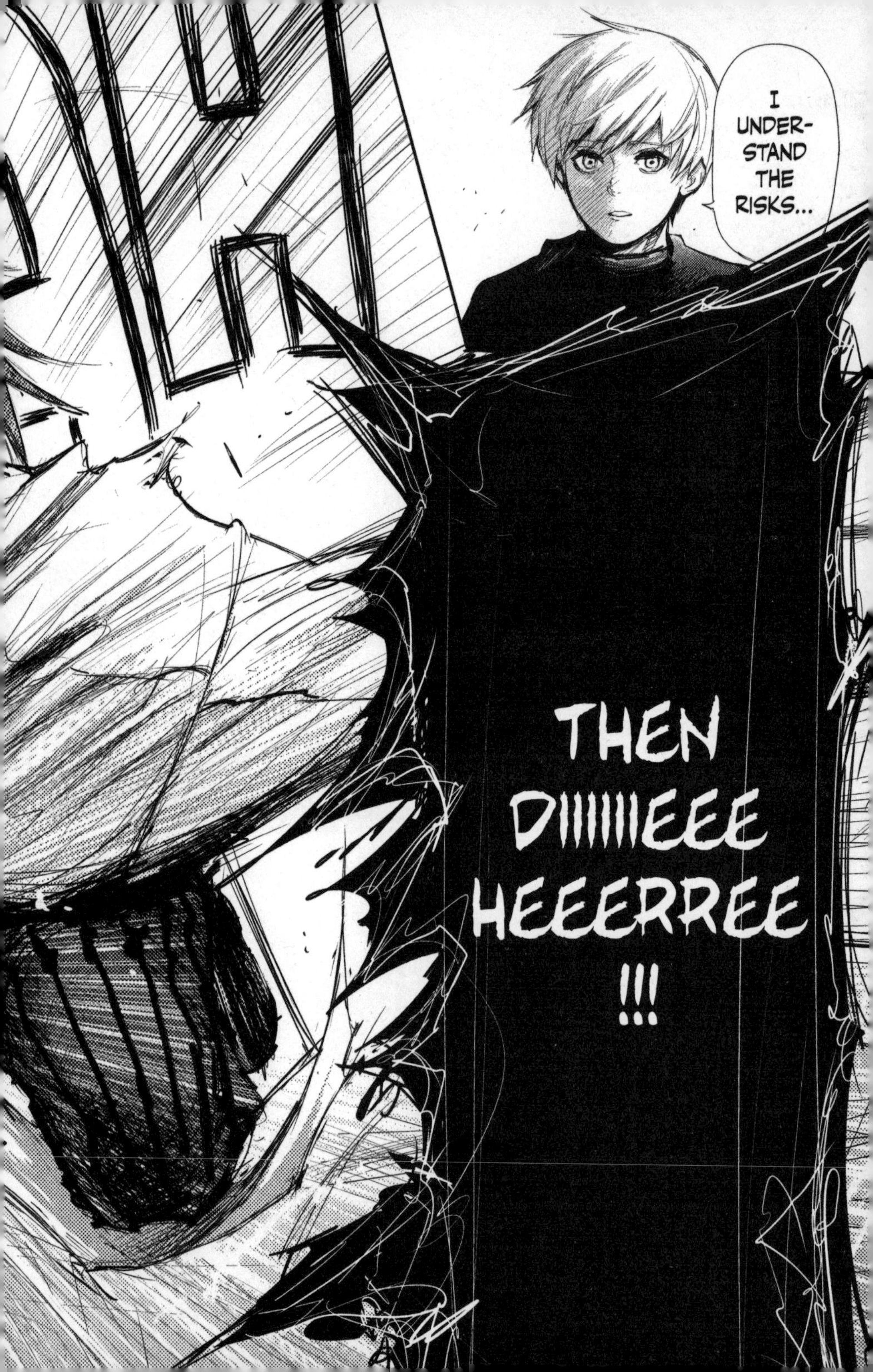
I UNDER-STAND THE RISKS...
THEN DIIIIIIEEE HEEERREE !!!

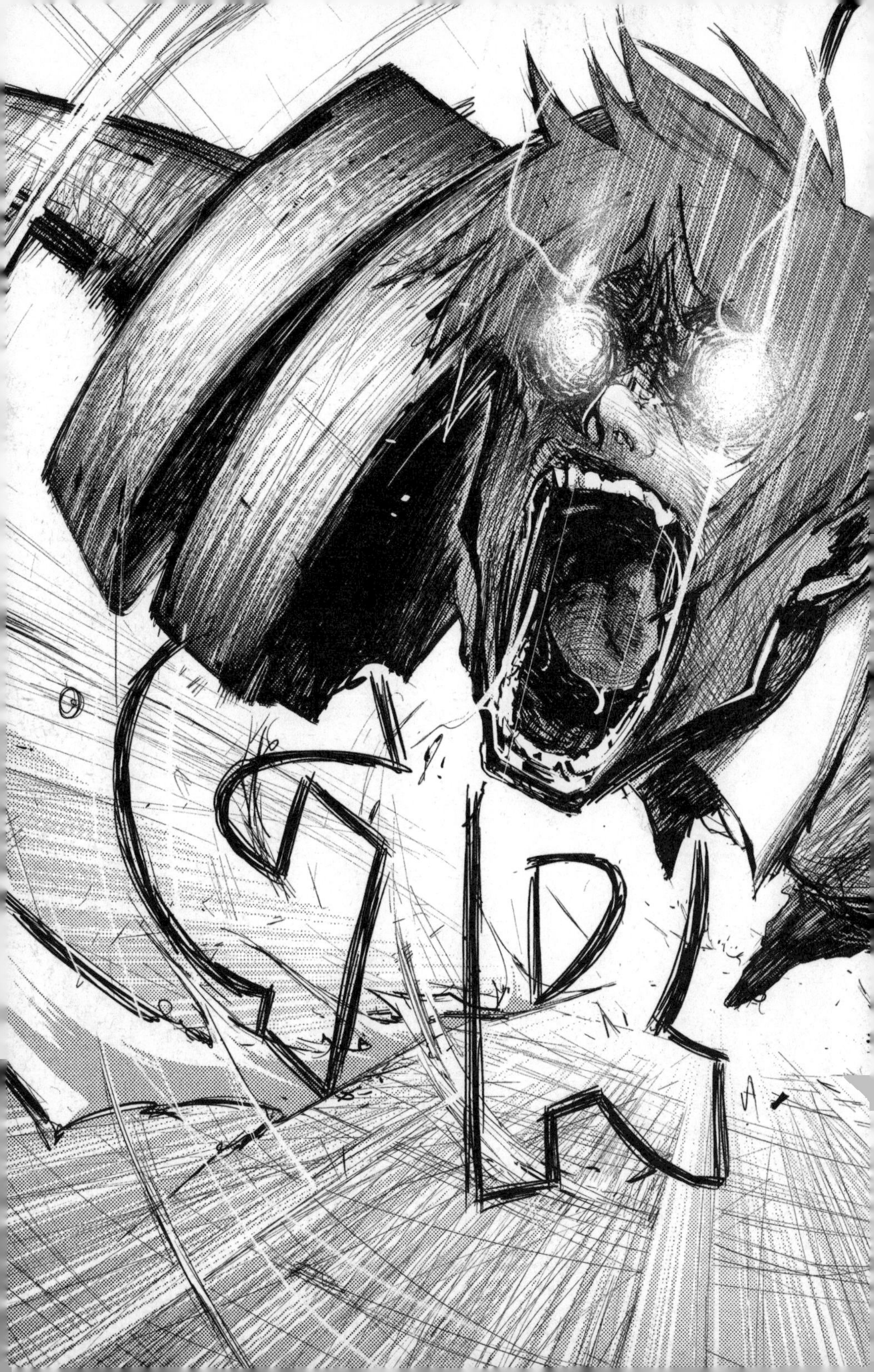

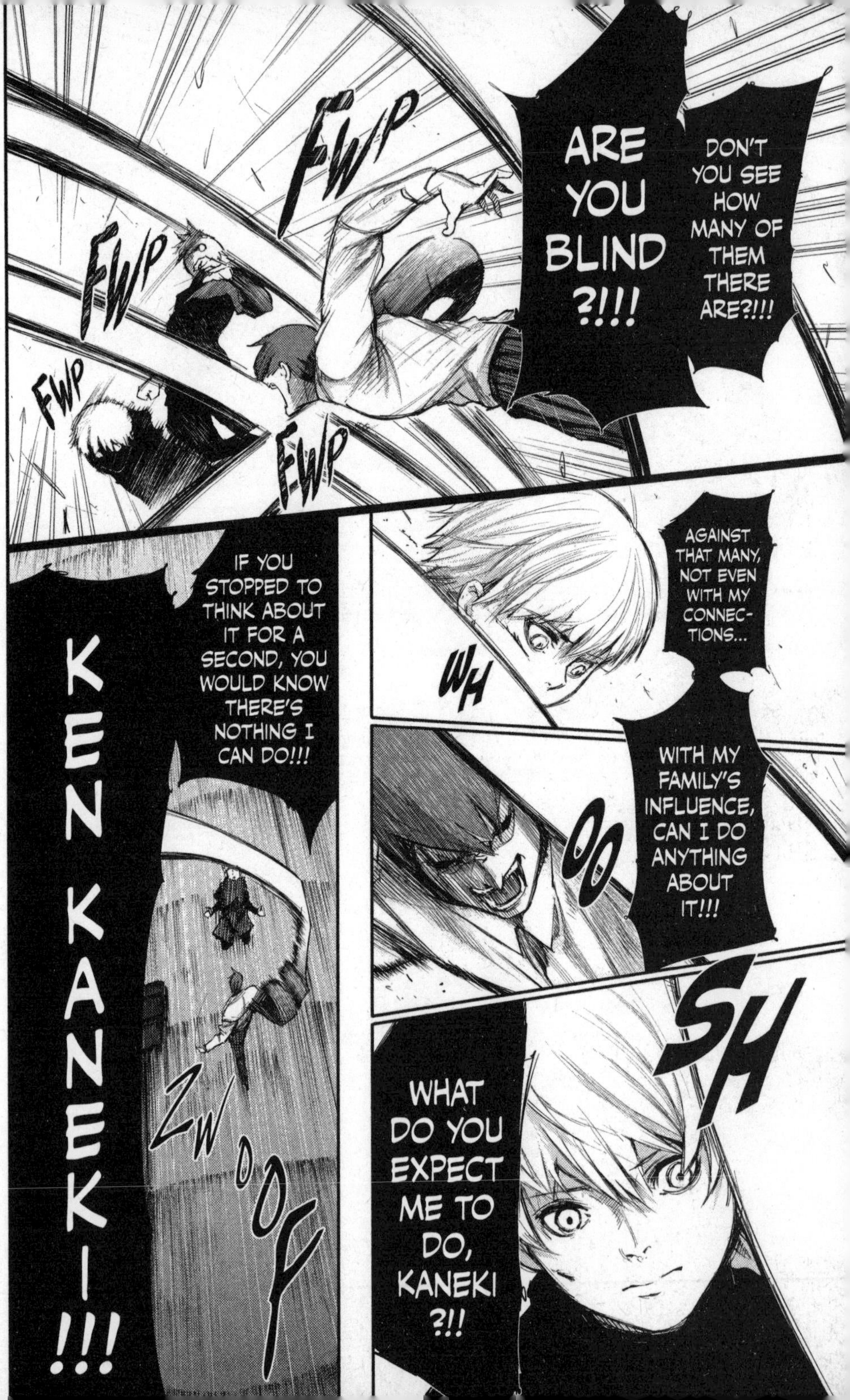
DON'T YOU SEE HOW MANY OF THEM THERE ARE?!!!
ARE YOU BLIND ?!!!
FWP
FWP
FWP
FWP
AGAINST THAT MANY, NOT EVEN WITH MY CONNEC-TIONS...
WH
WITH MY FAMILY'S INFLUENCE, CAN I DO ANYTHING ABOUT IT!!!
OO
SH
WHAT DO YOU EXPECT ME TO DO, KANEKI ?!!
IF YOU STOPPED TO THINK ABOUT IT FOR A SECOND, YOU WOULD KNOW THERE'S NOTHING I CAN DO!!!
KEN KANEKI!!!
ZWOOF

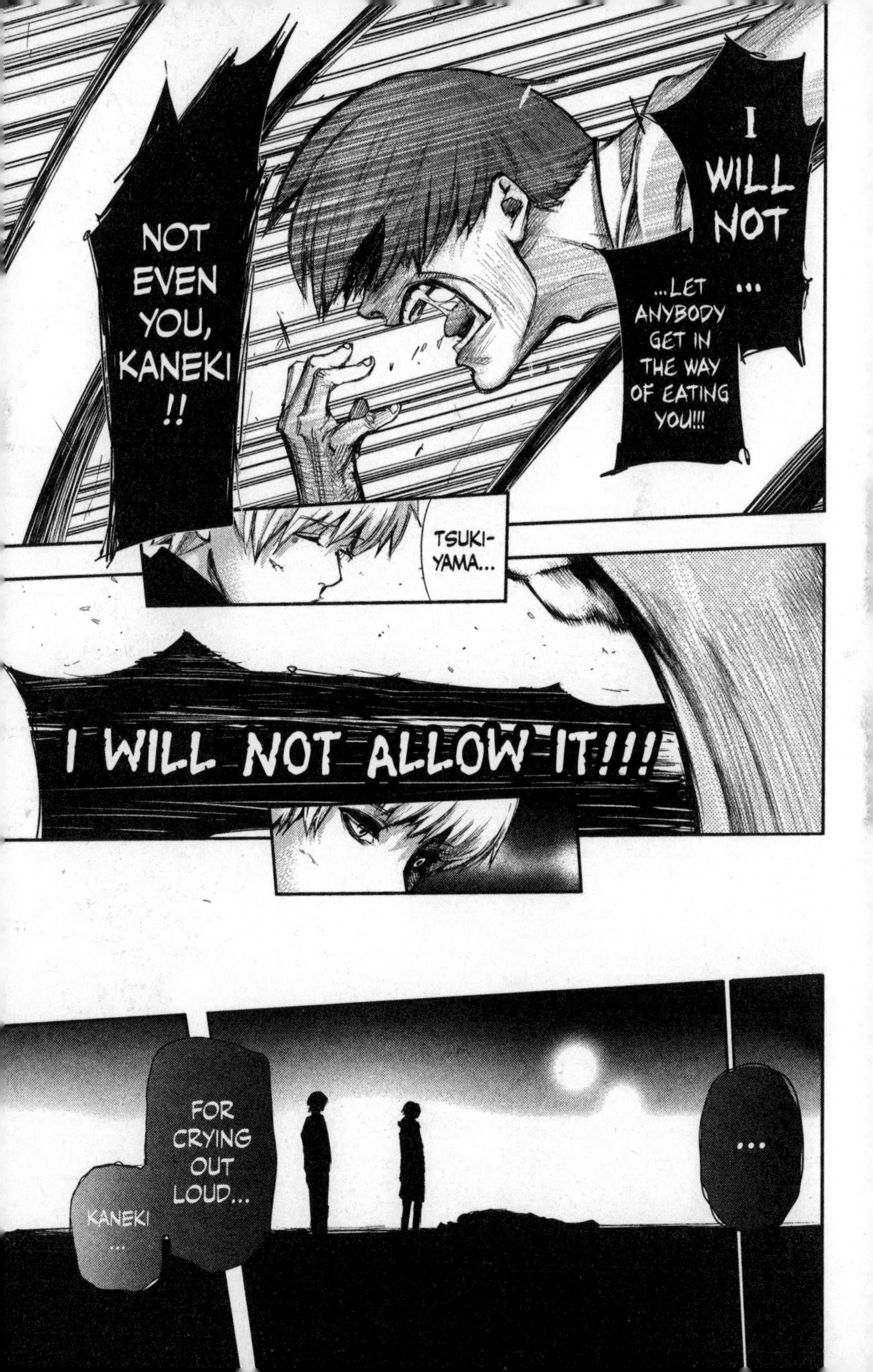
I WILL NOT ...
...LET ANYBODY GET IN THE WAY OF EATING YOU!!!
NOT EVEN YOU, KANEKI !!
TSUKI-YAMA...
I WILL NOT ALLOW IT!!!
...
FOR CRYING OUT LOUD...
KANEKI ...

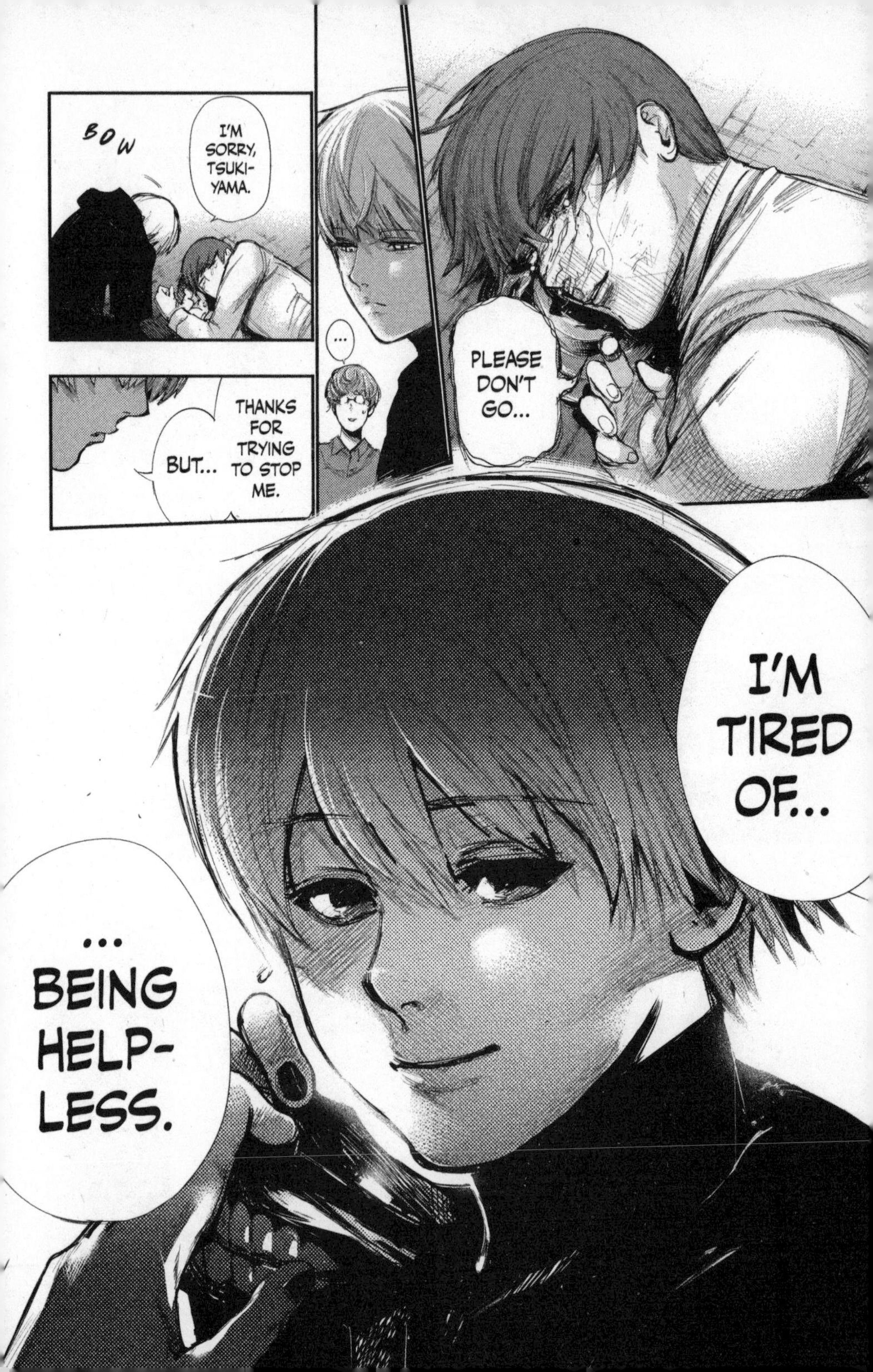
PLEASE DON'T GO...
...
BOW
I'M SORRY, TSUKIYAMA.
THANKS FOR TRYING TO STOP ME.
BUT...
I'M TIRED OF...
... BEING HELPLESS.

東京喰種
トーキョーグール
Tokyo
Ghoul

Poetry Time. (6)

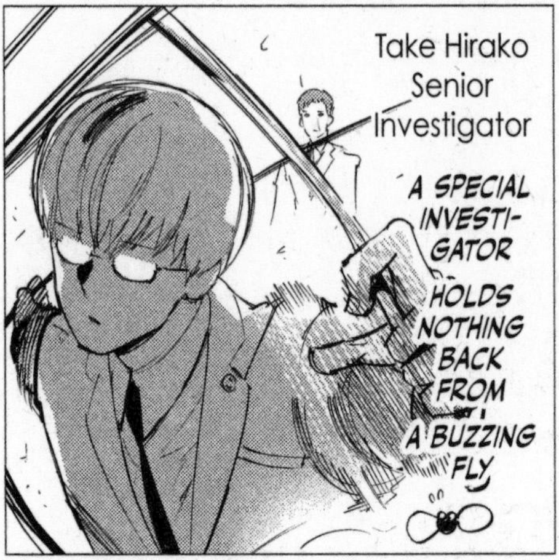
Take Hirako
Senior
Investigator
A SPECIAL INVESTIGATOR HOLDS NOTHING BACK FROM A BUZZING FLY

INVESTIGATOR ARIMA'S TWO-SWORD STYLE IS ALWAYS BREATHTAKING. (AKIRA)

THIS IS THE REASON WHY INVESTIGATOR ARIMA IS INVESTIGATOR ARIMA. (AMON)

I'M WORRIED IF THE FLY-SWATTER CAN WITHSTAND INVESTIGATOR ARIMA'S SNAP OF THE WRIST. (UI)

YOU GUYS ARE READING WAY TOO MUCH INTO IT. (SHINOHARA)

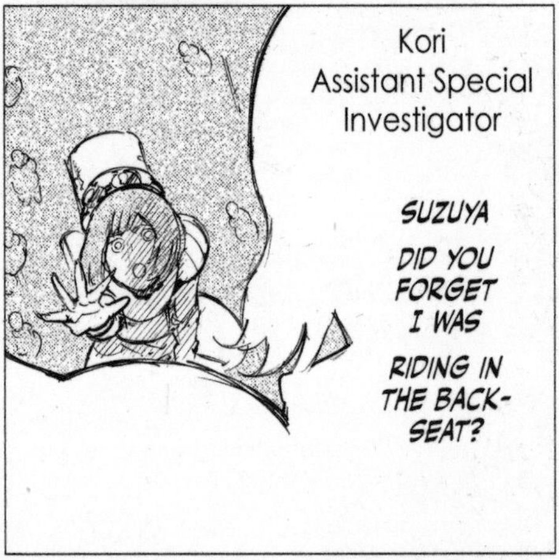
Kori
Assistant Special
Investigator
SUZUYA DID YOU FORGET I WAS RIDING IN THE BACKSEAT?

JUMP. (SUZUYA)

TOO LATE. (MARUDE@BOUGHT_A_NEW_BIKE)

MMM BOY! (TANAKAMARU)

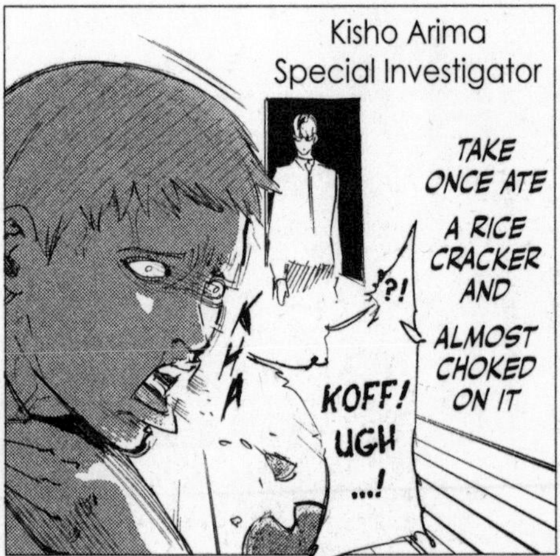
Kisho Arima
Special Investigator
TAKE ONCE ATE A RICE CRACKER AND ALMOST CHOKED ON IT
?!
KOFF! UGH ...!

WHAT IS THIS, A DIARY? (MARUDE)

I THOUGHT I WAS GOING TO DIE. (HIRAKO)

I WISHED I COULD'VE SEEN THAT. (UI)

MMM... BOY? (TANAKAMARU)

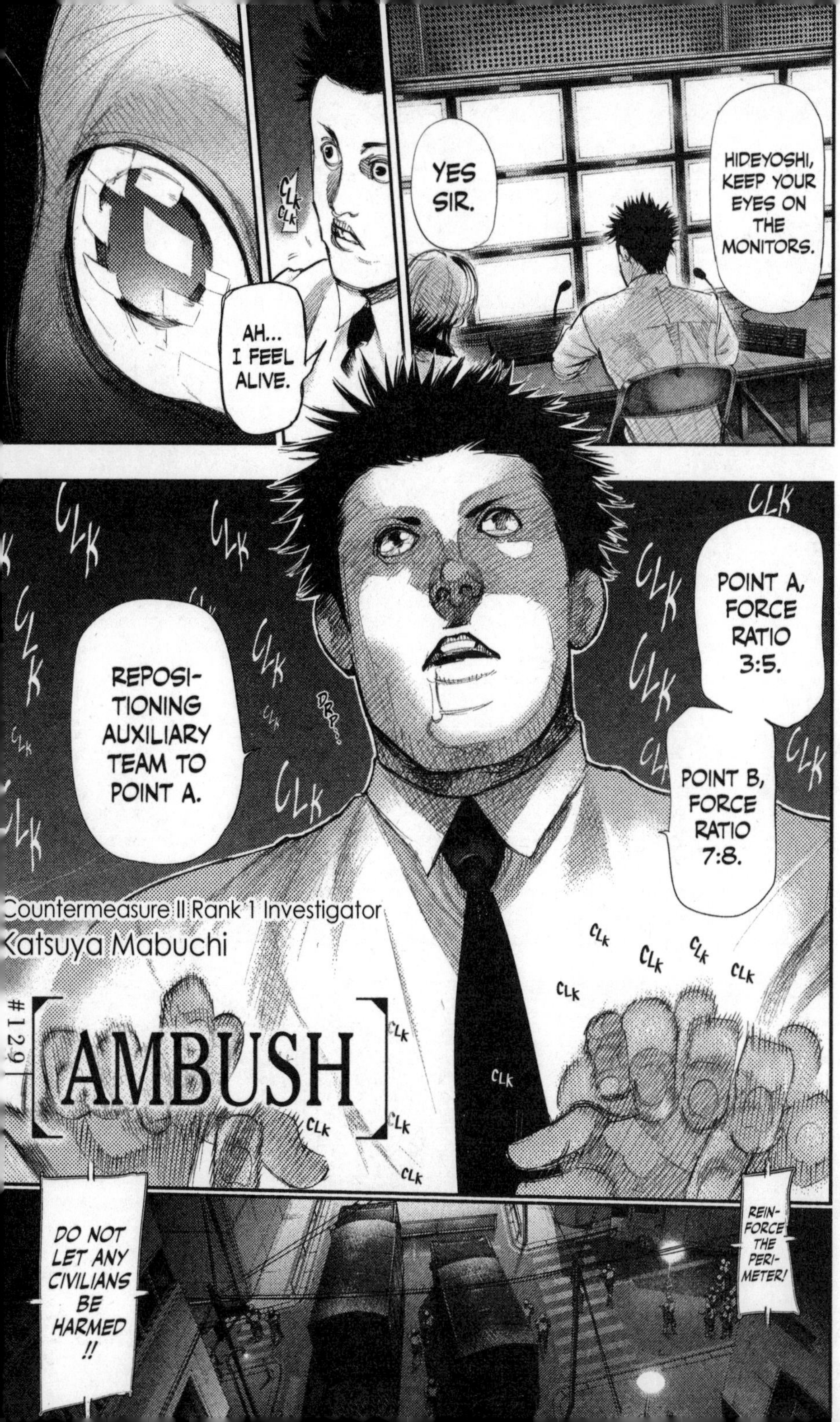
HIDEYOSHI, KEEP YOUR EYES ON THE MONITORS.
YES SIR.
CLK CLK
AH... I FEEL ALIVE.
CLK
POINT A, FORCE RATIO 3:5.
POINT B, FORCE RATIO 7:8.
REPOSITIONING AUXILIARY TEAM TO POINT A.
CLK
Countermeasure II Rank 1 Investigator
Katsuya Mabuchi
#129 AMBUSH
CLK
REIN-FORCE THE PERI-METER!
DO NOT LET ANY CIVILIANS BE HARMED!!

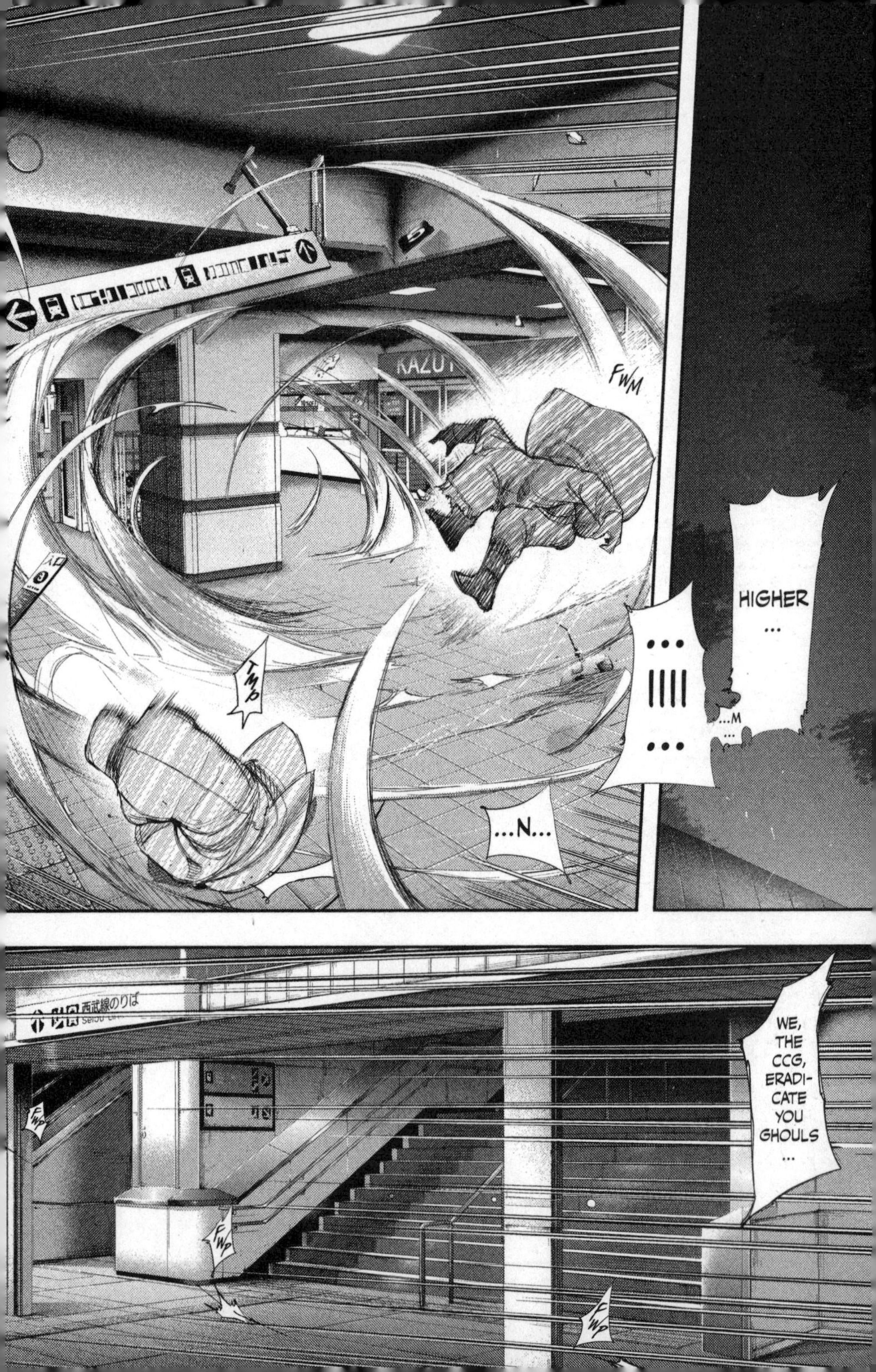
HIGHER ...
...M ...
FWM
...!!!!! ...
TMP
...N...
西武線のりば
WE, THE CCG, ERADICATE YOU GHOULS ...
FWP
FWP
FWP

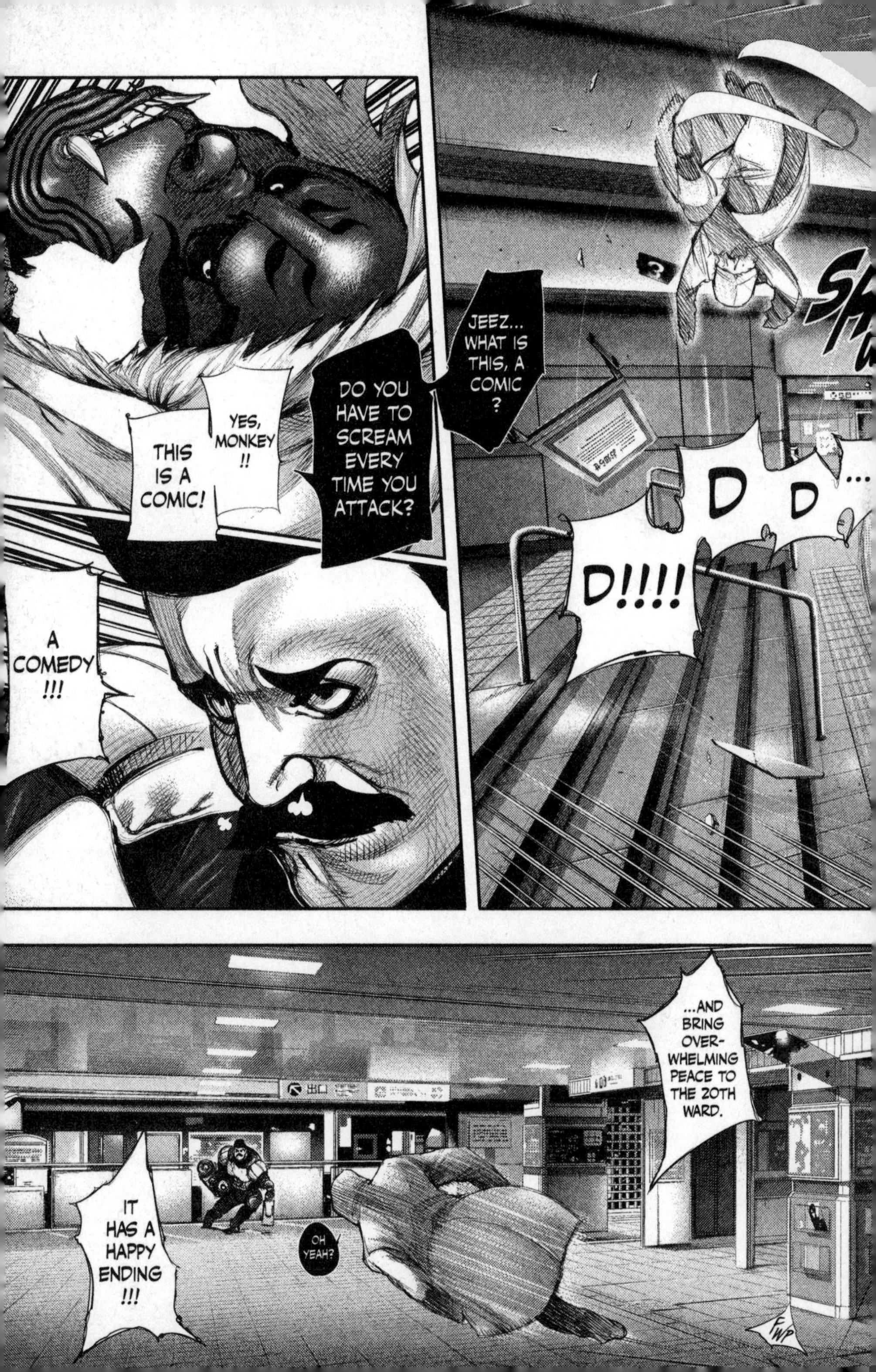
JEEZ... WHAT IS THIS, A COMIC ?
D D...
D!!!!
DO YOU HAVE TO SCREAM EVERY TIME YOU ATTACK?
YES, MONKEY !!
THIS IS A COMIC!
A COMEDY !!!
...AND BRING OVER-WHELMING PEACE TO THE 20TH WARD.
OH YEAH?
IT HAS A HAPPY ENDING !!!
FWP

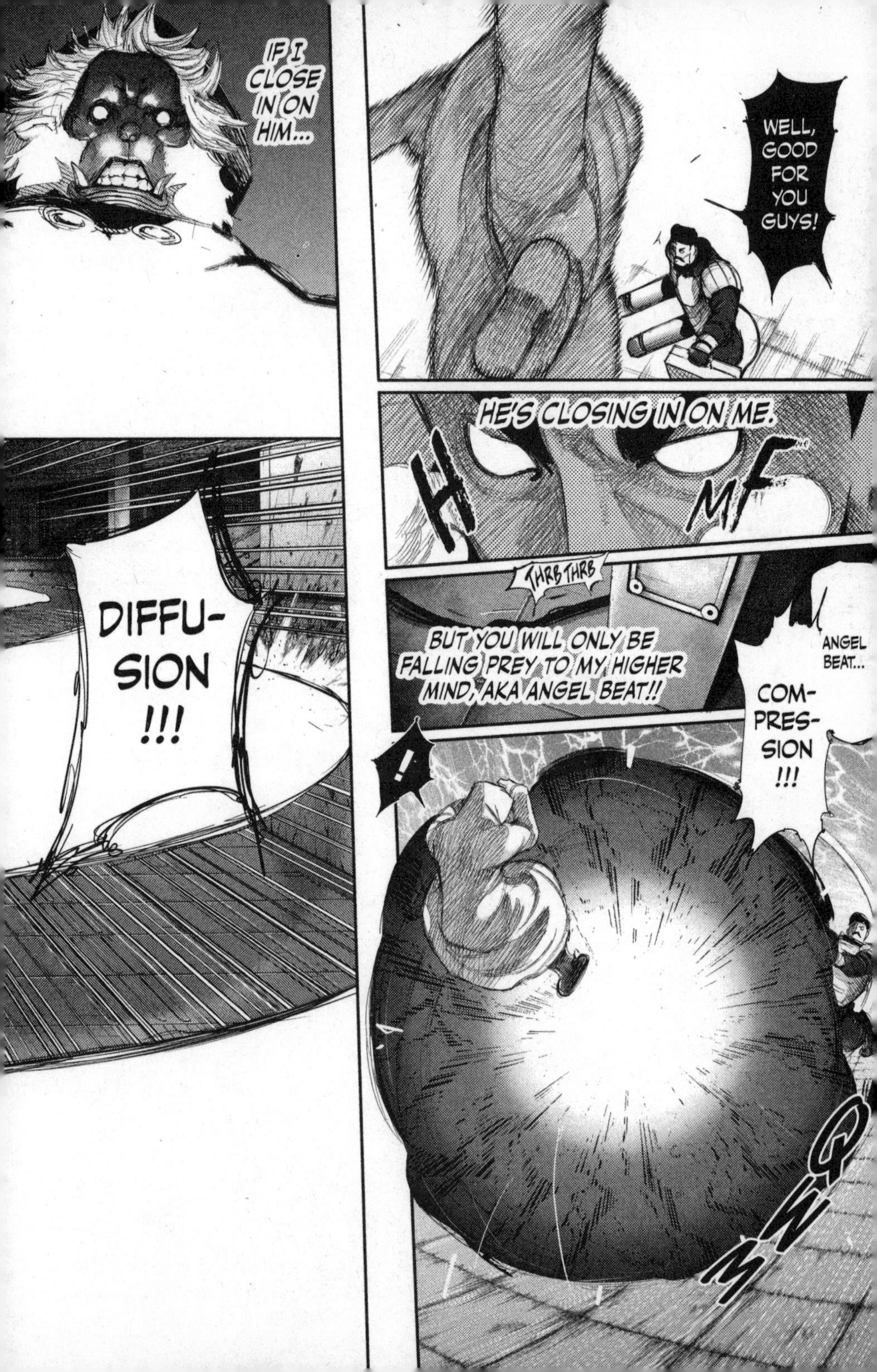
WELL, GOOD FOR YOU GUYS!
IF I CLOSE IN ON HIM...
HE'S CLOSING IN ON ME.
HMF
THRB THRB
BUT YOU WILL ONLY BE FALLING PREY TO MY HIGHER MIND, AKA ANGEL BEAT!!
ANGEL BEAT...
COMPRESSION!!!
!
DIFFUSION!!!

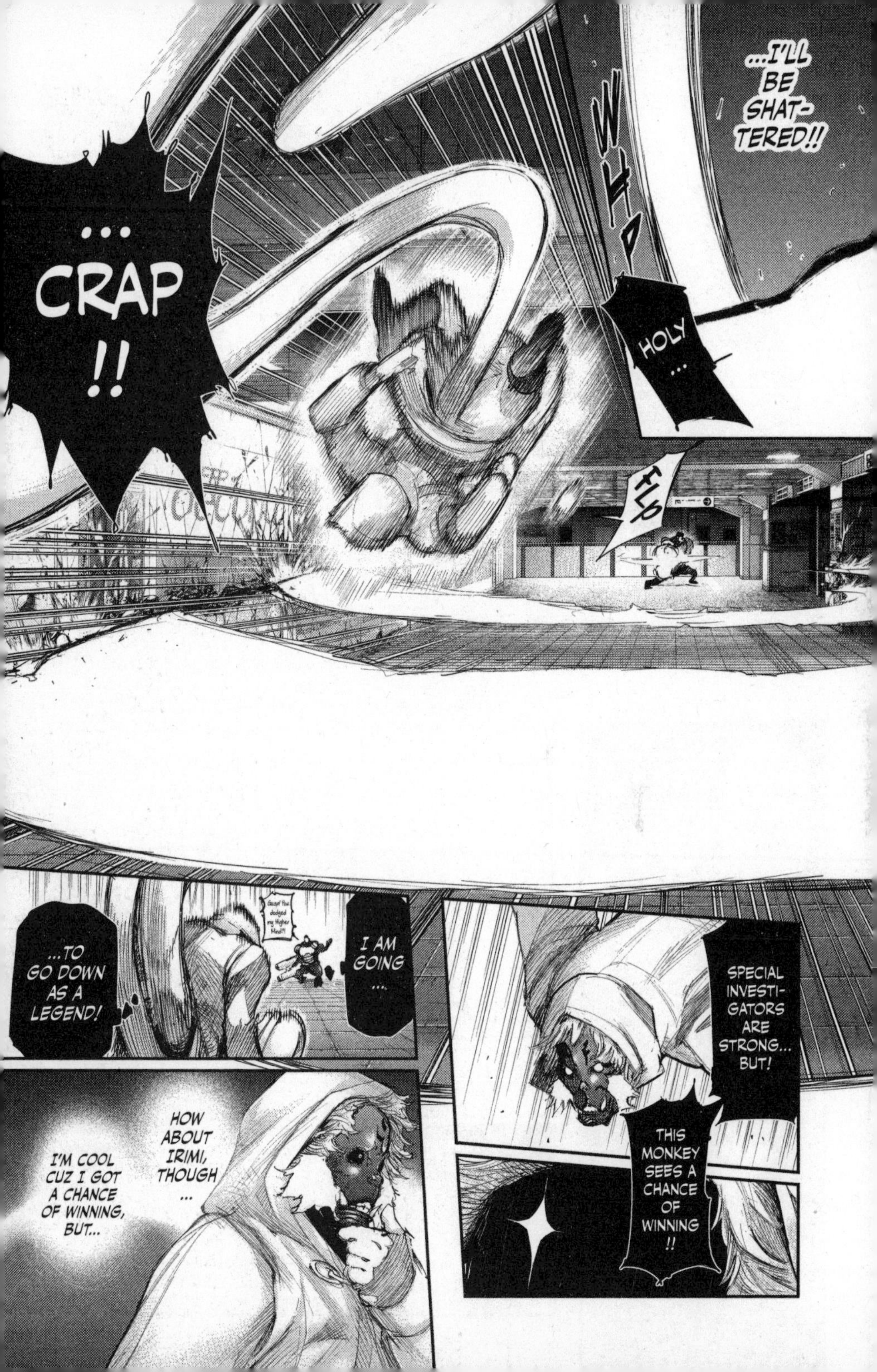
...I'LL BE SHAT-TERED!!
WHP
HOLY ...
... CRAP !!
FLP
SPECIAL INVESTI-GATORS ARE STRONG... BUT!
THIS MONKEY SEES A CHANCE OF WINNING !!
I AM GOING ...
...TO GO DOWN AS A LEGEND!
Gasp! You dodged my Higher Hind?!
HOW ABOUT IRIMI, THOUGH ...
I'M COOL CUZ I GOT A CHANCE OF WINNING, BUT...

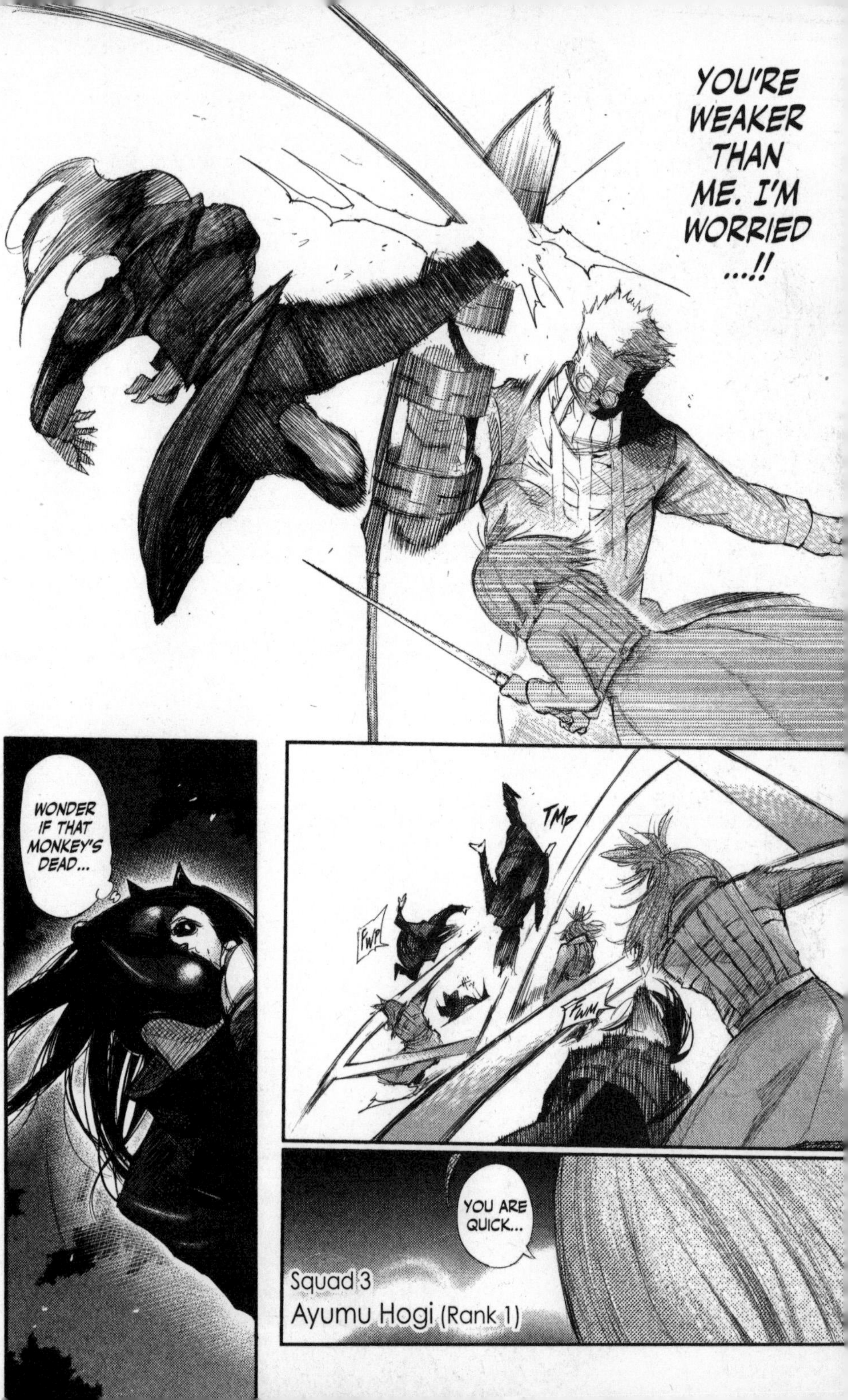
YOU'RE WEAKER THAN ME. I'M WORRIED ...!!
TMP
FWP
FWM
YOU ARE QUICK...
Squad 3
Ayumu Hogi (Rank 1)
WONDER IF THAT MONKEY'S DEAD...

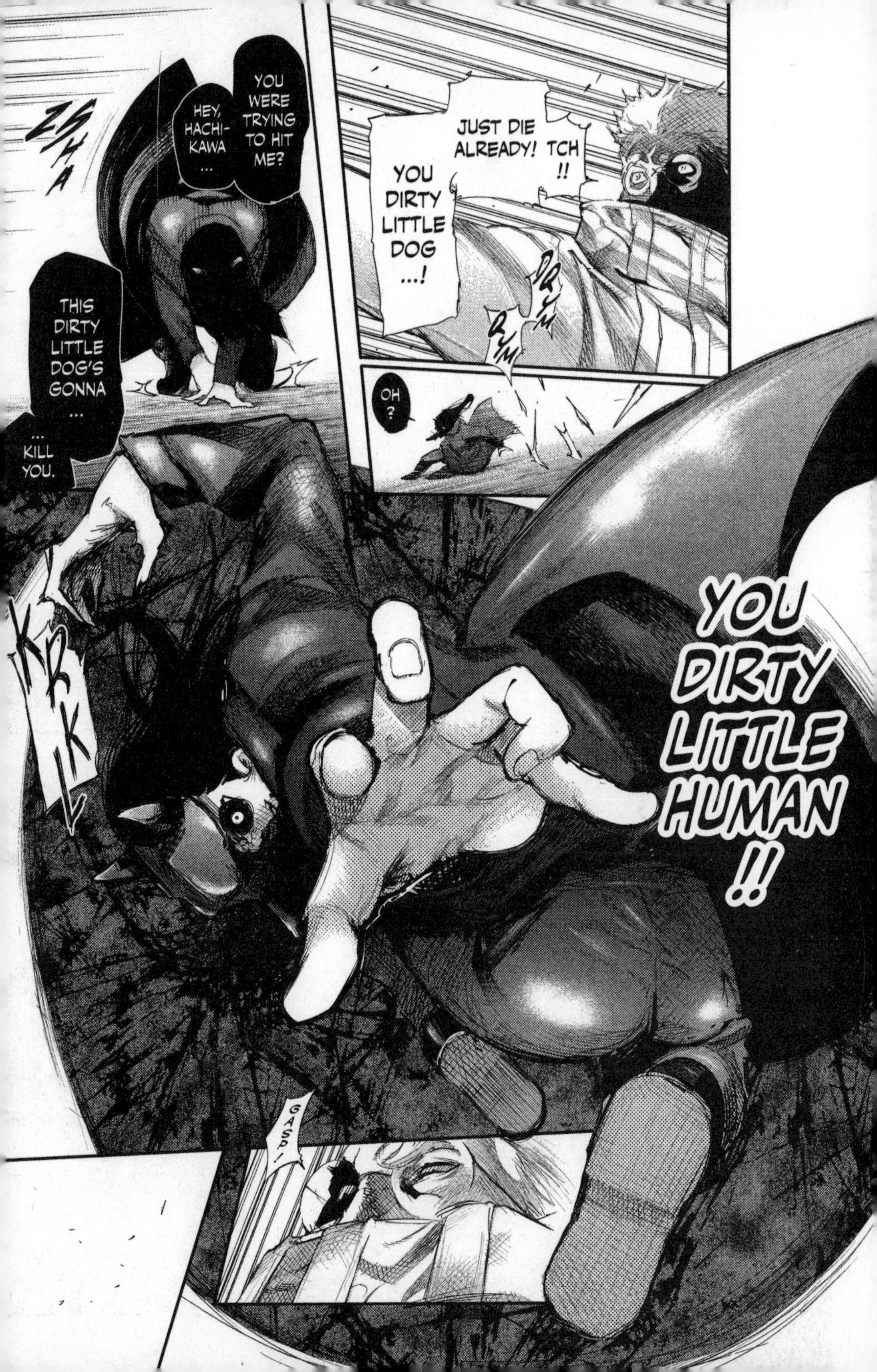
TCH !!
JUST DIE ALREADY!
YOU DIRTY LITTLE DOG ...!
DQ'M
DQ'M
OH ?
ZSHA
YOU WERE TRYING TO HIT ME?
HEY, HACHI-KAWA ...
THIS DIRTY LITTLE DOG'S GONNA ...
... KILL YOU.
YOU DIRTY LITTLE HUMAN !!
KRKL
GASP!

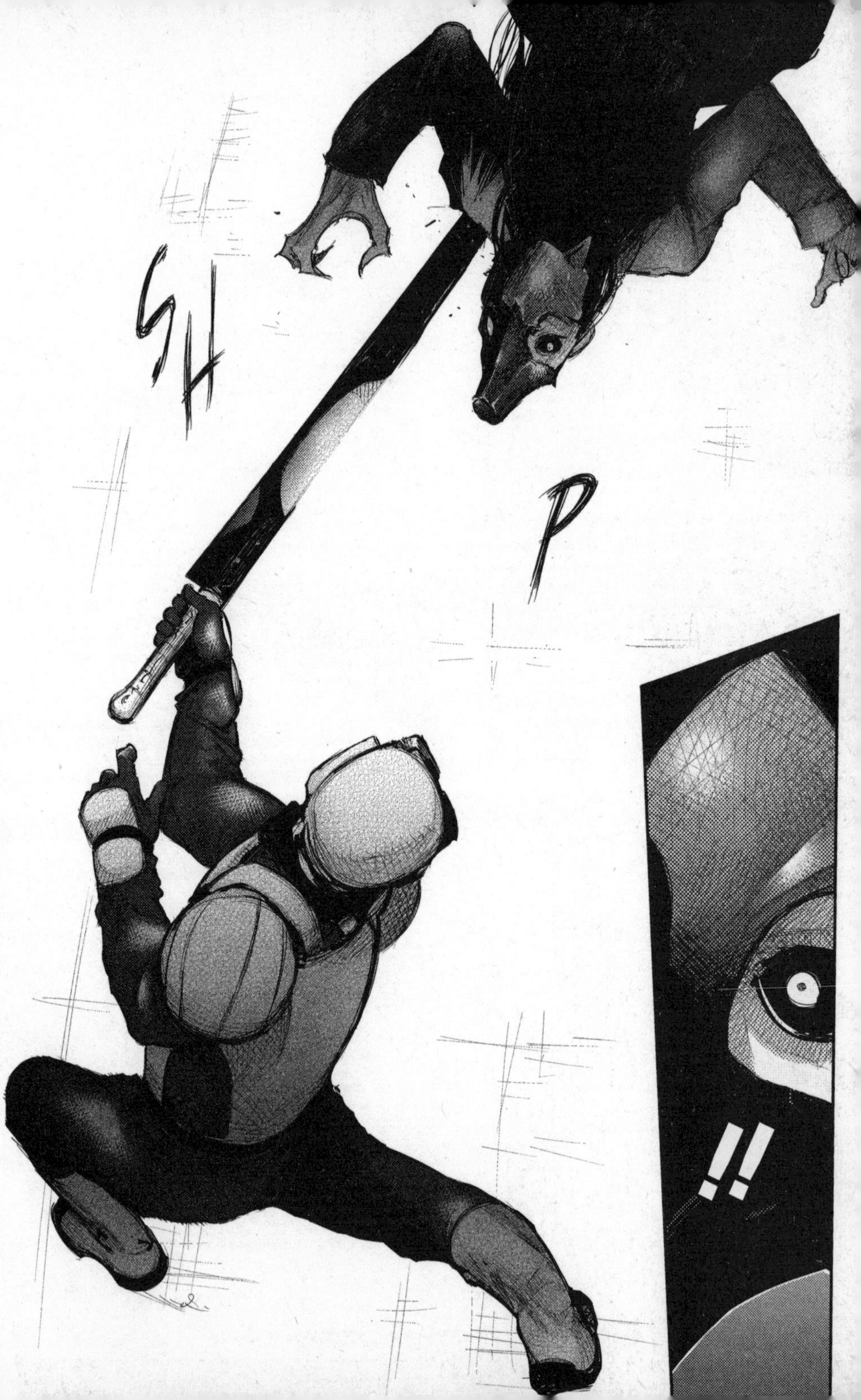
SHP
!!

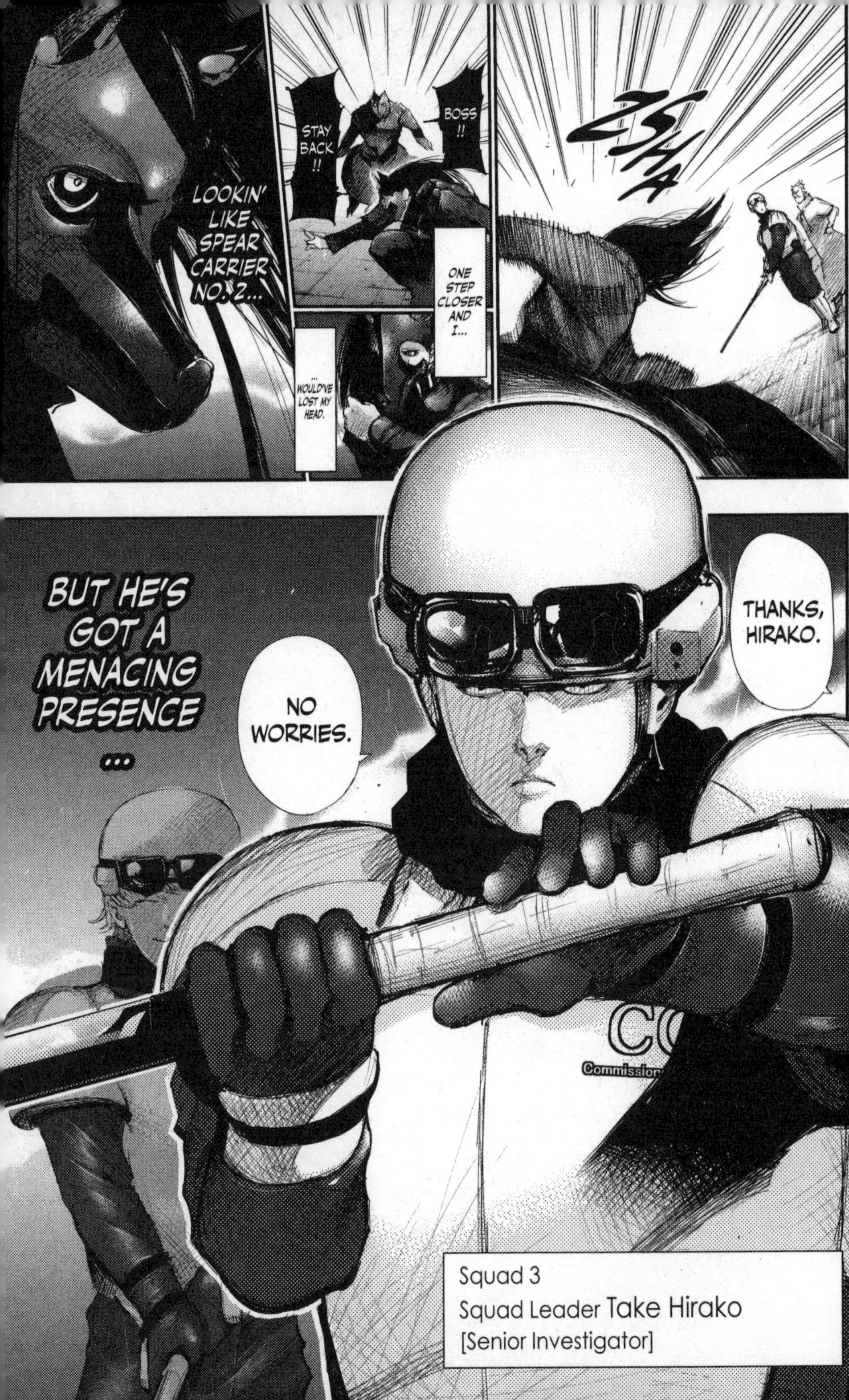
ZSHA
BOSS !!
STAY BACK !!
ONE STEP CLOSER AND I...
...WOULD'VE LOST MY HEAD.
LOOKIN' LIKE SPEAR CARRIER NO. 2...
THANKS, HIRAKO.
NO WORRIES.
BUT HE'S GOT A MENACING PRESENCE ...
Squad 3
Squad Leader Take Hirako
[Senior Investigator]

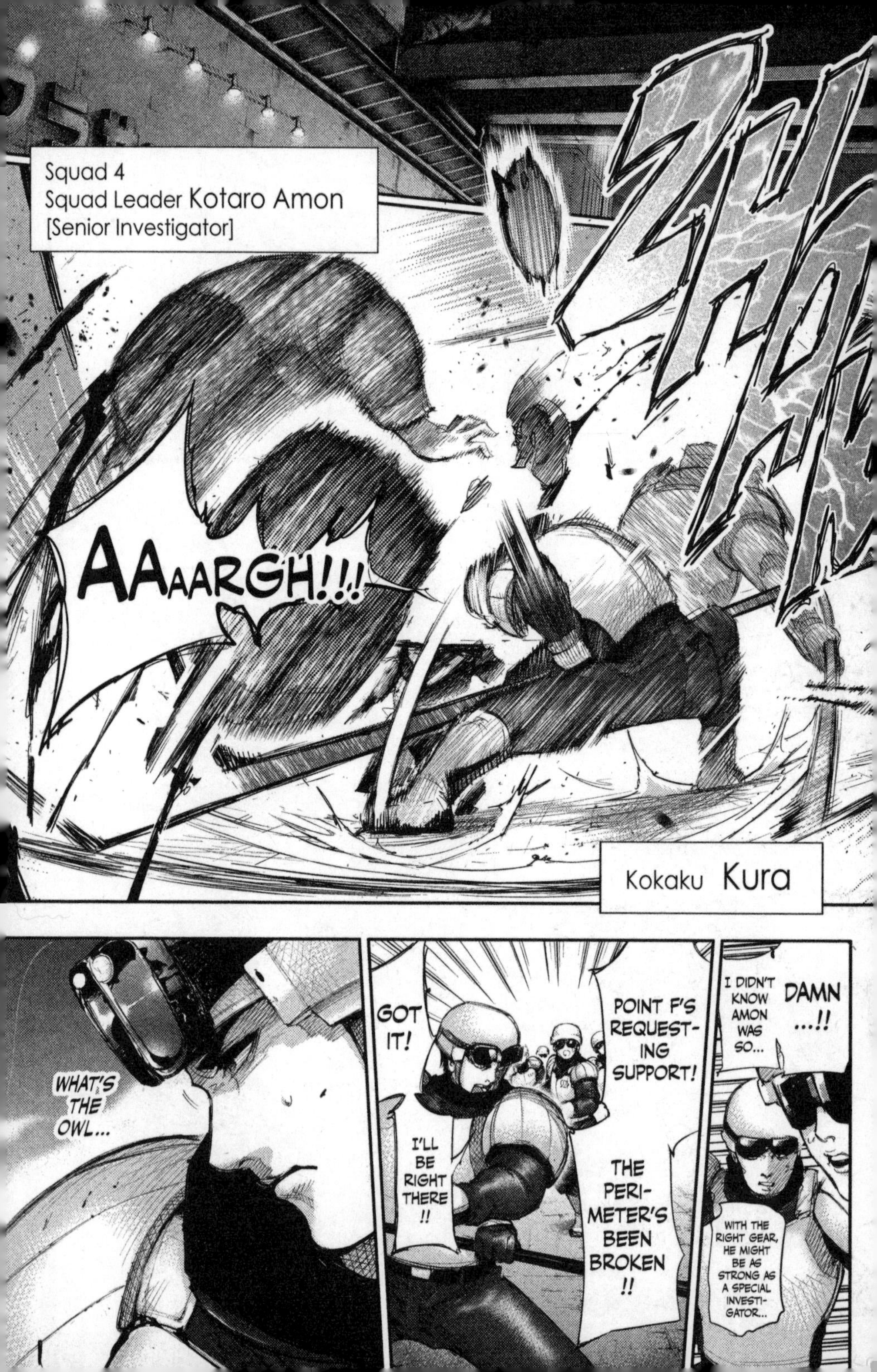
Squad 4
Squad Leader Kotaro Amon
[Senior Investigator]
AAAARGH!!!
Kokaku Kura
DAMN...!!
I DIDN'T KNOW AMON WAS SO...
WITH THE RIGHT GEAR, HE MIGHT BE AS STRONG AS A SPECIAL INVESTIGATOR...
POINT F'S REQUESTING SUPPORT!
GOT IT!
THE PERIMETER'S BEEN BROKEN!!
I'LL BE RIGHT THERE!!
WHAT'S THE OWL...

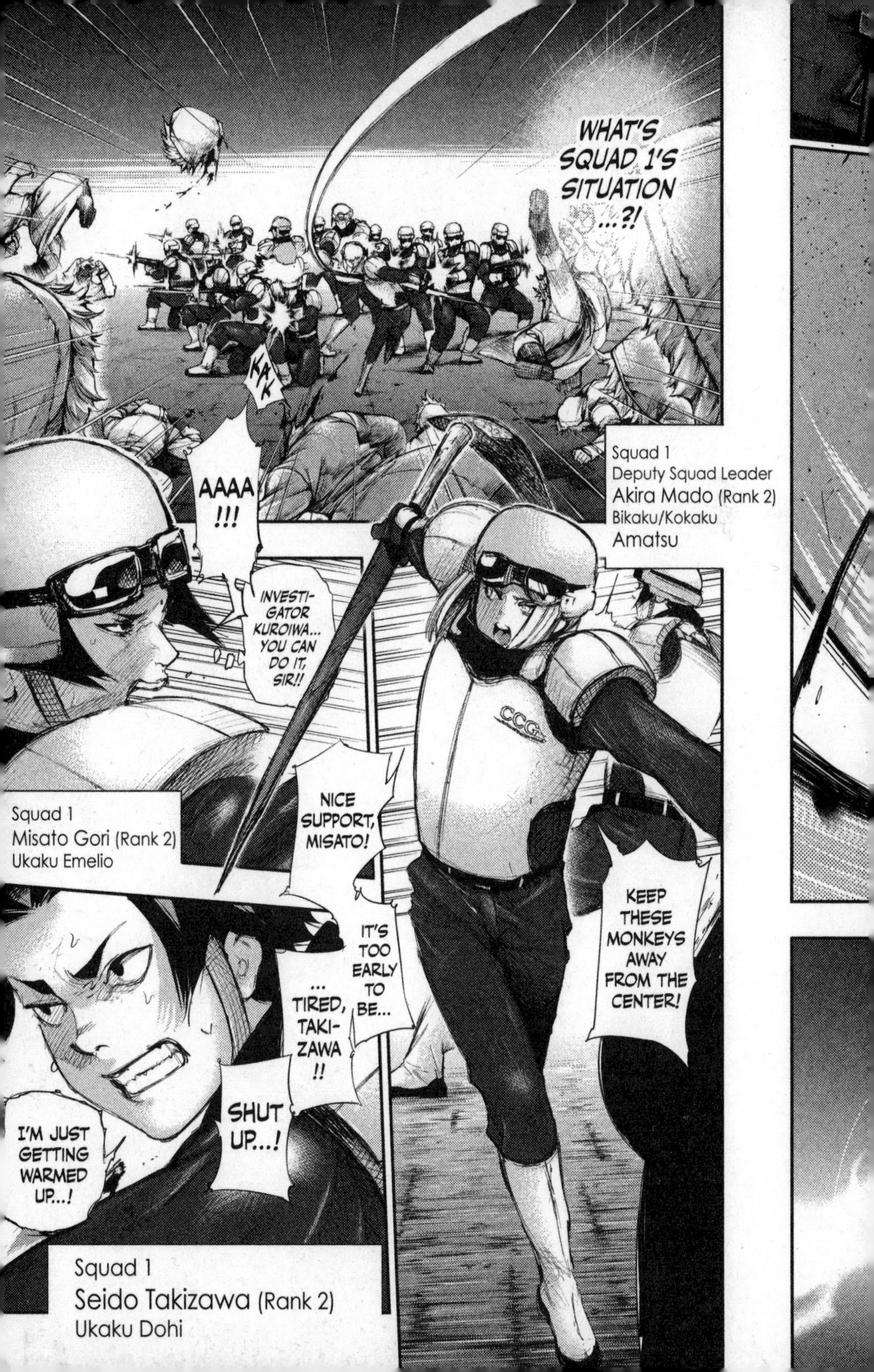

WHAT'S SQUAD 1'S SITUATION ...?!
KAK
AAAA!!!
Squad 1
Deputy Squad Leader
Akira Mado (Rank 2)
Bikaku/Kokaku
Amatsu
KEEP THESE MONKEYS AWAY FROM THE CENTER!
INVESTIGATOR KUROIWA... YOU CAN DO IT, SIR!!
Squad 1
Misato Gori (Rank 2)
Ukaku Emelio
NICE SUPPORT, MISATO!
IT'S TOO EARLY TO BE...
...TIRED, TAKIZAWA!!
SHUT UP...!
I'M JUST GETTING WARMED UP...!
Squad 1
Seido Takizawa (Rank 2)
Ukaku Dohi

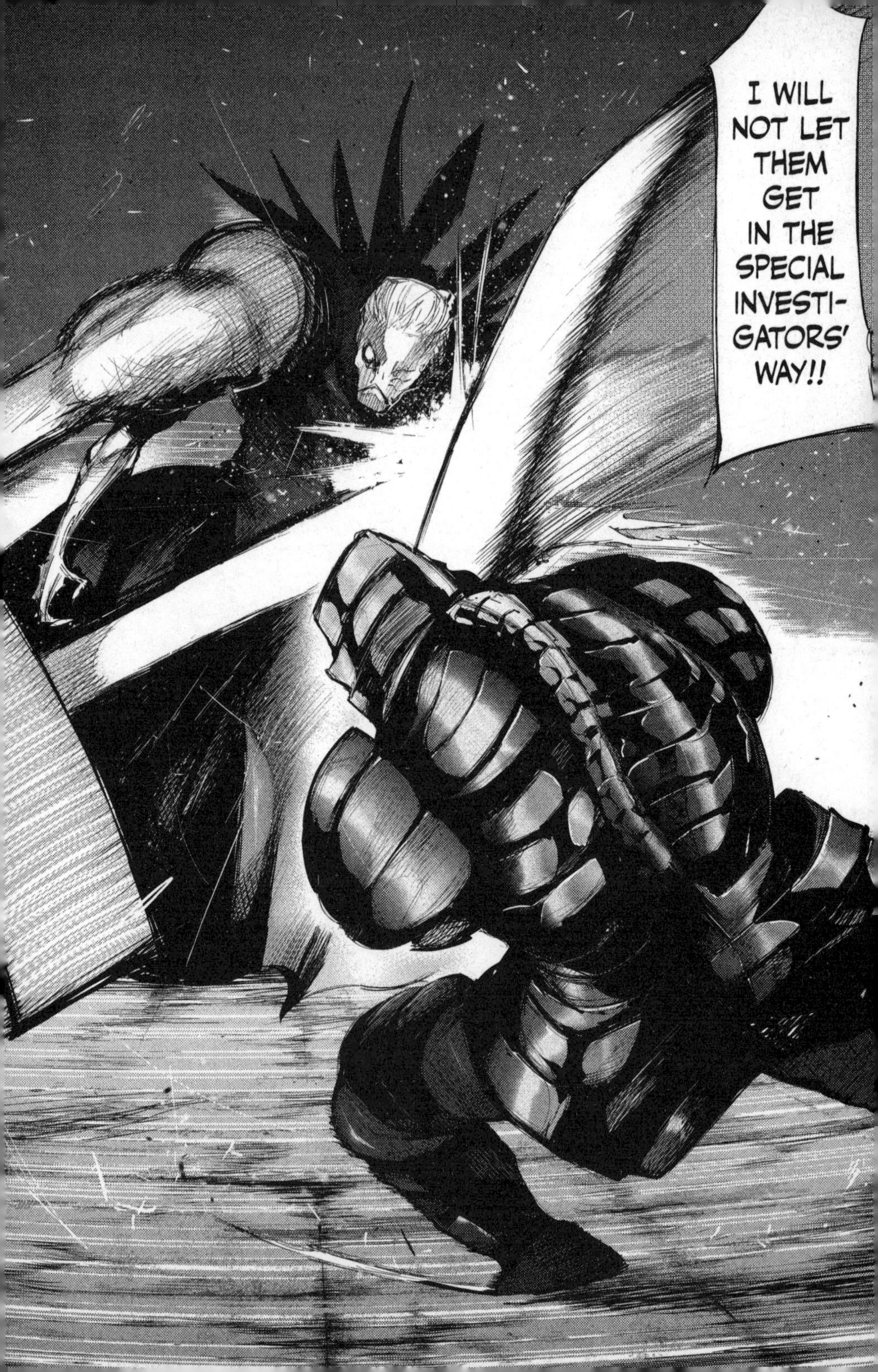
I WILL NOT LET THEM GET IN THE SPECIAL INVESTI- GATORS' WAY!!

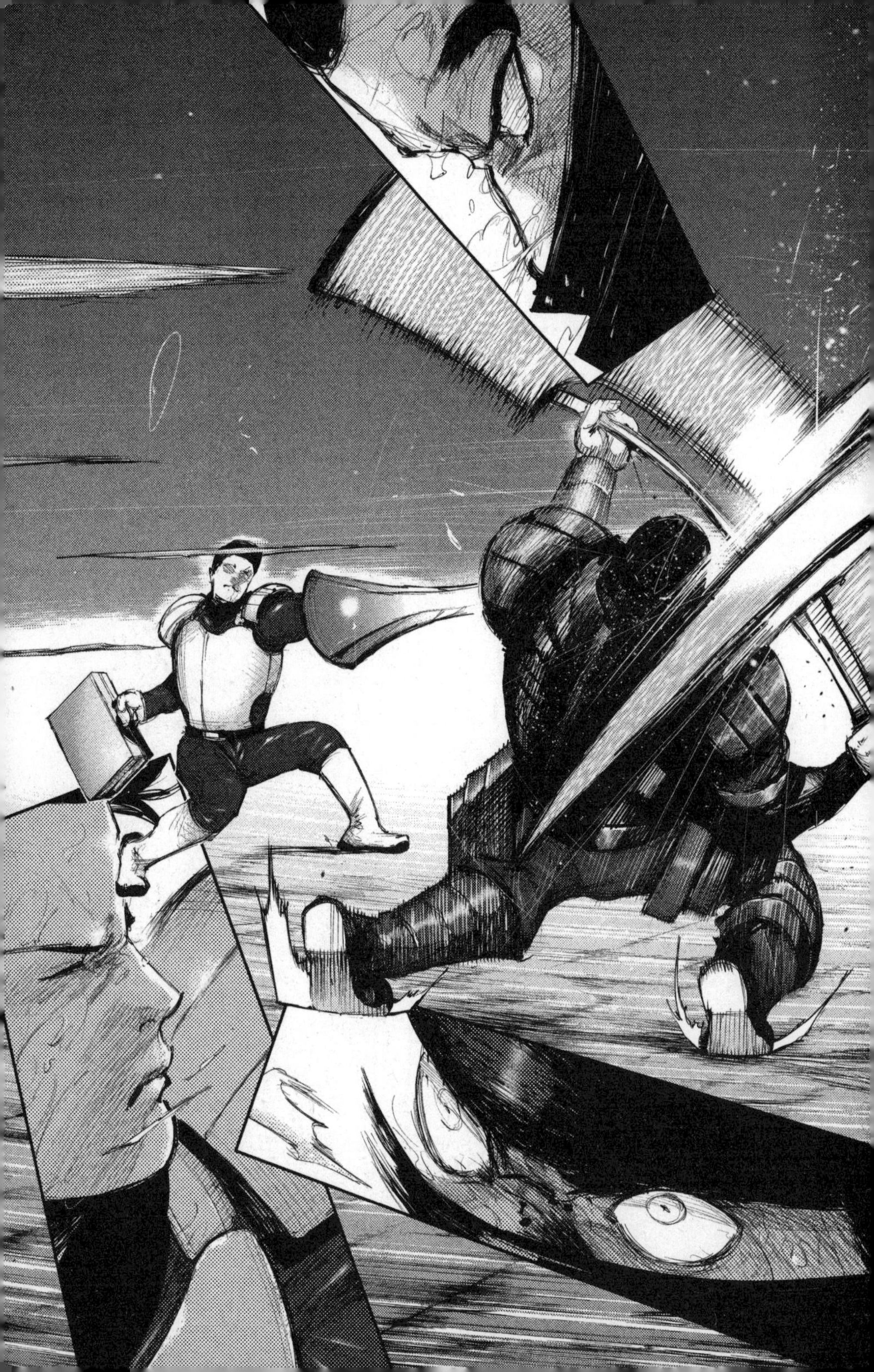

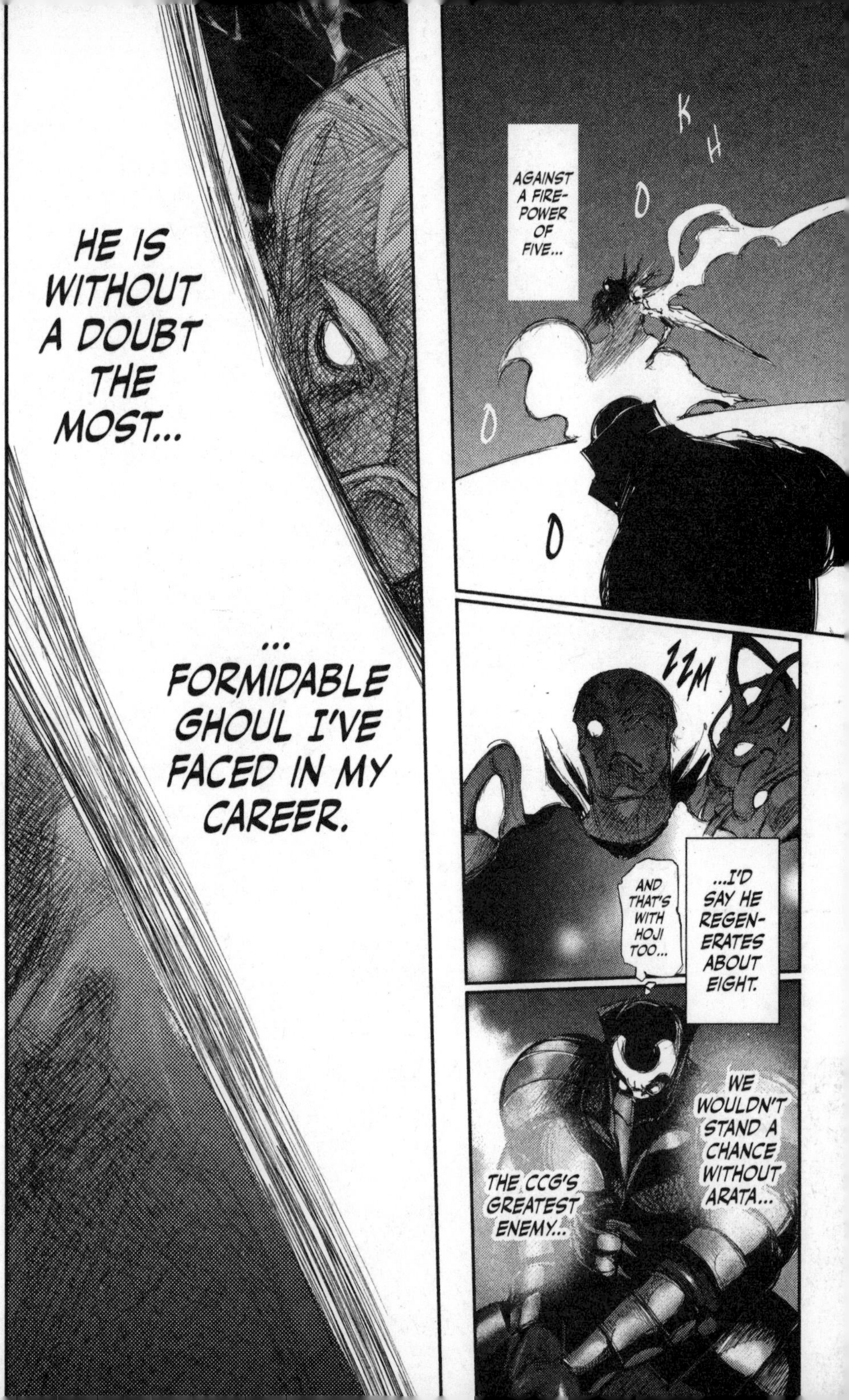
AGAINST A FIRE-POWER OF FIVE...
KHOOO
ZZM
...I'D SAY HE REGENER-ATES ABOUT EIGHT.
AND THAT'S WITH HOJI TOO...
WE WOULDN'T STAND A CHANCE WITHOUT ARATA...
THE CCG'S GREATEST ENEMY...
HE IS WITHOUT A DOUBT THE MOST...
...FORMIDABLE GHOUL I'VE FACED IN MY CAREER.

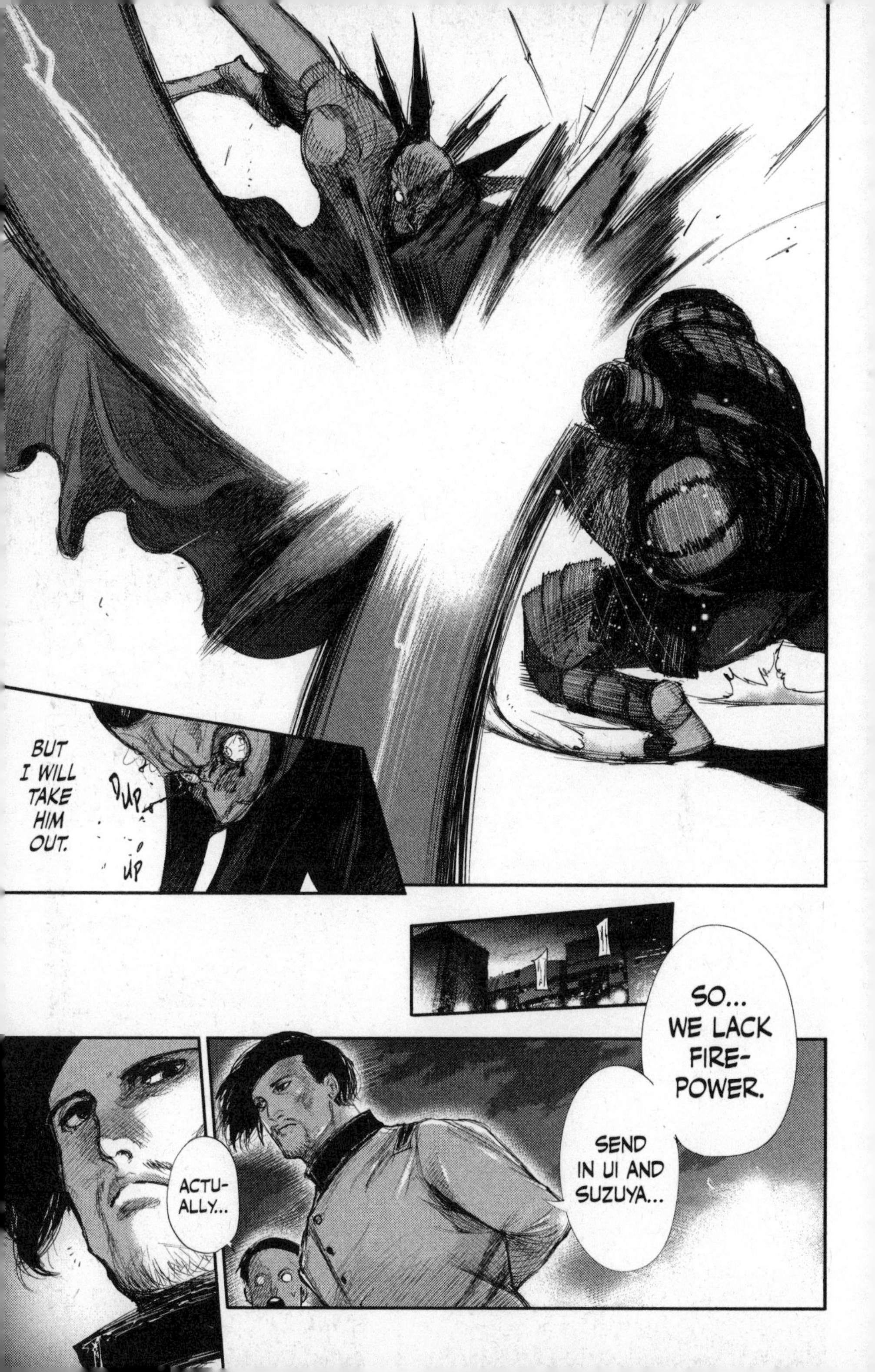
BUT I WILL TAKE HIM OUT.
SO... WE LACK FIRE-POWER.
SEND IN UI AND SUZUYA...
ACTU-ALLY...

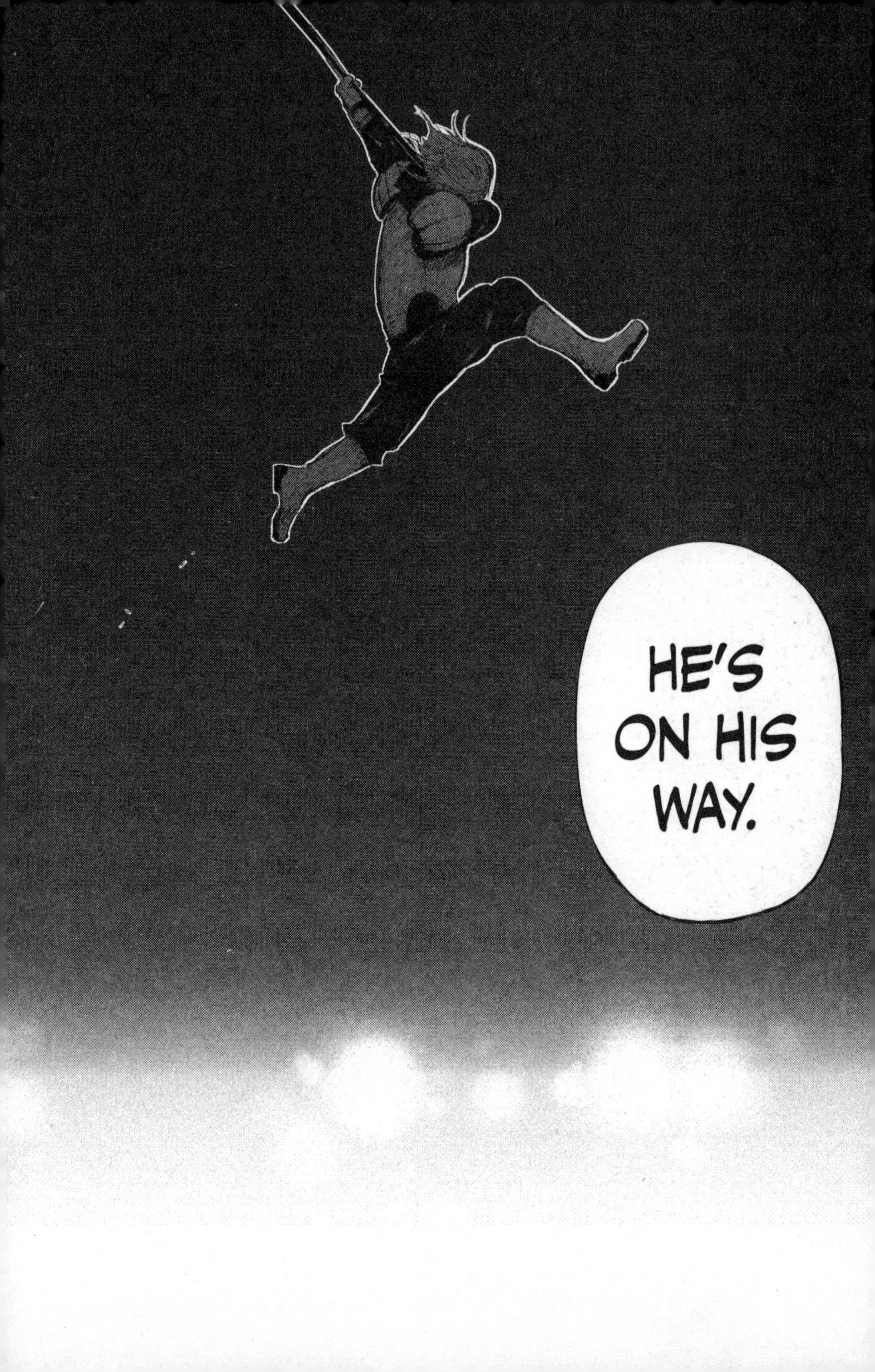
HE'S ON HIS WAY.

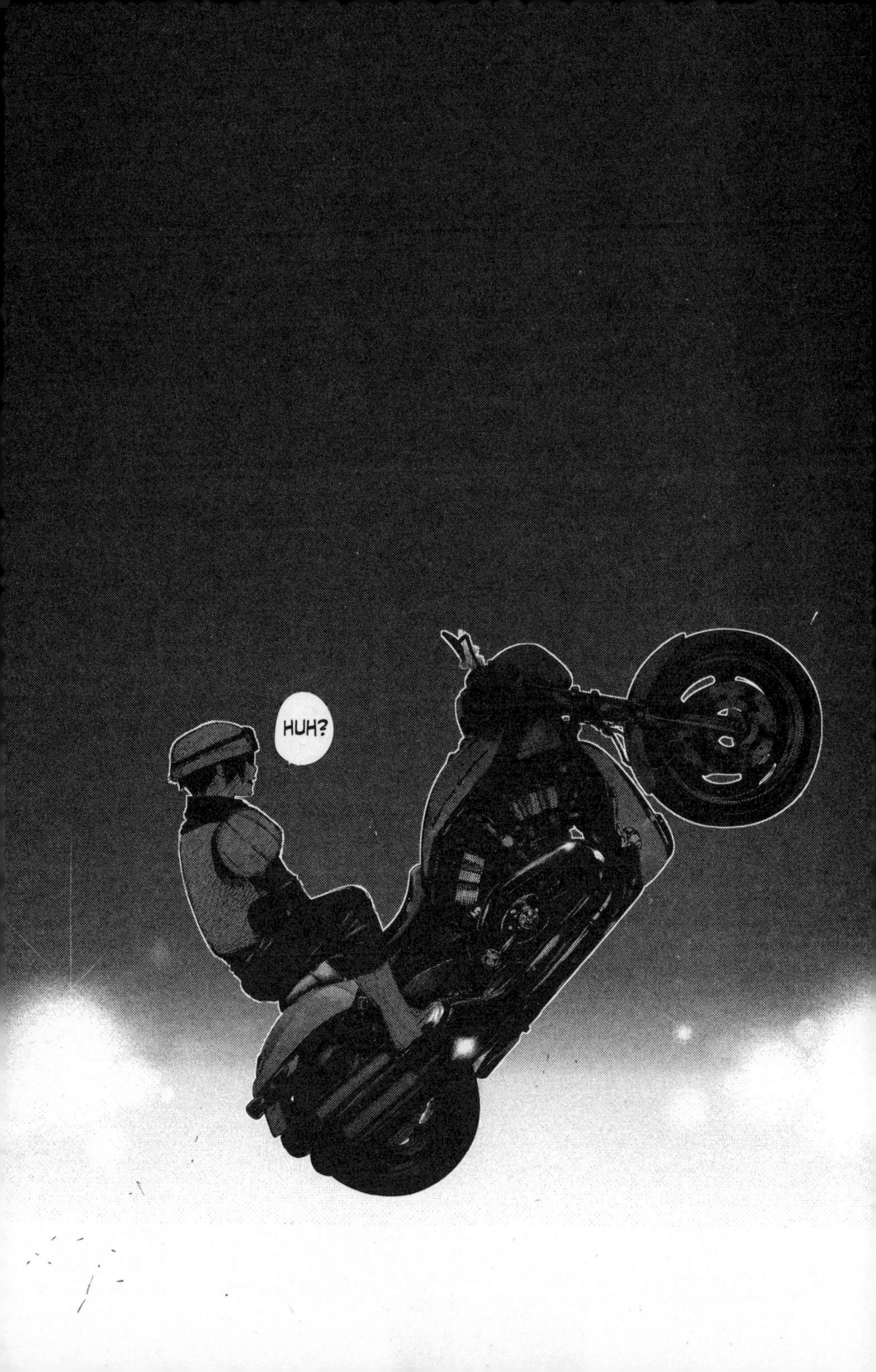
HUH?

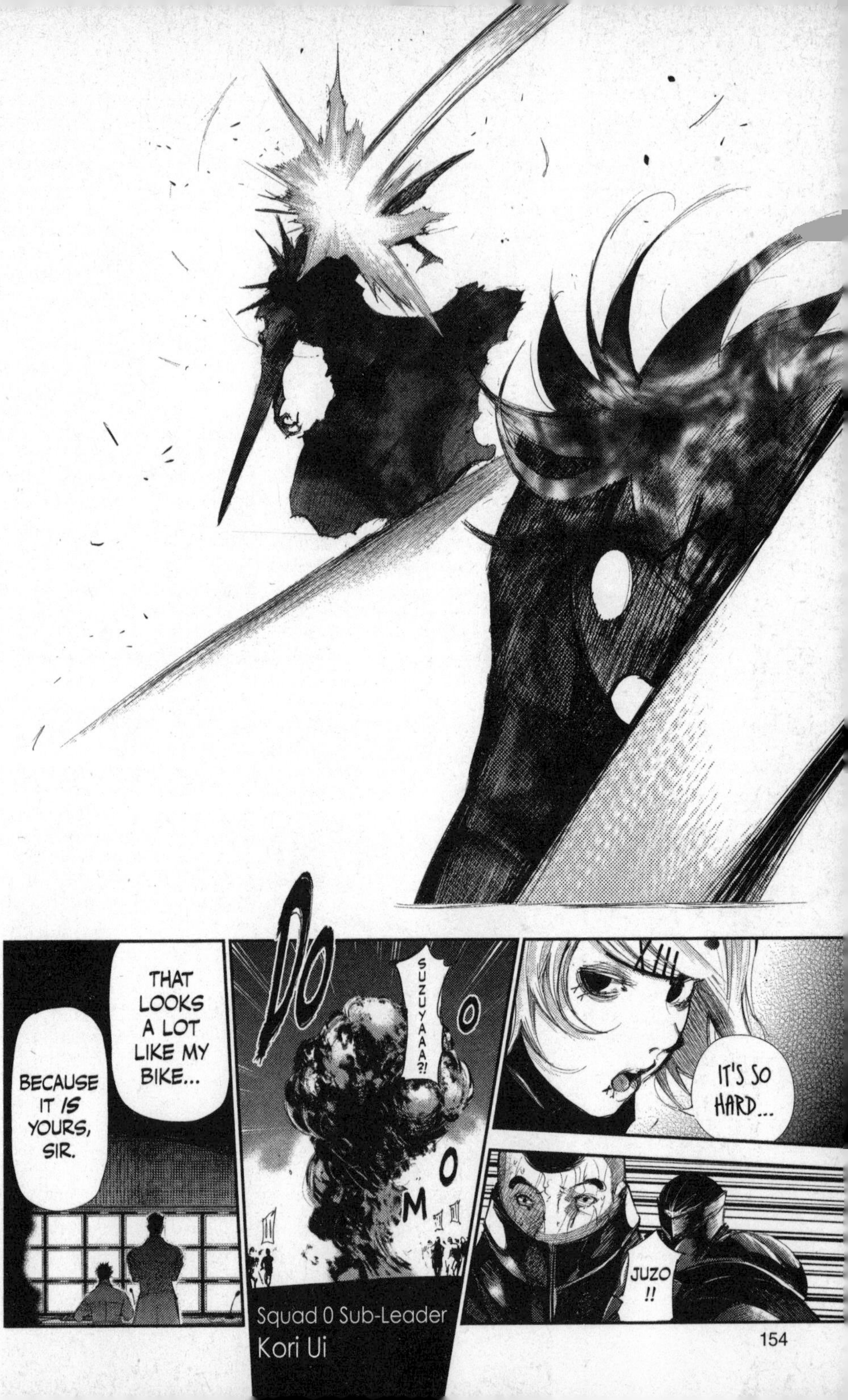
IT'S SO HARD...
JUZO !!
DOOOM
SUZUYAAA?!
Squad 0 Sub-Leader
Kori Ui
THAT LOOKS A LOT LIKE MY BIKE...
BECAUSE IT *IS* YOURS, SIR.

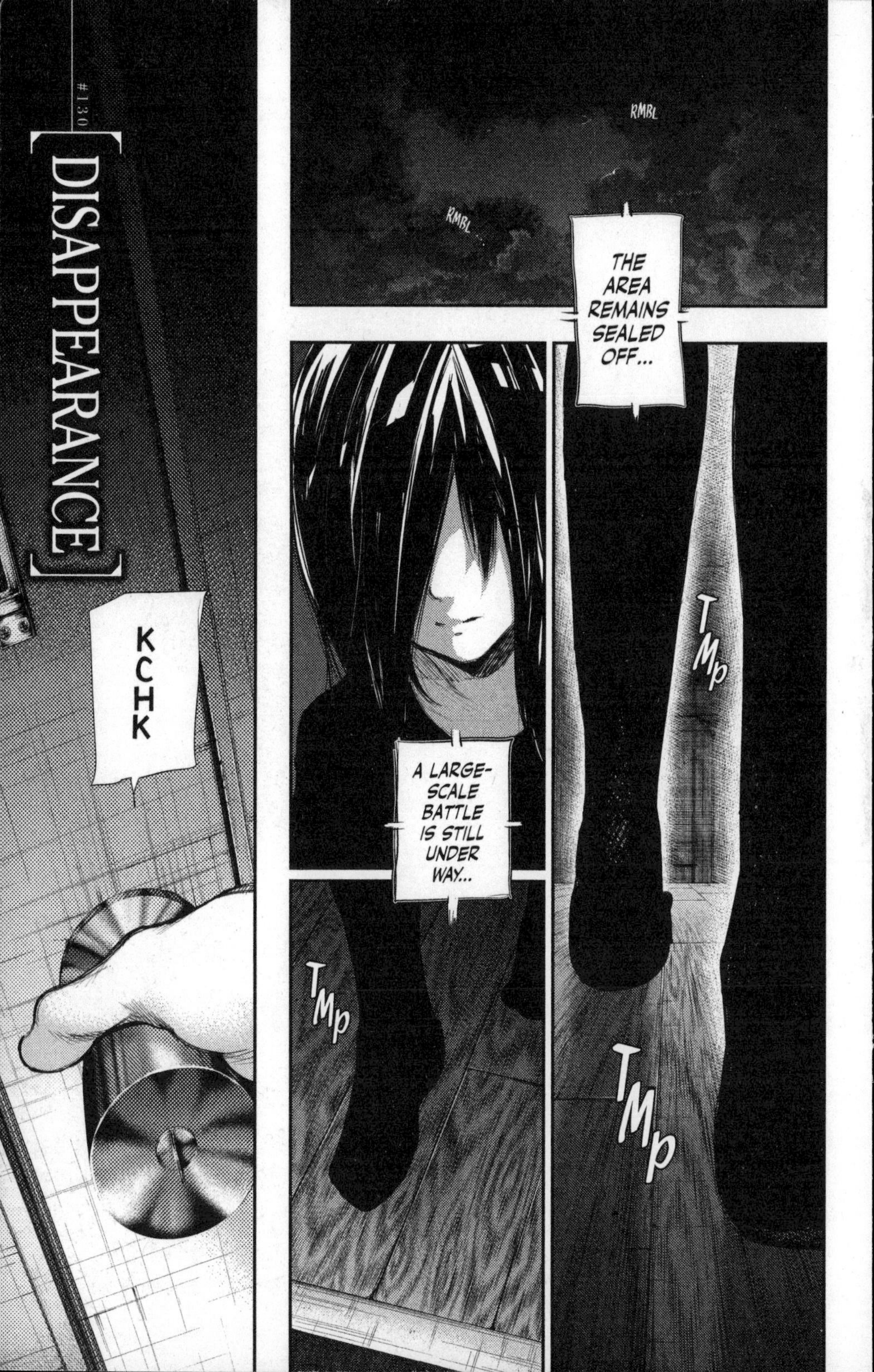
RMBL
RMBL
THE AREA REMAINS SEALED OFF...
TMp
TMp
A LARGE-SCALE BATTLE IS STILL UNDER WAY...
TMp
#130
[DISAPPEARANCE]
KCHK

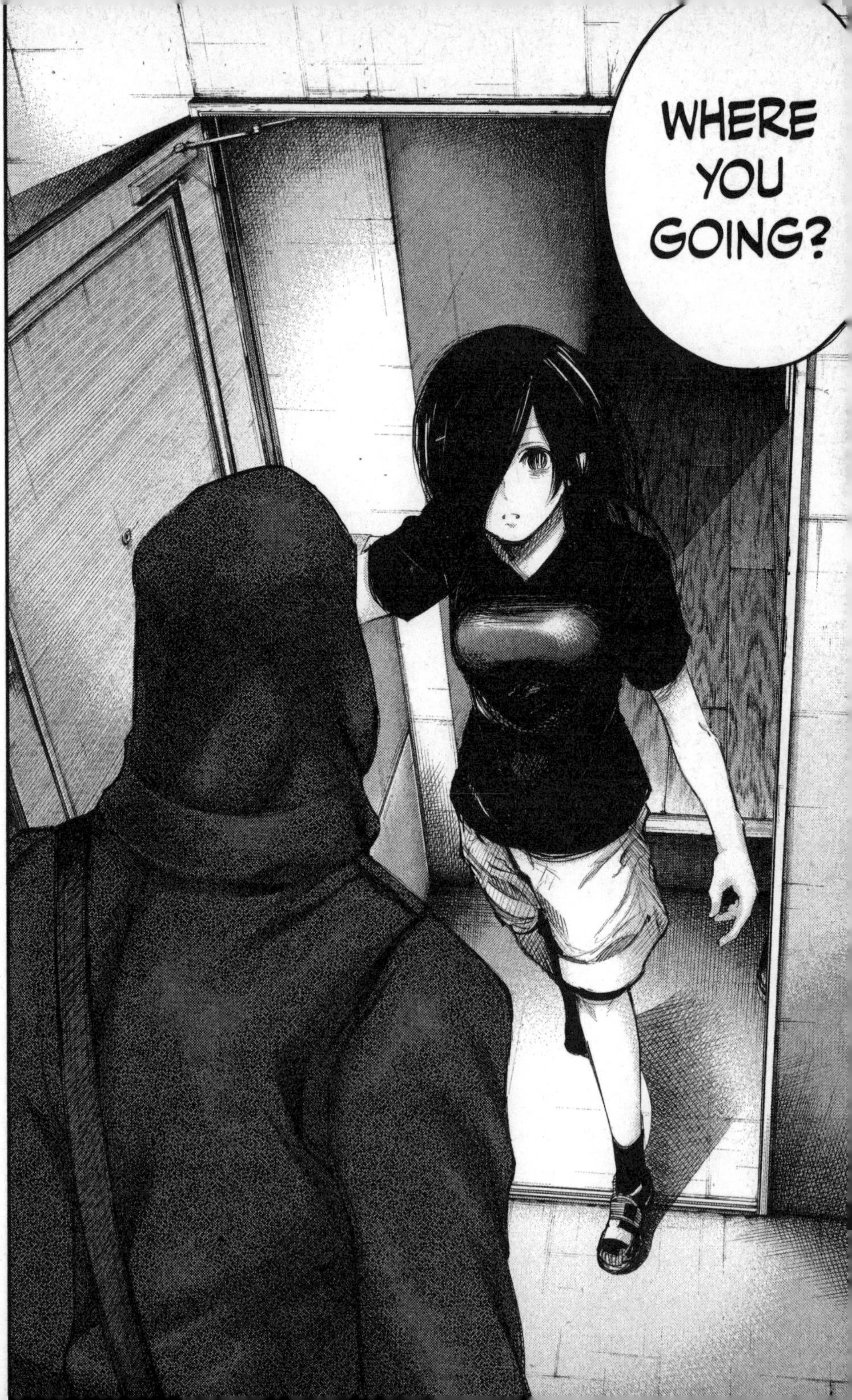
WHERE YOU GOING?

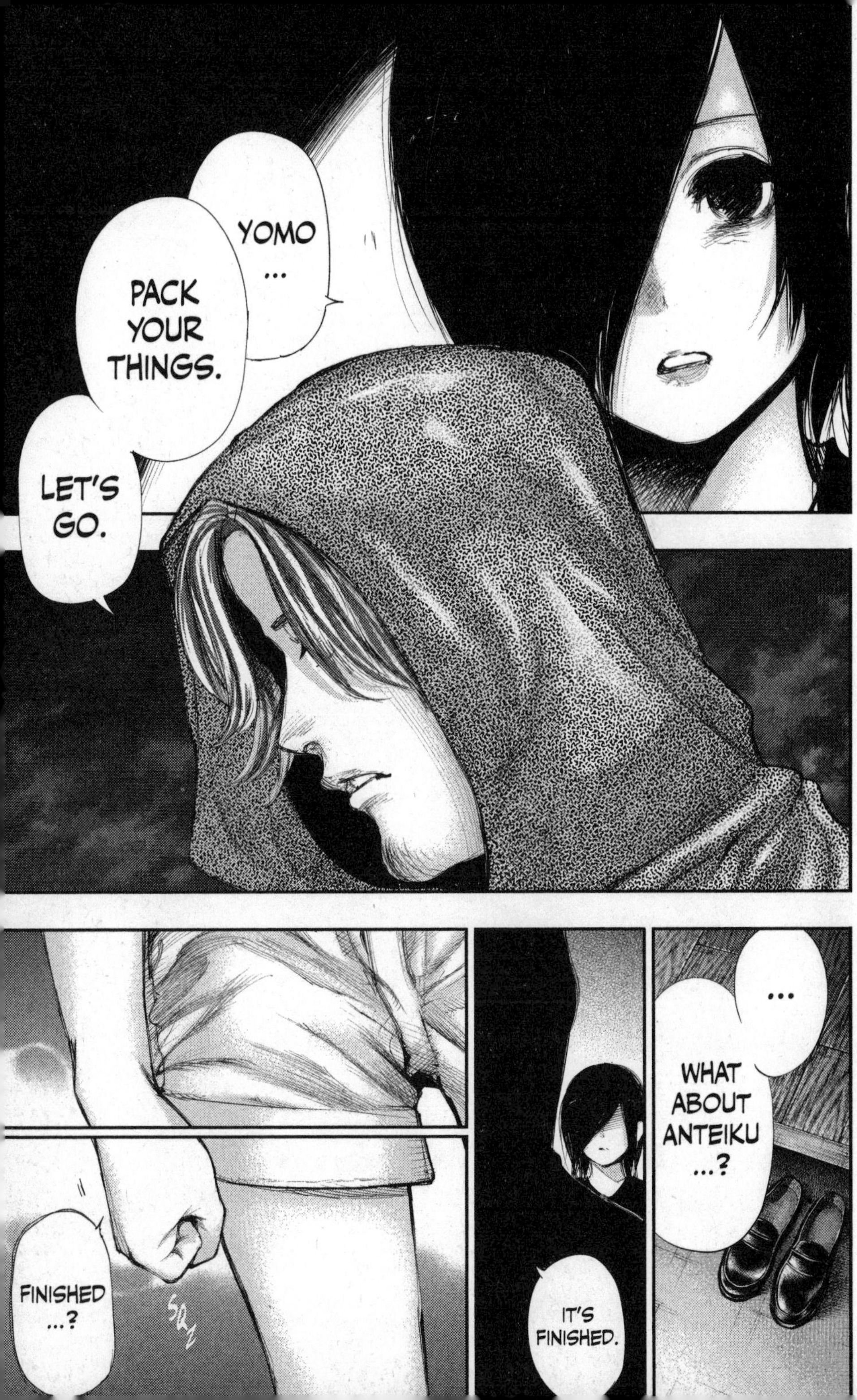
YOMO ...
PACK YOUR THINGS.
LET'S GO.
...
WHAT ABOUT ANTEIKU ...?
IT'S FINISHED.
FINISHED ...?

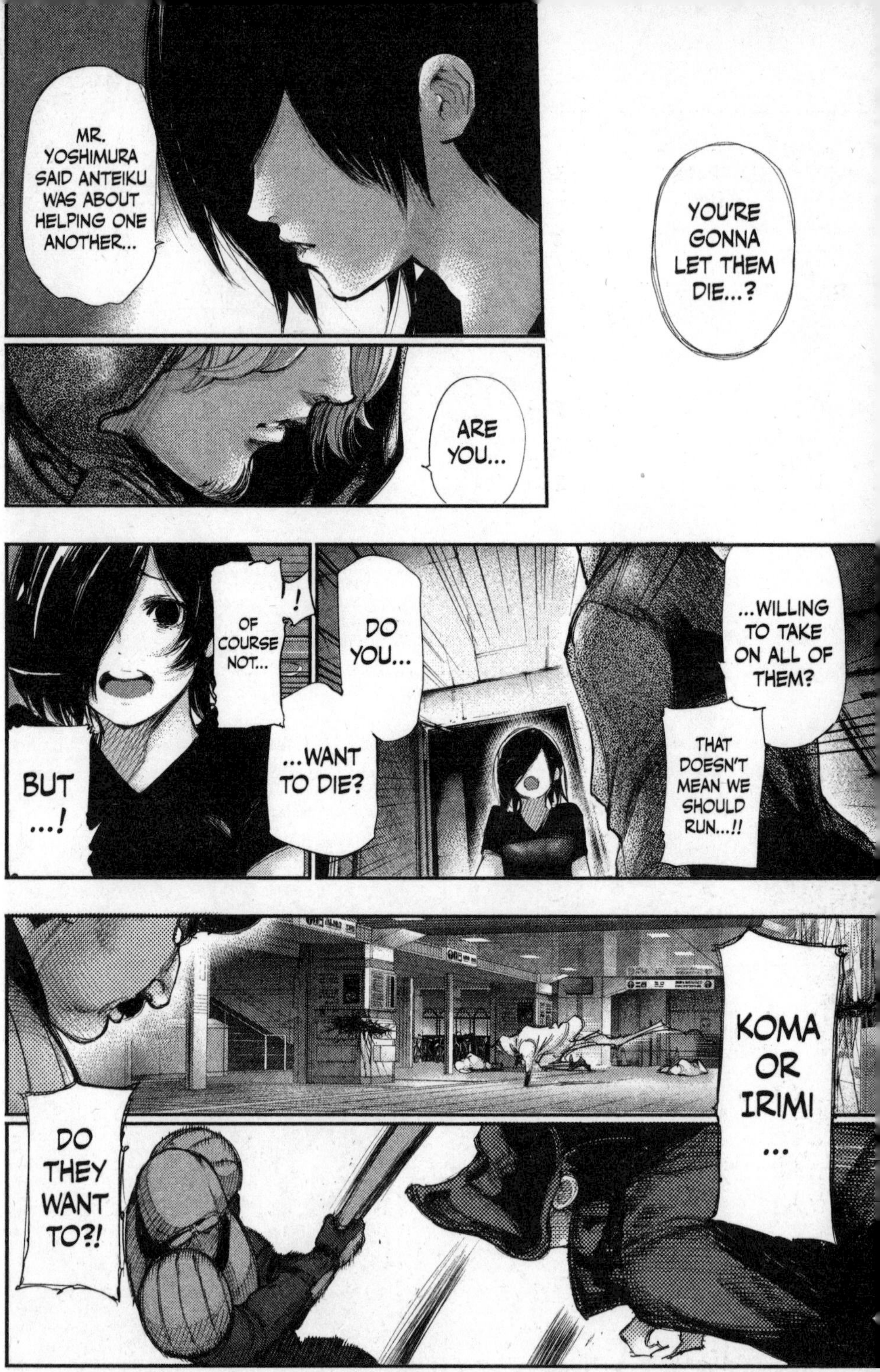
MR. YOSHIMURA SAID ANTEIKU WAS ABOUT HELPING ONE ANOTHER...
YOU'RE GONNA LET THEM DIE...?
ARE YOU...
...WILLING TO TAKE ON ALL OF THEM?
THAT DOESN'T MEAN WE SHOULD RUN...!!
DO YOU...
...WANT TO DIE?
!
OF COURSE NOT...
BUT ...!
KOMA OR IRIMI ...
DO THEY WANT TO?!

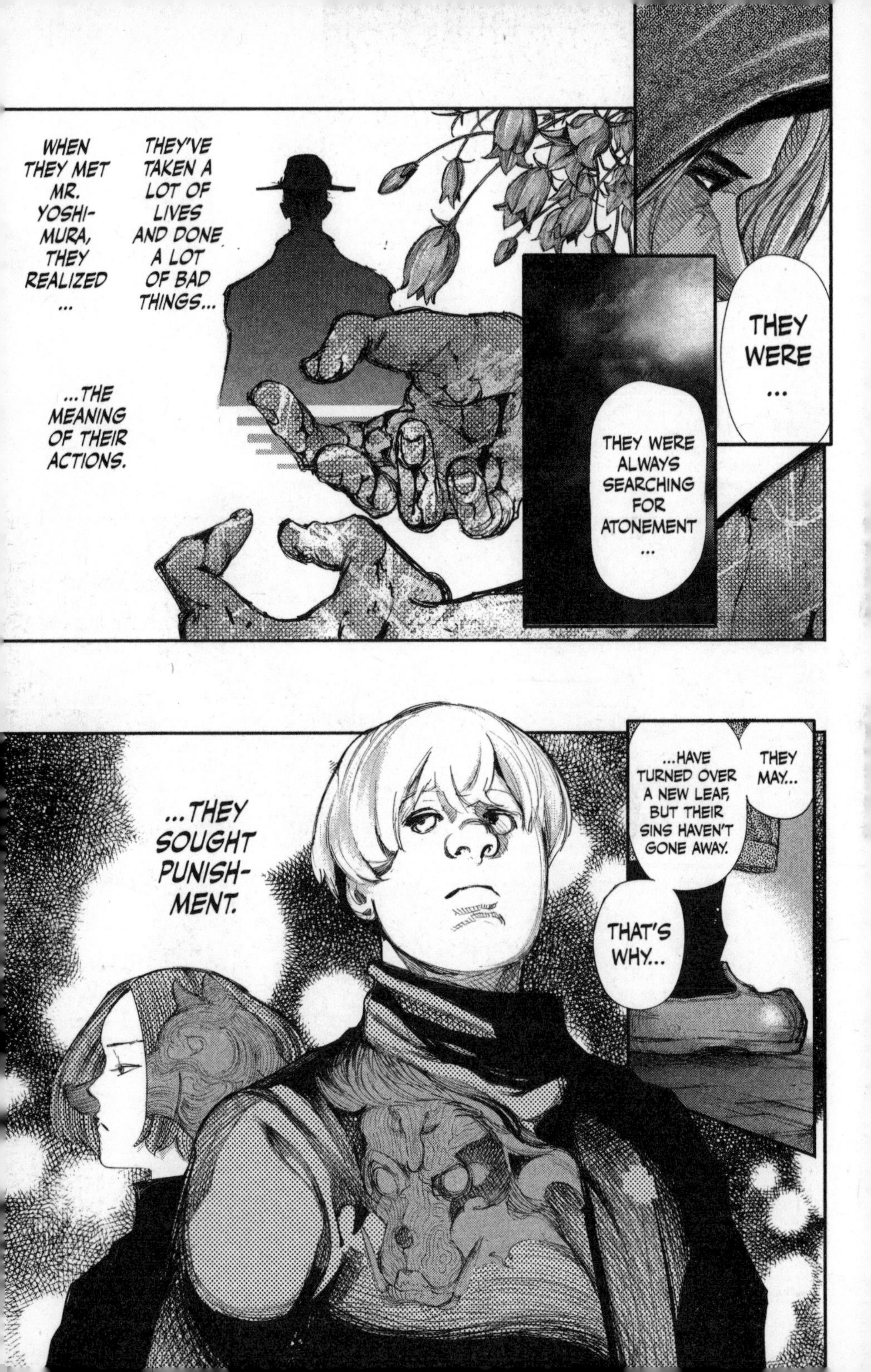
THEY WERE ...
THEY WERE ALWAYS SEARCHING FOR ATONEMENT ...
THEY'VE TAKEN A LOT OF LIVES AND DONE A LOT OF BAD THINGS...
WHEN THEY MET MR. YOSHIMURA, THEY REALIZED ...
...THE MEANING OF THEIR ACTIONS.
THEY MAY...
...HAVE TURNED OVER A NEW LEAF, BUT THEIR SINS HAVEN'T GONE AWAY.
THAT'S WHY...
...THEY SOUGHT PUNISHMENT.

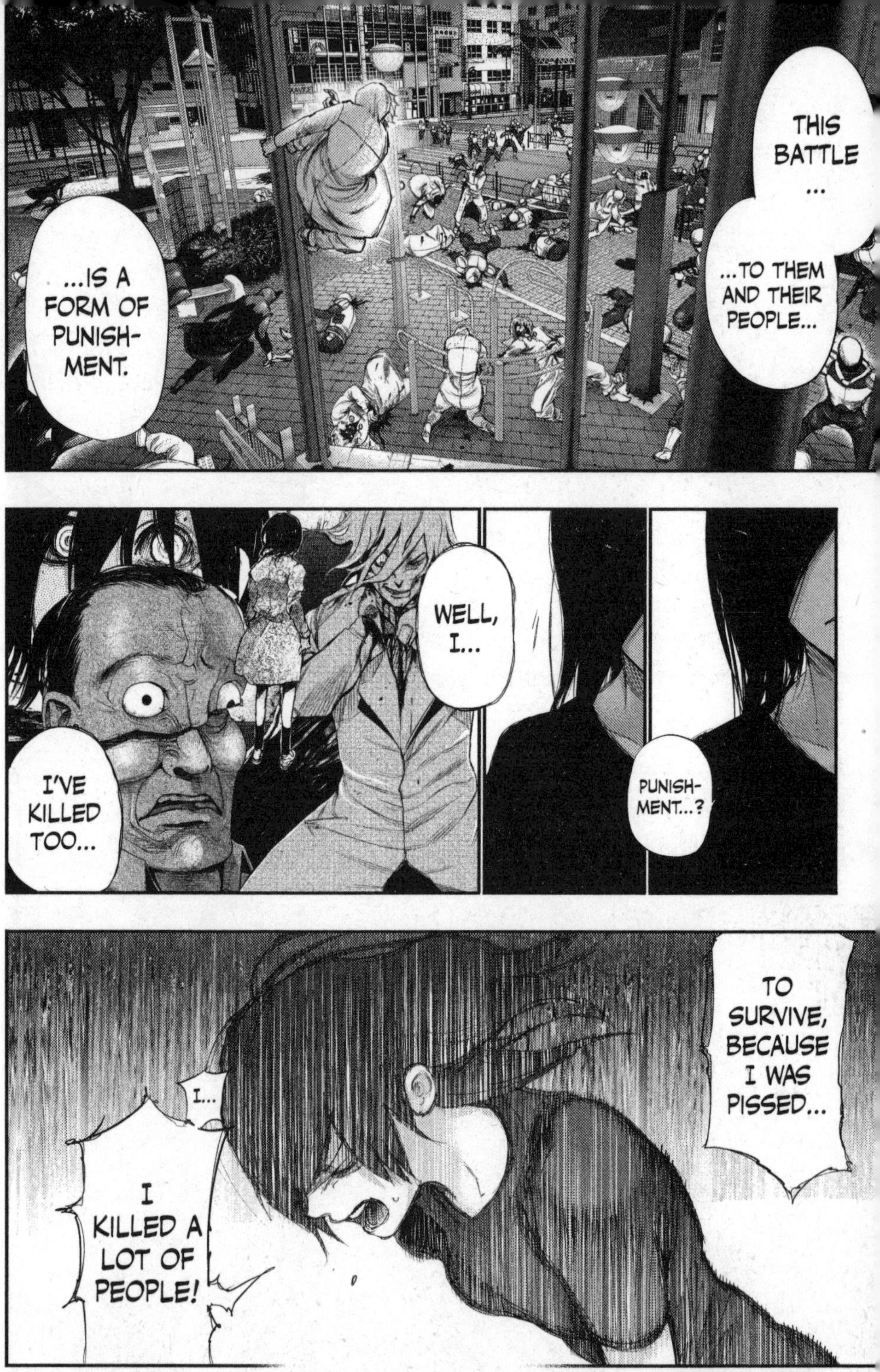
THIS BATTLE ...
...TO THEM AND THEIR PEOPLE...
...IS A FORM OF PUNISHMENT.
PUNISHMENT...?
WELL, I...
I'VE KILLED TOO...
TO SURVIVE, BECAUSE I WAS PISSED...
I...
I KILLED A LOT OF PEOPLE!

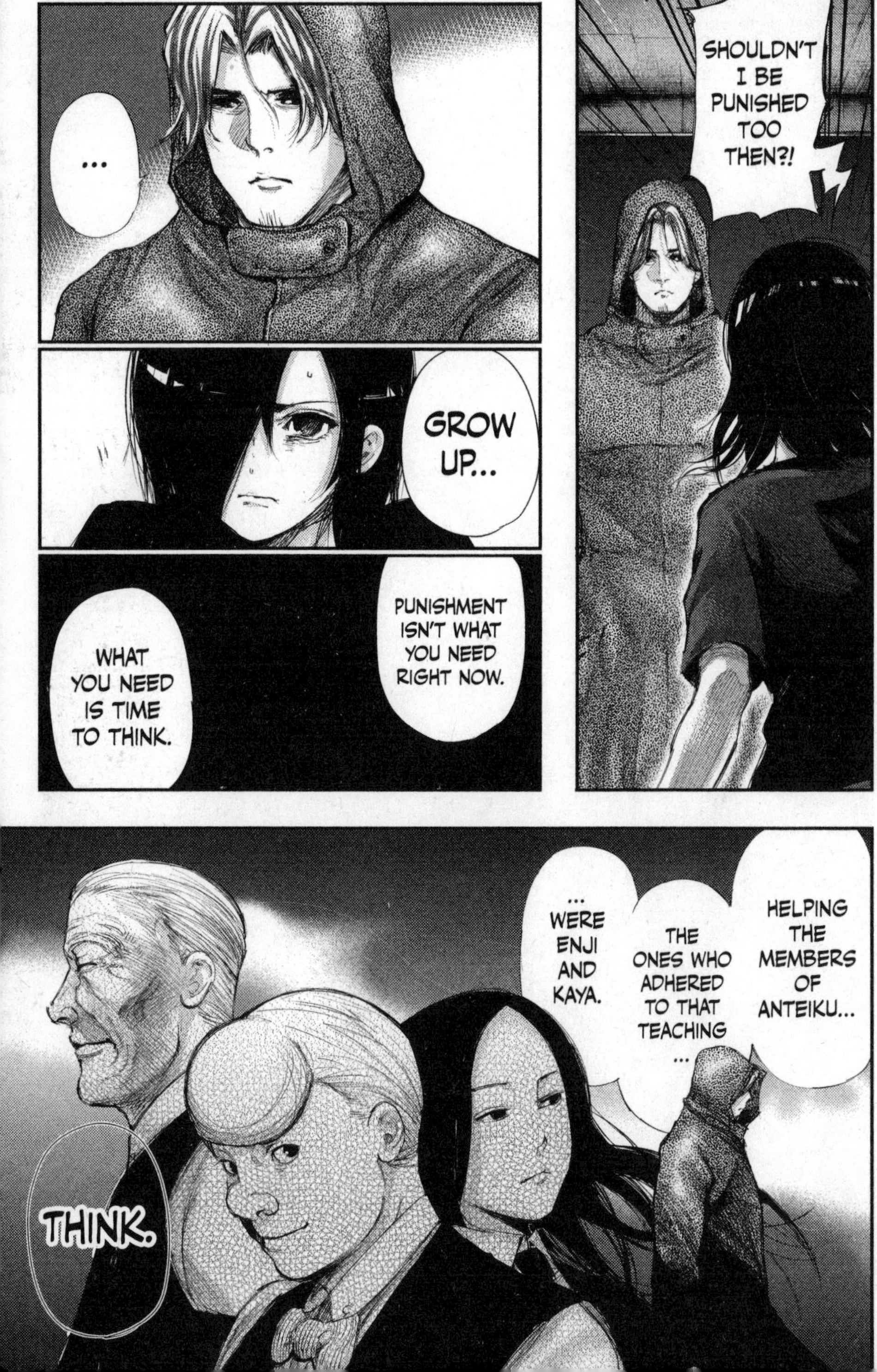
SHOULDN'T I BE PUNISHED TOO THEN?!
...
GROW UP...
PUNISHMENT ISN'T WHAT YOU NEED RIGHT NOW.
WHAT YOU NEED IS TIME TO THINK.
HELPING THE MEMBERS OF ANTEIKU...
THE ONES WHO ADHERED TO THAT TEACHING ...
... WERE ENJI AND KAYA.
THINK.

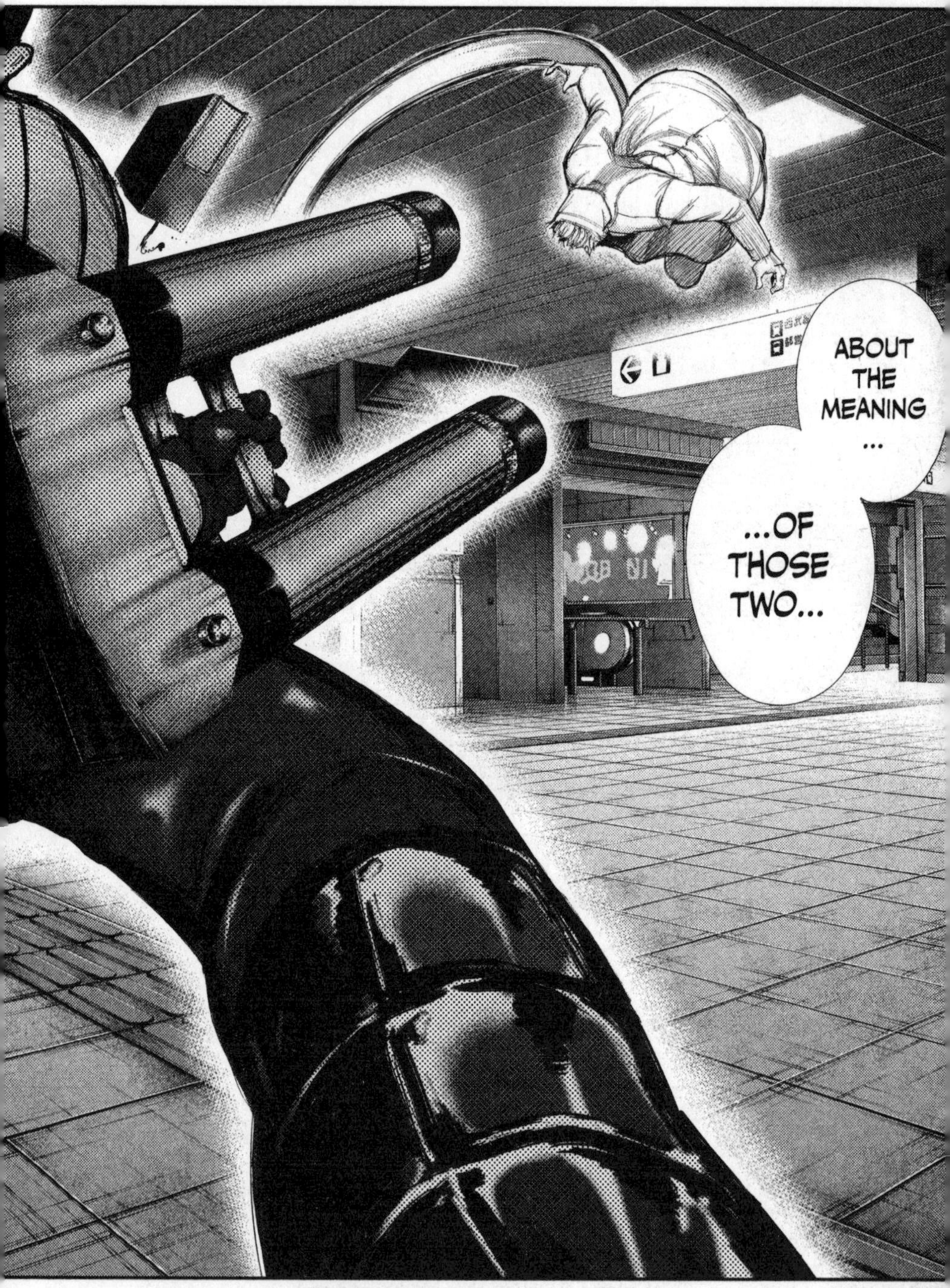
ABOUT THE MEANING ...
...OF THOSE TWO...

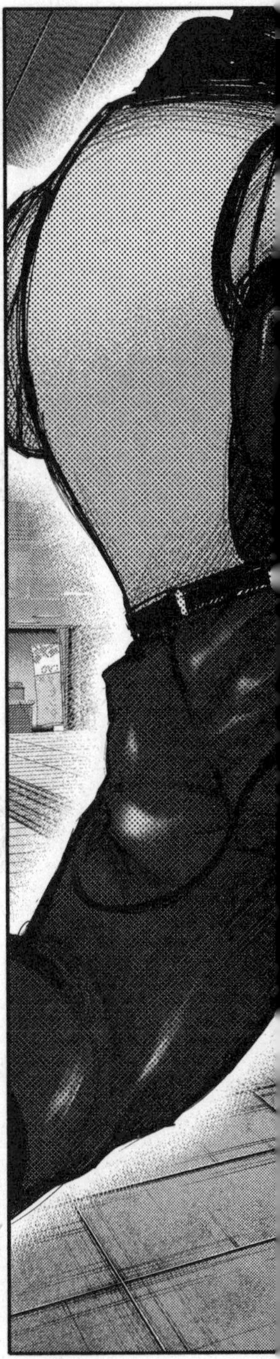

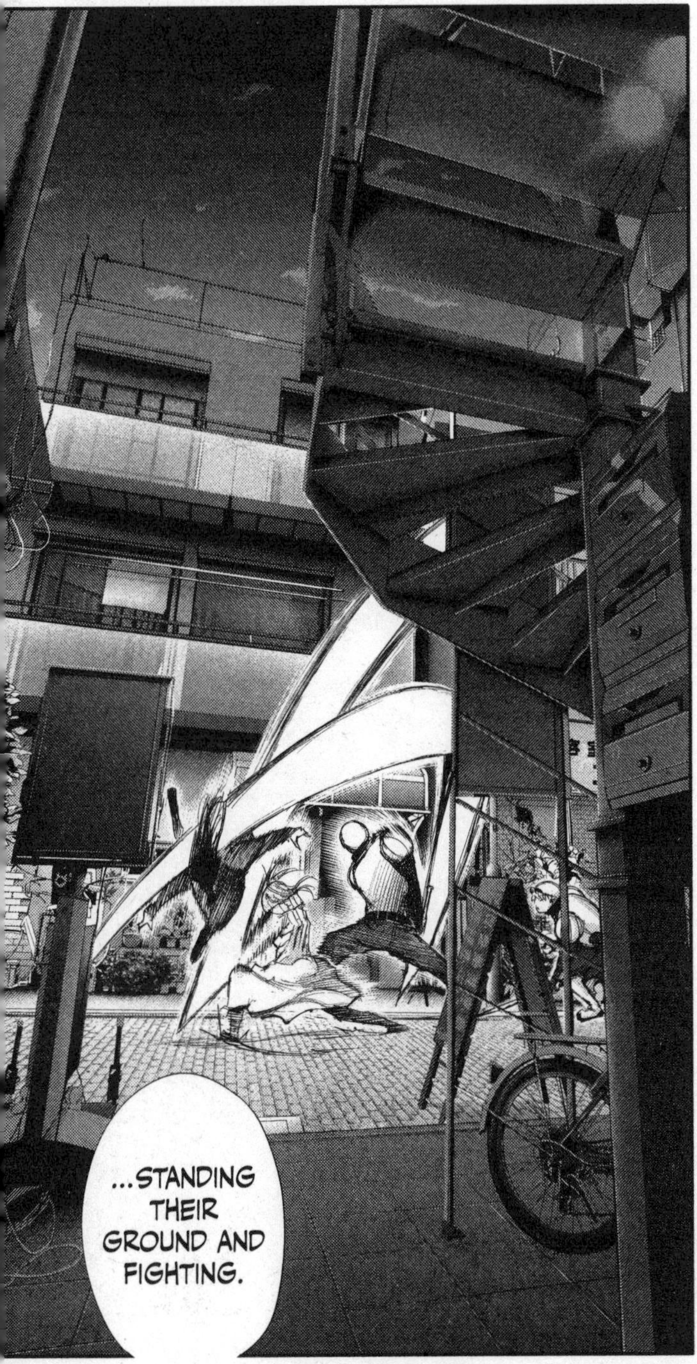

...STANDING THEIR GROUND AND FIGHTING.

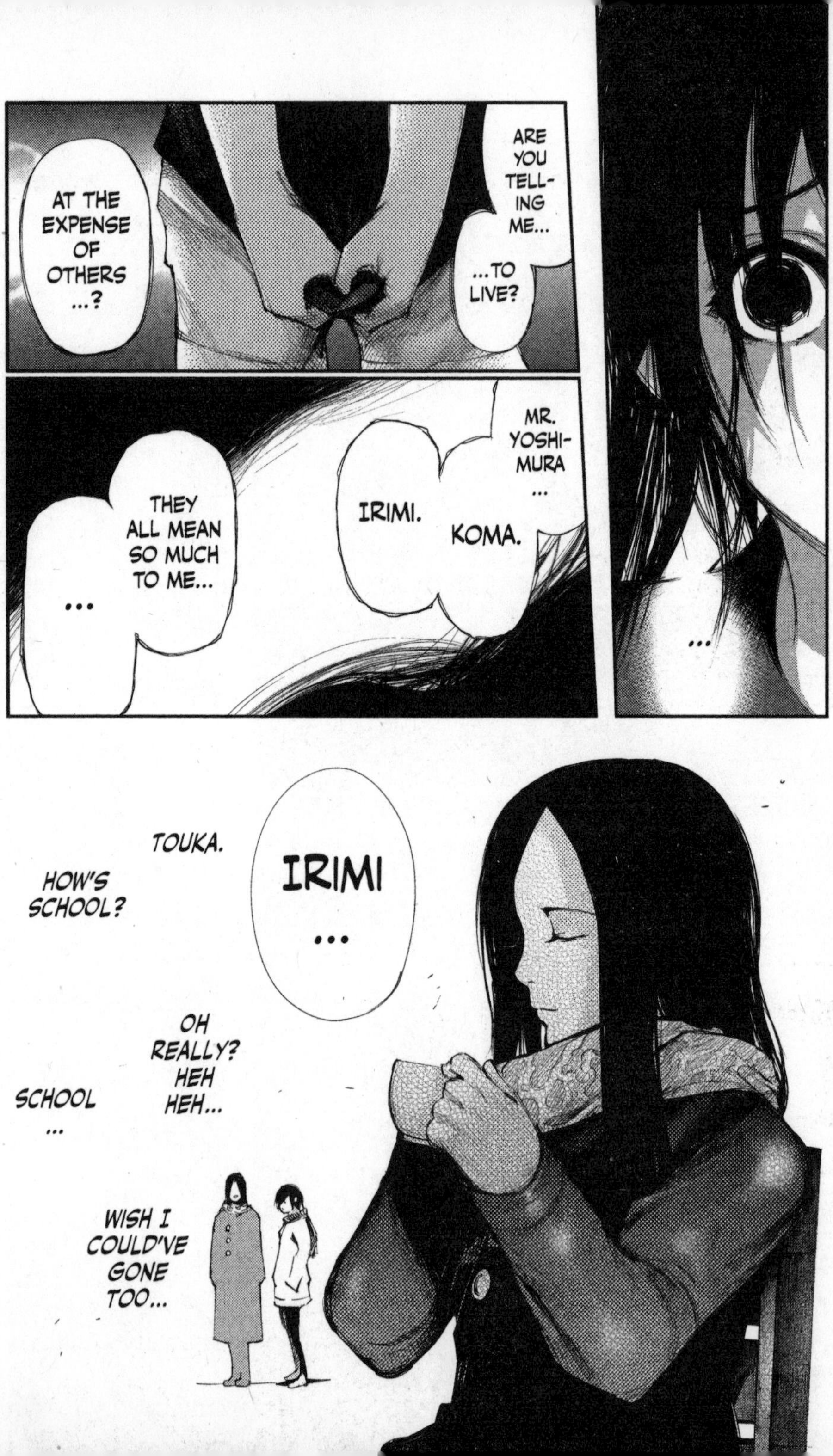
...
ARE YOU TELLING ME...
...TO LIVE?
AT THE EXPENSE OF OTHERS...?
MR. YOSHIMURA...
KOMA.
IRIMI.
THEY ALL MEAN SO MUCH TO ME...
...
IRIMI...
TOUKA.
HOW'S SCHOOL?
OH REALLY? HEH HEH...
SCHOOL...
WISH I COULD'VE GONE TOO...

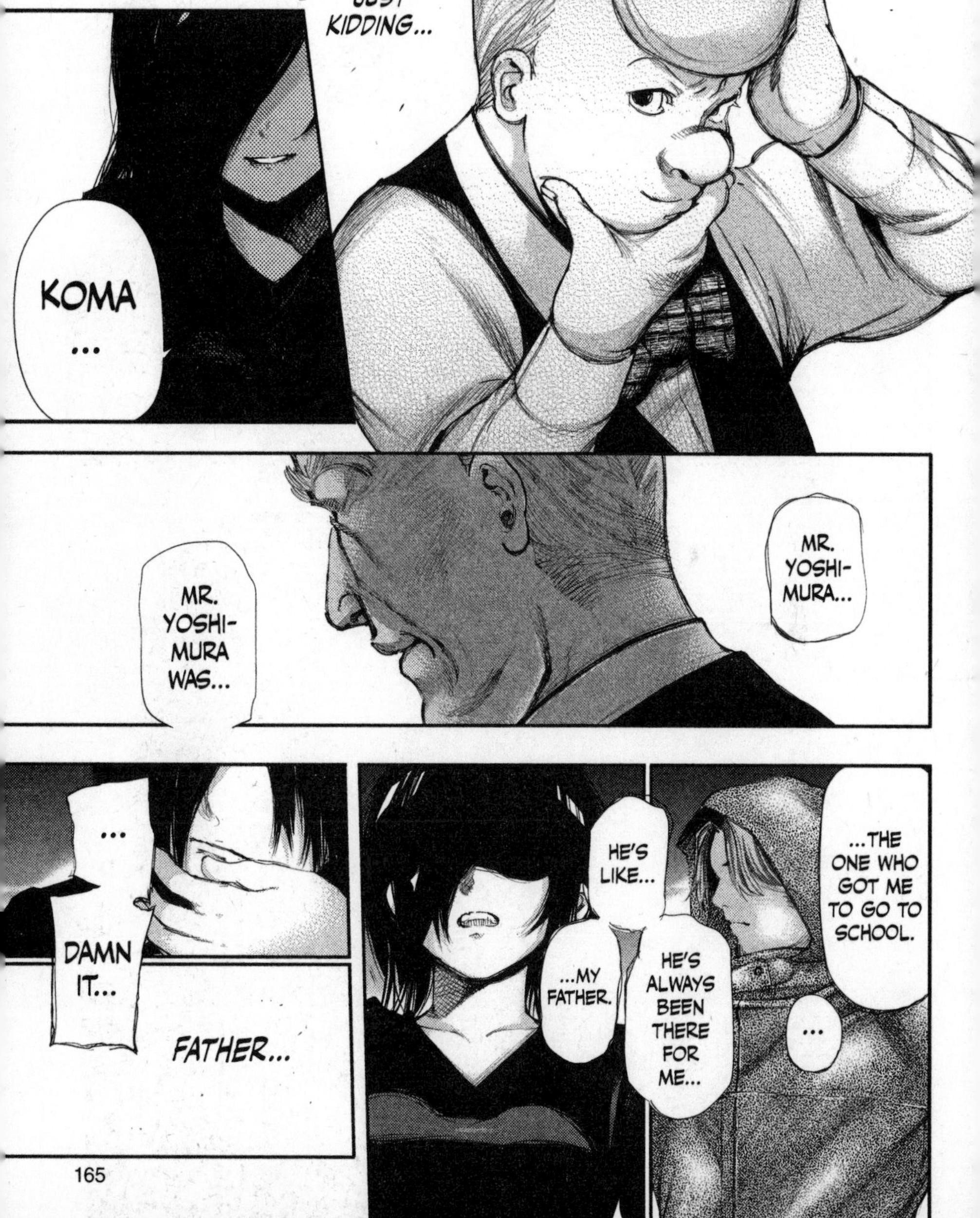
MM? YOU SAY MY TIE'S UGLY?
C'MON NOW, TOUKA...
I HOPE YOU'RE JUST KIDDING...
KOMA ...
MR. YOSHI-MURA...
MR. YOSHI-MURA WAS...
...THE ONE WHO GOT ME TO GO TO SCHOOL.
...
HE'S LIKE...
...MY FATHER.
HE'S ALWAYS BEEN THERE FOR ME...
...
DAMN IT...
FATHER...

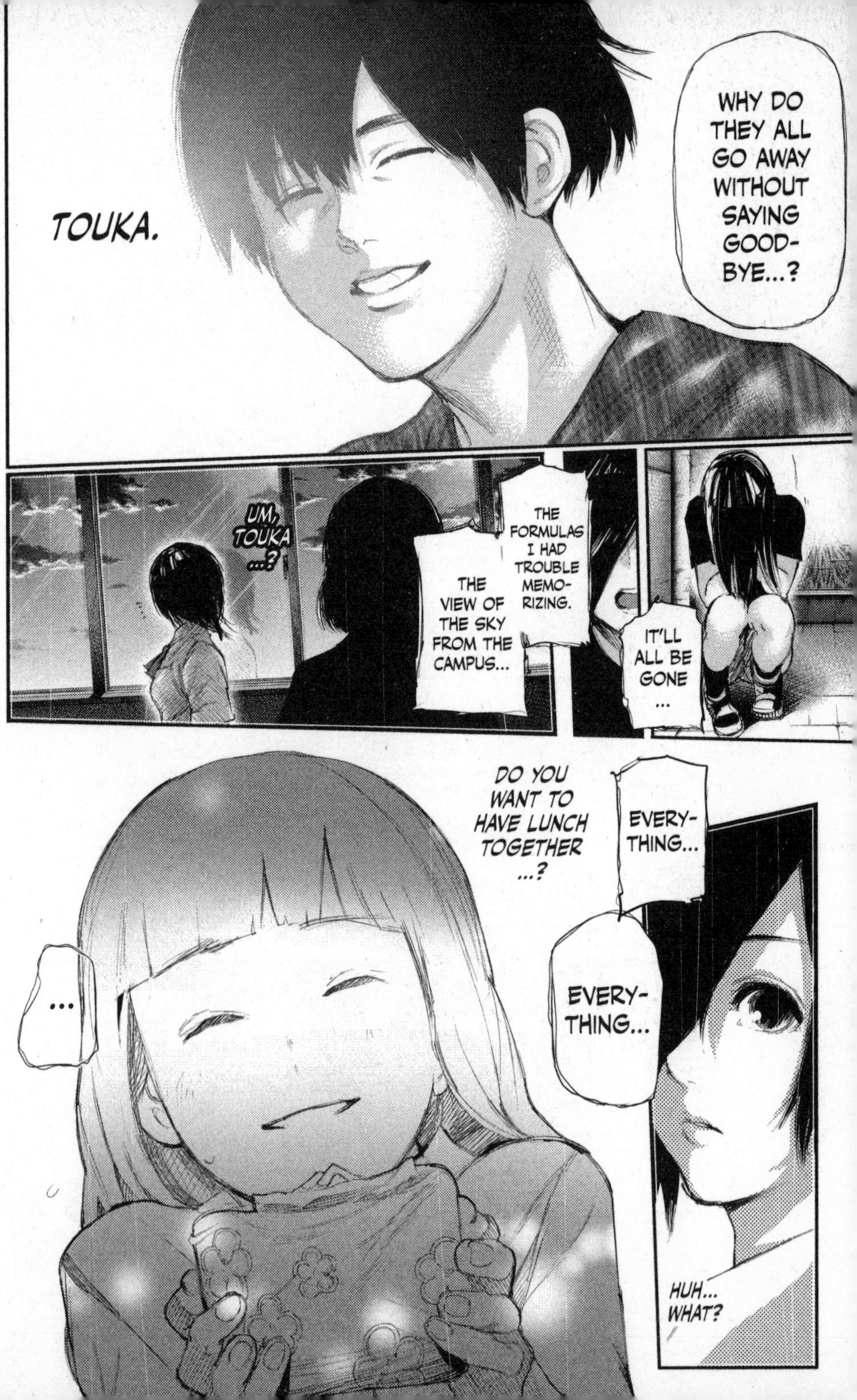
WHY DO THEY ALL GO AWAY WITHOUT SAYING GOOD-BYE...?
TOUKA.
IT'LL ALL BE GONE...
THE FORMULAS I HAD TROUBLE MEMORIZING.
THE VIEW OF THE SKY FROM THE CAMPUS...
UM, TOUKA...?
EVERYTHING...
DO YOU WANT TO HAVE LUNCH TOGETHER...?
EVERYTHING...
HUH... WHAT?
...

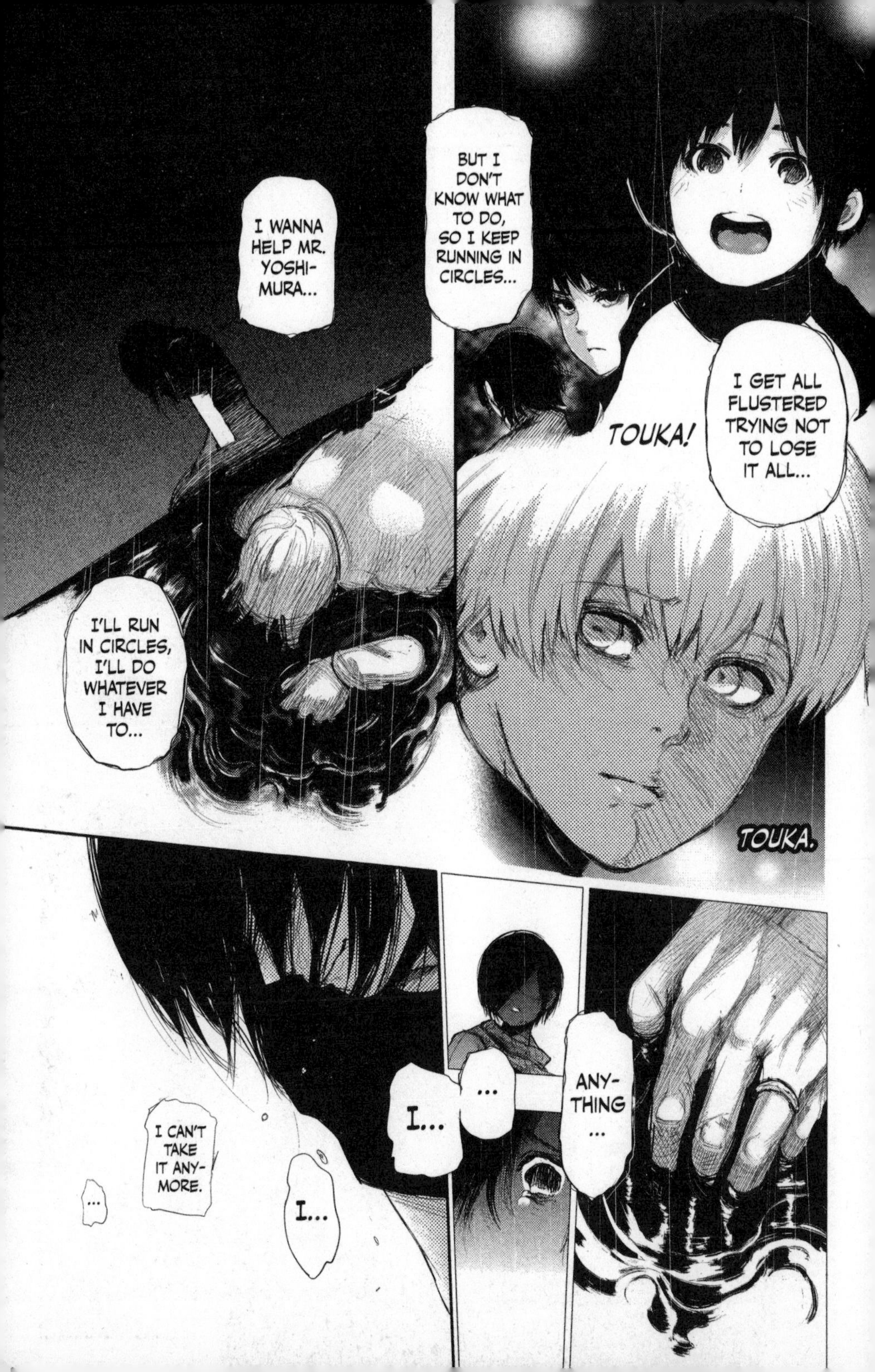
I WANNA HELP MR. YOSHI-MURA...
BUT I DON'T KNOW WHAT TO DO, SO I KEEP RUNNING IN CIRCLES...
I GET ALL FLUSTERED TRYING NOT TO LOSE IT ALL...
I'LL RUN IN CIRCLES, I'LL DO WHATEVER I HAVE TO...
TOUKA!
TOUKA.
ANY-THING...
...
I...
I...
I CAN'T TAKE IT ANY-MORE.
...

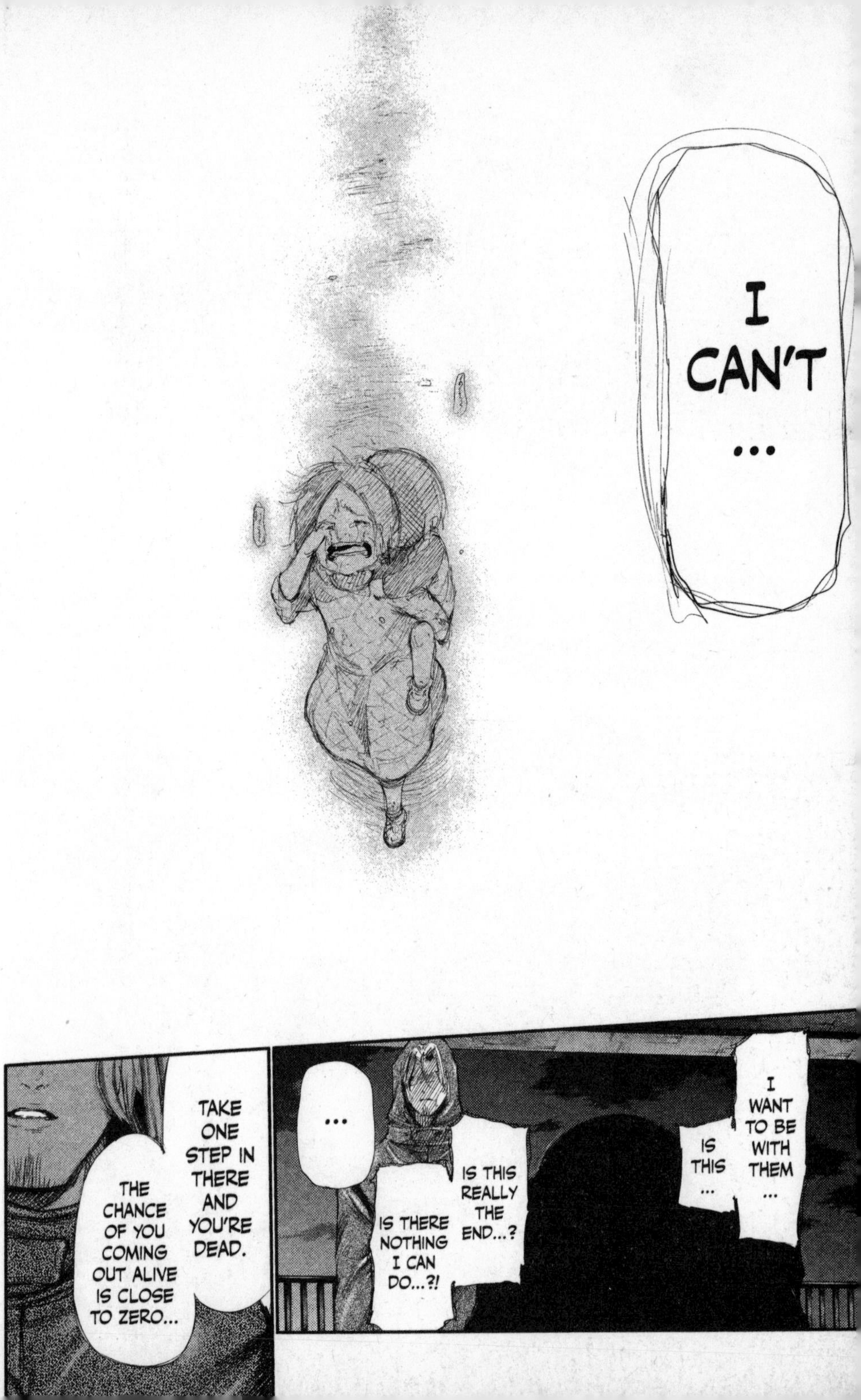
I CAN'T ...
I WANT TO BE WITH THEM ...
IS THIS ...
IS THIS REALLY THE END...?
IS THERE NOTHING I CAN DO...?!
...
TAKE ONE STEP IN THERE AND YOU'RE DEAD.
THE CHANCE OF YOU COMING OUT ALIVE IS CLOSE TO ZERO...

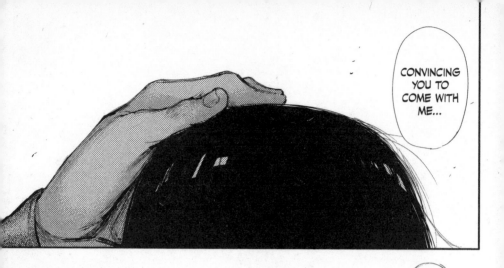

CONVINCING YOU TO COME WITH ME...

THAT'S MY LAST JOB FOR ANTEIKU.

TOUKA.

I KNOW HOW YOU FEEL...

BUT...

WE'RE MEANT TO...

...LIVE WITH THE LOSSES.

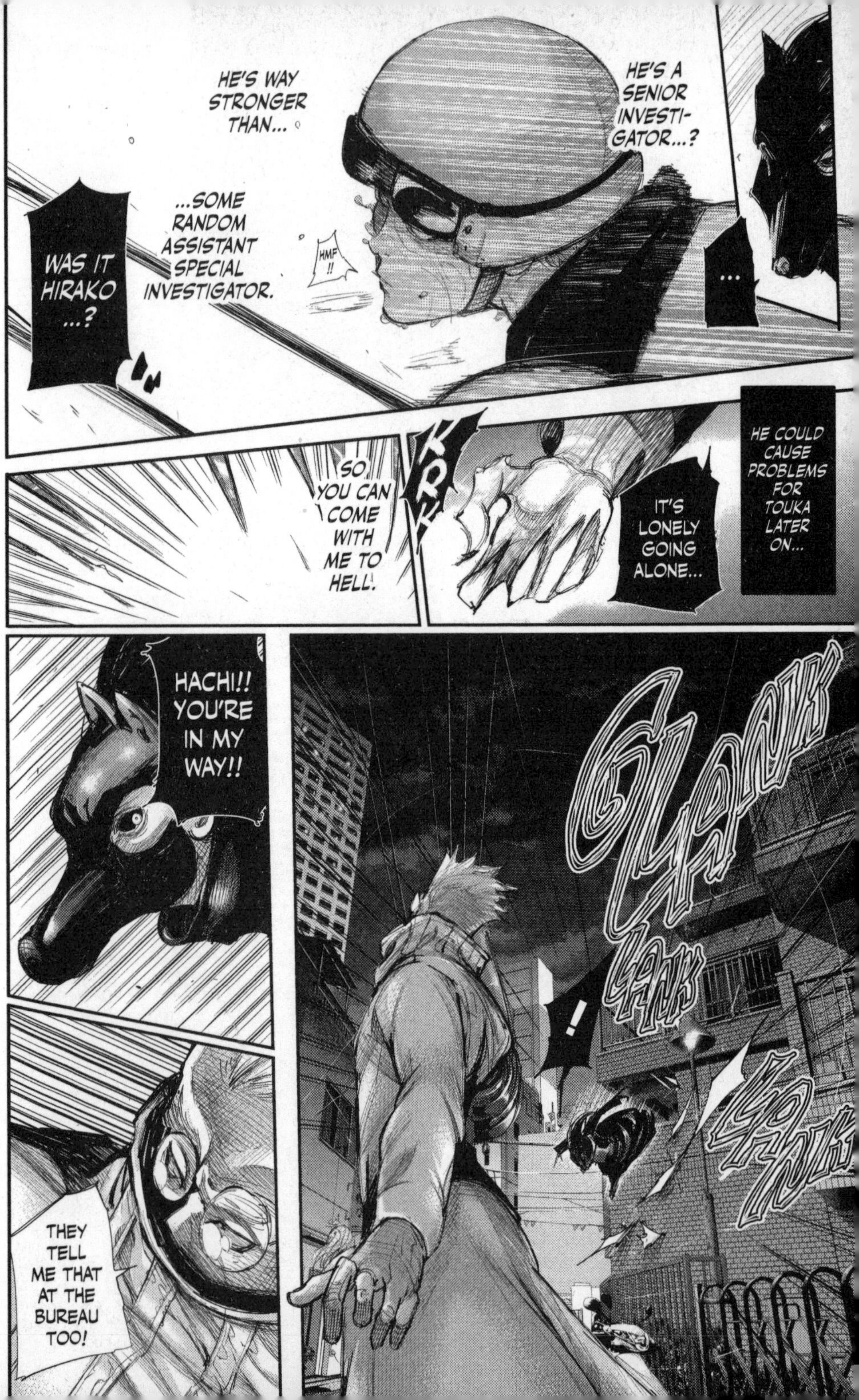
...
HE'S A SENIOR INVESTIGATOR...?
HE'S WAY STRONGER THAN...
...SOME RANDOM ASSISTANT SPECIAL INVESTIGATOR.
HMF!!
WAS IT HIRAKO...?
HE COULD CAUSE PROBLEMS FOR TOUKA LATER ON...
IT'S LONELY GOING ALONE...
KRK
SO YOU CAN COME WITH ME TO HELL.
!
HACHI!! YOU'RE IN MY WAY!!
THEY TELL ME THAT AT THE BUREAU TOO!

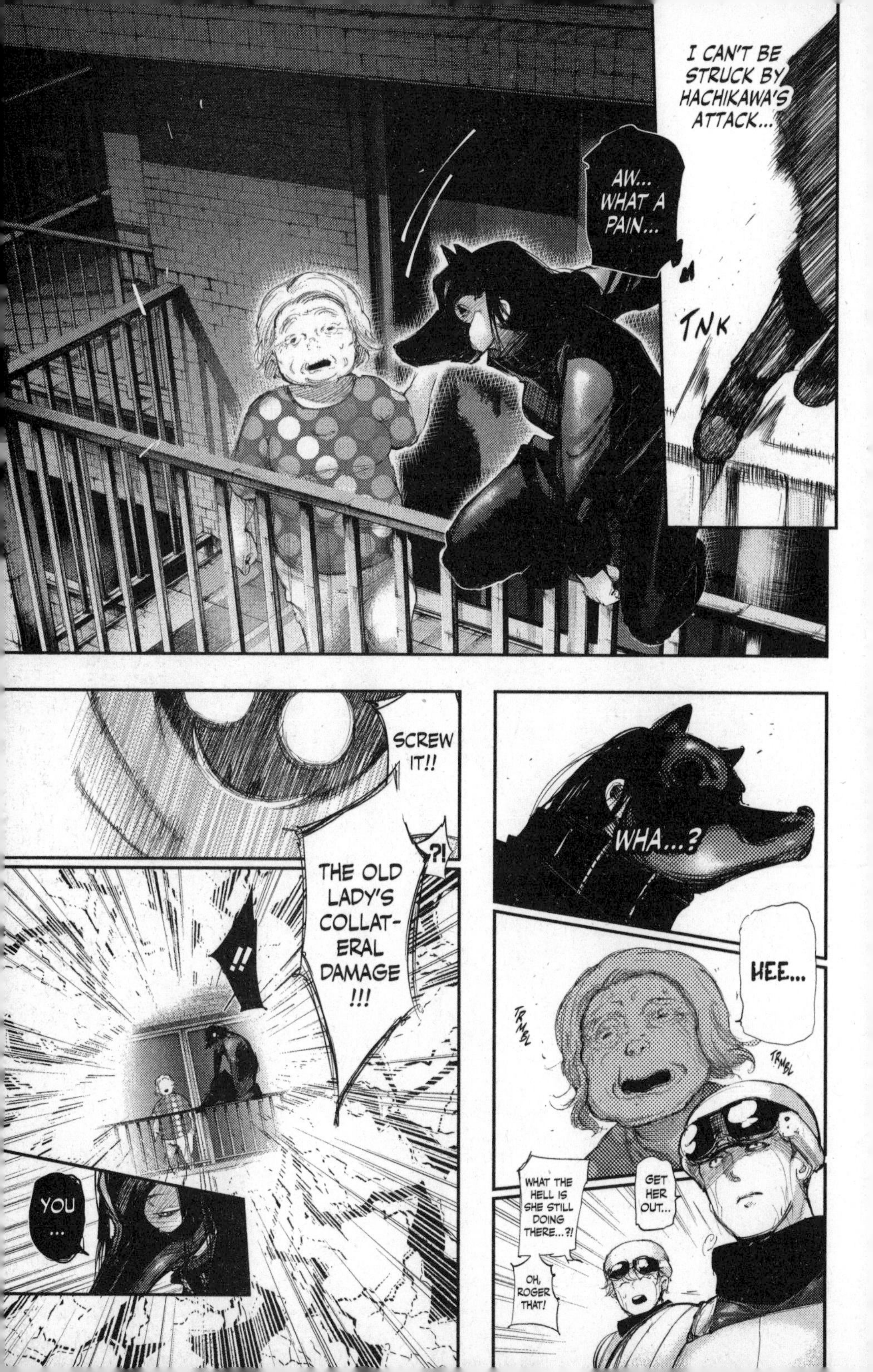
I CAN'T BE STRUCK BY HACHIKAWA'S ATTACK...
AW... WHAT A PAIN...
TNK
WHA...?
HEE...
TRMBL
TRMBL
GET HER OUT...
WHAT THE HELL IS SHE STILL DOING THERE...?!
OH, ROGER THAT!
SCREW IT!!
?!
THE OLD LADY'S COLLATERAL DAMAGE!!!
!!
YOU ...

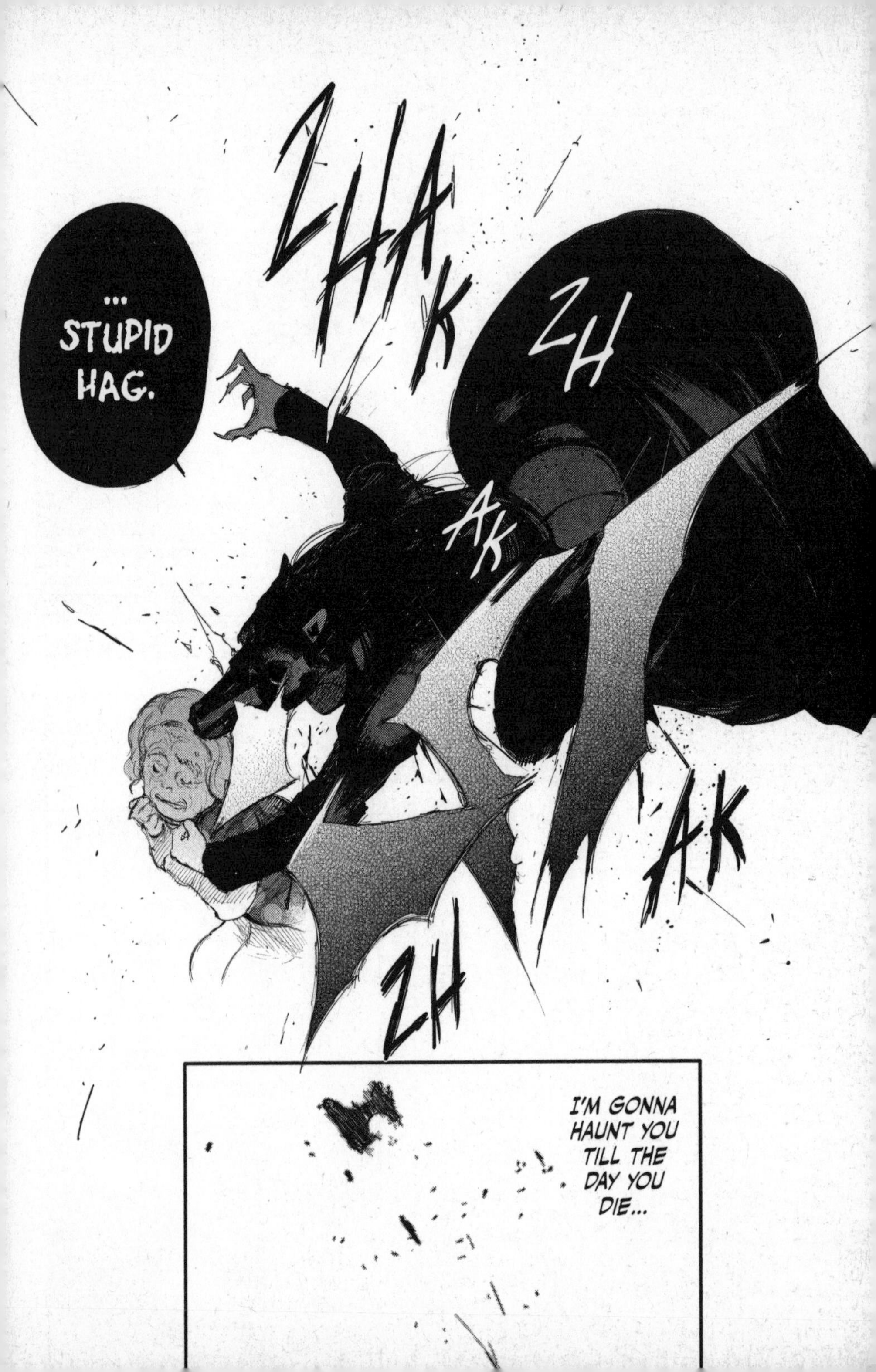
ZHAK
ZH
AK
... STUPID HAG.
AK
ZH
I'M GONNA HAUNT YOU TILL THE DAY YOU DIE...

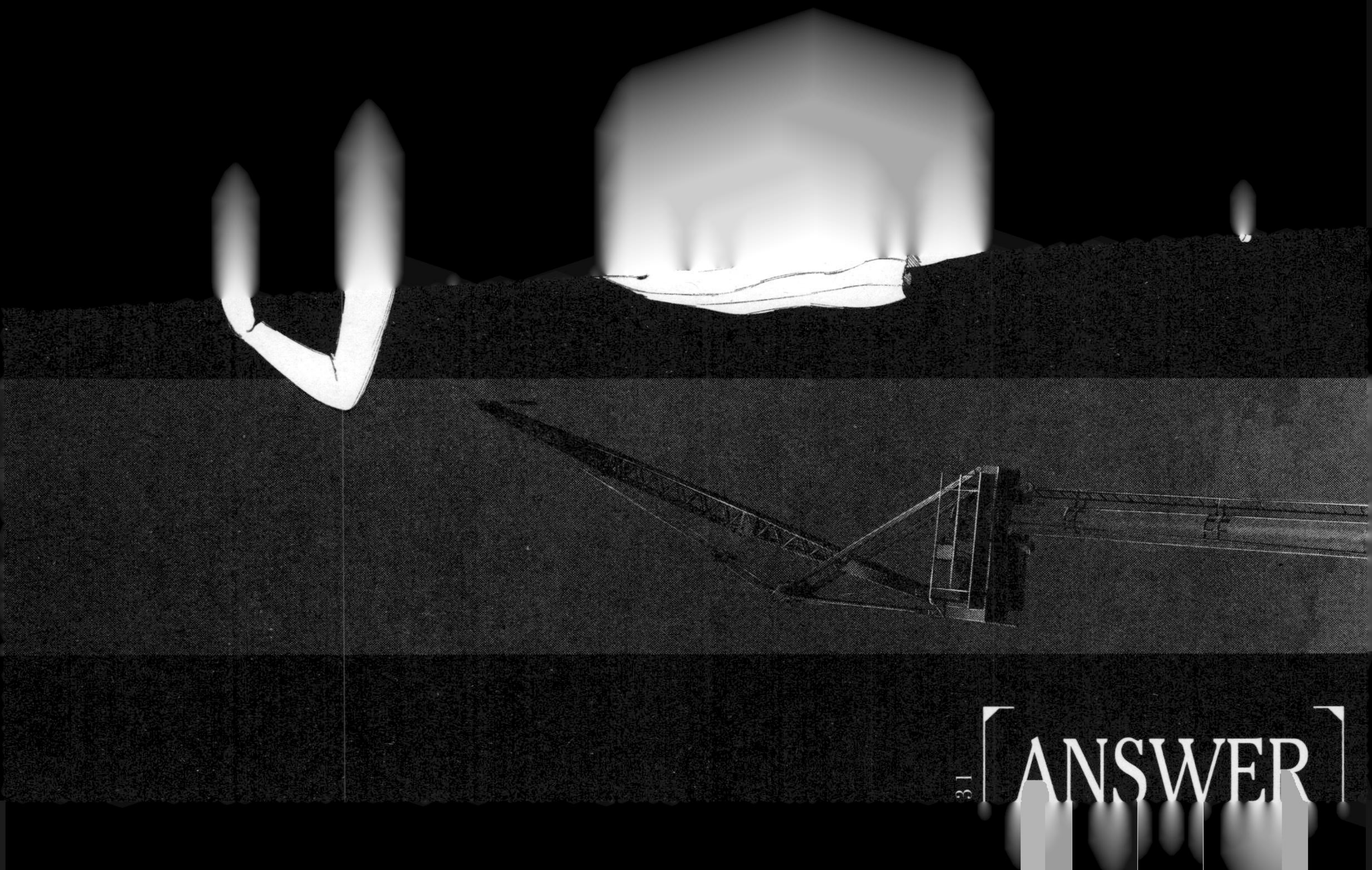
31
ANSWER

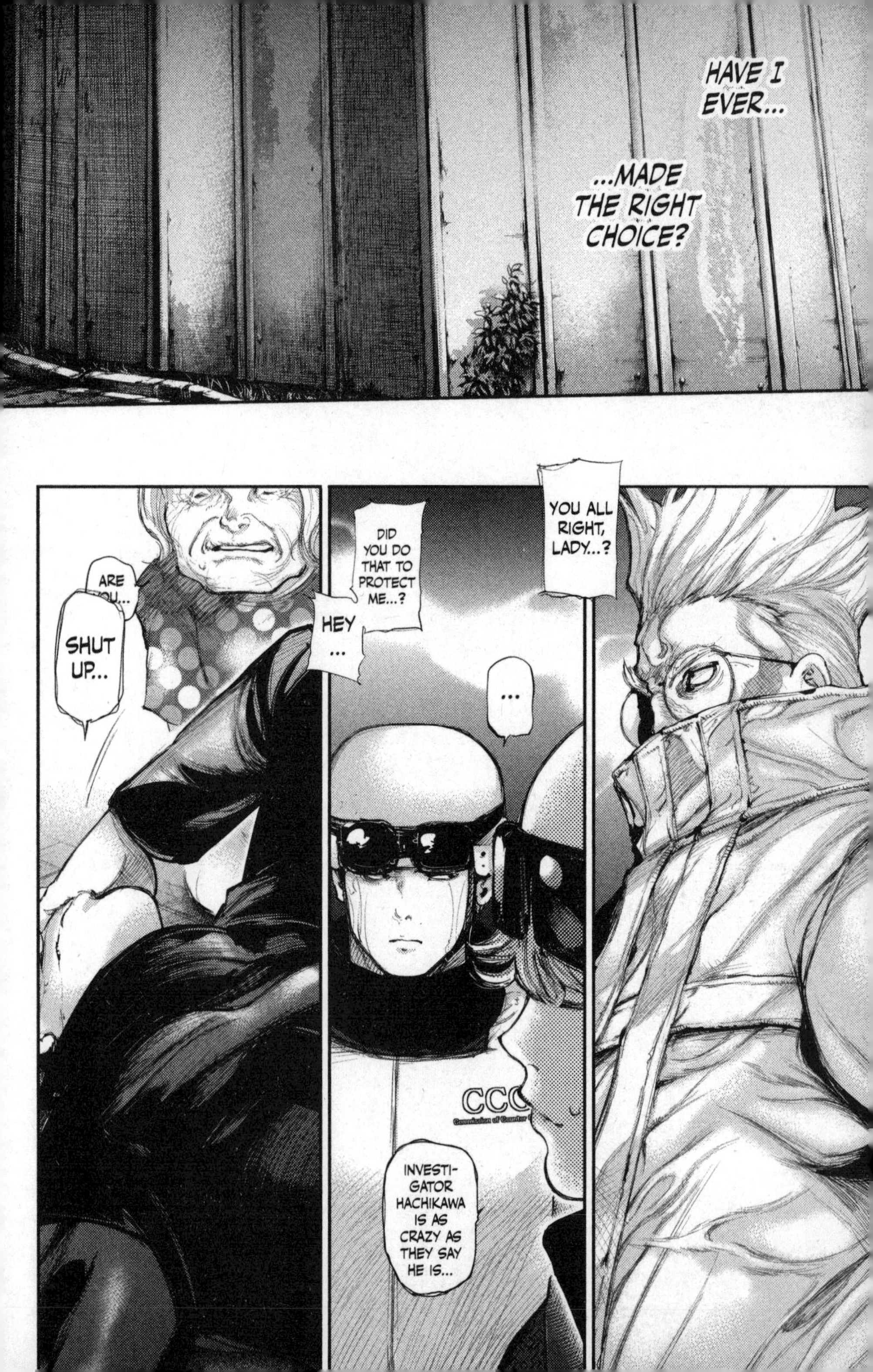
HAVE I EVER...
...MADE THE RIGHT CHOICE?
YOU ALL RIGHT, LADY...?
DID YOU DO THAT TO PROTECT ME...?
HEY ...
...
INVESTIGATOR HACHIKAWA IS AS CRAZY AS THEY SAY HE IS...
ARE YOU...
SHUT UP...

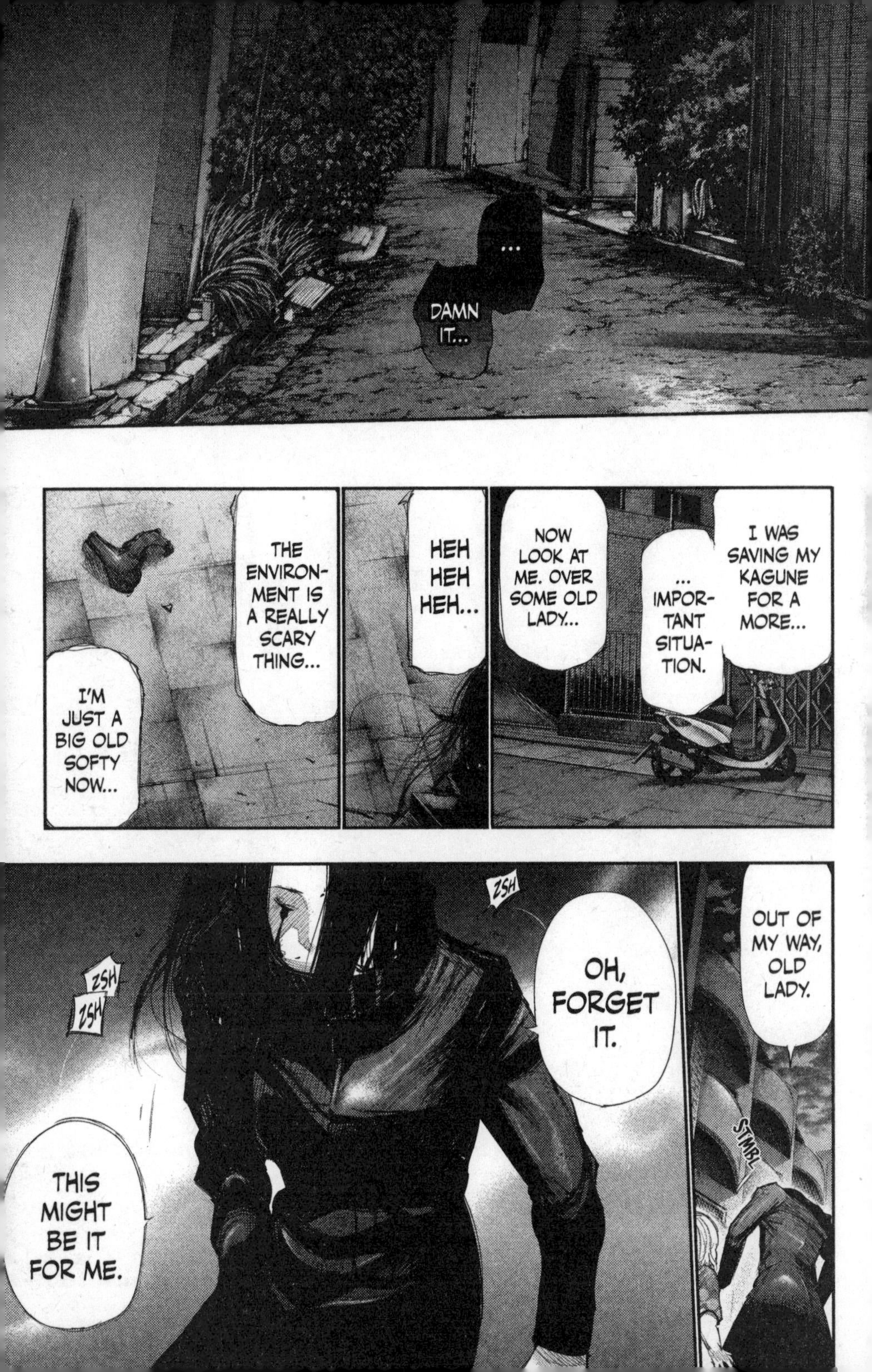
...
DAMN IT...
I WAS SAVING MY KAGUNE FOR A MORE...
... IMPORTANT SITUATION.
NOW LOOK AT ME. OVER SOME OLD LADY...
HEH HEH HEH...
THE ENVIRONMENT IS A REALLY SCARY THING...
I'M JUST A BIG OLD SOFTY NOW...
OUT OF MY WAY, OLD LADY.
STMBL
ZSH
OH, FORGET IT.
ZSH
ZSH
THIS MIGHT BE IT FOR ME.

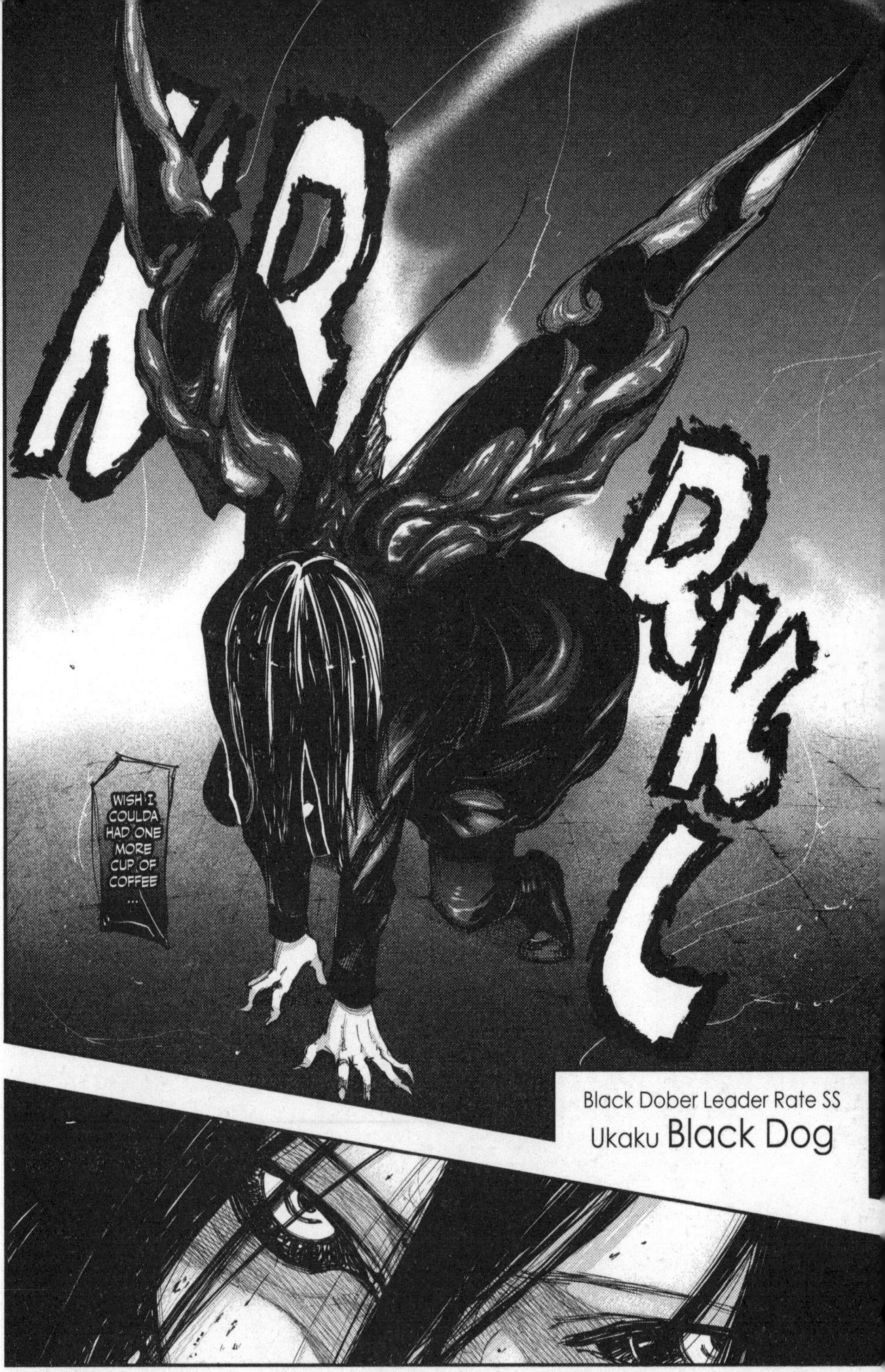
WISH I COULDA HAD ONE MORE CUP OF COFFEE ...
Black Dober Leader Rate SS
Ukaku Black Dog

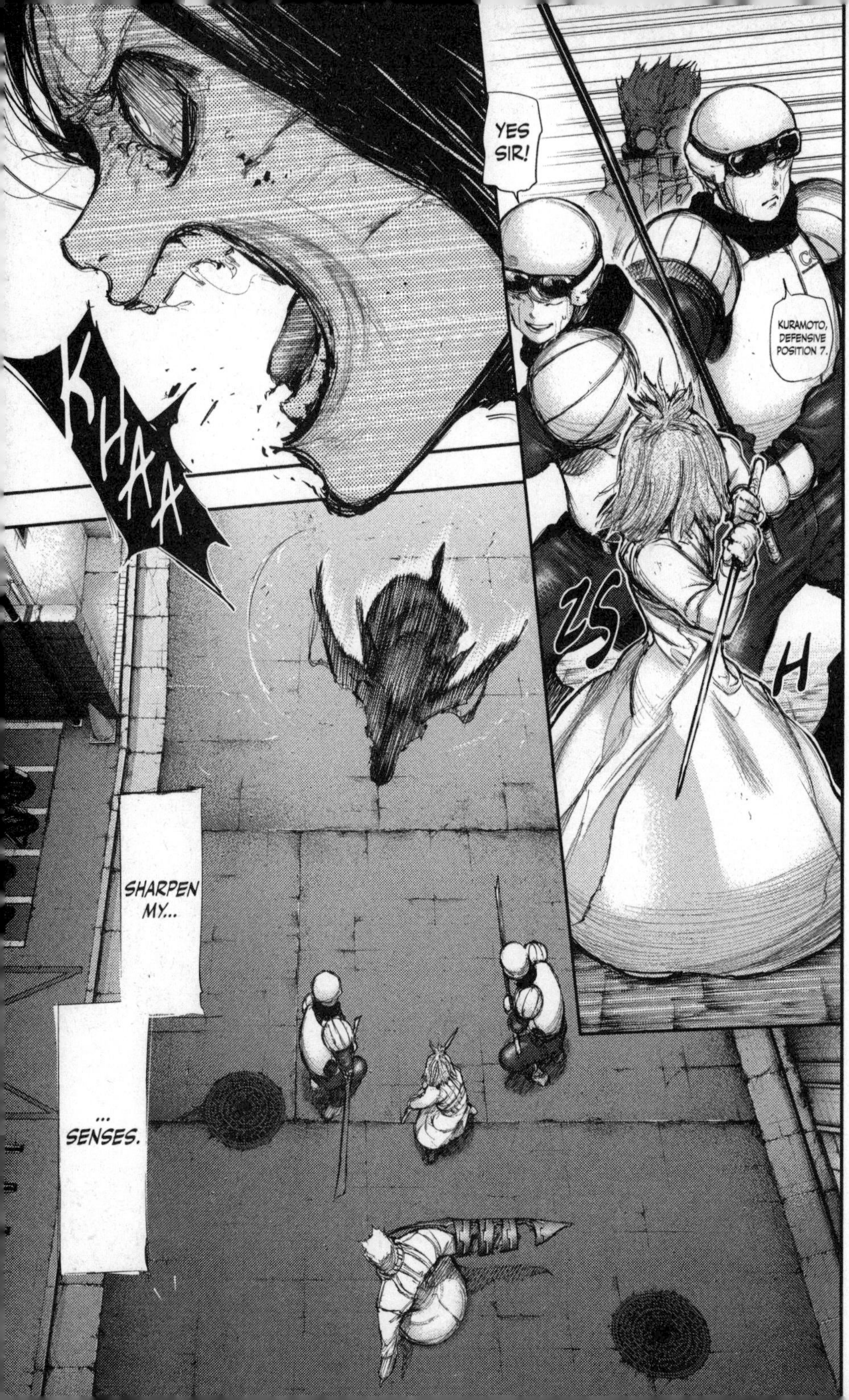
KURAMOTO, DEFENSIVE POSITION 7.
YES SIR!
ZS
H
KHAA
SHARPEN MY...
...SENSES.

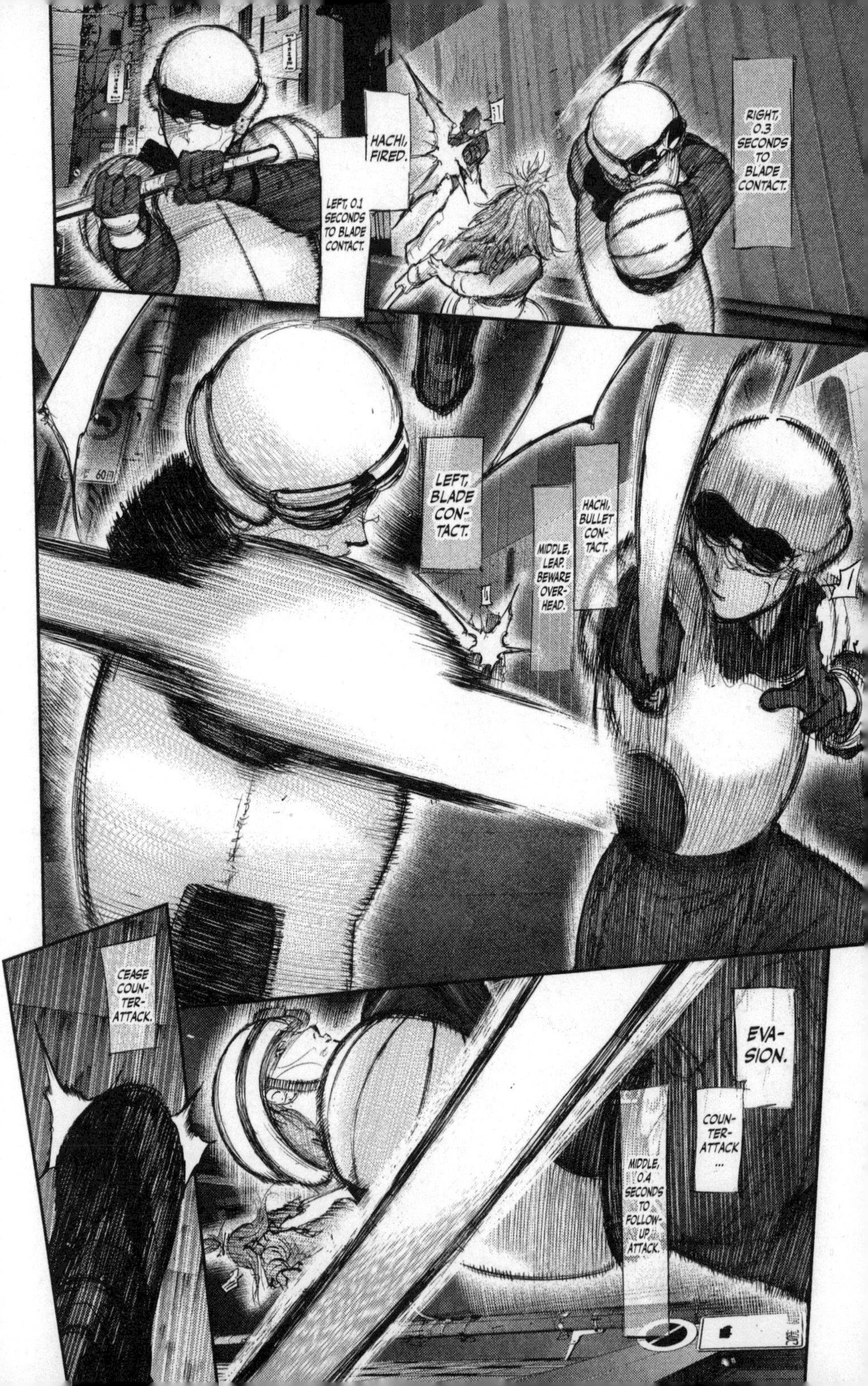
RIGHT, 0.3 SECONDS TO BLADE CONTACT.
HACHI, FIRED.
LEFT, 0.1 SECONDS TO BLADE CONTACT.
HACHI, BULLET CONTACT.
MIDDLE, LEAP. BEWARE OVERHEAD.
LEFT, BLADE CONTACT.
EVASION.
COUNTER-ATTACK...
MIDDLE, 0.4 SECONDS TO FOLLOW-UP ATTACK.
CEASE COUNTER-ATTACK.

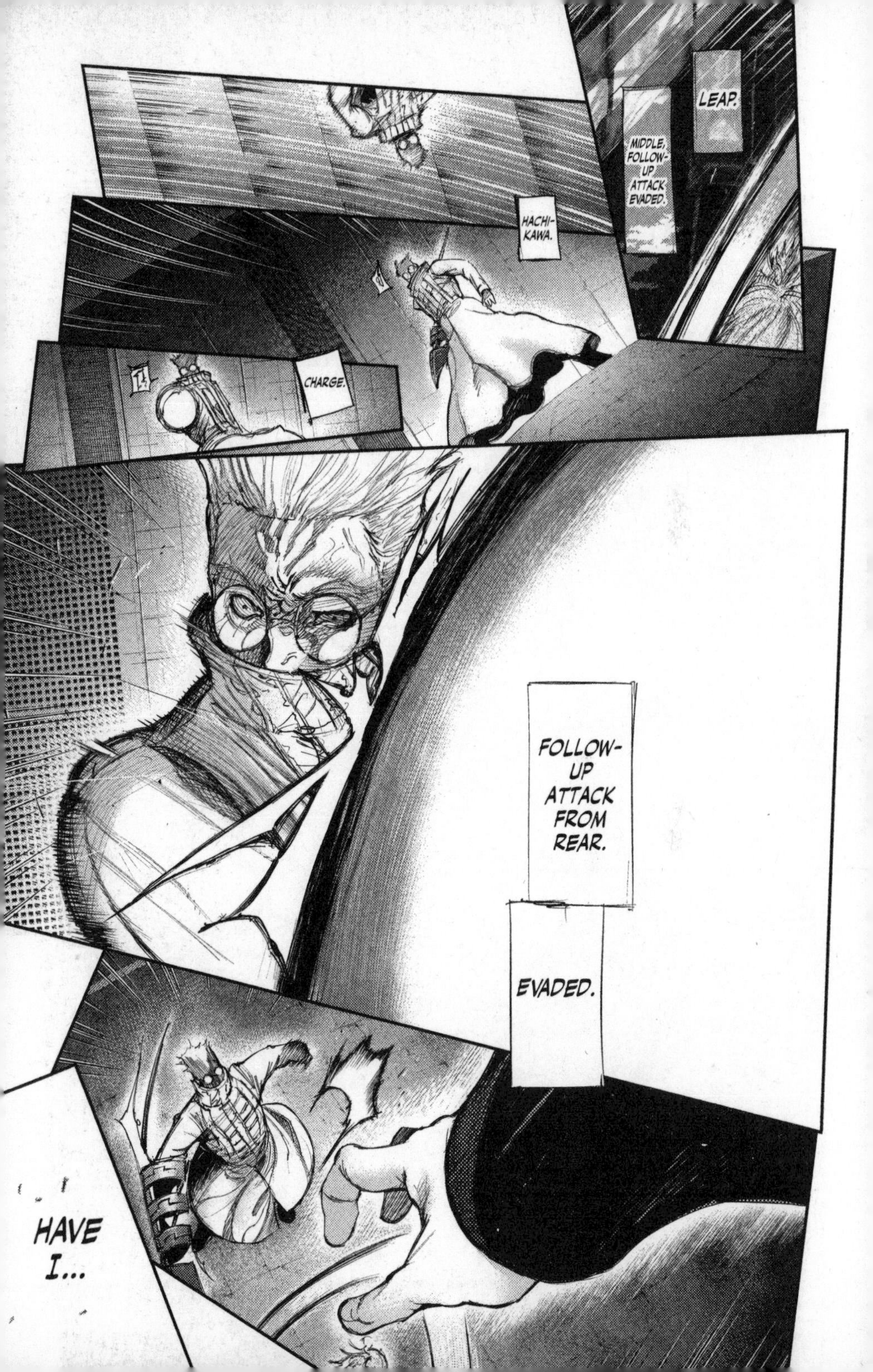
LEAP.
MIDDLE, FOLLOW-UP ATTACK EVADED.
HACHIKAWA.
CHARGE.
FOLLOW-UP ATTACK FROM REAR.
EVADED.
HAVE I...

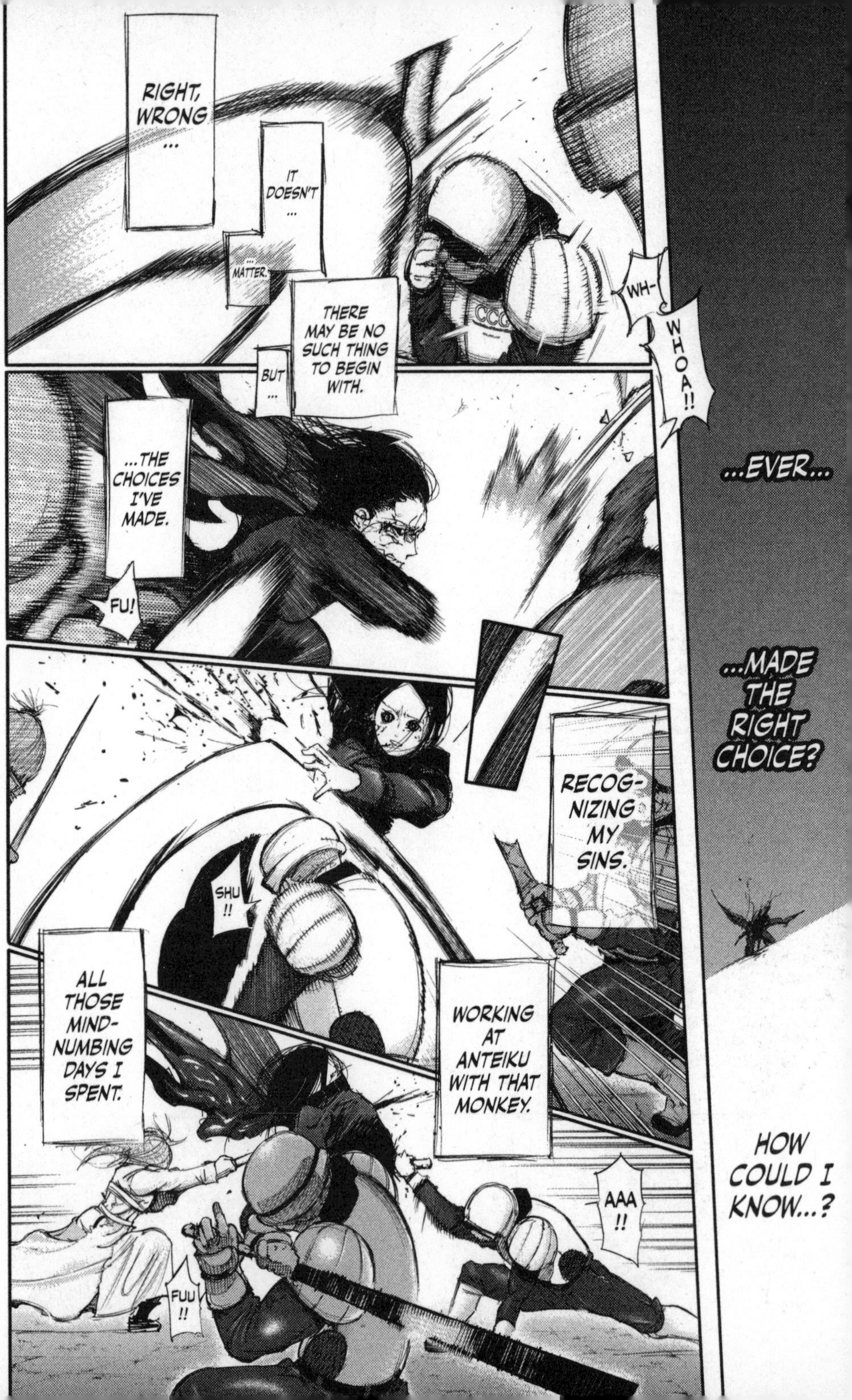
...EVER...
...MADE THE RIGHT CHOICE?
HOW COULD I KNOW...?
RIGHT, WRONG...
IT DOESN'T...
...MATTER.
WH-
WHOA!!
THERE MAY BE NO SUCH THING TO BEGIN WITH.
BUT...
...THE CHOICES I'VE MADE.
FU!
RECOG-NIZING MY SINS.
SHU!!
WORKING AT ANTEIKU WITH THAT MONKEY.
ALL THOSE MIND-NUMBING DAYS I SPENT.
AAA!!
FUU!!

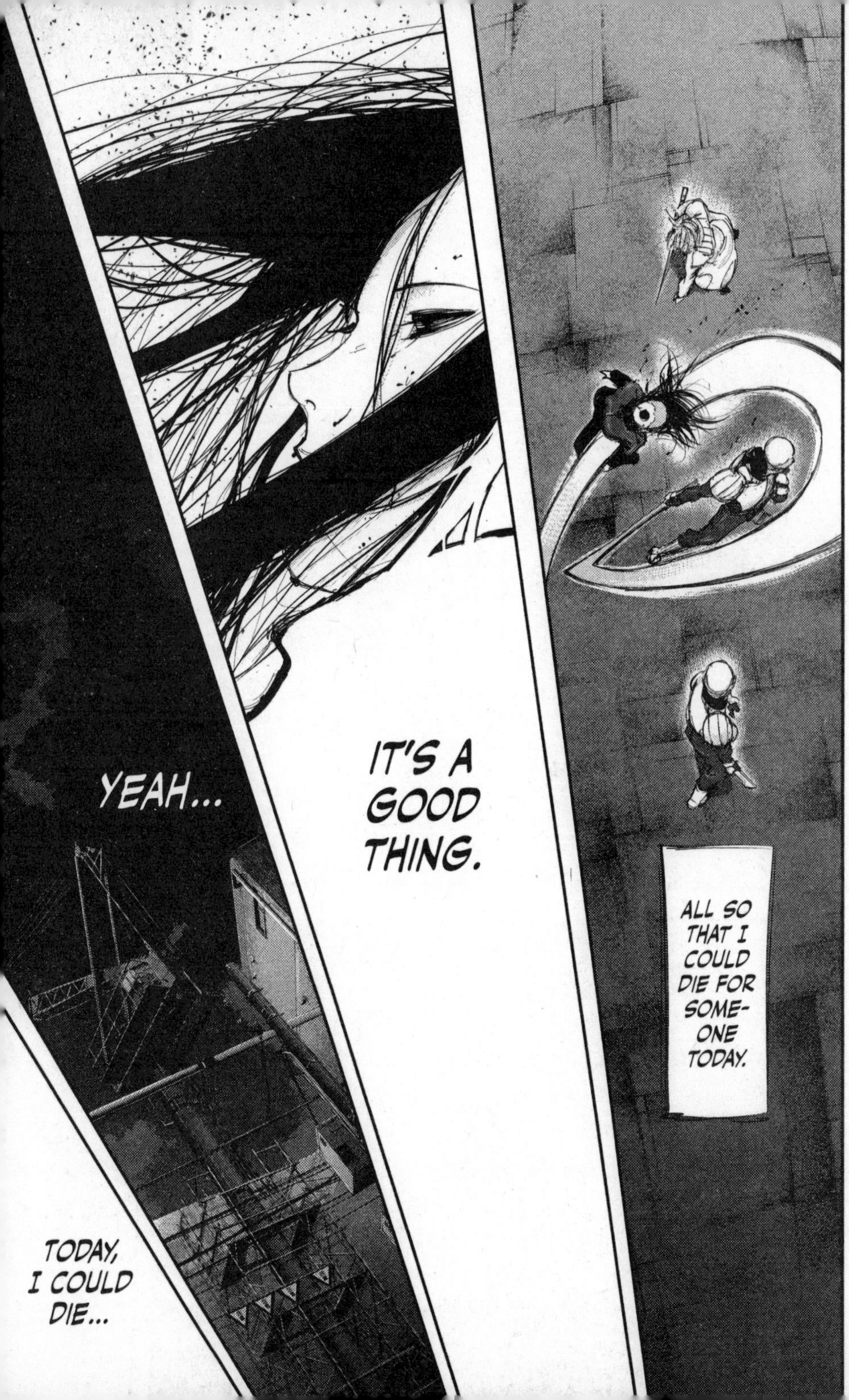
ALL SO THAT I COULD DIE FOR SOME-ONE TODAY.
IT'S A GOOD THING.
YEAH...
TODAY, I COULD DIE...

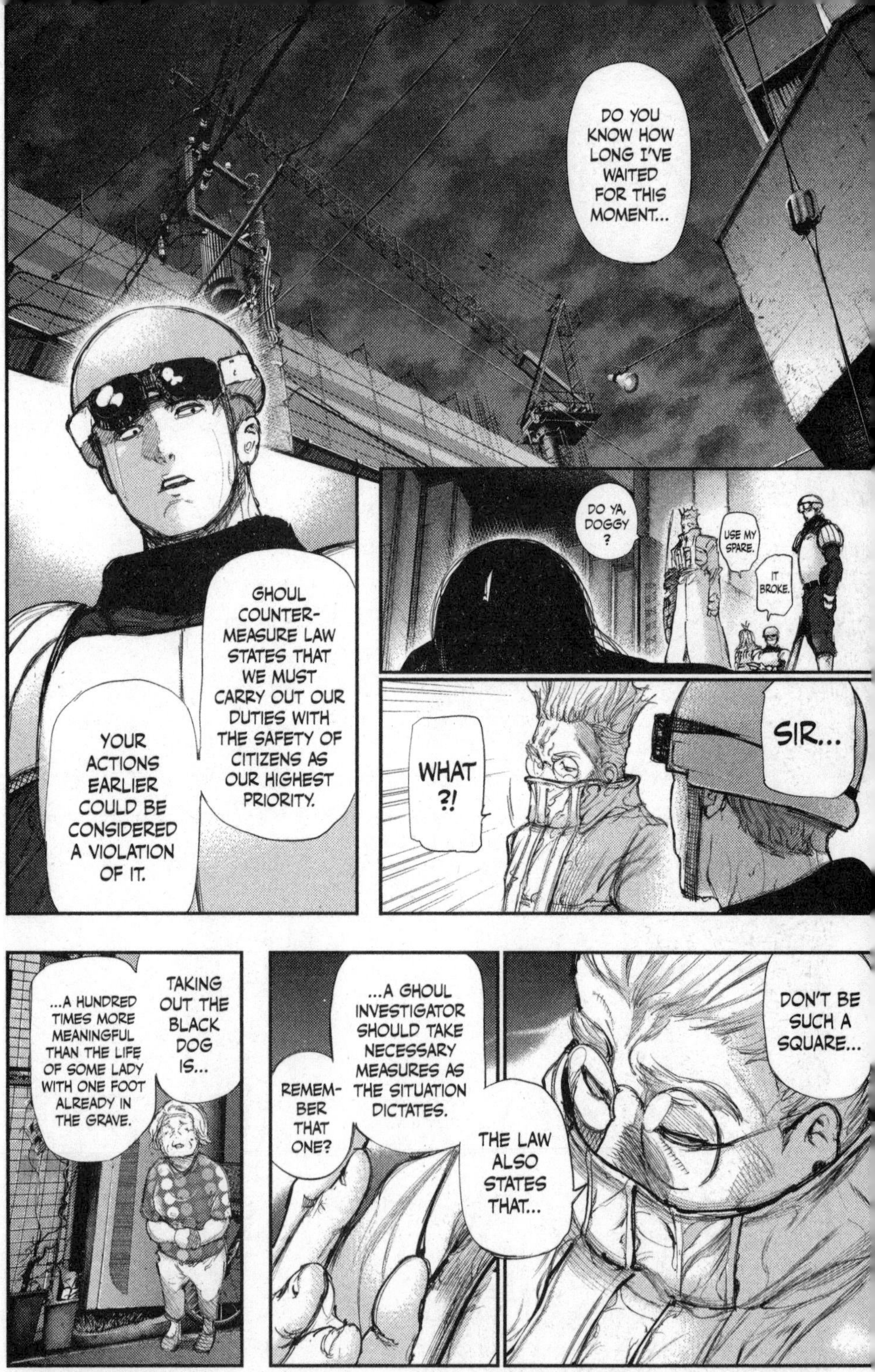
DO YOU KNOW HOW LONG I'VE WAITED FOR THIS MOMENT...
DO YA, DOGGY?
USE MY SPARE.
IT BROKE.
SIR...
WHAT?!
GHOUL COUNTER-MEASURE LAW STATES THAT WE MUST CARRY OUT OUR DUTIES WITH THE SAFETY OF CITIZENS AS OUR HIGHEST PRIORITY.
YOUR ACTIONS EARLIER COULD BE CONSIDERED A VIOLATION OF IT.
DON'T BE SUCH A SQUARE...
THE LAW ALSO STATES THAT...
...A GHOUL INVESTIGATOR SHOULD TAKE NECESSARY MEASURES AS THE SITUATION DICTATES.
REMEM-BER THAT ONE?
TAKING OUT THE BLACK DOG IS...
...A HUNDRED TIMES MORE MEANINGFUL THAN THE LIFE OF SOME LADY WITH ONE FOOT ALREADY IN THE GRAVE.

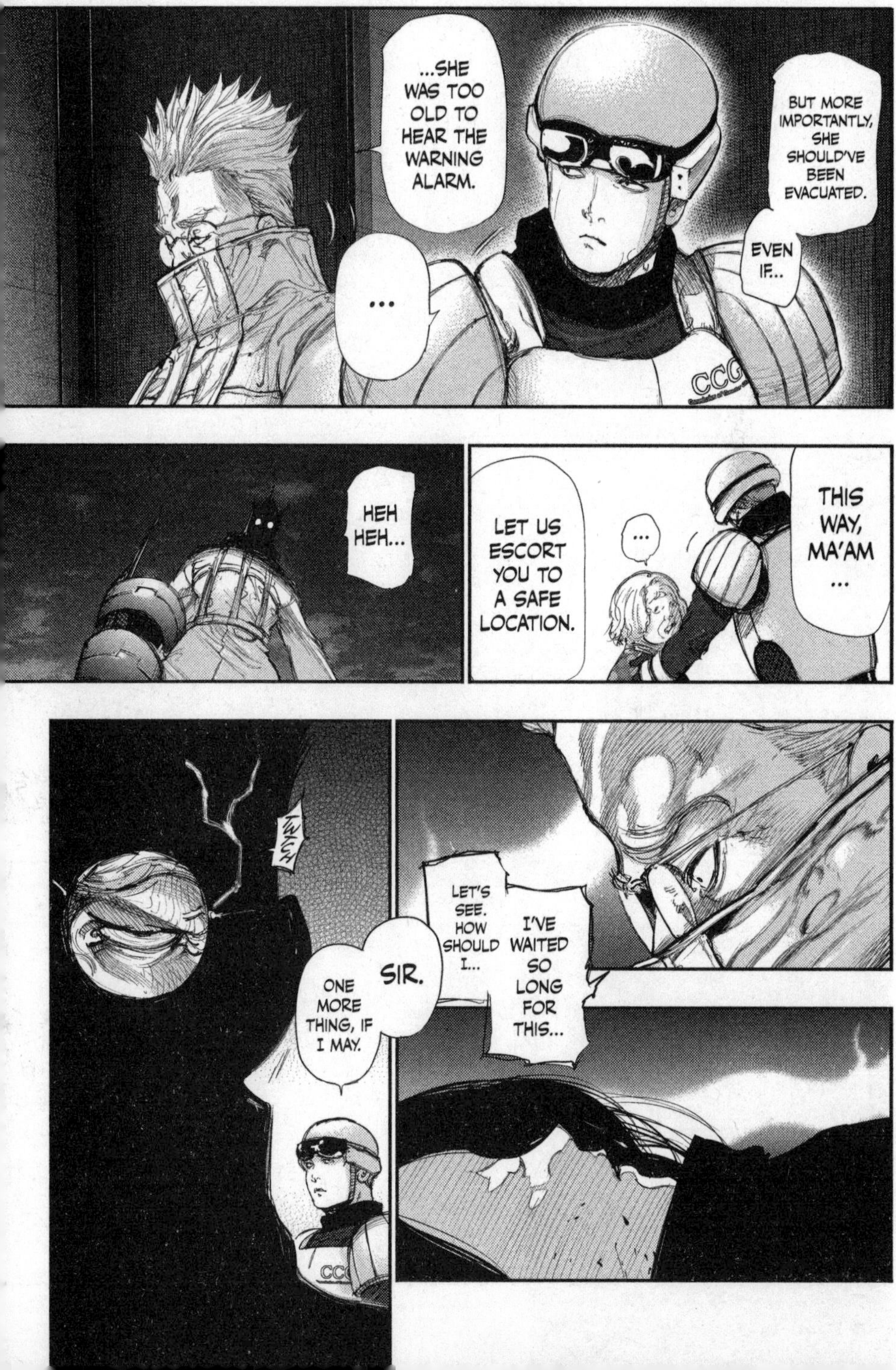
BUT MORE IMPORTANTLY, SHE SHOULD'VE BEEN EVACUATED.
EVEN IF...
...SHE WAS TOO OLD TO HEAR THE WARNING ALARM.
...
THIS WAY, MA'AM ...
LET US ESCORT YOU TO A SAFE LOCATION.
...
HEH HEH...
I'VE WAITED SO LONG FOR THIS...
LET'S SEE. HOW SHOULD I...
TWITCH
SIR.
ONE MORE THING, IF I MAY.

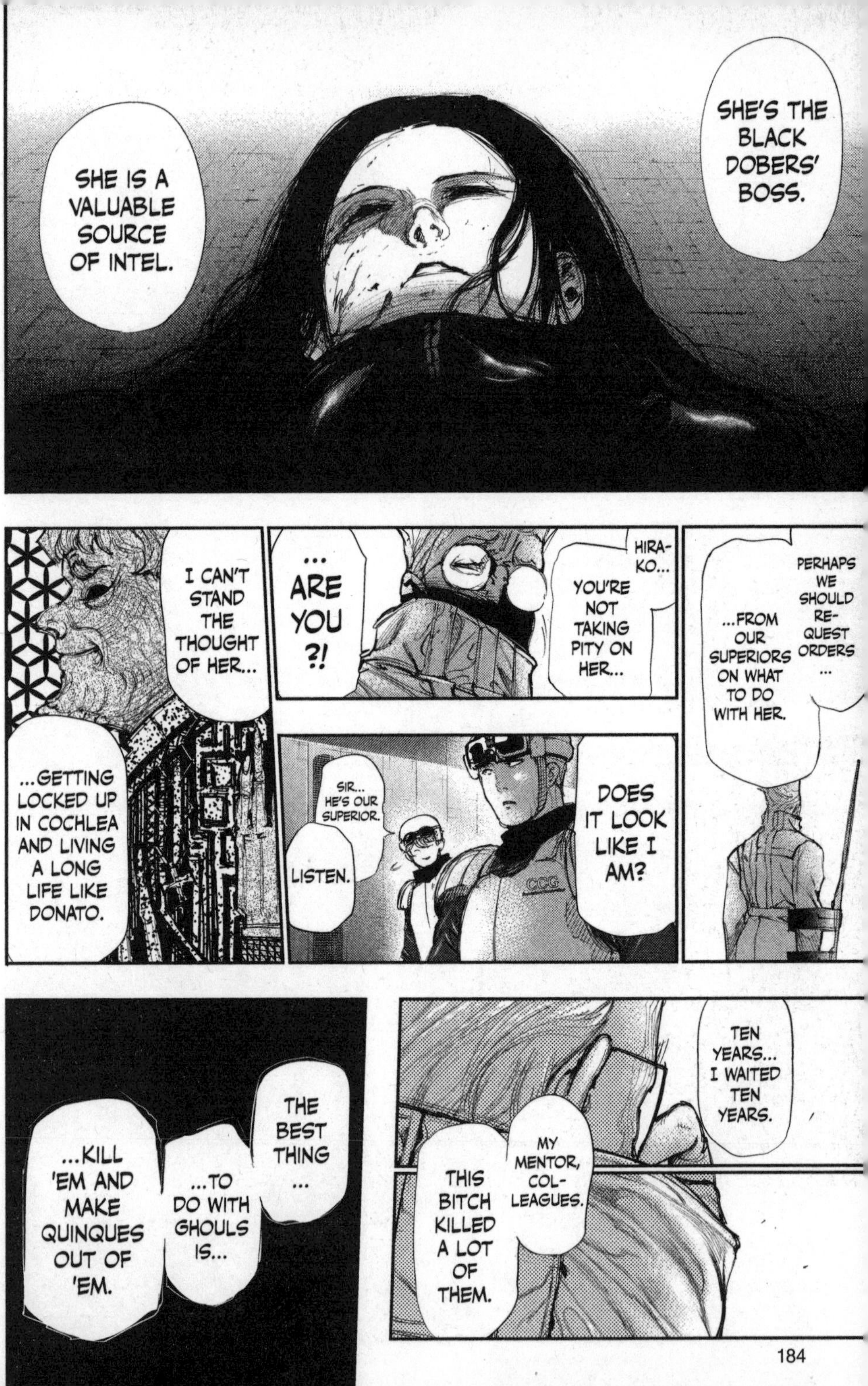
SHE'S THE BLACK DOBERS' BOSS.
SHE IS A VALUABLE SOURCE OF INTEL.
PERHAPS WE SHOULD REQUEST ORDERS...
...FROM OUR SUPERIORS ON WHAT TO DO WITH HER.
HIRAKO... YOU'RE NOT TAKING PITY ON HER...
...ARE YOU?!
DOES IT LOOK LIKE I AM?
SIR... HE'S OUR SUPERIOR.
LISTEN.
I CAN'T STAND THE THOUGHT OF HER...
...GETTING LOCKED UP IN COCHLEA AND LIVING A LONG LIFE LIKE DONATO.
TEN YEARS... I WAITED TEN YEARS.
MY MENTOR, COLLEAGUES.
THIS BITCH KILLED A LOT OF THEM.
THE BEST THING...
...TO DO WITH GHOULS IS...
...KILL 'EM AND MAKE QUINQUES OUT OF 'EM.

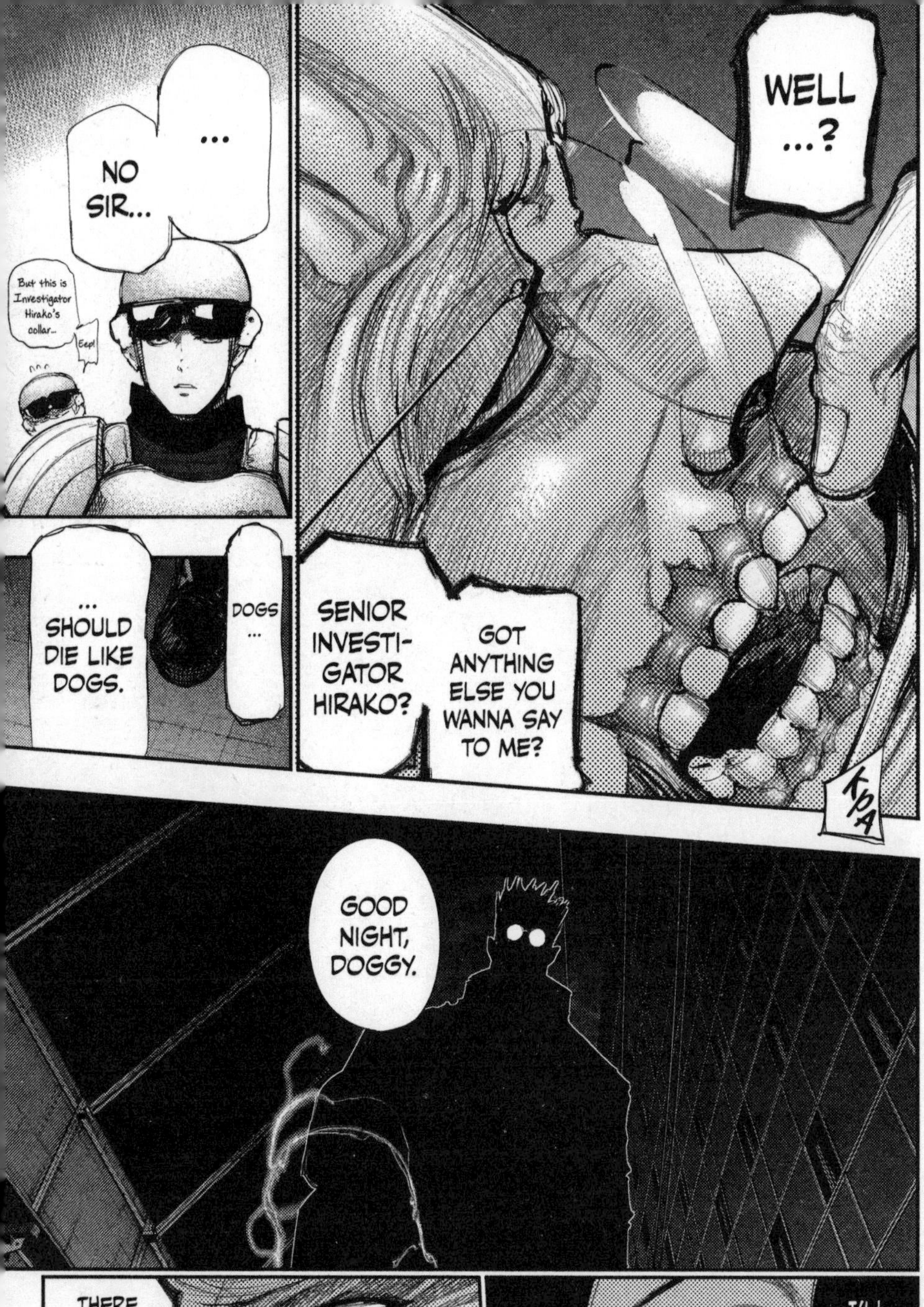
WELL ...?
SENIOR INVESTI-GATOR HIRAKO?
GOT ANYTHING ELSE YOU WANNA SAY TO ME?
KPA
...
NO SIR...
But this is Investigator Hirako's collar...
Eep!
DOGS ...
... SHOULD DIE LIKE DOGS.
GOOD NIGHT, DOGGY.
I'LL SEE YOU IN HELL...
GRN
THERE AIN'T NO AFTER-LIFE FOR GHOULS.

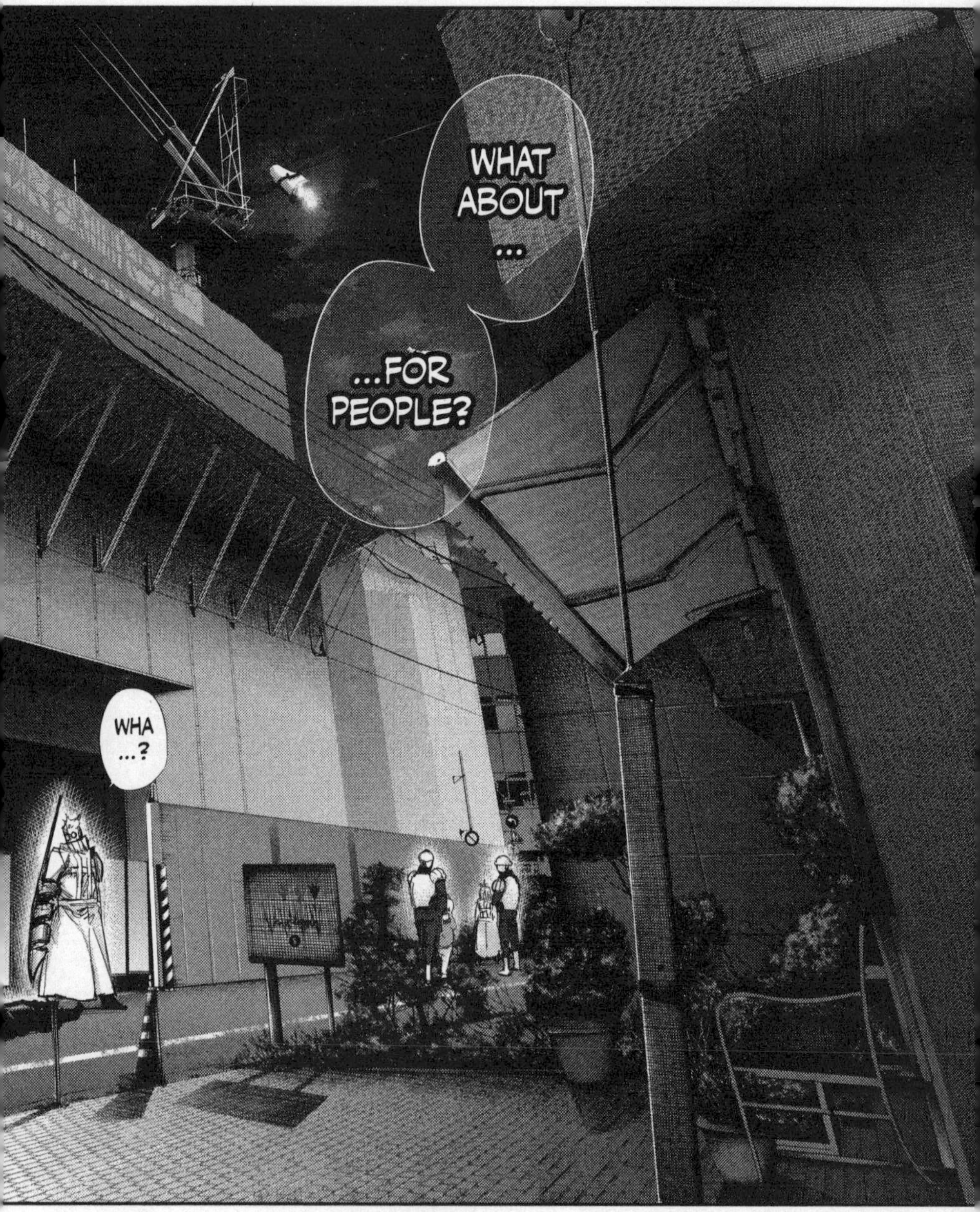
WHAT ABOUT ...
...FOR PEOPLE?
WHA ...?

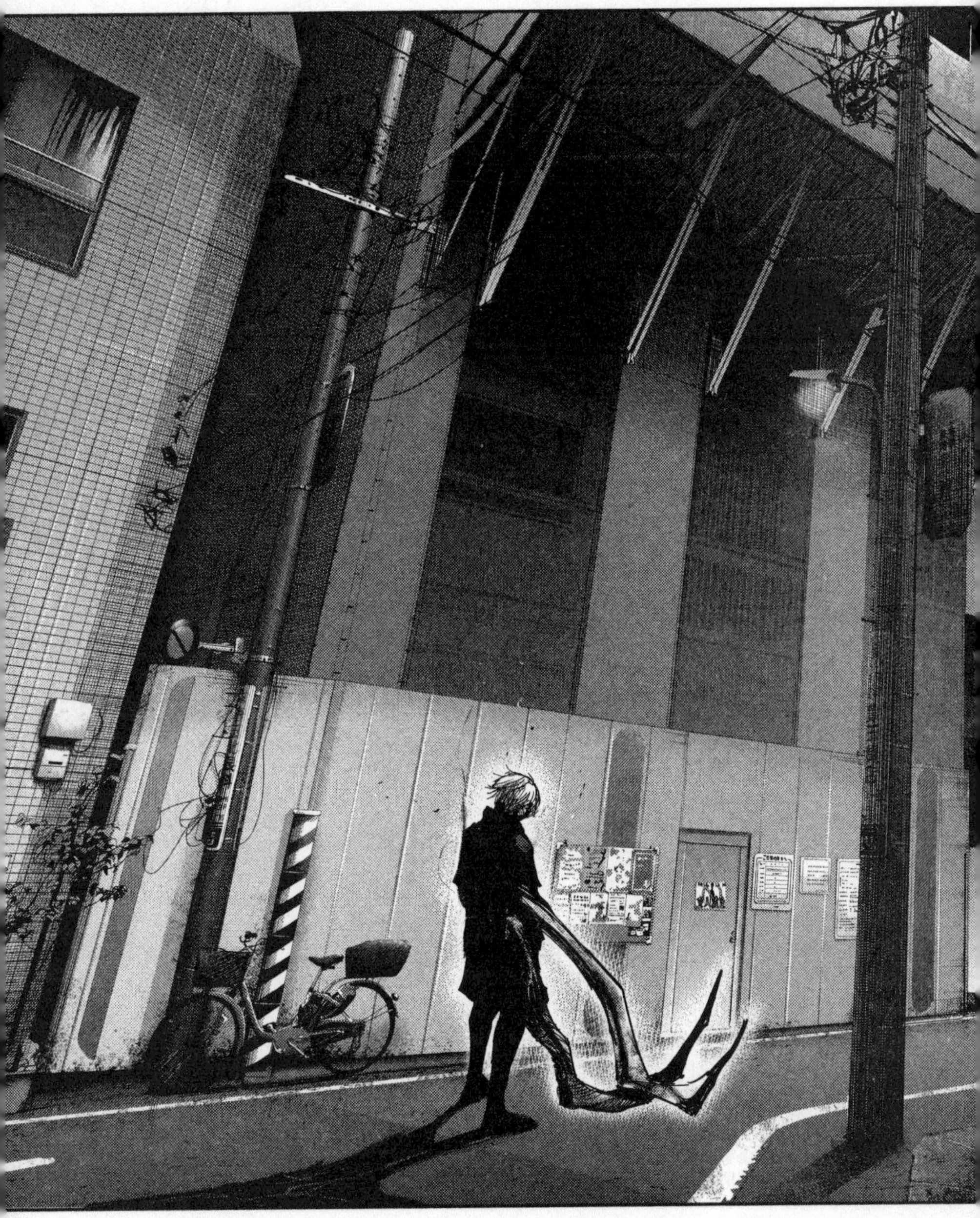

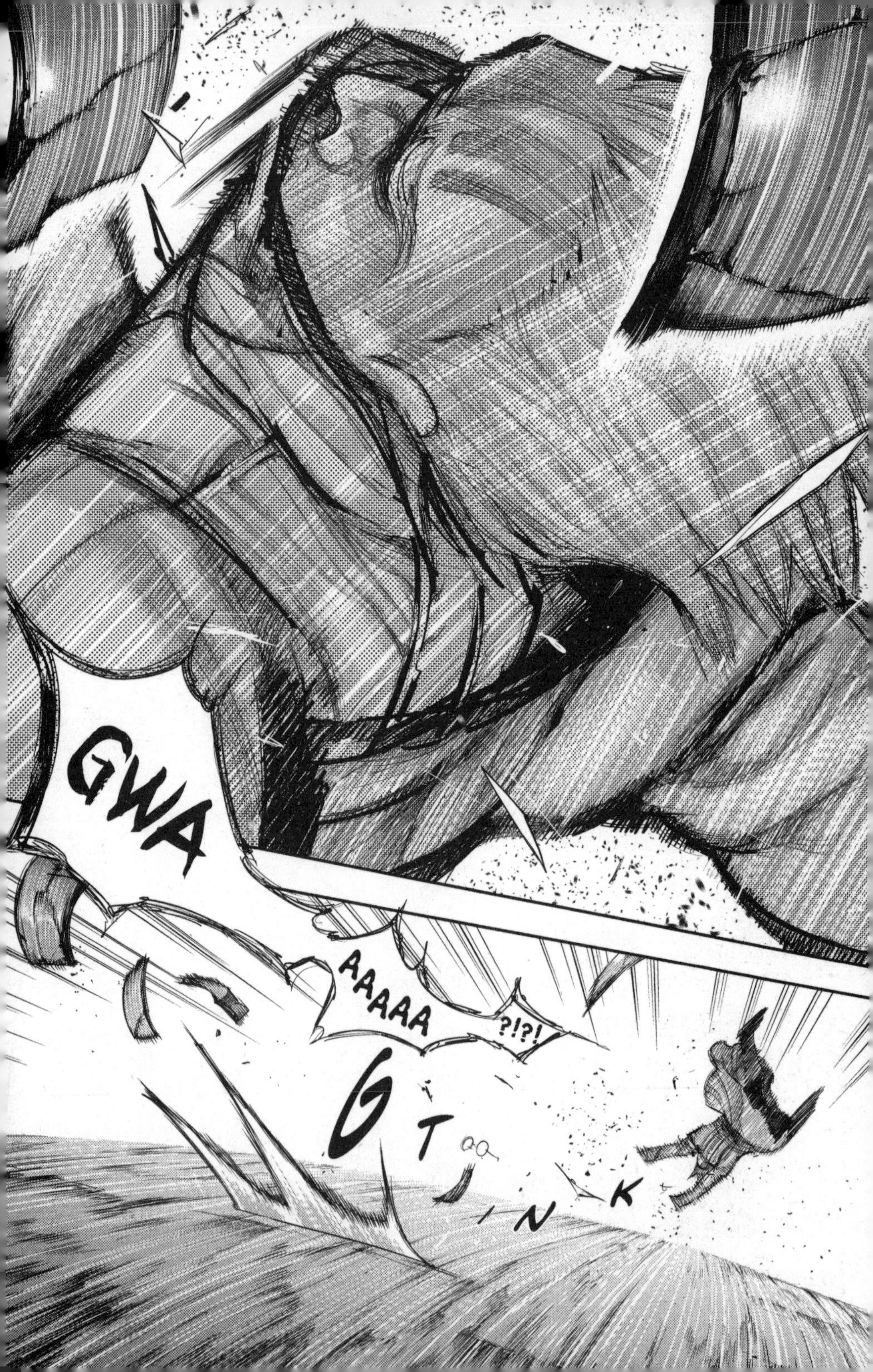
GWA
AAAAAA
?!?!
GTINK

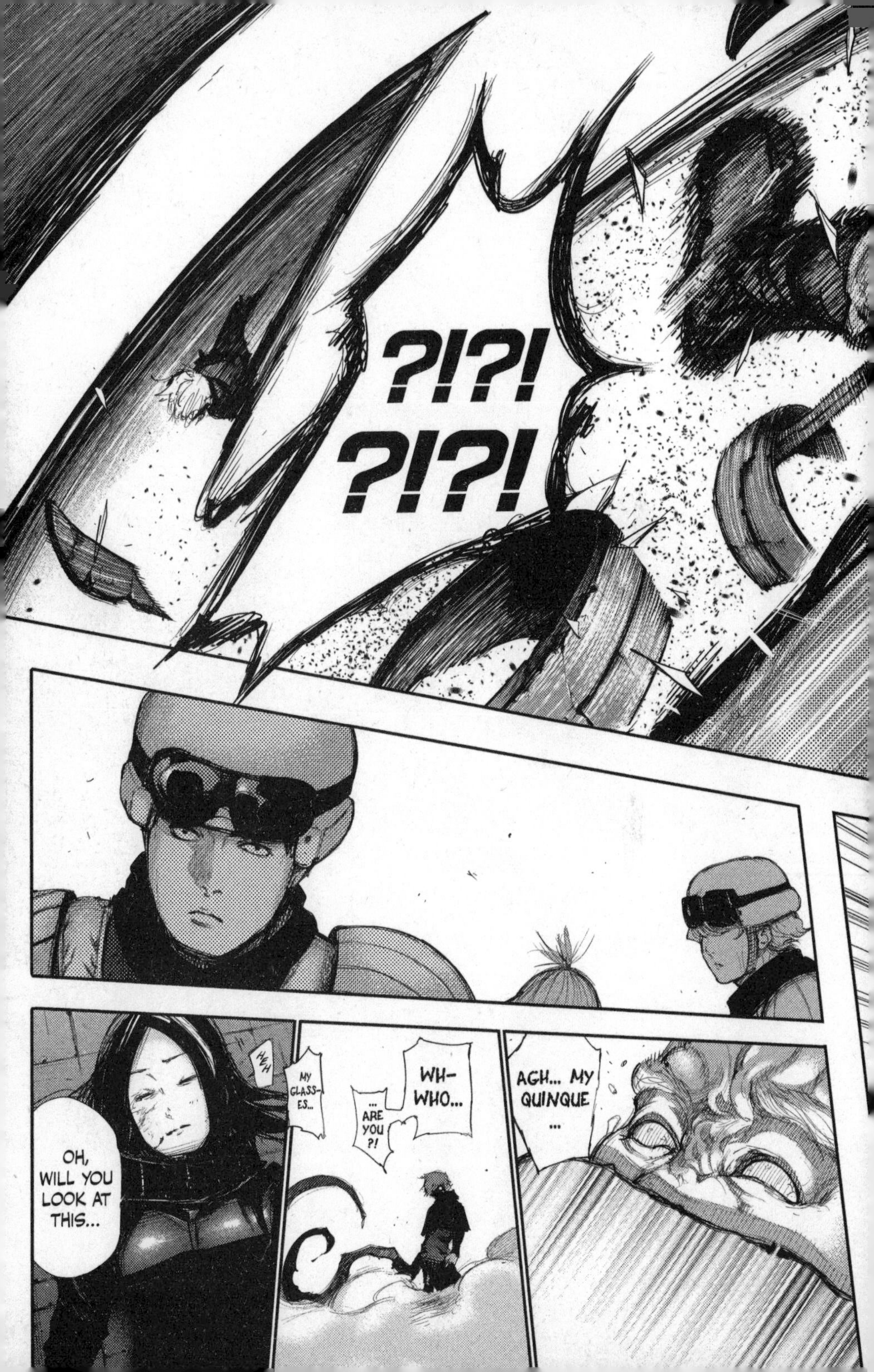
?!?!
?!?!
AGH... MY QUINQUE ...
WH- WHO...
... ARE YOU ?!
MY GLASS- ES...
HEH
OH, WILL YOU LOOK AT THIS...

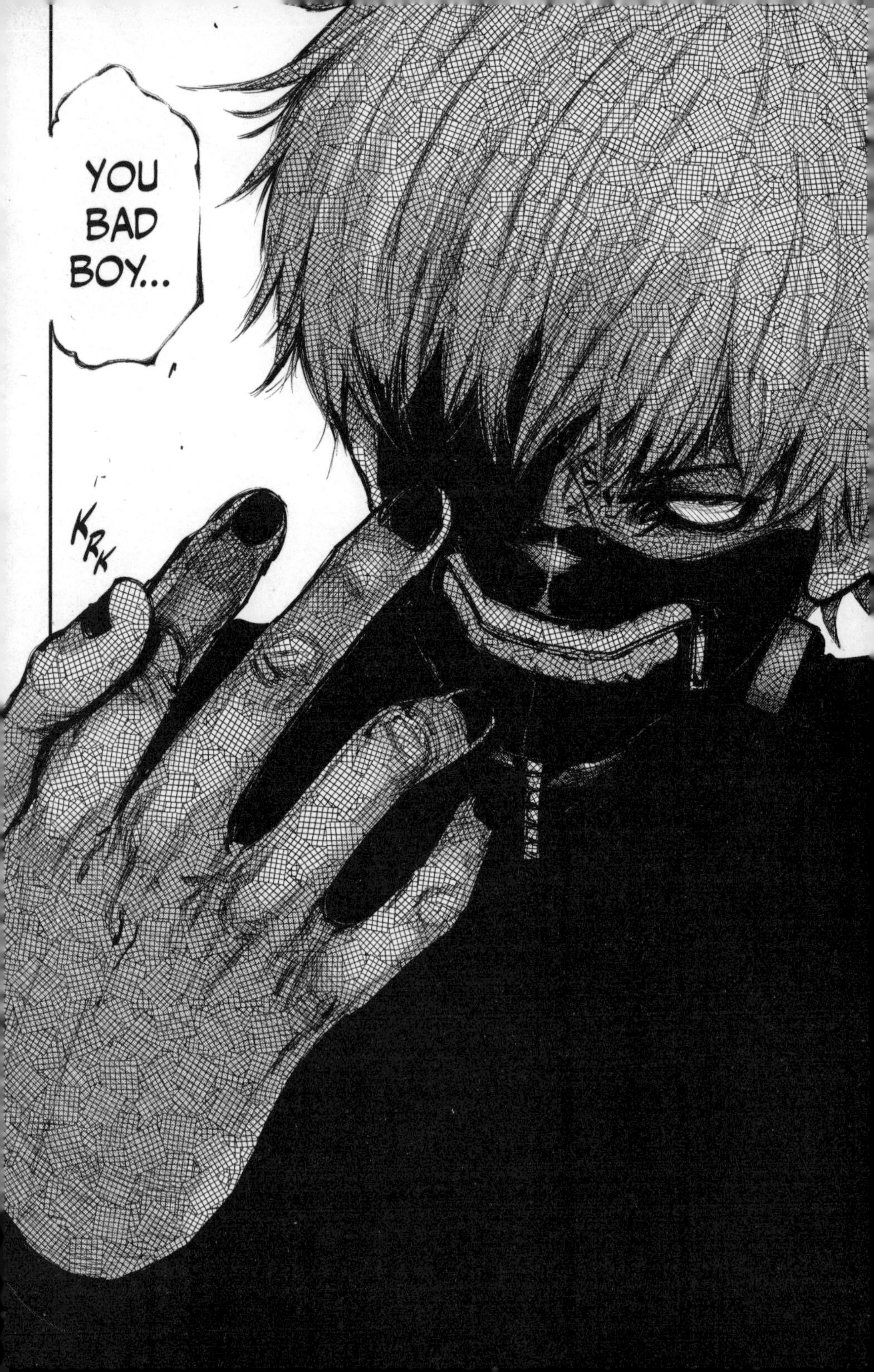
YOU BAD BOY...
KRK

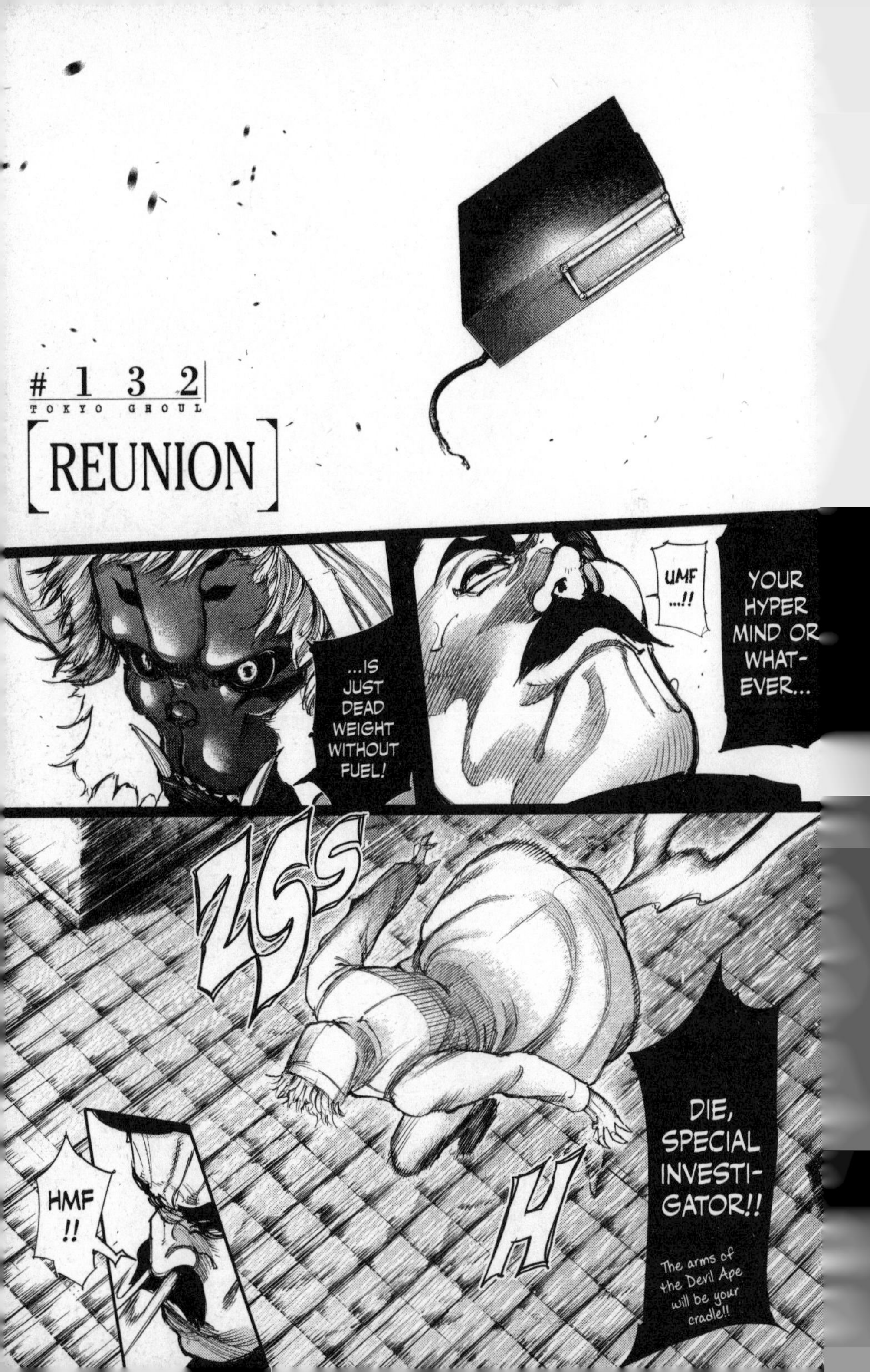
#132
TOKYO GHOUL
[REUNION]
YOUR HYPER MIND OR WHATEVER...
UMF ...!!
...IS JUST DEAD WEIGHT WITHOUT FUEL!
ZSS
DIE, SPECIAL INVESTIGATOR!!
The arms of the Devil Ape will be your cradle!!
H
HMF !!

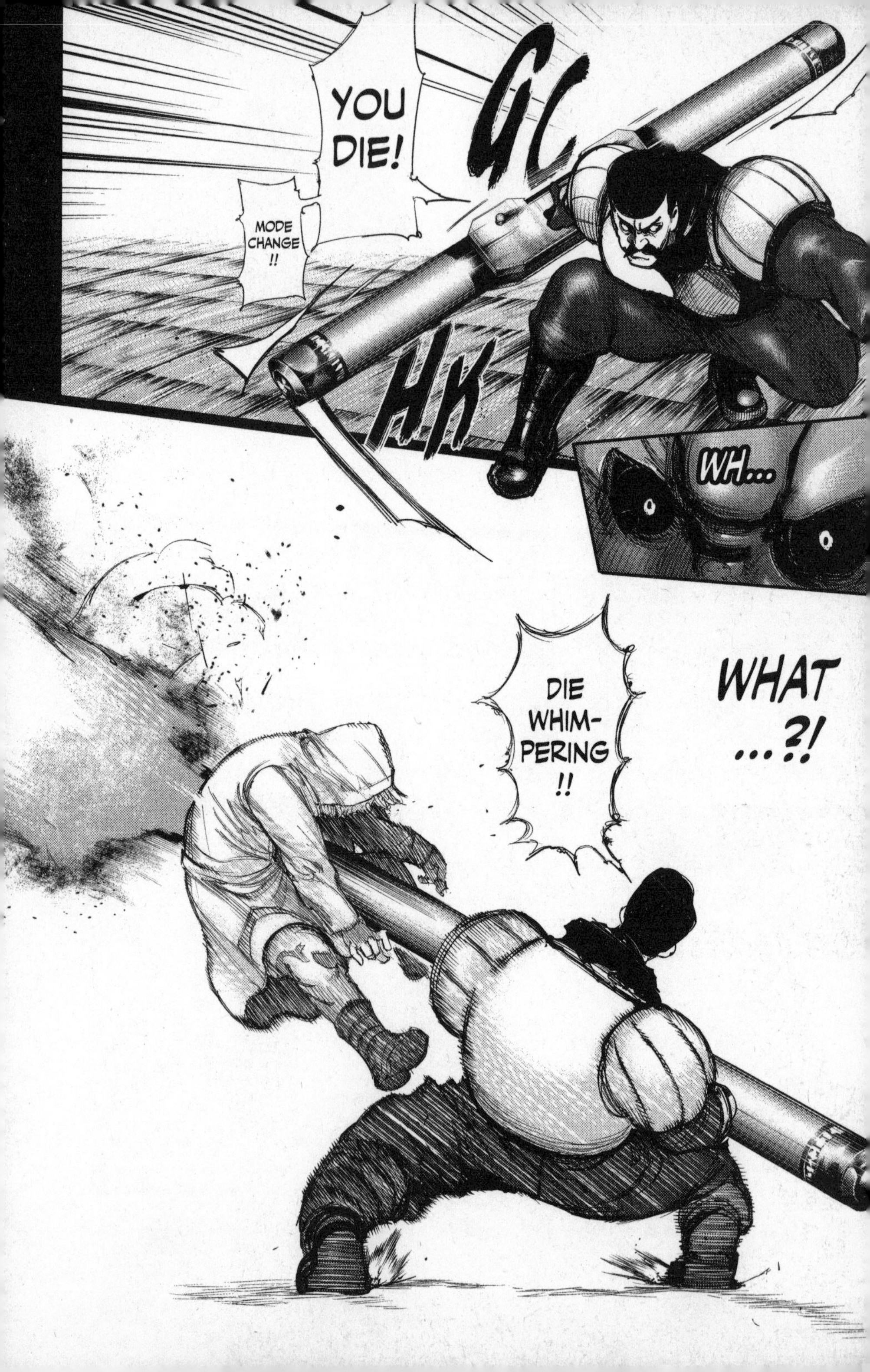
GC
YOU DIE!
MODE CHANGE !!
HK
WH...
WHAT ...?!
DIE WHIM-PERING !!

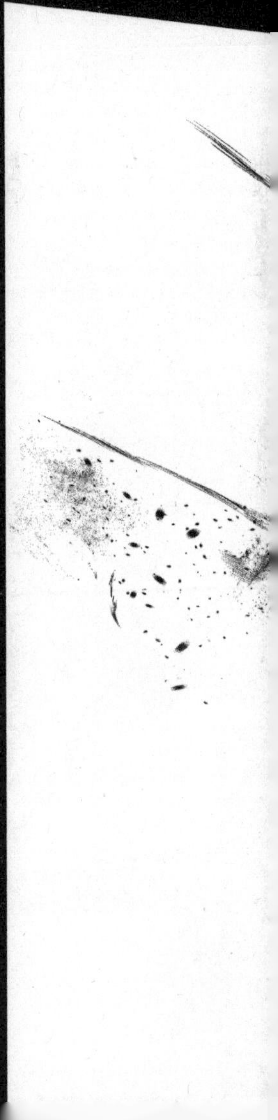

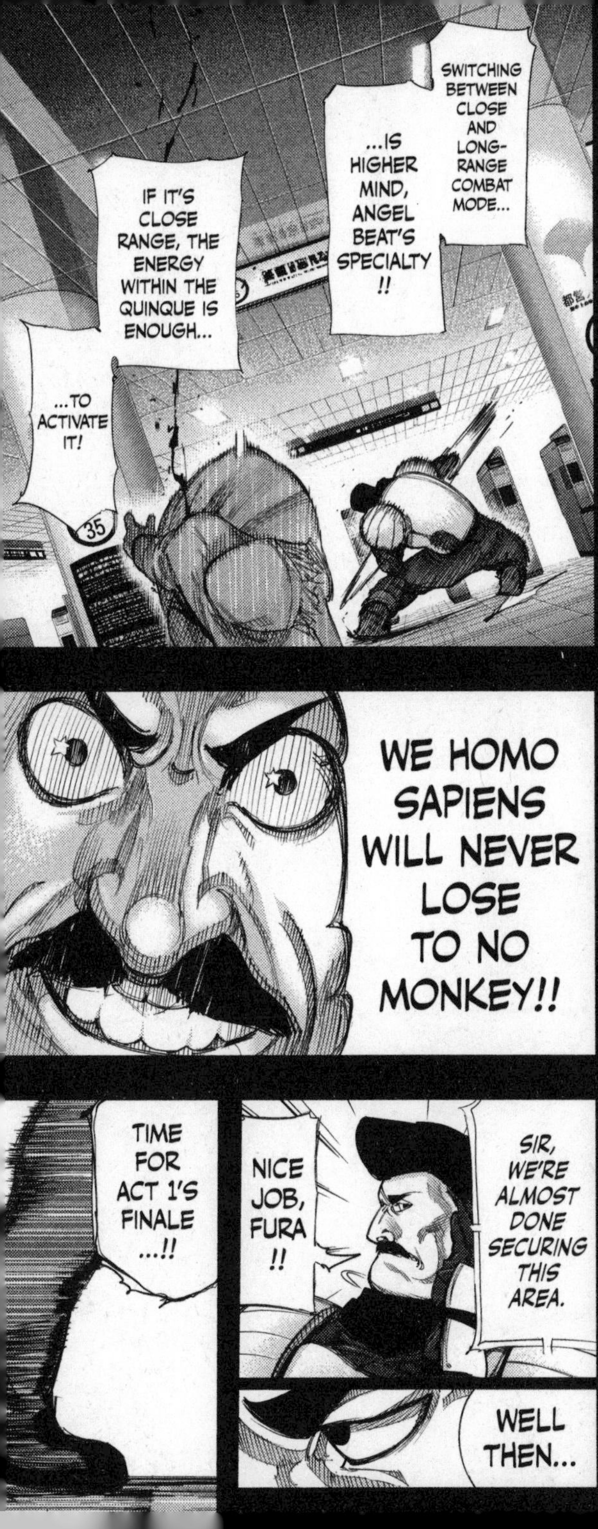
SWITCHING BETWEEN CLOSE AND LONG-RANGE COMBAT MODE...
...IS HIGHER MIND, ANGEL BEAT'S SPECIALTY!!
IF IT'S CLOSE RANGE, THE ENERGY WITHIN THE QUINQUE IS ENOUGH...
...TO ACTIVATE IT!
35
WE HOMO SAPIENS WILL NEVER LOSE TO NO MONKEY!!
SIR, WE'RE ALMOST DONE SECURING THIS AREA.
NICE JOB, FURA!!
WELL THEN...
TIME FOR ACT 1'S FINALE...!!

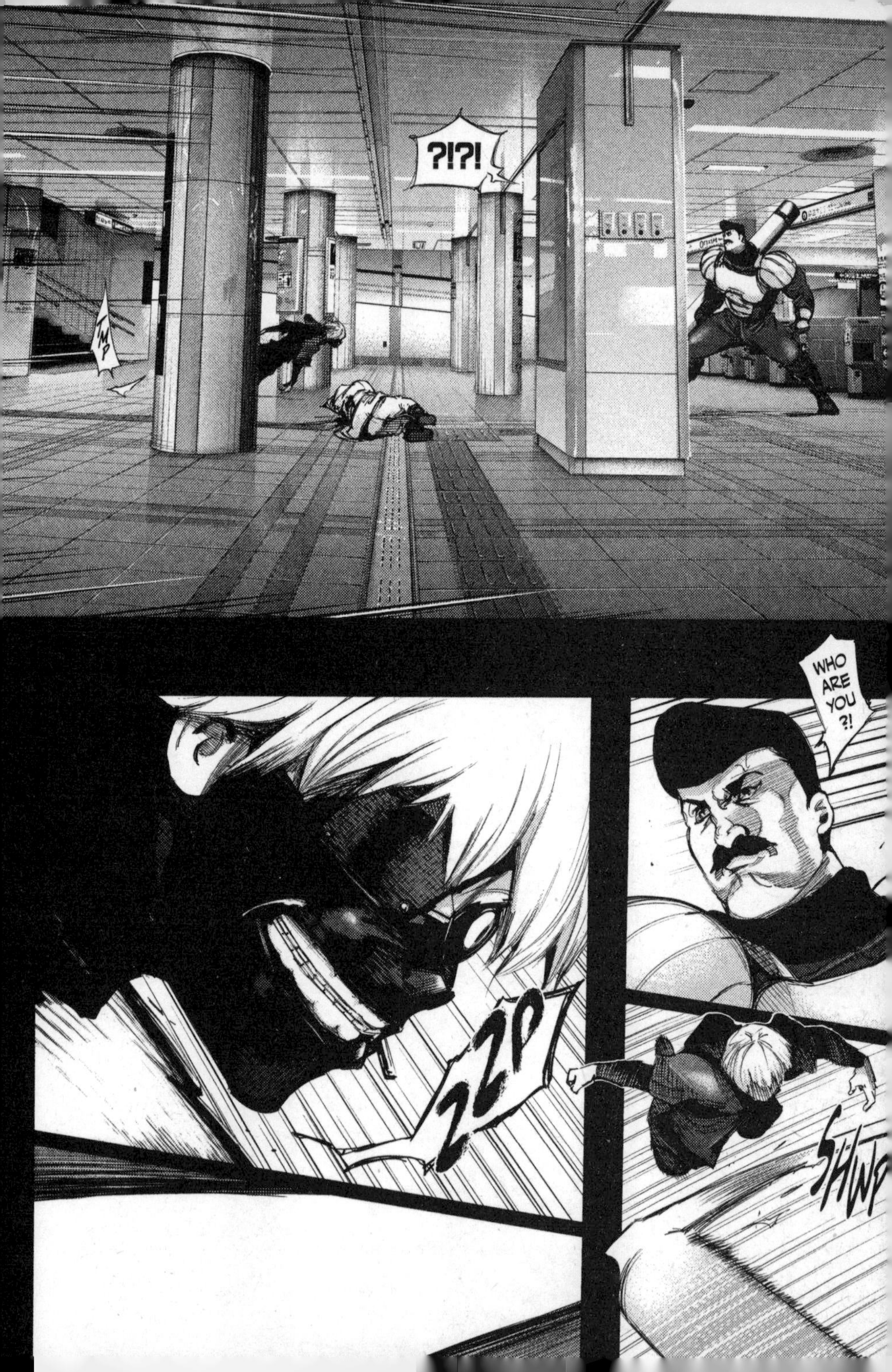
?!?!
TMP
WHO ARE YOU ?!
SHWP
ZZP

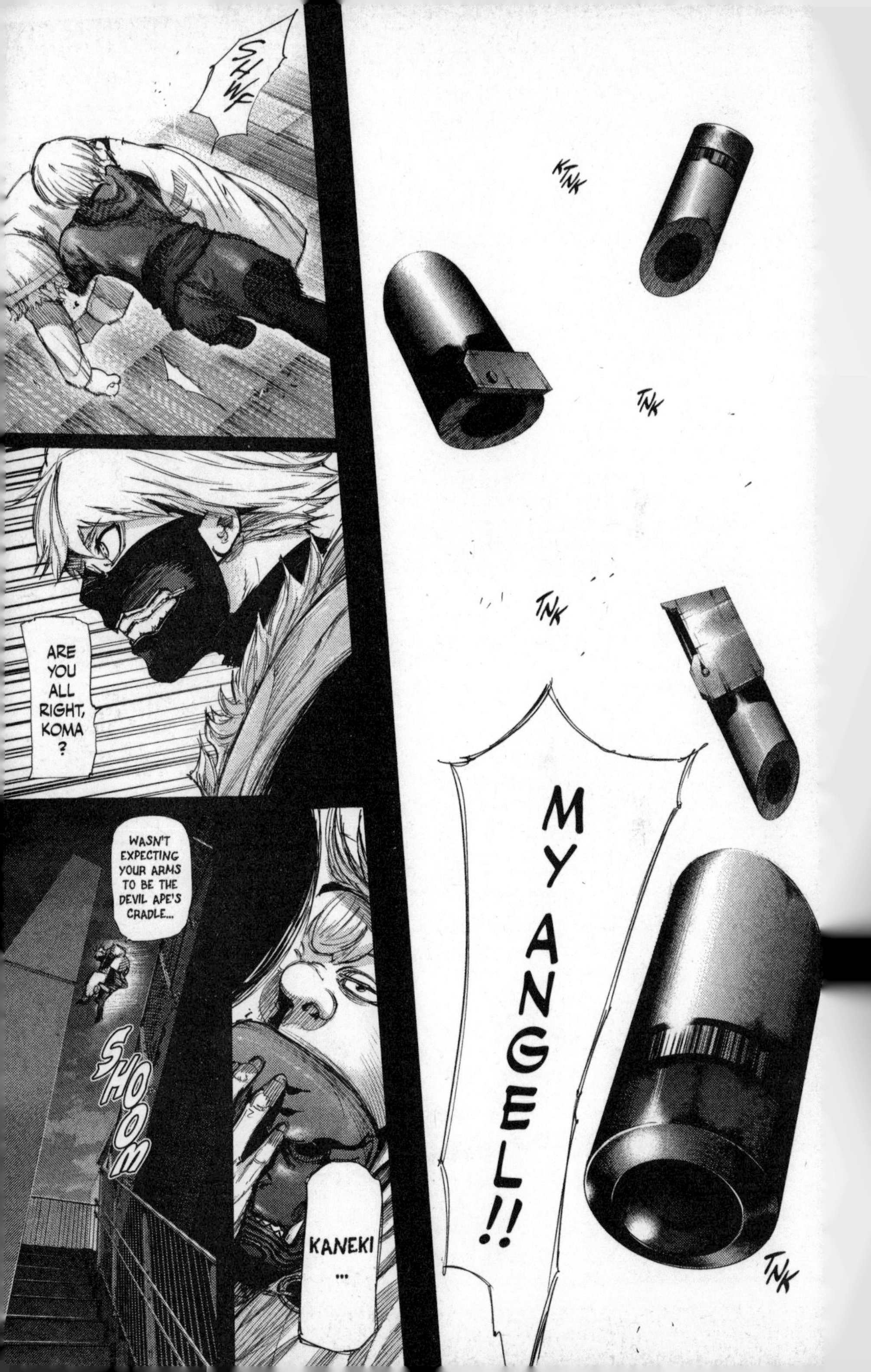
KTNK
TNK
TNK
MY ANGEL!!
TNK
SHWF
ARE YOU ALL RIGHT, KOMA?
KANEKI...
WASN'T EXPECTING YOUR ARMS TO BE THE DEVIL APE'S CRADLE...
SHOOM

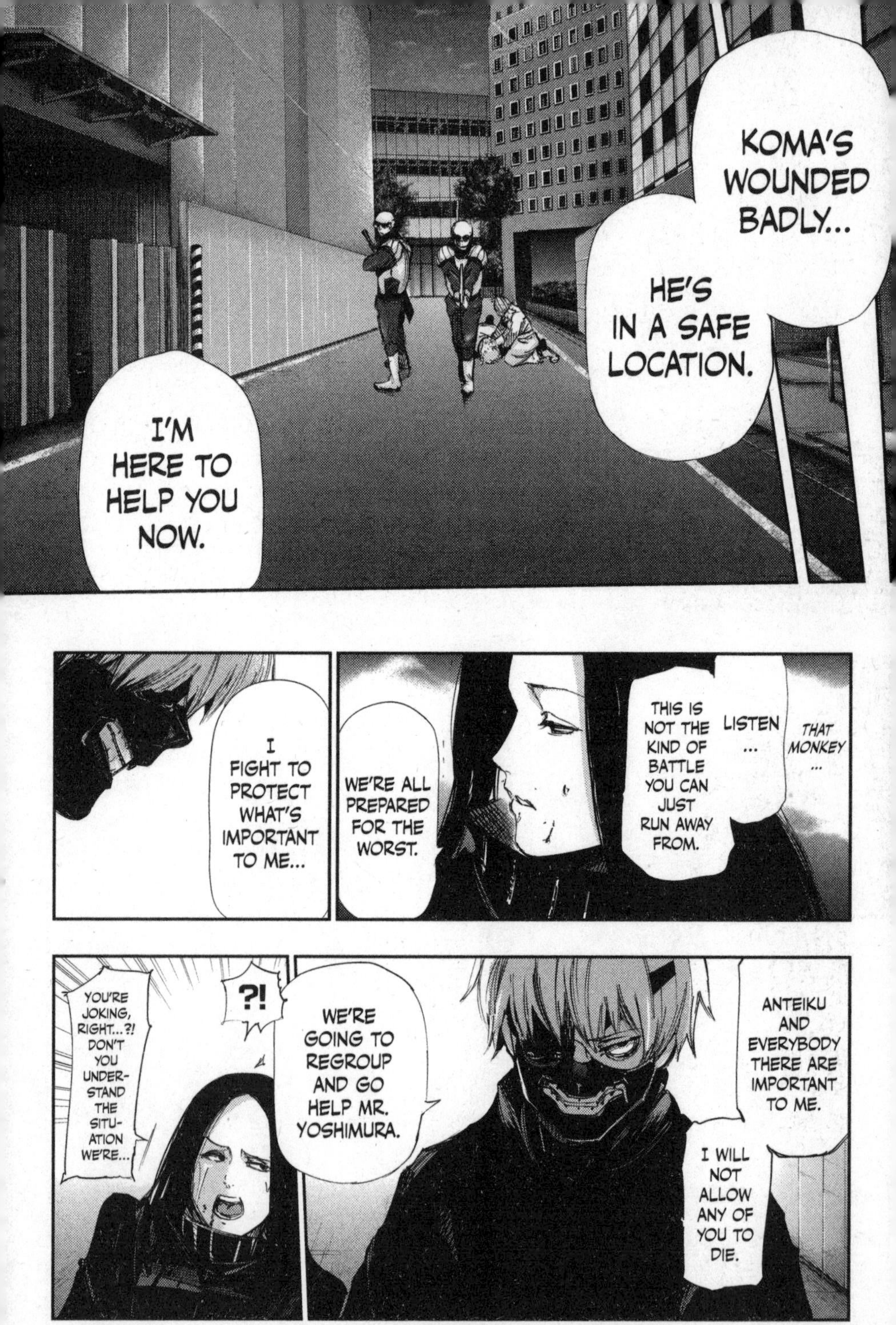
KOMA'S WOUNDED BADLY...
HE'S IN A SAFE LOCATION.
I'M HERE TO HELP YOU NOW.
THAT MONKEY ...
LISTEN ...
THIS IS NOT THE KIND OF BATTLE YOU CAN JUST RUN AWAY FROM.
WE'RE ALL PREPARED FOR THE WORST.
I FIGHT TO PROTECT WHAT'S IMPORTANT TO ME...
ANTEIKU AND EVERYBODY THERE ARE IMPORTANT TO ME.
I WILL NOT ALLOW ANY OF YOU TO DIE.
WE'RE GOING TO REGROUP AND GO HELP MR. YOSHIMURA.
?!
YOU'RE JOKING, RIGHT...?! DON'T YOU UNDER-STAND THE SITU-ATION WE'RE...

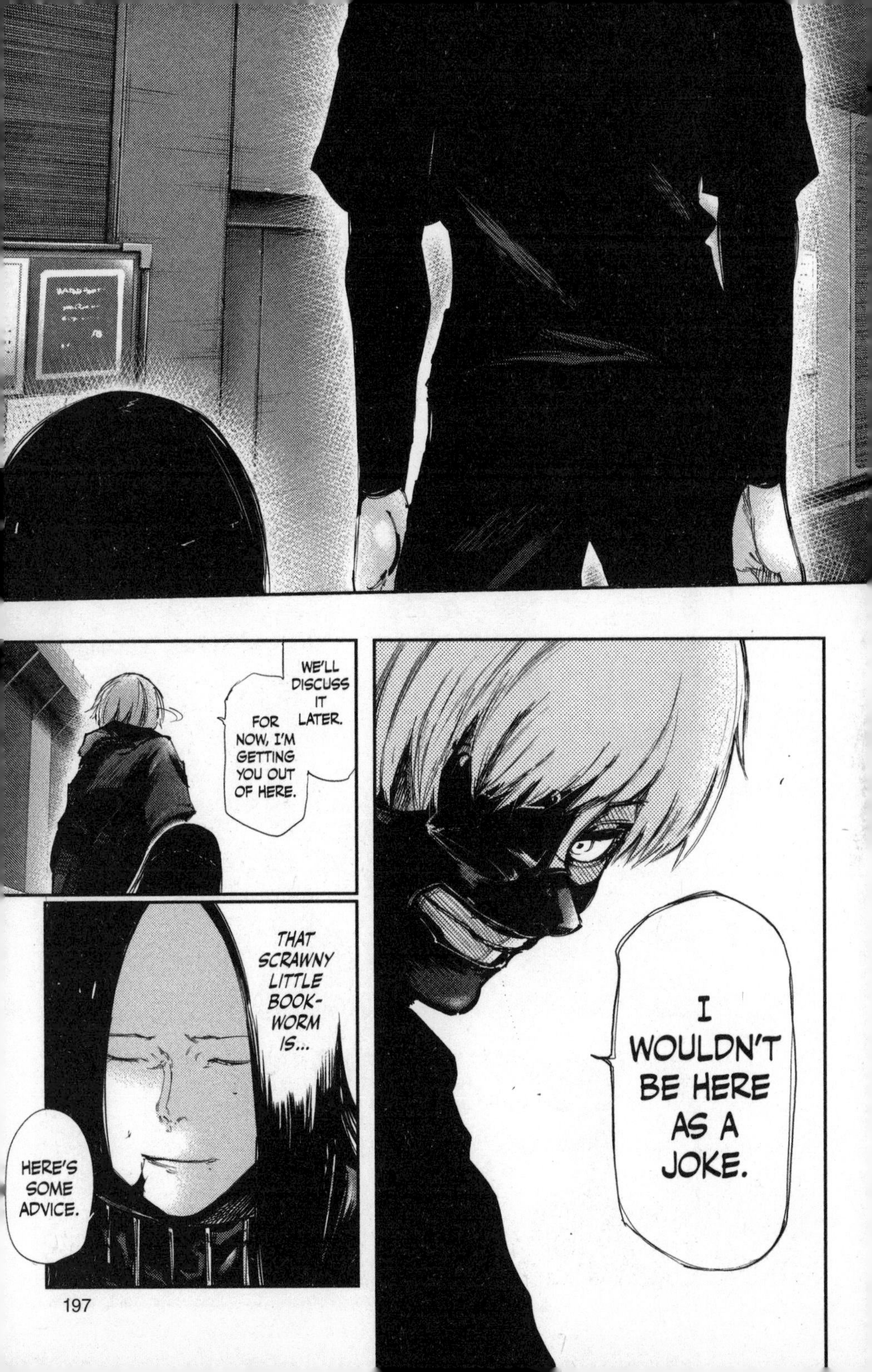
I WOULDN'T BE HERE AS A JOKE.
WE'LL DISCUSS IT LATER.
FOR NOW, I'M GETTING YOU OUT OF HERE.
THAT SCRAWNY LITTLE BOOK-WORM IS...
HERE'S SOME ADVICE.

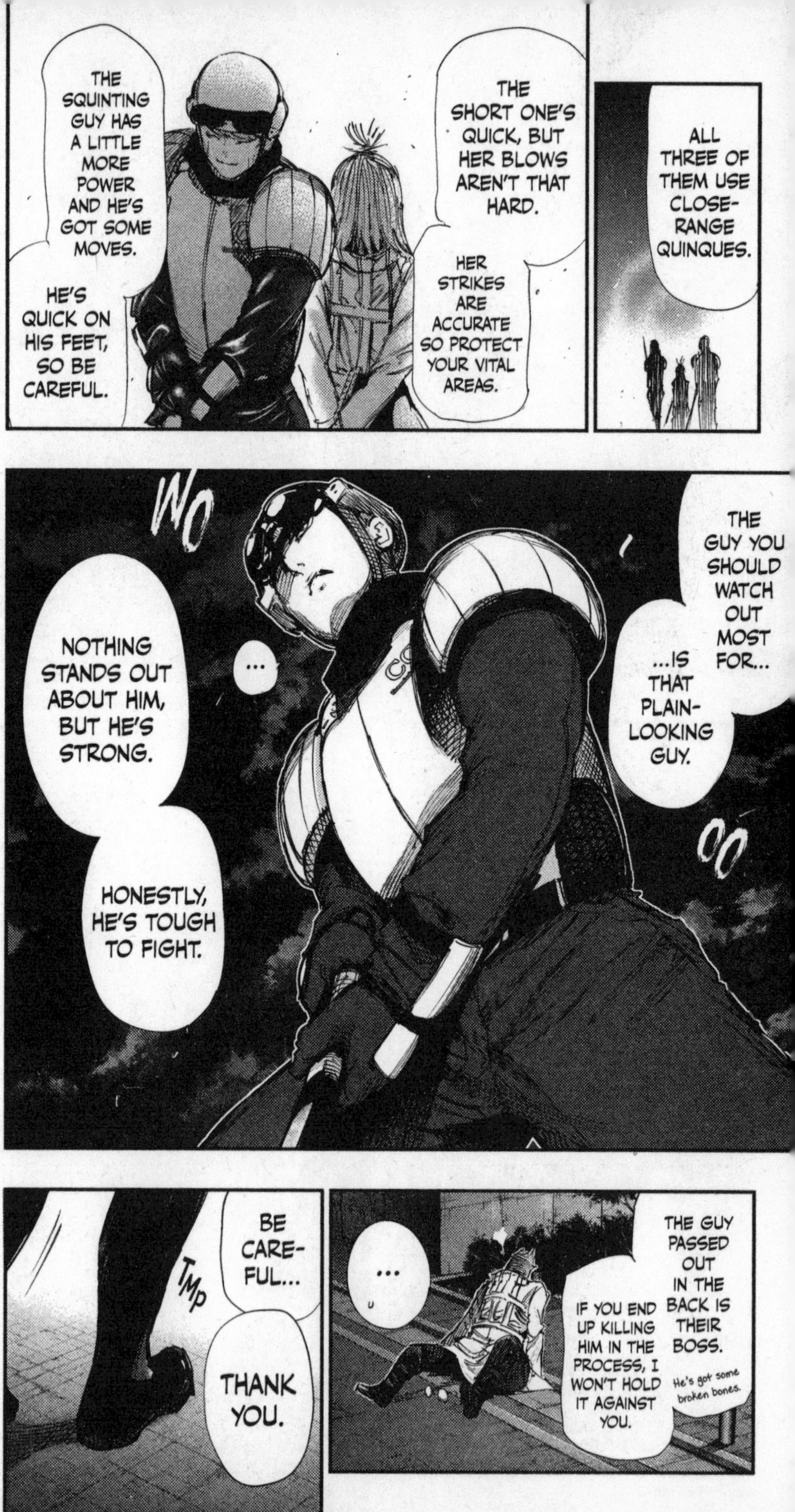
ALL THREE OF THEM USE CLOSE-RANGE QUINQUES.
THE SHORT ONE'S QUICK, BUT HER BLOWS AREN'T THAT HARD.
HER STRIKES ARE ACCURATE SO PROTECT YOUR VITAL AREAS.
THE SQUINTING GUY HAS A LITTLE MORE POWER AND HE'S GOT SOME MOVES.
HE'S QUICK ON HIS FEET, SO BE CAREFUL.
THE GUY YOU SHOULD WATCH OUT MOST FOR...
...IS THAT PLAIN-LOOKING GUY.
WO
OO
...
NOTHING STANDS OUT ABOUT HIM, BUT HE'S STRONG.
HONESTLY, HE'S TOUGH TO FIGHT.
THE GUY PASSED OUT IN THE BACK IS THEIR BOSS.
He's got some broken bones.
IF YOU END UP KILLING HIM IN THE PROCESS, I WON'T HOLD IT AGAINST YOU.
...
BE CARE-FUL...
TMP
THANK YOU.

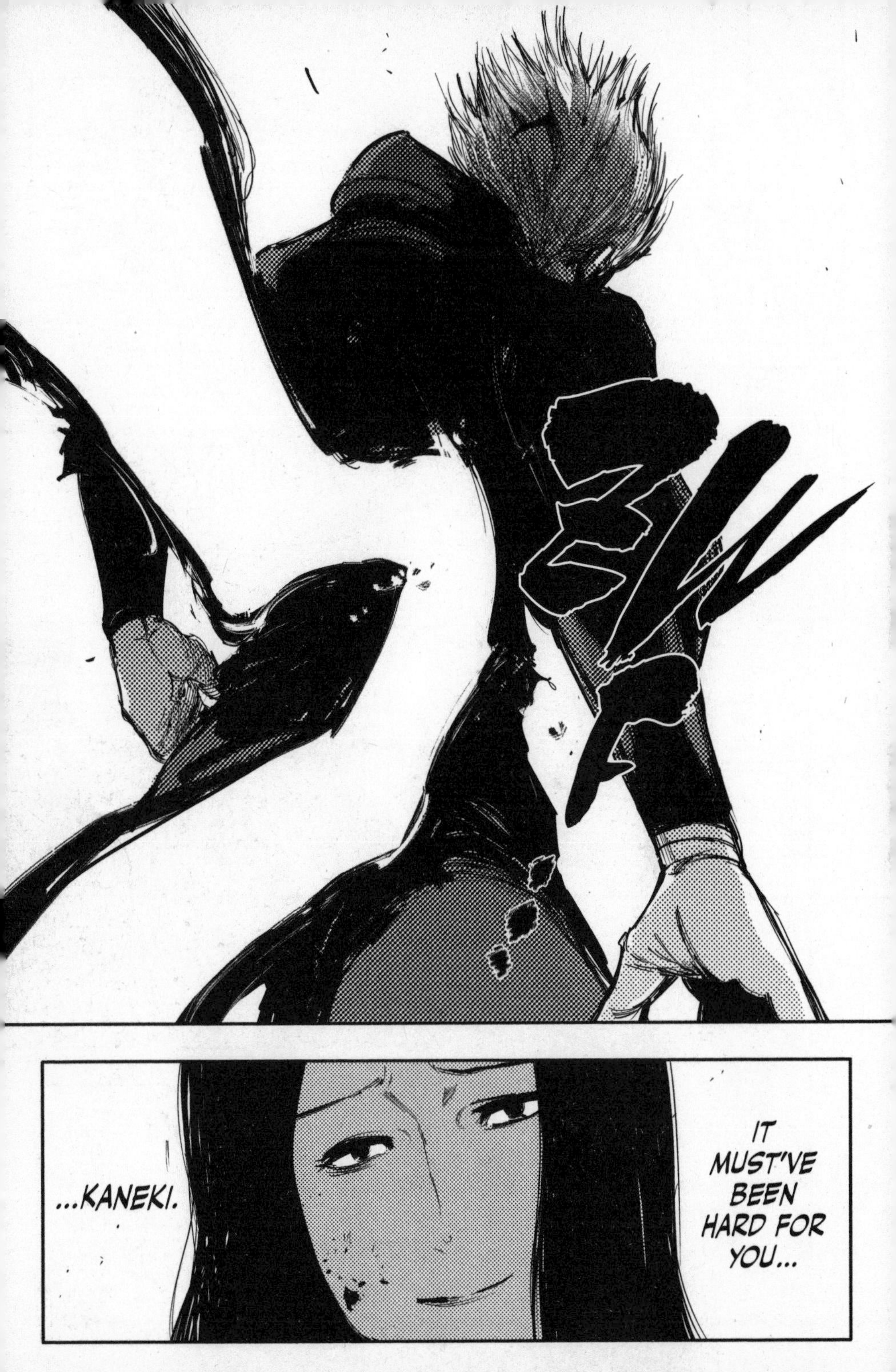
IT MUST'VE BEEN HARD FOR YOU...
...KANEKI.

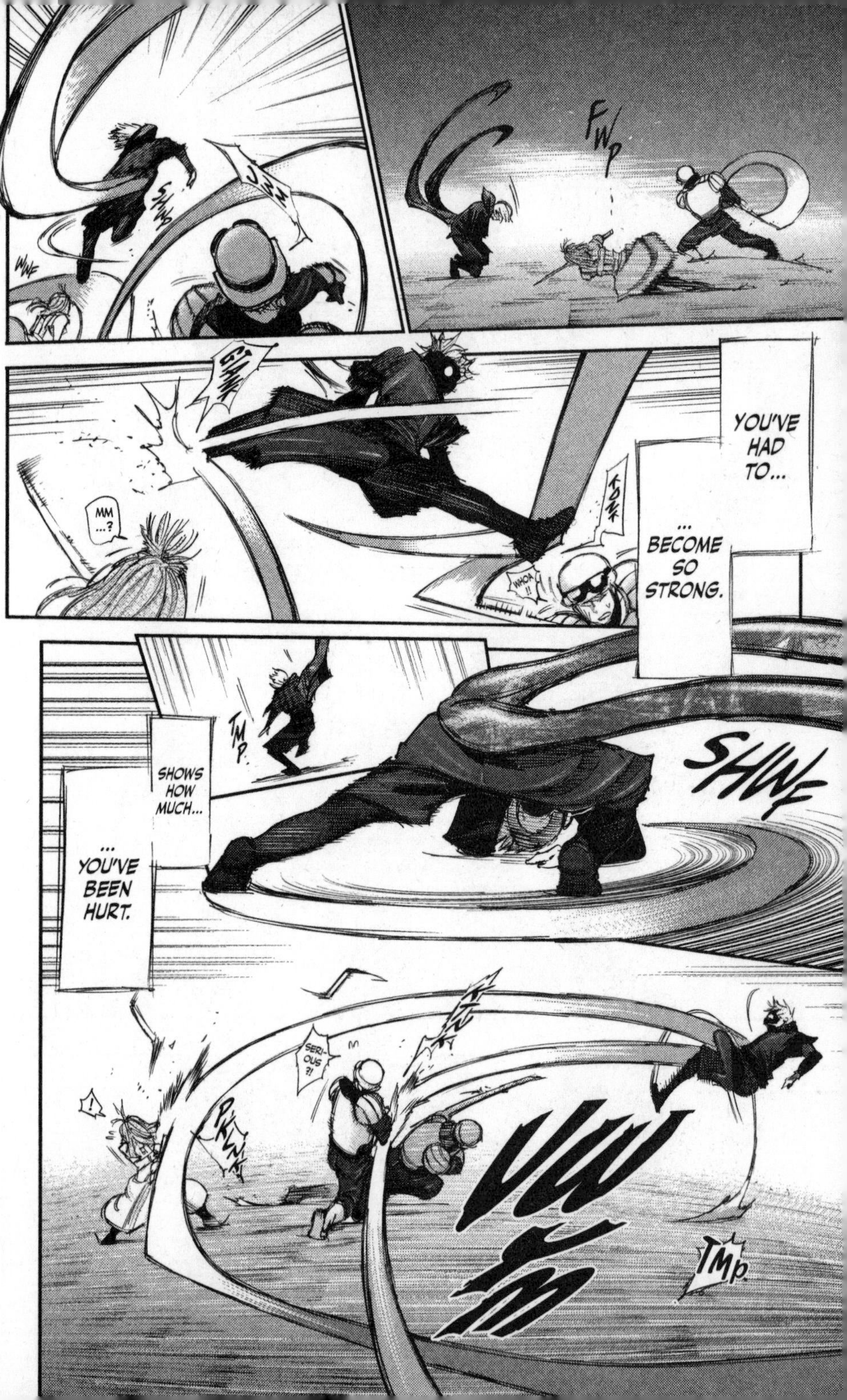
FWP
JZZ
WNF
YOU'VE HAD TO...
... BECOME SO STRONG.
KONK
WHOA!!
GLANK
MM ...?
SHWF
TMP.
SHOWS HOW MUCH...
... YOU'VE BEEN HURT.
TMP.
SERI-OUS?!
PKLNK!
!

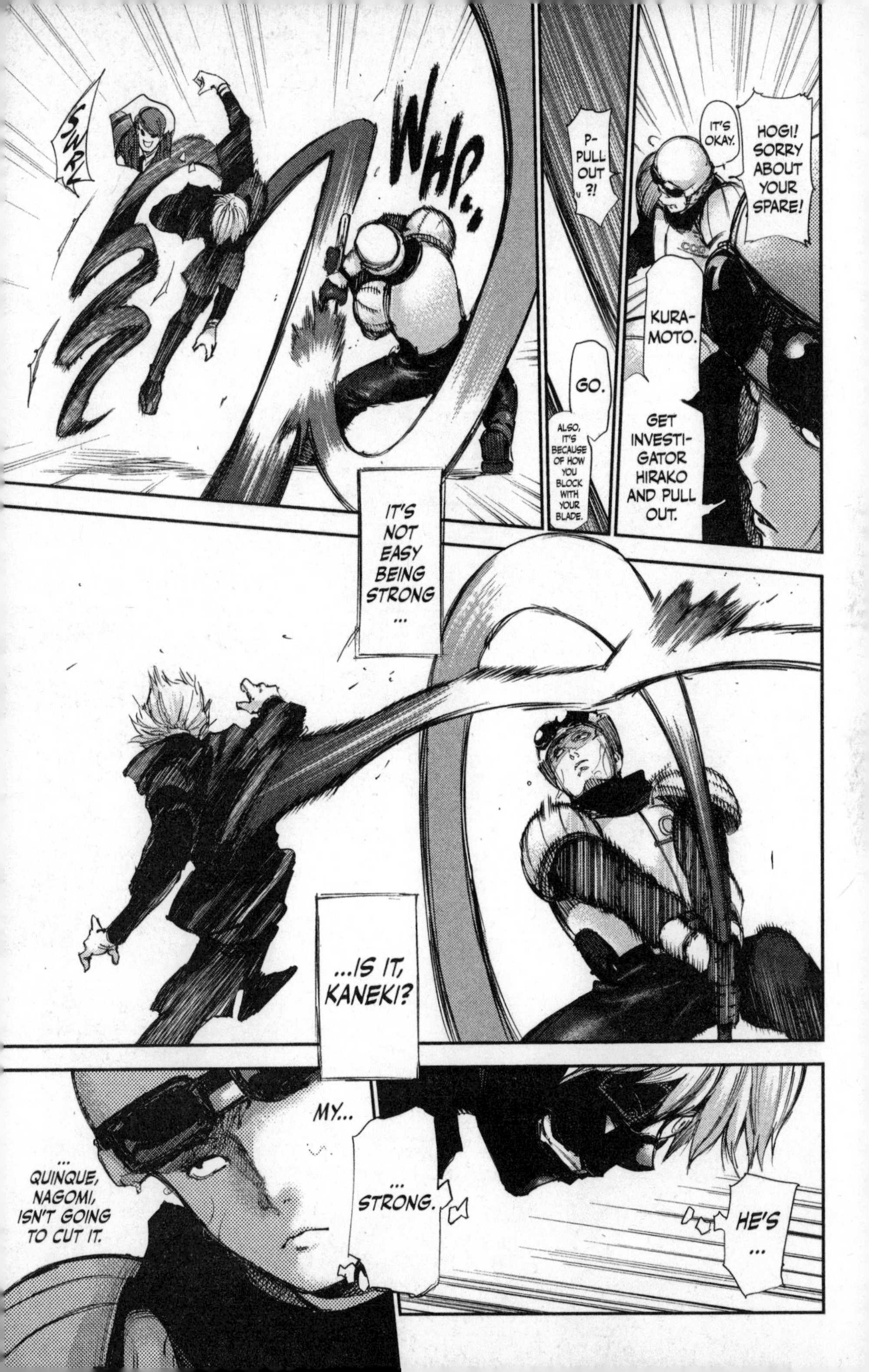

HOGI! SORRY ABOUT YOUR SPARE!
IT'S OKAY.
KURA-MOTO.
GET INVESTI-GATOR HIRAKO AND PULL OUT.
P-PULL OUT ?!
GO.
ALSO, IT'S BECAUSE OF HOW YOU BLOCK WITH YOUR BLADE.
WHP...
SWRK
IT'S NOT EASY BEING STRONG ...
...IS IT, KANEKI?
HE'S ...
... STRONG.
MY...
... QUINQUE, NAGOMI, ISN'T GOING TO CUT IT.

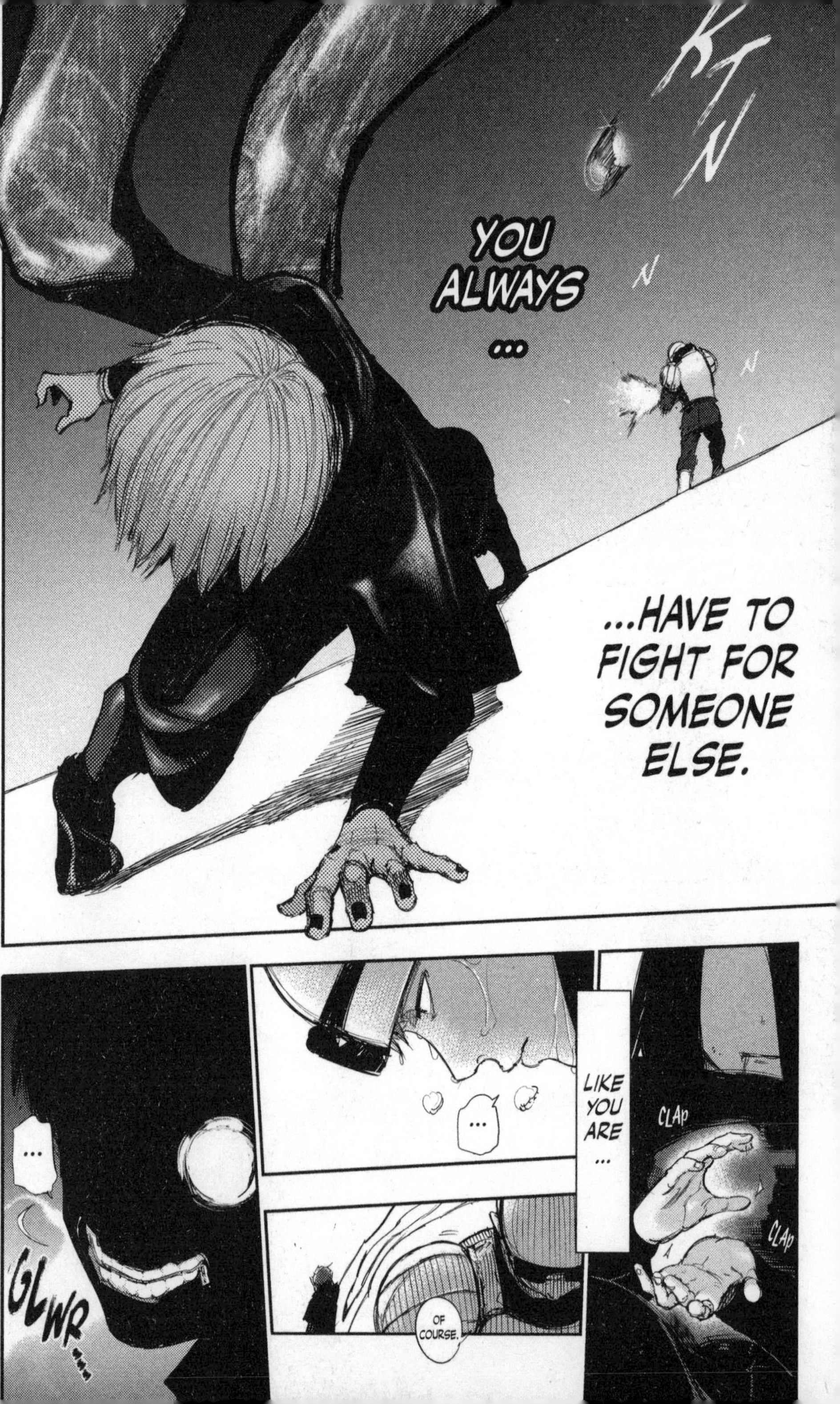
KTINNNK
YOU ALWAYS...
...HAVE TO FIGHT FOR SOMEONE ELSE.
LIKE YOU ARE...
CLAP
CLAP
...
OF COURSE.
...
GLWR

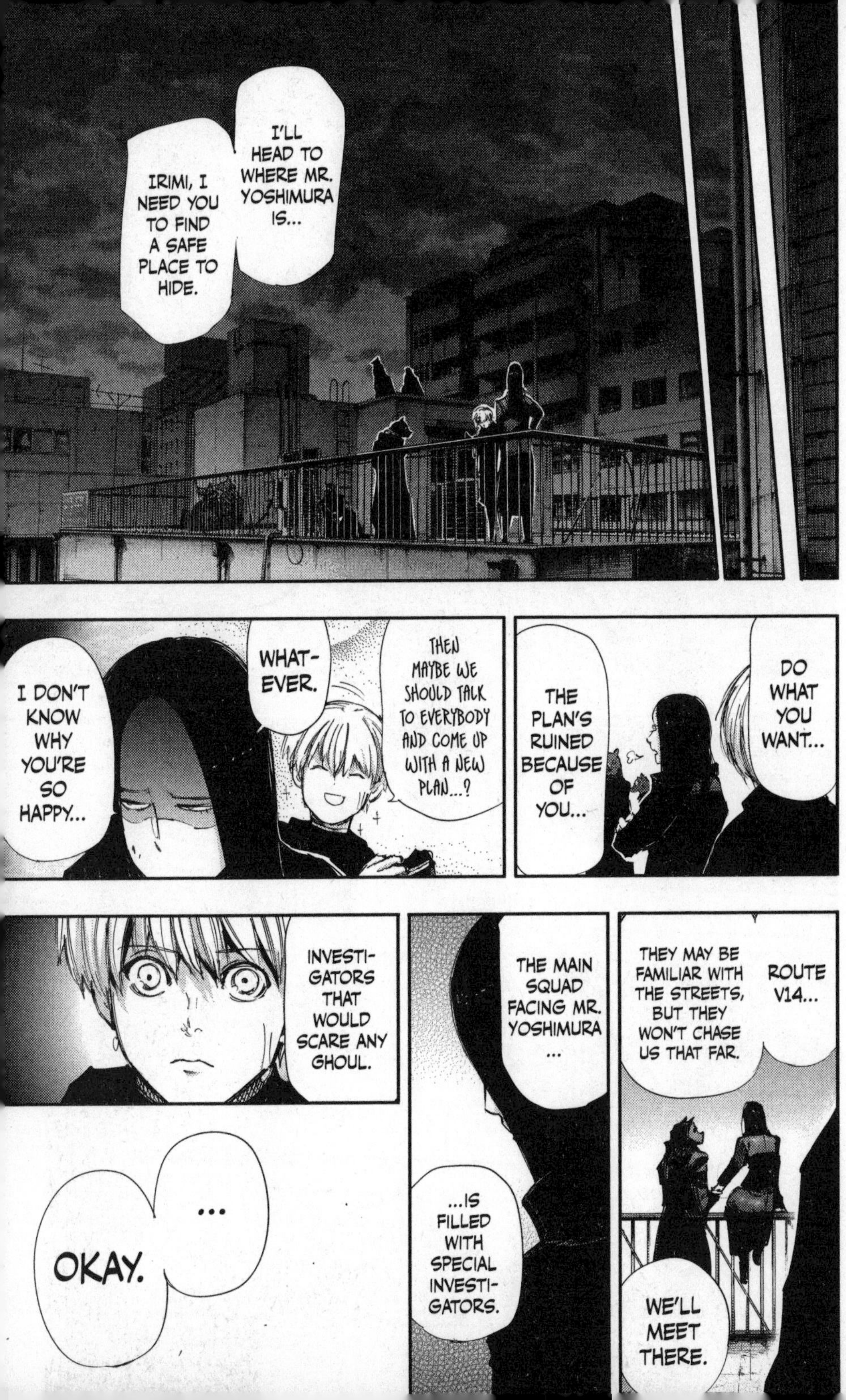
I'LL HEAD TO WHERE MR. YOSHIMURA IS...
IRIMI, I NEED YOU TO FIND A SAFE PLACE TO HIDE.
DO WHAT YOU WANT...
THE PLAN'S RUINED BECAUSE OF YOU...
THEN MAYBE WE SHOULD TALK TO EVERYBODY AND COME UP WITH A NEW PLAN...?
WHAT-EVER.
I DON'T KNOW WHY YOU'RE SO HAPPY...
ROUTE V14...
THEY MAY BE FAMILIAR WITH THE STREETS, BUT THEY WON'T CHASE US THAT FAR.
WE'LL MEET THERE.
THE MAIN SQUAD FACING MR. YOSHIMURA...
...IS FILLED WITH SPECIAL INVESTIGATORS.
INVESTIGATORS THAT WOULD SCARE ANY GHOUL.
...
OKAY.

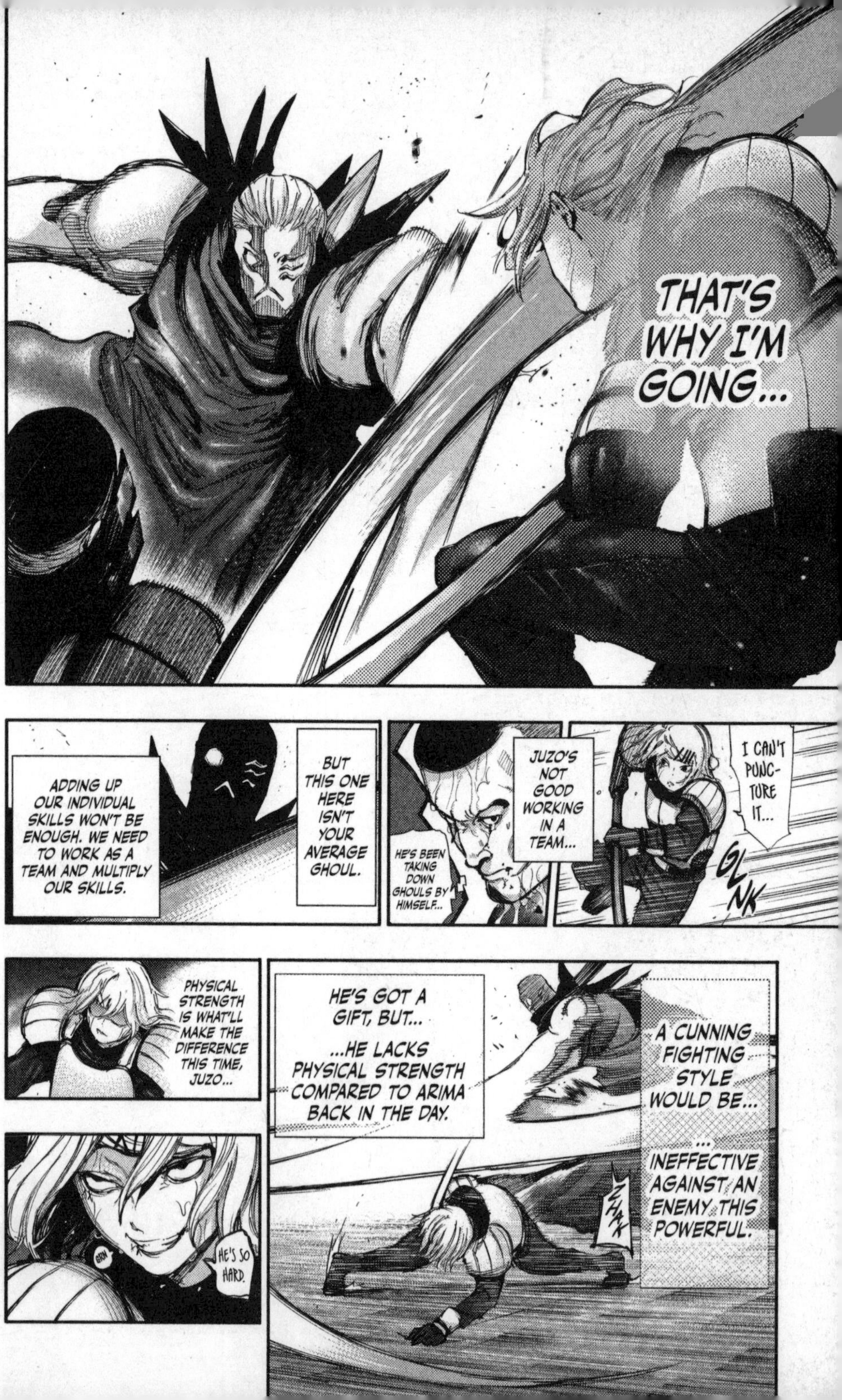
THAT'S WHY I'M GOING...
I CAN'T PUNC-TURE IT...
GLNK
JUZO'S NOT GOOD WORKING IN A TEAM...
HE'S BEEN TAKING DOWN GHOULS BY HIMSELF...
BUT THIS ONE HERE ISN'T YOUR AVERAGE GHOUL.
ADDING UP OUR INDIVIDUAL SKILLS WON'T BE ENOUGH. WE NEED TO WORK AS A TEAM AND MULTIPLY OUR SKILLS.
HE'S GOT A GIFT, BUT...
...HE LACKS PHYSICAL STRENGTH COMPARED TO ARIMA BACK IN THE DAY.
A CUNNING FIGHTING STYLE WOULD BE...
...INEFFECTIVE AGAINST AN ENEMY THIS POWERFUL.
SHAK
PHYSICAL STRENGTH IS WHAT'LL MAKE THE DIFFERENCE THIS TIME, JUZO...
HE'S SO HARD.

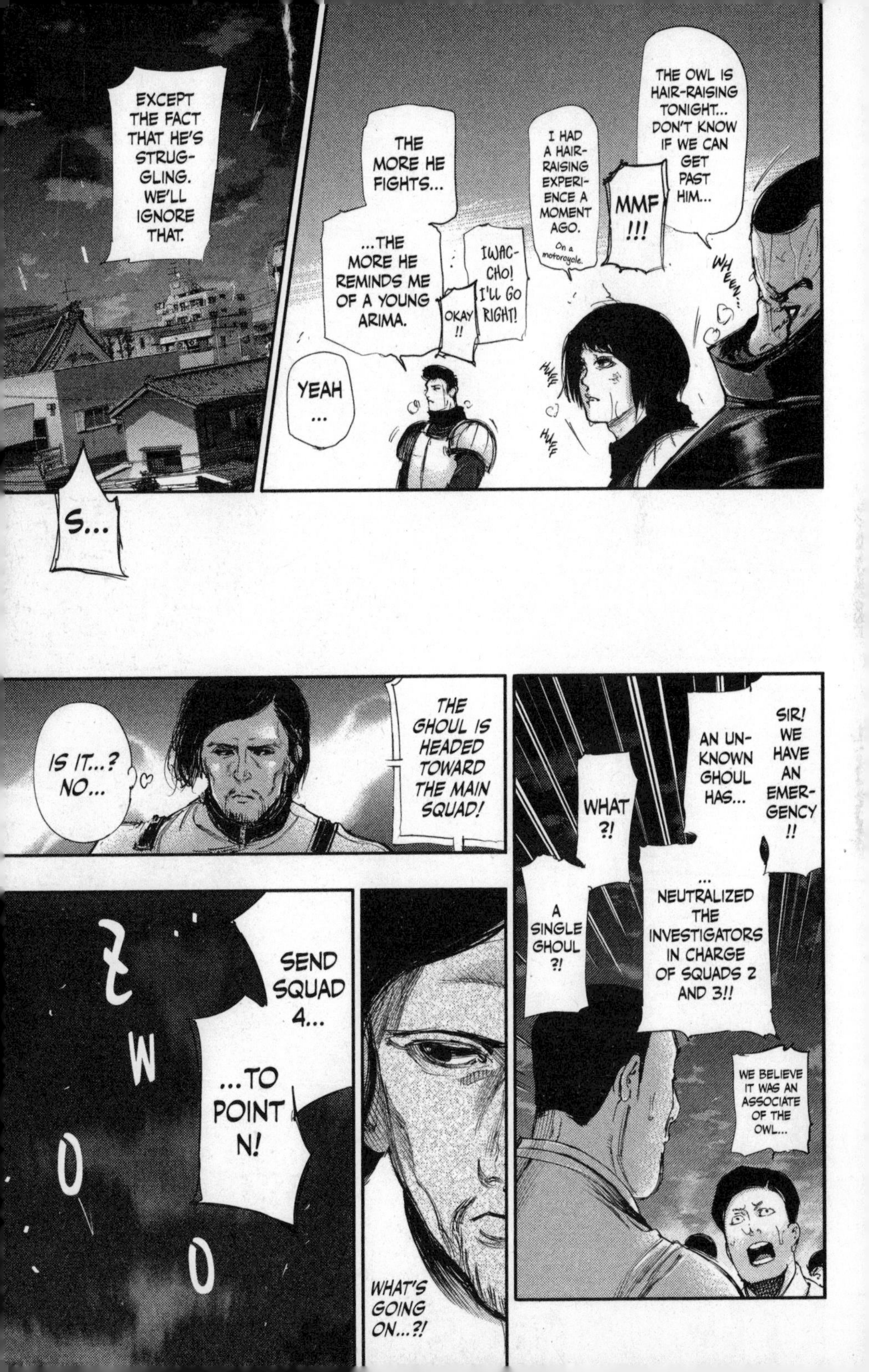
THE OWL IS HAIR-RAISING TONIGHT... DON'T KNOW IF WE CAN GET PAST HIM...
WHEEN...
MMF!!!
I HAD A HAIR-RAISING EXPERIENCE A MOMENT AGO.
On a motoroyale.
HUFF
HUFF
IWAC-CHO! I'LL GO RIGHT!
OKAY!!
THE MORE HE FIGHTS...
...THE MORE HE REMINDS ME OF A YOUNG ARIMA.
YEAH...
EXCEPT THE FACT THAT HE'S STRUG-GLING. WE'LL IGNORE THAT.
S...
SIR! WE HAVE AN EMER-GENCY!!
AN UN-KNOWN GHOUL HAS...
WHAT?!
...NEUTRALIZED THE INVESTIGATORS IN CHARGE OF SQUADS 2 AND 3!!
A SINGLE GHOUL?!
WE BELIEVE IT WAS AN ASSOCIATE OF THE OWL...
THE GHOUL IS HEADED TOWARD THE MAIN SQUAD!
IS IT...? NO...
WHAT'S GOING ON...?!
SEND SQUAD 4...
...TO POINT N!

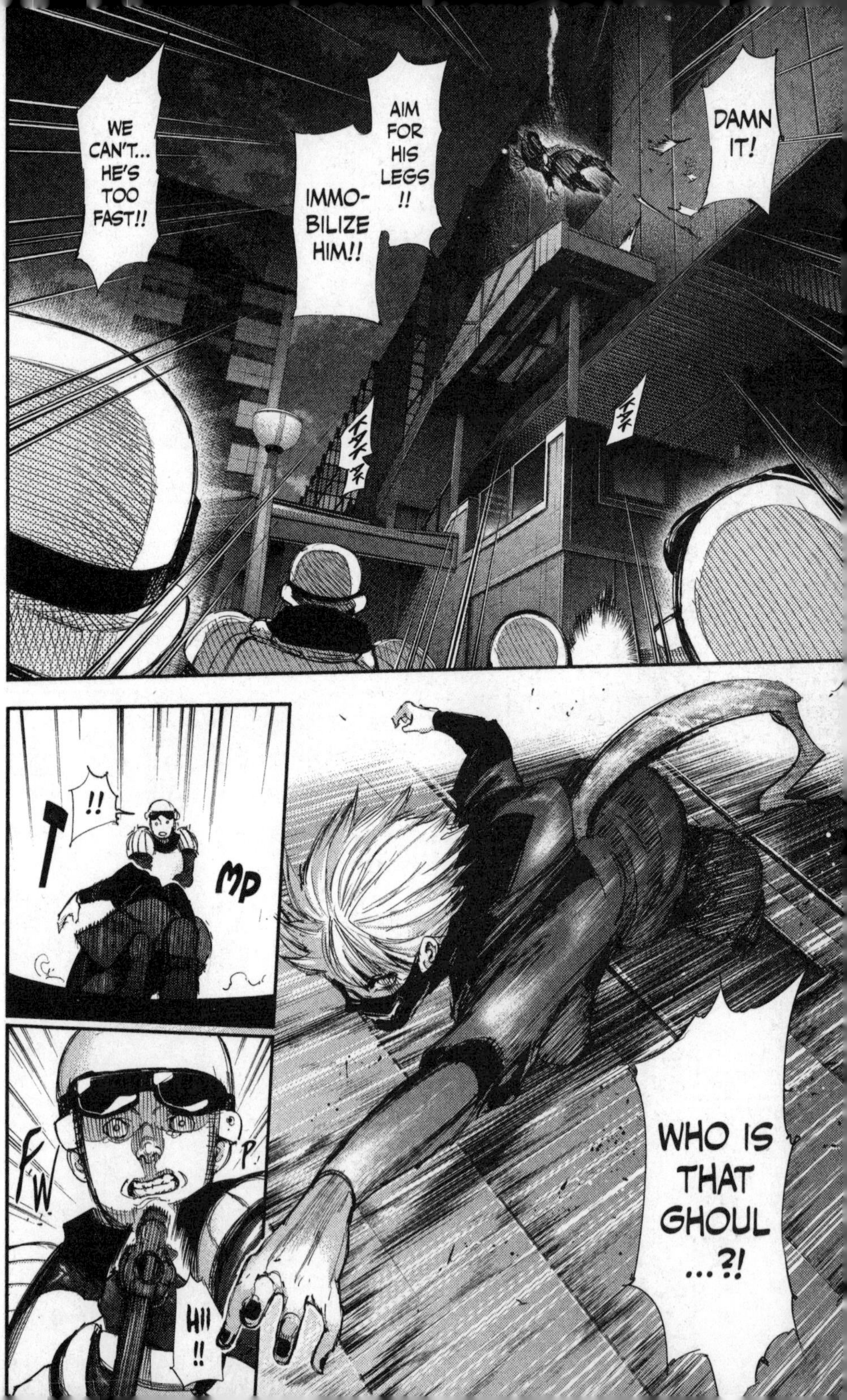
DAMN IT!
AIM FOR HIS LEGS!!
IMMO-BILIZE HIM!!
WE CAN'T... HE'S TOO FAST!!
KAK
KAK KAK
WHO IS THAT GHOUL ...?!
!!
MP
P
FW
HII!!

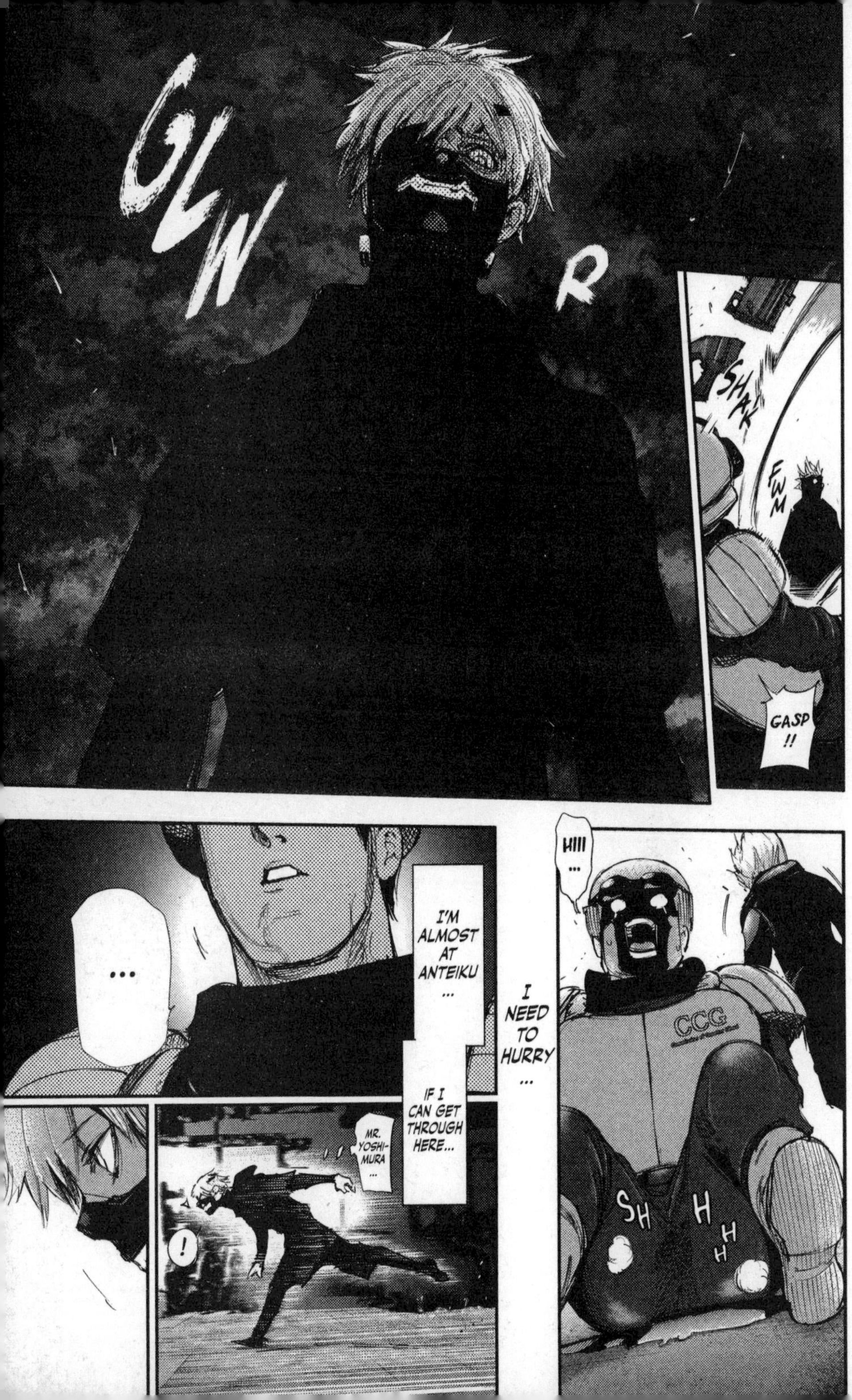
SHAK
FWM
GASP!!
GLWR
HIII...
I NEED TO HURRY...
SH HHHH
I'M ALMOST AT ANTEIKU...
...
IF I CAN GET THROUGH HERE...
MR. YOSHIMURA...
!

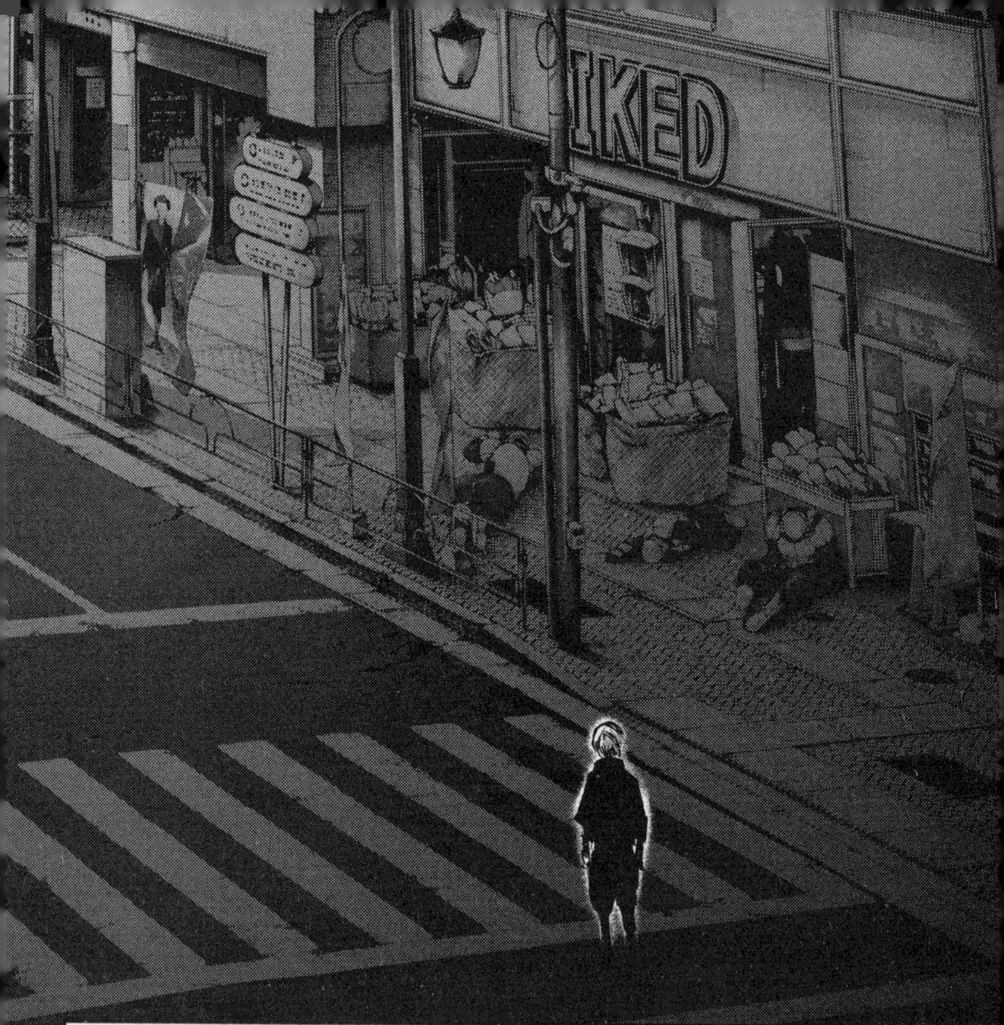
IKED

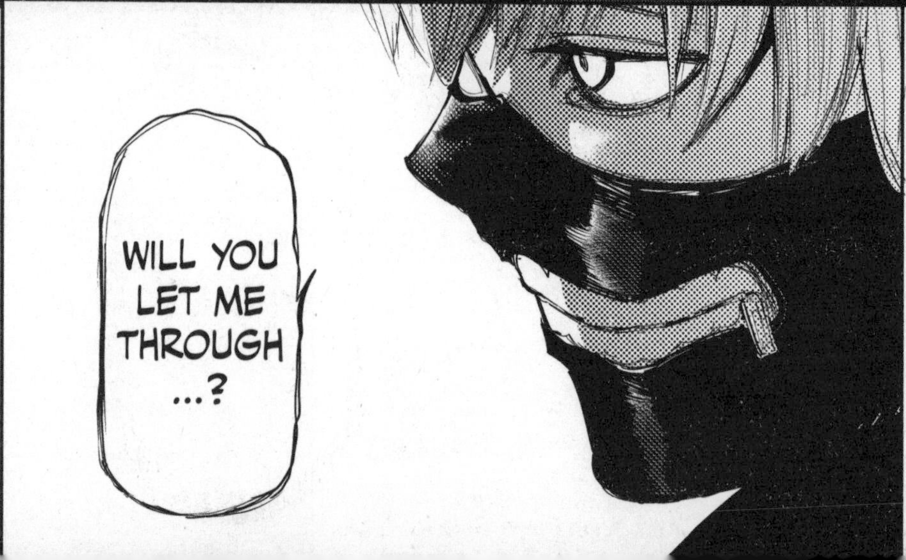
WILL YOU LET ME THROUGH ...?

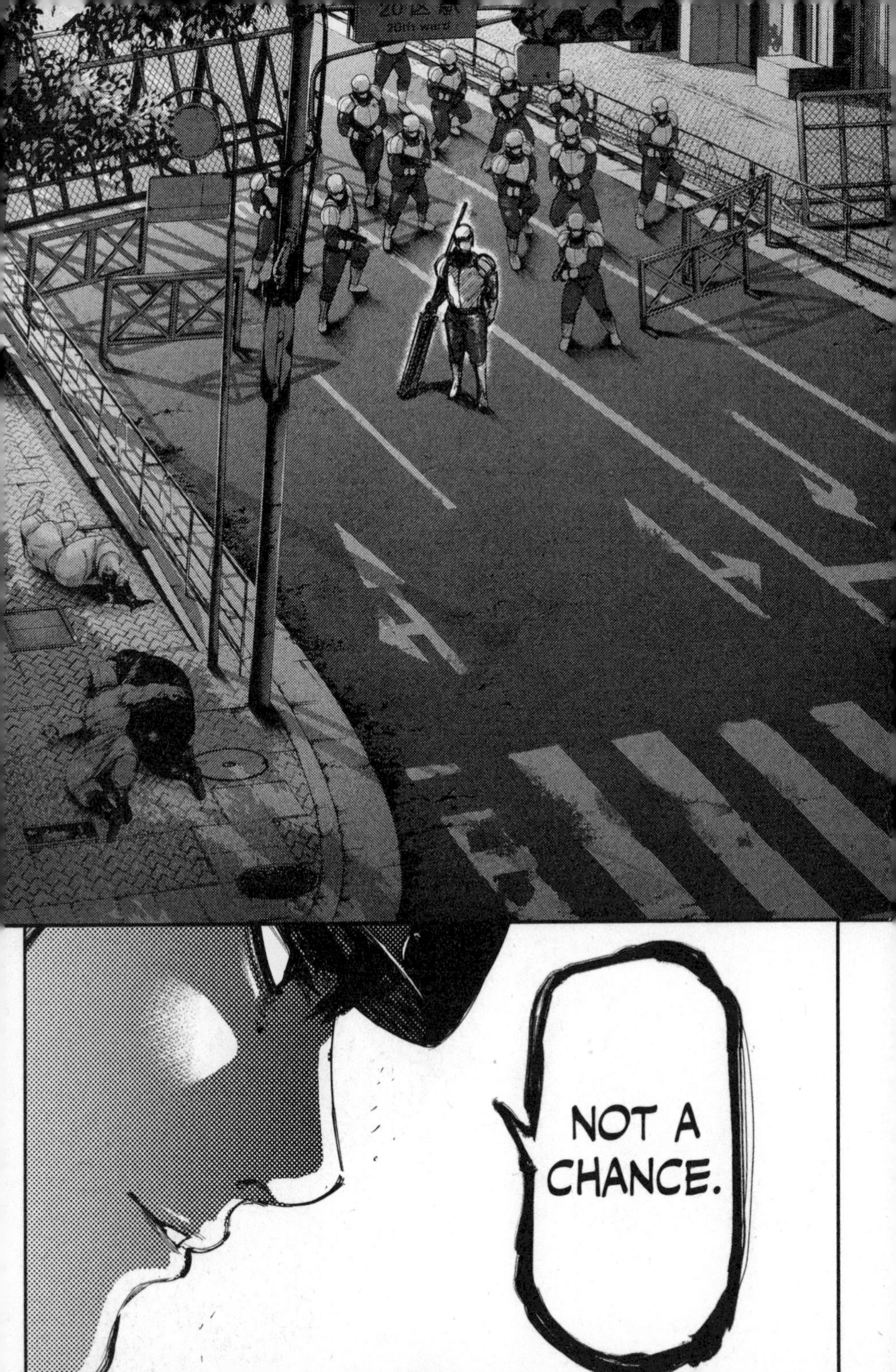
NOT A CHANCE.

To be continued in *Tokyo Ghoul* vol. 14.

STAFF
Ryuji Miyamoto
Mizuki Ide
Matsuzaki
Kota Shugyo
Hashimoto
Haraguchi

Design
Hideaki Shimada 〈L.S.D.〉

Cover
Miyuki Takaoka 〈Pocket〉

Editor
Jumpei Matsuo

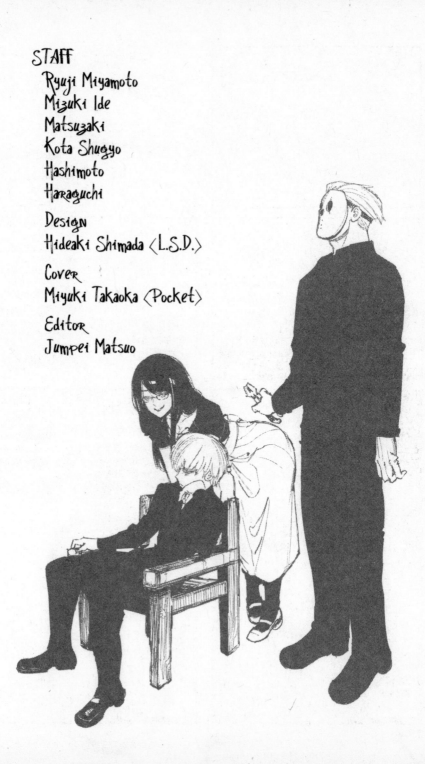

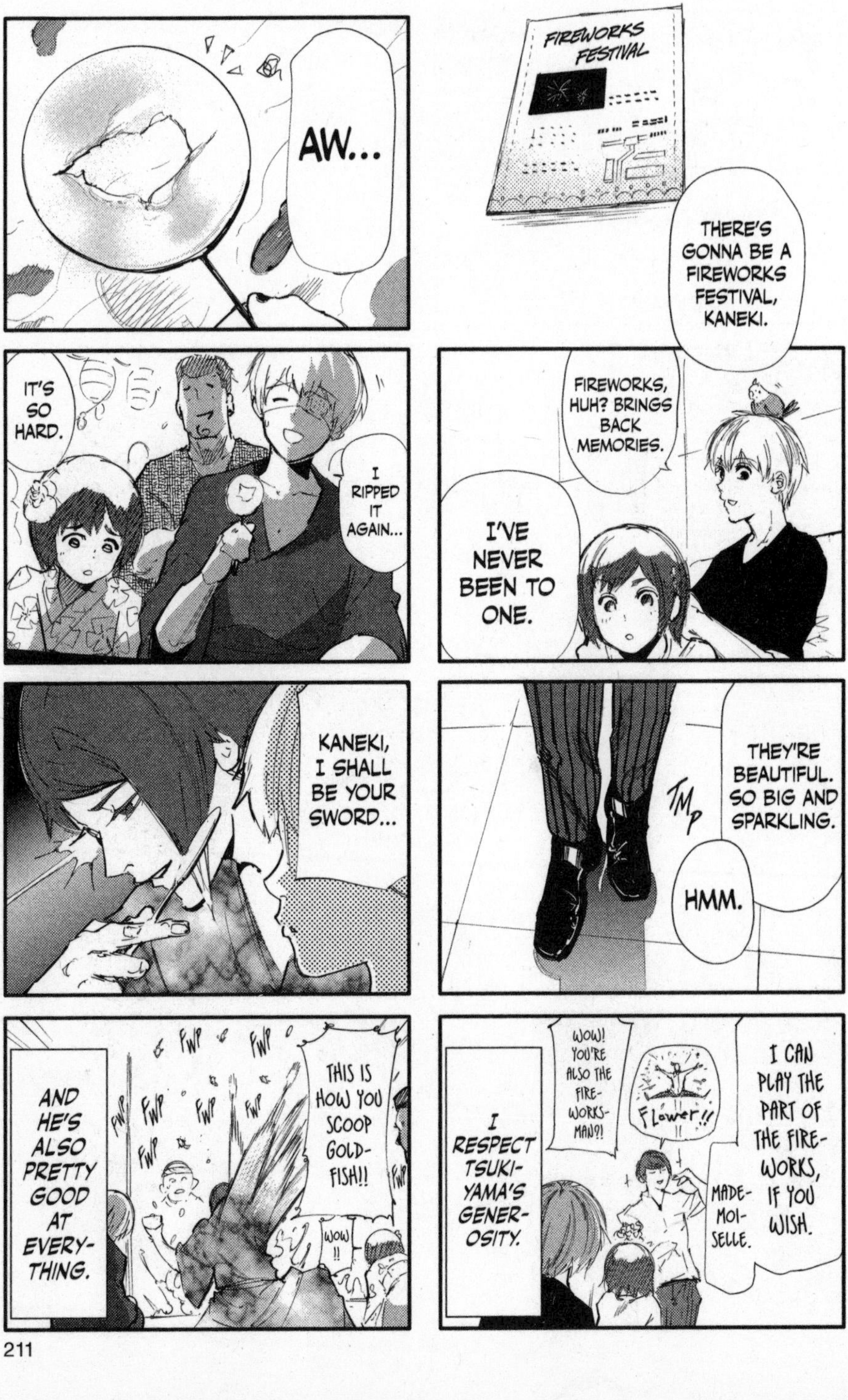
FIREWORKS FESTIVAL
THERE'S GONNA BE A FIREWORKS FESTIVAL, KANEKI.
FIREWORKS, HUH? BRINGS BACK MEMORIES.
I'VE NEVER BEEN TO ONE.
THEY'RE BEAUTIFUL. SO BIG AND SPARKLING.
TMP
HMM.
I CAN PLAY THE PART OF THE FIRE-WORKS, IF YOU WISH.
MADE-MOI-SELLE.
WOW! YOU'RE ALSO THE FIRE-WORKS-MAN?!
Flower!!
I RESPECT TSUKI-YAMA'S GENER-OSITY.
AW...
IT'S SO HARD.
I RIPPED IT AGAIN...
KANEKI, I SHALL BE YOUR SWORD...
THIS IS HOW YOU SCOOP GOLD-FISH!!
FWP FWP FWP FWP FWP FWP FWP FWP
WOW!!
AND HE'S ALSO PRETTY GOOD AT EVERY-THING.

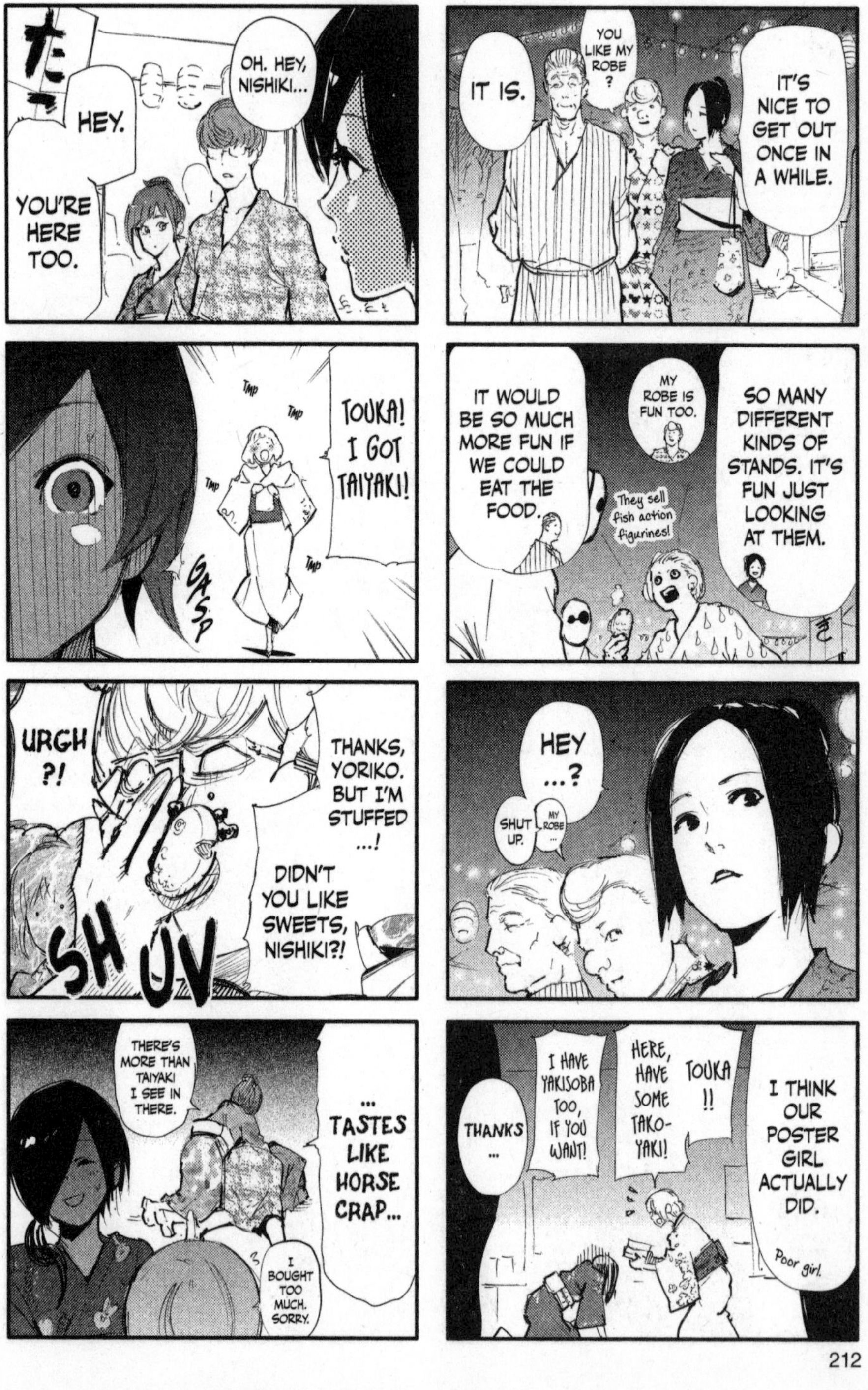
IT'S NICE TO GET OUT ONCE IN A WHILE.
YOU LIKE MY ROBE?
IT IS.
OH. HEY, NISHIKI...
HEY.
YOU'RE HERE TOO.
SO MANY DIFFERENT KINDS OF STANDS. IT'S FUN JUST LOOKING AT THEM.
MY ROBE IS FUN TOO.
IT WOULD BE SO MUCH MORE FUN IF WE COULD EAT THE FOOD.
They sell fish action figurines!
TOUKA! I GOT TAIYAKI!
GASP
HEY ...?
MY ROBE ...
SHUT UP.
THANKS, YORIKO. BUT I'M STUFFED ...!
DIDN'T YOU LIKE SWEETS, NISHIKI?!
URGH ?!
SHUV
I THINK OUR POSTER GIRL ACTUALLY DID.
TOUKA !!
HERE, HAVE SOME TAKO-YAKI!
I HAVE YAKISOBA TOO, IF YOU WANT!
THANKS ...
Poor girl.
... TASTES LIKE HORSE CRAP...
THERE'S MORE THAN TAIYAKI I SEE IN THERE.
I BOUGHT TOO MUCH. SORRY.

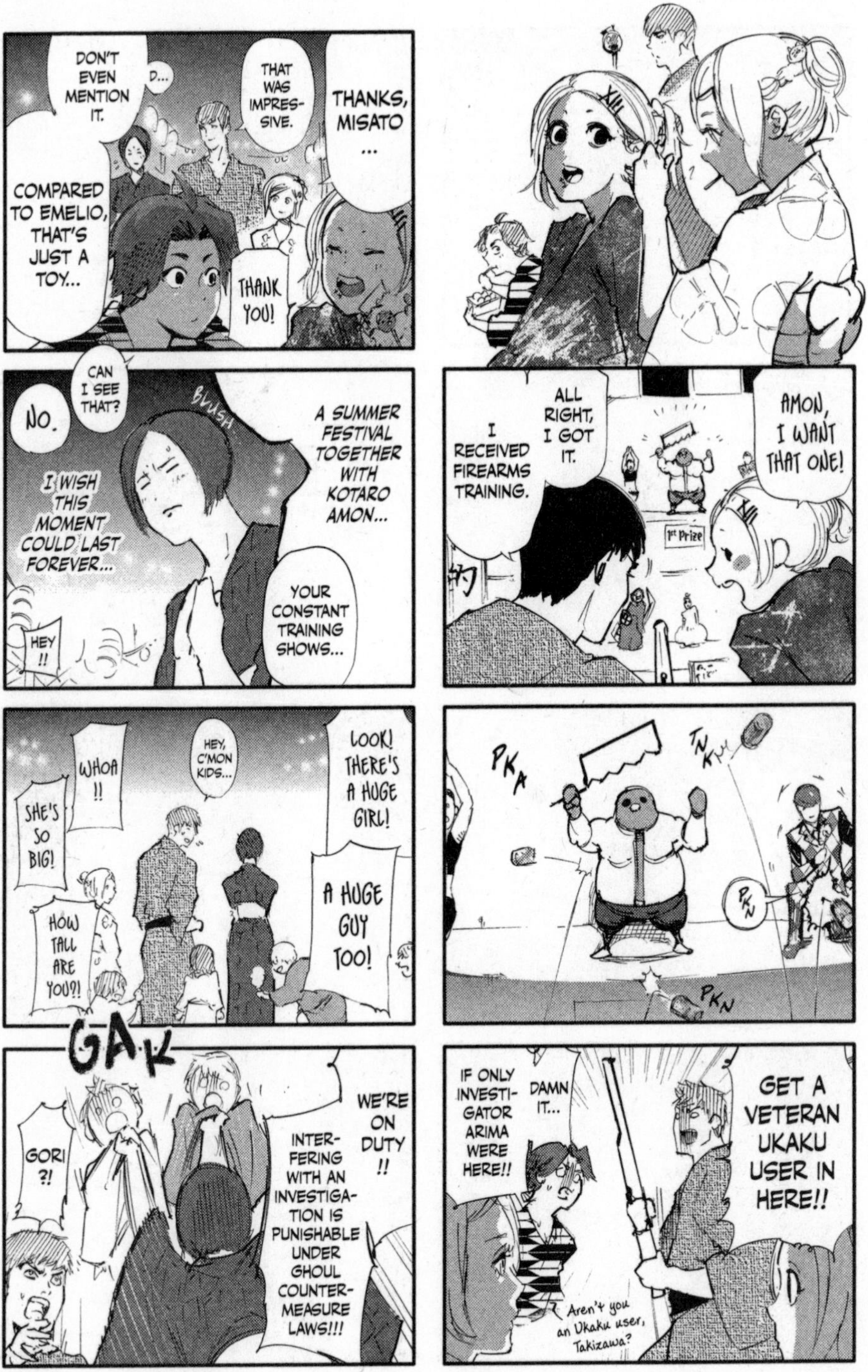
AMON, I WANT THAT ONE!
ALL RIGHT, I GOT IT.
I RECEIVED FIREARMS TRAINING.
1st Prize
PKA
TNK
PKN
PKN
GET A VETERAN UKAKU USER IN HERE!!
DAMN IT...
IF ONLY INVESTIGATOR ARIMA WERE HERE!!
Aren't you an Ukaku user, Takizawa?
THANKS, MISATO...
THAT WAS IMPRESSIVE.
D...
DON'T EVEN MENTION IT.
COMPARED TO EMELIO, THAT'S JUST A TOY...
THANK YOU!
A SUMMER FESTIVAL TOGETHER WITH KOTARO AMON...
CAN I SEE THAT?
BLUSH
NO.
I WISH THIS MOMENT COULD LAST FOREVER...
YOUR CONSTANT TRAINING SHOWS...
HEY!!
LOOK! THERE'S A HUGE GIRL!
HEY, C'MON KIDS...
WHOA!!
SHE'S SO BIG!
A HUGE GUY TOO!
HOW TALL ARE YOU?!
GAK
WE'RE ON DUTY!!
INTERFERING WITH AN INVESTIGATION IS PUNISHABLE UNDER GHOUL COUNTERMEASURE LAWS!!!
GORI?!

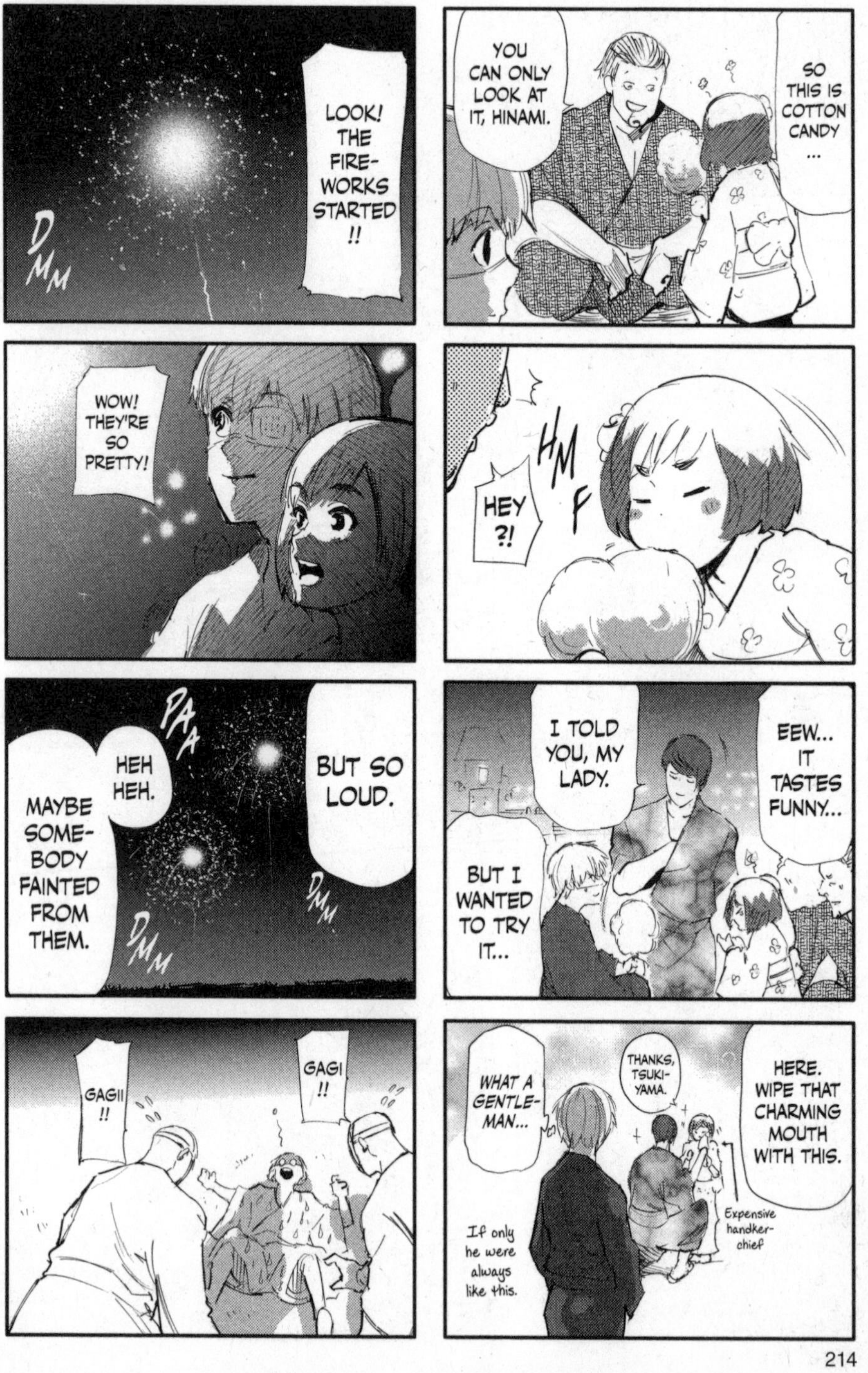
SO THIS IS COTTON CANDY ...
YOU CAN ONLY LOOK AT IT, HINAMI.
HMF
HEY ?!
EEW... IT TASTES FUNNY...
I TOLD YOU, MY LADY.
BUT I WANTED TO TRY IT...
HERE. WIPE THAT CHARMING MOUTH WITH THIS.
Expensive handkerchief
THANKS, TSUKIYAMA.
WHAT A GENTLEMAN...
If only he were always like this.
LOOK! THE FIREWORKS STARTED !!
DMM
WOW! THEY'RE SO PRETTY!
BUT SO LOUD.
PAA
HEH HEH.
MAYBE SOMEBODY FAINTED FROM THEM.
DMM
DMM
GAGI !!
GAGII !!

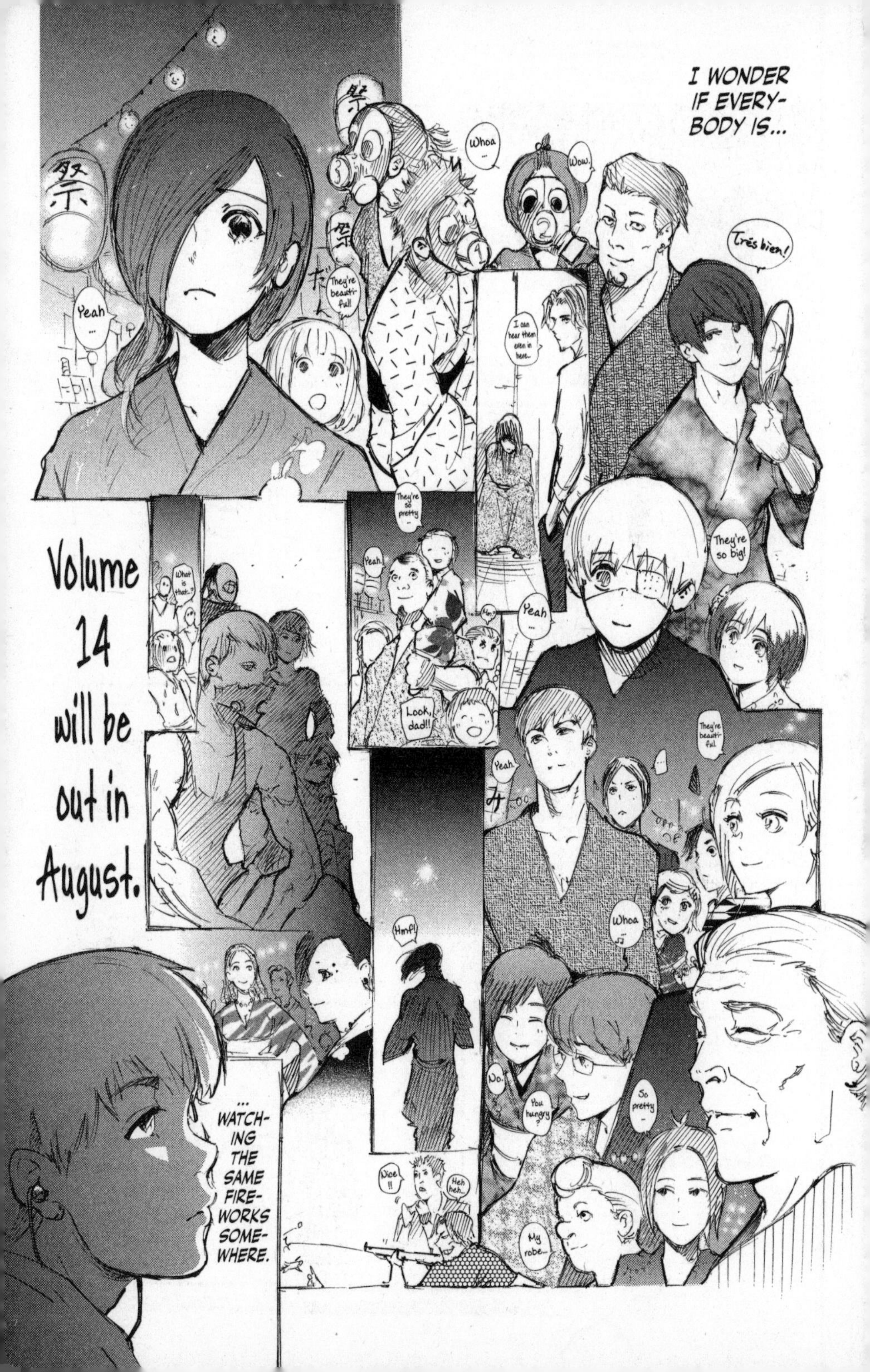
I WONDER IF EVERY-BODY IS...
Trés bien!
Wow.
Whoa...
I can hear them even in here...
They're beautiful!
Yeah...
They're so big!
Yeah...
Hm?
They're so pretty...
Yeah.
Look, dad!!
What is that...?
Volume 14 will be out in August.
They're beautiful.
Yeah.
...
Whoa
So pretty...
You hungry
No.
My robe...
Hmf!
Heh heh...
Nice!!
...WATCHING THE SAME FIREWORKS SOMEWHERE.

TOKYO GHOUL

東 京 喰 種

VOLUME 13
VIZ Signature Edition

Story and art by
SUI ISHIDA

TOKYO GHOUL © 2011 by Sui Ishida
All rights reserved.
First published in Japan in 2011 by
SHUEISHA Inc., Tokyo.
English translation rights arranged by
SHUEISHA Inc.

TRANSLATION. Joe Yamazaki

TOUCH-UP ART AND LETTERING. Vanessa Satone

DESIGN. Shawn Carrico

Printed in the U.S.A.

Published by VIZ Media, LLC
P.O. Box 77010
San Francisco, CA 94107

10 9 8 7 6 5 4 3 2 1
First printing, June 2017

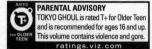

AUG   2017